CULTURE, PLACE, AND NATURE
STUDIES IN ANTHROPOLOGY AND ENVIRONMENT

Devon Peña and K. Sivaramakrishnan,

Series Editors

CULTURE, PLACE, AND NATURE

Centered in anthropology, the Culture, Place, and Nature series encompasses new interdisciplinary social science research on environmental issues, focusing on the intersection of culture, ecology, and politics in global, national, and local contexts. Contributors to the series view environmental knowledge and issues from multiple and often conflicting perspectives of various cultural systems.

The Kuhls of Kangra:
Community-Managed Irrigation
in the Western Himalaya,
by Mark Baker

The Earth's Blanket:
Traditional Teachings for Sustainable Living,
by Nancy Turner

Property and Politics in Sabah, Malaysia:
Native Struggles over Land Rights,
by Amity A. Doolittle

Border Landscapes:
The Politics of Akha Land Use
in China and Thailand
by Janet C. Sturgeon

From Enslavement to Environmentalism:
Politics on a Southern African Frontier
by David McDermott Hughes

Ecological Nationalisms:
Nature, Livelihoods, and Identities in South Asia
edited by Gunnel Cederlöf and
K. Sivaramakrishnan

ECOLOGICAL NATIONALISMS

Nature, Livelihoods, and Identities
in South Asia

Edited by
GUNNEL CEDERLÖF AND
K. SIVARAMAKRISHNAN

UNIVERSITY OF WASHINGTON PRESS

Seattle and London

THIS PUBLICATION WAS SUPPORTED IN PART
BY THE DONALD R. ELLEGOOD INTERNATIONAL
PUBLICATIONS ENDOWMENT.

Copyright © 2006 by the University of Washington Press
Printed in the United States of America
12 11 10 09 08 07 06 5 4 3 2 1

Published in the United States of America
by University of Washington Press,
PO Box 50096, Seattle, WA 98145-5096, U.S.A.
www.washington.edu/uwpress

Published in South Asia by Permanent Black
D-28 Oxford Apts., 11 I.P. Extension, Delhi 110092

All rights reserved. No part of this publication may be
reproduced or transmitted in any form or by any means,
electronic or mechanical, including photocopy, recording,
or any information storage or retrieval system, without
permission in writing from the publisher.

Library of Congress Cataloging-in-Publication Data
Ecological nationalisms: nature, livelihoods, and
identities in South Asia / edited by Gunnel Cederlöf
and K. Sivaramakrishnan.
    p. cm. — (Culture, place, and nature)
Includes bibliographical references and index.
ISBN 0-295-98531-3 (hardback : alk. paper)
    1. Political science—South Asia.
    2. Political ecology—South Asia.
    3. National state.
    I. Cederlöf, Gunnel.
    II. Sivaramakrishnan, K., 1957–
    III. Series
JA84.S64E27 2006   320.54'0954—dc22   2005014154

Typeset in Minion by
Guru Typograph Technology, New Delhi 110075

The paper used in this publication is acid-free and 90 percent
recycled from at least 50 percent post-consumer waste. It meets
the minimum requirements of American National Standard
for Information Sciences—Permanence of Paper for Printed
Library Materials, ANSI Z39.48–1984.

CONTENTS

Preface and Acknowledgments   vii

Notes on Contributors   xi

1 Introduction
 Ecological Nationalisms: Claiming Nature for Making History   1
 K. SIVARAMAKRISHNAN AND GUNNEL CEDERLÖF

I. REGIONAL NATURES, NATION, AND EMPIRE

2 Environmental History, the Spice Trade, and the State in South India
 KATHLEEN D. MORRISON   43

3 The Toda Tiger: Debates on Custom, Utility, and Rights in Nature, South India 1820–1843
 GUNNEL CEDERLÖF   65

4 Contested Forests in North-West Pakistan: The Bureaucracy between the "Ecological," the "National," and the Realities of a Nation's Frontier
 URS GEISER   90

II. COMPETING NATIONALISMS

5 Indigenous Forests: Rights, Discourses, and Resistance in Chotanagpur, 1860–2002
 VINITA DAMODARAN   115

6 Nature and Politics: The Case of Uttarakhand, North India
 ANTJE LINKENBACH   151

7 Indigenous Natures: Forest and Community Dynamics
   in Meghalaya, North-East India
   Bengt G. Karlsson   170

8 Sacred Forests of Kodagu: Ecological Value and Social Role
   Claude A. Garcia and J.-P. Pascal   199

III. COMMODIFIED NATURE AND NATIONAL VISIONS

9 Knowledge Against the State: Local Perceptions of
   Government Interventions in the Fishery (Kerala, India)
   Götz Hoeppe   233

10 Shifting Cultivation, Images, and Development in the
   Chittagong Hill Tracts of Bangladesh
   Wolfgang Mey   255

11 Forest Management in a Pukhtun Community:
   The Constructions of Identities
   Sarah Southwold-Llewellyn   274

12 "There Is No Life Without Wildlife": National Parks and
   National Identity in Bardia National Park, Western Nepal
   Nina Bhatt   297

   Bibliography   326

   Index   373

PREFACE AND ACKNOWLEDGMENTS

THIS PROJECT BEGAN AS A PANEL AT THE ANNUAL SOUTH ASIA CONFErence at the University of Wisconsin, Madison in 2001. At that meeting a small group of anthropologists and historians of South Asia, working from academic institutions in the USA and Europe, began to explore the relationship of struggles over nature, and its conservation, to issues of citizenship, subjecthood, and nationalism. We initially juxtaposed, in a comparative spirit, historical and ethnographic research on India and Nepal over the last two hundred years. Our geographical span has since then grown to include also Bangladesh and Pakistan.

From a European perspective, expansion on other continents, and the possibilities perceived in emerging scientific disciplines, multiplied the encounters with nature and therefore further delineated an imagined geography of the natural environment in South Asia. Colonial government enabled some of the earliest, modern, grand schemes that were launched in the name of Improvement and for the conservation of nature. However, in spite of Nature's preference, both nature and people tended to be seen as getting in the way of national Progress.

Modern nations have pursued further experiments in defining, utilizing and conserving an elusive South Asian nature. Projects of colonial state formation, national development, monarchic consolidation, and democratic reform have configured regimes of nature's utility and conservation in particular ways. Over the last century, the South Asian states' claim on the environment—as articulated in ideas, policy and implementation for utilizing and preserving nature—has moved away from consecrating and protecting wild, rare, and threatened territories. Conservation is now increasingly linked to regimes of environmental management that require more complex associations of natural heritage with collective identity, regional aspiration, and communal and individual rights.

Remarkable continuities as well as changes have characterized the relationship of the long twentieth century to questions of rights in nature and environmental politics in South Asia. Examining some of these new developments, and the ways in which they were enmeshed in various histories, led to a focus that emerged out of this panel and was pursued in a larger gathering and more sustained discussion at the 17th European Conference on Modern South Asian Studies, held in Heidelberg, during September 2002. Some of the original panelists from Madison were joined by many other scholars, mostly based in European institutions, at this scenic venue on the banks of the Neckar River. In meeting rooms near the river, and on a memorable boat ride down it, this group of scholars discussed the hitherto scantily addressed connections between nature, social conflict, nation-ness, and nationalism. An area of common interest that emerged was the relationships between ideas about nature, as well as ideas about social relations with contested natures in South Asia, and how both these sets of ideas are refracted through nationalist prisms in the different countries on which all of us worked; these informed much of the discussion. Papers in this panel considered national parks, forest management and ethnic strife, and the technologies of nation-state building deployed in community-based conservation in order to elucidate how contested natures mediate the formation of nations, subjects, and citizens. A related theme that was explored led some of the participants to reflect on the relations between the making of colonial empire in the context of land and nature, and how this shaped, or simply compared with, the making of nation in the context of what must be considered postcolonial land relations and postcolonial ideas of nature.

By the end of the Heidelberg conference it was clear we had the makings of an interesting book on a topic surprisingly neglected in the vast and growing scholarship on the environmental history and anthropology of South Asia. We defined the topic as *ecological nationalism*. What we mean by this term is amply discussed in the first chapter of the book, so we will leave our readers to discover that meaning there. But it is worth noting here that, by working on this book, some of us have come to realize how salient it is to talk of ecological nationalism in a variety of contexts, i.e. ecological nationalisms.

Discussions of ecological security and natural assets circulate a lot in scholarly and policy discourse. These terms require elucidation as well. Presumably, security, assets, and affect (in many ways our primary interest in this book) are all meaningful when we are talking not merely of the individual but also of the groups to which the individual inevitably belongs and in which s/he participates. Examined closely, security, assets, and futures are imagined in the context of multiple collectives. When the environment or nature is the organizing concern, these collectives, on a grand scale, can be global—the world's climate, international petrochemical futures, war, the decimation of natural resources in economically poor but ecologically rich regions, and so forth. But it seems that managerial justifications for the environment or conservation of nature, and claims to home and heritage (place attachments of residents and non-residents) are rarely able to escape some form of nationalist associative logic when they are mobilized in the service of some environmental or nature-related cause. So, it appears, we are in the happy position of feeling that our project is just the beginning of what may become a larger exploration which some of us, and many others who read this book, will likely undertake.

For this energy-giving experience we have to thank first our collaborators, who have made the journey, through two meetings and innumerable email exchanges, rewarding and pleasant. Their essays are the heart of the book, and we begin by thanking them for putting their hearts into these. Bengt G. Karlsson, who has been with us from the start, and actually put us together, deserves special thanks for his initial efforts and enthusiasm and gracious participation later. Chris Tarnowski was with us at Madison, but could not continue. We thank him for early support to this project.

For reading, discussing, and commenting on versions of the introductory chapter we would like to thank, in addition to the other authors in this book, Neeladri Bhattacharya, Rosemary Coombe, Ann Gold, Thomas Blom Hansen, Stig Toft Madsen, Mahesh Rangarajan, Eric Worby, and various participants in the two conferences where these ideas were presented. Anonymous reports from readers for the publishers—Permanent Black and University of Washington Press—helped us revise and sharpen the arguments, while making the collection more cohesive. Our editors, Rukun Advani and Lorri Hagman, guided the manuscript expertly into production and helped us with a variety of tasks, including the illustrations.

Individually, Sivaramakrishnan would like to thank the Graduate School, University of Washington, for a travel grant that helped him attend the Heidelberg conference in 2002, and the American Council of Learned Societies Fellowship that earned him the leave in 2004–5 to finish writing and performing the editorial tasks that finally sent the script to press.

Cederlöf would like to thank the Bank of Sweden Tercentenary Foundation and the Swedish International Development Cooperation Agency for financially supporting her participation in the two conferences. She would also like to thank Björn Wittrock, Barbro Klein, Göran Therborn, and Heléne Andersson at the Swedish Collegium of Advanced Study in the Social Sciences, Uppsala University, for generously providing a research environment in which her initial ideas along these lines took root.

We would both like to thank our families for their patience and love, as we travelled and corresponded to complete this project over the last four years.

GUNNEL CEDERLÖF
Uppsala, May 2005

K. SIVARAMAKRISHNAN
Seattle, May 2005

NOTES ON CONTRIBUTORS

Nina Bhatt works at the Social Development Department of the World Bank in Washington, DC. She completed her PhD thesis, entitled "King of the Jungle: An Ethnographic Study of Identity, Power and Politics among Nepali National Park Officials," in the Department of Anthropology at Yale University in 2002.

Gunnel Cederlöf is Associate Professor of History at Uppsala University. Her work focuses on South Indian modern history, particularly agrarian labor relations, and the politics of land conflicts in forest and hill tracts. Her publications include *Bonds Lost: Subordination, Conflict and Mobilisation in Rural South India, c.1900–1970* (1997).

Vinita Damodaran is Senior Lecturer in the Department of History at the University of Sussex, UK. She is the author of *Broken Promises: Popular Protest, Indian Nationalism, and the Congress Party in Bihar, 1935–1946* (1992); co-editor (with Richard Grove and Satpal Sangwan) of *Nature and the Orient: The Environmental History of South and Southeast Asia* (1998); and co-editor (with Maya Unnithan-Kumar) of *Postcolonial India: History, Politics and Culture* (2000).

Claude A. Garcia completed his PhD, entitled "Sacred Forests of Kodagu: Ecological Value, Social Role and Implications for Conservation Biology" (University of Lyon I, France), in 2003. He is currently working for the French development-oriented research organization Centre de Coopération Internationale en Recherche Agronomique pour le Développement (CIRAD), in the field of biodiversity conservation and tropical forest management.

Urs Geiser, PhD, is Senior Researcher at the Development Study Group and Lecturer, Department of Geography, University of Zurich. His research focuses on the political ecology of natural resource use and rural development, and on development as practice. His ongoing research is located in northwest Pakistan, and in Kerala, India.

Götz Hoeppe, PhD in social anthropology, is editor of the astronomy magazine *Sterne und Weltraum* (Heidelberg) and part-time lecturer in social anthropology at Heidelberg University. His publications include *Blau: Die Farbe des Himmels* (1999) and *Conversations on the Beach: Debating Local Knowledge and Environmental Change in South India* (in press).

Bengt G. Karlsson is Research Fellow at the Department of Cultural Anthropology, Uppsala University. His work deals mainly with issues concerning indigenous peoples and environment in India, above all in the north-eastern region. His publications include *Contested Belonging: An Indigenous People's Struggle for Forest and Identity in Sub-Himalayan Bengal* (2000).

Antje Linkenbach, PhD, is a social anthropologist and sociologist currently working at the Institute of Social Anthropology, University of Heidelberg. She has published in the fields of social theory, ecology and development, and social movements, with a regional focus on South Asia, particularly the Himalaya.

Wolfgang Mey is Deputy of the Museum Service of Hamburg and a staff member of the Museum für Völkerkunde Berlin, Linden-Museum Stuttgart, Museum für Völkerkunde Hamburg. He lectures at the Institutes of Anthropology at the universities of Berlin, Tübingen, Mainz, and Hamburg. He has published on the Chittagong Hill Tracts, minority and human rights issues, rituals in Sri Lanka, and museology. His field research includes Austria, France, Bangladesh, and Sri Lanka.

Kathleen Morrison is Professor of Anthropology and Director of the Center for International Studies at the University of Chicago. Her research combines approaches from archeology, history, and paleoenvironmental analysis to address problems of agricultural change and landscape transformation, and their relations to political and economic organization. She is the author of *Fields of Victory: Vijayanagara and the Course of Intensification* (2000), co-editor of *Empires: Perspectives from Archaeology and History* (2001), and co-editor also of *Forager-Traders in South and Southeast Asia: Long-Term Perspectives* (2002).

J.-P. Pascal is Director of Research at the National Center for Scientific Research, and former Director of the French Institute at Pondicherry. He is the author of many books and maps of the Western Ghats in India. His publications include *Wet Evergreen Forests of the Western Ghats of India*

(1988), *Atlas of Endemics of the Western Ghats, India* (1997), and *Forest Map of South India* (six sheets, 1982–2002).

K. Sivaramakrishnan is Professor of Anthropology and International Studies, and Director, South Asia Center, University of Washington, Seattle. He is the author of *Modern Forests: Statemaking and Environmental Change in Colonial Eastern India* (1999, rpt. 2002); and co-editor (with Arun Agrawal) of two collections: *Agrarian Environments: Resources, Representations and Rule in India* (2000) and *Regional Modernities: The Cultural Politics of Development in India* (2003).

Sarah Southwold-Llewellyn is an economic anthropologist and Assistant Professor of Rural Development Sociology at Wageningen University. Her research in Pakistan has focused on the management of natural resources among agro-pastoralists in the Hindu Kush, with particular reference to dispute settlements. Currently, she researches the public–private management of marine fisheries in Andhra Pradesh.

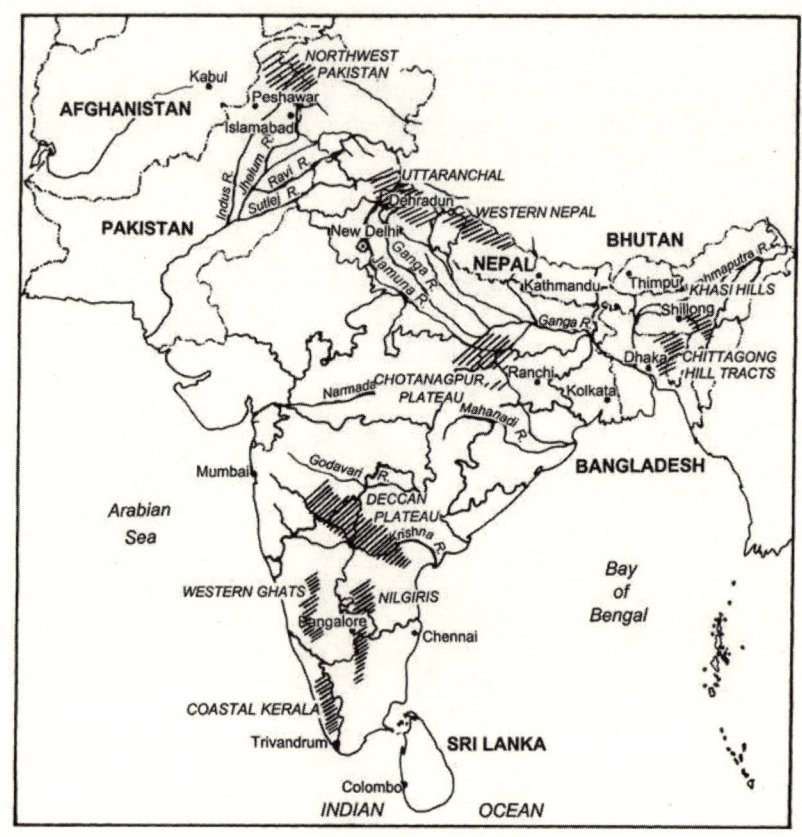

Map Showing Regions Discussed

1

INTRODUCTION

Ecological Nationalisms: Claiming Nature for Making History

K. Sivaramakrishnan and Gunnel Cederlöf

I

AT THE TIME OF WRITING, MILLIONS OF PEOPLE IN BANGLADESH and in east and north-east India have been displaced by floods, while yet another monsoon has failed in South India. Even at this time, a development project that has been called "the largest artificial water network in the world"—the Interlinking of Major Rivers—is on the planning board of the Indian government and has been declared top priority. Fourteen tributaries of the Ganges and Brahmaputra rivers in North India and Nepal are expected to distribute up to 1500 cubic meters of water per second via canals and pumping stations to seventeen rivers in the dry South.[1] In the process, flooding will be extensive and will drown the homes and livelihoods of a great number of people. The chief ministers of various states in the North fear farmers' unrest as water may become scarce, environmentalists speak of the spread of polluted waters, and popular movements protest the privatization of water resources. In a searing criticism of the scheme, Arundhati Roy observes: "the river-linking project makes big dams look like enlightenment itself. It will become to development debate what the Ram mandir in Ayodhya is to the communal debate [. . .] it is destructive even if it is never realized. It will be used to block every other local, more effective, more democratic irrigation project."[2] The valorization of secularism and democracy, the affirmation of small and local and nature-mindful solutions to natural resources needed by the citizenry, are all themes implicit in Roy's strong words. They invoke a vision of nationalist possibilities sacrificed in pursuit of more cosmopolitan, yet chauvinist, and centrist, approaches to the same problems. However, the first chairman of the project enthusiastically envisioned a private-sector boost and a ten percent growth in India's GDP, the creation of jobs in the farming, manufacturing and service sectors, and support for reforestation. Ultimately, the project is expected to spur national integration.

From quite different perspectives, the issues at stake center on the integrity and prosperity of the Indian nation. Once again, a state in the South Asian region plans to manifest its capacity to solve climatic, environmental, and distribution problems in firm, technological mega-scale solutions, while critics foresee dramatic and devastating social and environmental transformations. Many questions can be asked about linking rivers in India, but what the example highlights for us is the continuing struggle to define the nation in terms of massive projects of landscape and social engineering orchestrated by a central government. Some of these are enterprises, frequently centering on the redirection of water in India, that started soon after independence with the Damodar Valley Corporation.[3]

Manifestations of nationality and nationhood have long and complex histories in South Asia. As shared memories of mother nature, or as appropriated economic, political and religious geographies, terrestrial entities have been imagined in terms of dense ecological networks of relationship and often been the space or reference point for national aspirations. In recent times, different particularistic interests have claimed and appropriated landscapes and territories for the purpose of locating and justifying a specific and utopian version of the nation by accommodating its origin in the ancient past. Often, such claims are made to assert political space, and to place supposedly ancient national identities historically in the present. By identifying their roots in "time immemorial" or in "the beginning of creation," conflicting communities aim at legitimizing a variety of identity claims located in the unbounded time of eternity and nature.[4] Images have come to play a crucial role. The iconography of megafauna, and the spectacular avian species of known endemicity that nations adopt, quite apart from the sacred geographies of pilgrimage sites, can all now map the imaginary boundaries of nations.

Such references to creation and to virgin nature for the purpose of political recognition are not, however, recent phenomena. A similar rhetoric was deployed two centuries ago, when land conflicts emerged in new forms as the British East India Company moved into the forests and hills of the Indian subcontinent. Recent developments have only made the language of nature politically potent once again. So, we ask ourselves: what are the apparent relations between contested natures and multiple, often competing, nationalisms in the aftermath of the colonial encounter in South Asia? How are abiding concerns of sovereignty, self-determination, and place-based collective identities played out in the entanglement of nature devotion and nationalist aspirations in different parts of the subcontinent?

Moving from national utopian visions to state development interventions, we find that these are histories of nations in which wilderness and wild people have been brought into the fold of progressive possibilities. One may argue that this has been a way of domesticating popular social forces that critically phrase their agendas in terms of "region," "nation" or "people," because of their inability to find space within the political project of the nation-state. Hence, given these multiple communities and their varying agendas, aspirations and articulations of nation and nationhood come into conflict.

Such conflicts became acute in the last decades of the twentieth century precisely because of a growing disjuncture between the territorial, geo-political and economic spaces occupied by development projects, and the nation-state's reproductive infrastructure, respectively. As Ludden notes: "development projects are now most often outside state control. Yet national states also authorize most development projects; national boundaries inscribe the public sphere; and national systems of law, politics and culture implicate every locality."[5]

To argue a specific relationship to nature—to the ecology and landscape and to the place of origin, whether still living on this land or having been displaced from there—means to legitimize a right to this place by asserting specified close links between humanity and nature. However, many of the movements speaking from within or on behalf of people living within South Asian forests—people threatened by the nation-state's large-scale projects and global transnational interventions—face counterarguments and blame for land degradation. Such counterarguments target the usual suspects: paddy farmers, tropical shifting cultivators, woodcutters, and pastoralists, all of whom have come into the sights of world environmentalists once again. South Asian seasons are now viewed more intently through a global prism than ever before. This has happened not least because world climate historians have revived the study of linkages between ocean currents, temperature, rainfall, and food security that had first captured the imagination of colonial governments in tropical Asia and Africa during the nineteenth century.[6] Further, invasive species and exotic plants have been attacked both for representing the biotic advance of secular nationalism and the weakening consequences for more intimate forms of community fostered in villages and small towns—imagined as regions of greater authenticity and antiquity.[7]

But these are elements of ecological nationalism also present in other parts of the world. What is distinctive, we must ask, within the South Asian experience?

Apart from their distinctive monsoonal oscillations, South Asian regional environments are also distinguishably the product of large political entities and empires, emerging from Mughal unifications of land classification and purposive settlement of frontiers and the result of consolidations of the same enterprise—carried on with greater intensity—under the aegis of Britain's imperium.[8] In Pakistan, India and Bangladesh, colonial engineering, cartography, and the taxonomic schematization of landscapes ensured that a shared legacy of value hierarchies and esthetic prisms was bequeathed to these postcolonial nations, which began to explore ways, over the past five decades, to clarify or muddy the relations between territorial allegiances and natural boundaries. Nepal, though not so directly a part of this historical legacy in the early twentieth century, certainly got drawn into its influence in the latter part of the twentieth century, as development and nature conservation enterprises in the mountain monarchy grew within the shadow of postcolonial plains experiences nearby.

Within this distinct South Asian pattern we can make further fine distinctions relating to the different political trajectories that emerged in each nation-state. For instance, in India the inherent contradictions of federalism, and the suspicion with which state governments are regarded in relation to grand central schemes, have ensured that trans-regional and mega projects have always been hamstrung by the workings of democratic processes. This point is well illustrated in a fine study of the command area development schemes introduced in eastern India soon after World War II. As Klingensmith shows in the case of the Damodar Valley Corporation, such modern "temples" were not easy to build when the political powers of state legislatures and local bodies were circumscribed by the supposed importance of such monuments to the nation.[9]

Conflicting nationalisms, as Partha Chatterjee notes, are generated in postcolonial societies like South Asia when multiple nations are simultaneously constructed. A variety of assertions to nationhood and national identity thereby deny the common nation-state project as it is ideally imagined. In contrast to the "utopian homogeneous time of capital" in which nationhood, identity, and progress may be imagined as part of a shared space of lived experience, heterogeneous and conflicting nationalisms are located in real space; or, in Chatterjee's terms, in the "heterogeneous time of governmentality," in the Foucauldian sense. Chatterjee draws our attention to different temporal frames that shape ideas of nation in postcolonial societies. [10] Commenting on the need to consider these varied temporalities, often divergent and always present in the imagining of nations within specific historical periods, Akhil Gupta notes that "nationalism always has a utopian or messianic time [. . .] in the Third World, the utopian time of the nation is profoundly shaped by a sense of lag and a historical consciousness of lack."[11] We would like to add to this observation that different senses of urgency, deprivation, and complacence operate within individual postcolonial nations as regions and communities assess themselves on a scale of accomplishment naturalized by the developmental state. In these assessments, the extent and form of control over nature as resources or heritage (the two ideas are also at times conflated) become a measure of losses and aspirations.

For instance, much of north-east India is wracked by insurgency, political unrest, and social anxiety over interlopers and foreigners. The struggle over land and identity in these north-eastern regions is often described by participants and observers in the language of native belonging and elusive sovereignty.[12] This language works within and across nation-state boundaries. Frequently, such struggles are also depicted, in the press and in scholarship on sub-national movements, as a struggle over natural resources. But such analysis can miss facets of the struggles that are revealed when we notice how they sometimes work through the language of regional pride and cultural affiliation. The predicament of the All Bodo Students Union in Assam illustrates this point. Since 1989, this militant organization has destroyed infrastructure in the Manas tiger sanctuary as a way of attacking central authority, which opposes their demands for regional autonomy. In 2003, some factions within the organization resolved to recover "the lost glory of their region" by supporting the tiger conservation program and its efforts to restore forests and wildlife habitats as both conservation and commercial prospect.[13]

To us, as this example of the struggles in Bodo-land suggests, there is an additional point to be made in relation to the plural imaginings at work in postcolonial nations, and particularly in places like India that are committed to pluralism as an aspect of their constitutional identity. This refers to the other issue raised by Benedict Anderson about styles of imagination, and its modification by Satish Deshpande, who points to a dominant economic style and many undercurrents of cultural styles that were present in India from the late colonial period.[14] The capacity of regional and local social forces to exercise power by drawing upon various cultural styles—including nature-mediated ones of belonging and affinity to landscapes—by realizing the weakness of the nation-state and its economistic imaginings (which were shaped by anti-colonial struggle) is an underlying problematic in many of the contributions to this volume. Several of the essays here observe that varieties of ecological nationalism are summoned to work again, more so than ever before. Clearly, the problematic we are articulating needs to be addressed in the plural as ecological nationalisms.

Ecological nationalism, in our usage, refers to a condition where both cosmopolitan and nativist versions of nature devotion converge and express themselves as a form of nation-pride in order to become part of processes legitimizing and consolidating a nation. This concept of ecological nationalism links cultural and political aspirations with programs of nature conservation or environmental protection, while noting their expression in, and through, a rhetoric of rights that includes civil, human, and intellectual property rights.[15] We would like to suggest that the concept of ecological nationalism enables us to distinguish between civic and ethnic nationalism in a new and more productive way, in as much as it does not give to the civic version sole power to generate debates on the different classes of rights in a modern liberal political context. It is the argument of this essay, and of several contributions to this volume (cf. Damodaran, Karlsson, and Linkenbach), that the varieties of ethnic nationalism we identify, describe and discuss in India during the late twentieth century are complex products of a discourse of rights enmeshed in a discourse of regional or adivasi identity. This key recognition—of the hybrid nature of identity politics in a political universe of rights-based government and political activism—leads us to refuse the insistence that all indigenous and traditionalist claims are merely acts of strategic self-essentializing cultural identity politics. We argue the crucial importance of recognizing that these are so clearly also claims to territory, resources, and the desire to maintain subsistence livelihoods. The language of nature intimacy, stewardship, and respect for lived landscapes, as also other claims that affirm affinities between cultural identity and the environment, are perhaps "new political performatives" that seek to assert forms of sovereignty that groups and communities hope to establish on the hitherto unelaborated ground of human rights mediated by place attachments.[16]

In elaborating this concept we are aware that, at first glance, ecology may be equated with ecologism—namely, seeking to preserve nature in absolute terms without making allowance for human beings. But this is not the case. Ecological nationalism presupposes a radical change in human relations with the environment, which may imply changes in social and political life. In this sense ecologism contrasts with environmentalism, which seeks to manage externalities brought by contemporary patterns of production and consumption.[17] This is why ecology may appear antithetical to nationalism, of which the core vales are anthropocentric. But in fact ecology is understood by us in its broader sense, as the interrelatedness of environment and organisms. Nor is nationalism a universal ideology. As has been acknowledged by many theorists, every particular nationalism appropriates ideological values that circulate in many contexts but always does so in a distinct location in time and space. In the process, a specific idea of nationalism may of course employ durable concepts such as self-determination and sovereignty, which transcend particular varieties of nationalism.[18] But essentially, nationalism is a parasite that "preys upon other ideologies, forming new amalgams suitable for use by political entrepreneurs."[19]

There can thus be many different ways in which ecological nationalism is expressed. Two contrasting views of it can fruitfully be explored. One is the metropolitan-secular view of nature and its economistic and material uses for the nation. The other is an indigenist, or regionalist, reaction to the expansion of the high-modern nation-state in its imperial or post-Independence forms, or to the forces of globalization that intervene from outside the realms of nation-states. This problematic becomes especially relevant as it emerges at specific historical conjunctures in the era of modernity or global capitalism.[20]

A major characteristic of the metropolitan-secular appropriation of nature is that it claims to secure national integration and legitimacy for politics and projects generated or located in the heart of the nation-state. The proponents may be politicians, state bureaucrats, businessmen, or other interest groups, and the means may vary—for example, the appropriations may be political, institutional, military, or social. International agencies, or the forces of economic globalization, may also accommodate their appropriation of natural resources within a metropolitan-secular agenda, arguing that their actions, or the impacts of their activity, benefit the nation. Cultural differences, local histories, and regional geographical spaces need here to be overcome in favor of processes wherein romantic visions of nature via iconographic images may dramatically be seen to oversee or supervise a large-scale and forceful management of natural resources. The "secular" as it operates in this form of appropriation of nature does not hinder religious sentiments that may be expressed in nationalist terms. Rather, metropolitan-secular ecological nationalism works through an emphasis on the constitutional underpinnings of the liberal modern state in its colonial, imperial, or independent form, and its appropriation of nature for the good of the nation or the "public." As a community evolving from state formations claiming large geographical areas, this singular "nation" therefore expresses and redefines what it means to be a subject or a citizen: an "Indian," "Pakistani," "Nepali," and so on. When considered from the perspective of ecological nationalism, these redefinitions are also about the proper uses of natural bounties available in the territorial confines of the nation-state. The cultural constructions implicit in these claims are erased by erasing the people who may have inhabited these "enclaves of nature," and by viewing landscapes largely separated from histories of their production.[21] Cosmopolitan-secular ecological nationalism actively weds the self-conscious newness of the modern nation to the antiquity of its lands by arguing for the nation-state, and for its leaders as the repository of all the wisdom needed to hold an ancient heritage within a beneficial relationship of service to the new citizenry.

In contrast, indigenist or regionalist expressions of ecological nationalism are mostly, but not always, a reaction to the predatory state or to global encroachments on the life and livelihoods of communities being marginalized by such expansion. The distinctive features of such ecological nationalism include its notions of authenticity, its physical attachments to place and nature, and its historical memories that are forms of attachment to and solidarity with a specific environment. Adivasi assertion, of indigeneity, for the sake of securing rights in lands and forests that they inhabit, come to mind when we think of examples of this kind of ecological nationalism. But the historical record equally reveals that regionally dominant communities or particular cultural and ethnic political groups may symbolically and materially appropriate nature for the sake of increasing their own political and economic control within a region. A good example of this is provided by the political agency shown by Roman Catholic Mukkuvar fisherfolk in Kanyakumari district of South India. These fisherfolk have supported the Hindu-rightist Bharatiya Janata Party in their efforts to secure access to fishing rights and assert their claims over such rights by deploying the language of belonging—at once in the locality and in the nation. As Ajantha Subramanian shows, regional community alignment with specific large-scale development projects can, in certain historical moments, serve as a form of local cultural assertion. "Coastal modernity had emerged as a variant of national modernity, and the modern Mukkuvar as a fisher who understood technological progress, not in an abstract sense, but as a means to caste and religious minority empowerment."[22] She goes on to argue that community and place-making at the local level rest on the points of intersection where forms of ecological mobilization and nationalist sentiment meet, as either antagonists or friends.[23]

Our point is that, in either case, the landscape becomes the place for contested identities. References to "tradition" can be made, but these should not necessarily be understood as reactionary visions of golden pasts or as the objects of nostalgic yearning. For claims to putative tradition are often made to define and assert rights that were promised by the liberal state as the consequence of full and equal citizenship and political representation, and the state itself is often used as a space to achieve particular aims. The changing character of the nation-state has serious implications for citizenship, as Seyla Ben-Habib reminds us. She identifies many of the changes with the end of unitary citizenship, and the concomitant demands "for pluralization of cultural identities [. . .] decentering of administrative uniformities [. . .] and the weakening of bonds between continuing territorial residency and citizenship responsibilities."[24] While much of this is happening in South Asia too, the lens of ecological nationalism enables us to see those occasions when citizenship is claimed precisely by combining plural cultural identities with renewed bonds of territorial affiliation or affinity. These are the arguments that a supple modern nation-state should accommodate apparently incongruous claims of culture on the idea of the nation and its places in the environment, or in nature.

In pursuing this important qualification to the general terms of argument mapped in relation to the globalization literature by Ben-Habib, our discussion also draws upon, but modifies, earlier discussions of civic and ethnic nationalism, while relating these forms of nationalism to ecological consciousness. Civic nationalists who may seek to manage and direct nature in environmentally profitable ways can, paradoxically, be simultaneously more likely to find their values and goals compatible with those of contemporary ecologism. In contrast, the goals and values of ethnic nationalism can be incompatible with ecologism—which risks displacing people for the sake of ecology—and are also often incompatible with the values of Green political actors. Ethnic nationalists are rather able to appropriate naturalistic discourses.[25] In this way, ecological nationalism expresses processes as well as conditions, for it refers to the ways in which varieties of nationalism are mediated and constructed via reference to the natural.[26]

To conclude this first section, in which we have sought to define our term ecological nationalism, we would like to underline that the easy dichotomy between civic and ethnic nationalism is complicated by our concept and by our cases, in two clear ways. One relates to rights-based notions of collective identity and citizenship, which we argue are present in ethnic nationalism within South Asia for a variety of reasons which have to do with modern political formations of the region in the aftermath of British colonial rule and anticolonial freedom struggles. Thus, ethnic nationalisms, we argue, do not necessarily define a space where rights-based identities are refused, but in fact may provide a space where such identities are produced in combination with place-based identities mediated by claims on nature. The other point we wish to make relates to the often counterintuitive relationship that we find between civic nationalism, ethnic nationalism, and ecologism. Several essays herein show that civic nationalists (in the guise of metropolitan secularists) can ally with forms of ecologism that deny a more complex web of claims, rights, and sovereignties favoring unitary nationalism. In contrast, ethnic nationalism can generate the political space for a different ecologism which seeks to accommodate "rights of nature" and "rights of livelihood" in a constructive, mutualist relationship.

II

Our consideration of ecological nationalisms is relevant to questions that scholars of patriotism and nationalism in South Asia are asking toward understanding these collective aspirations for a history deeper than the history of colonialism.[27] One promise of ecological nationalism, as an analytical perspective, is its recognition that identities which are shared and mediated by attachments to places are always produced in the context of the formation of polities, and that these political processes are not unique to colonialism, even if they took distinctive forms in that period. Exploring this promise takes the study of modern identity formation in South Asia into a more dialogic relationship with "colonial knowledge" and its construction via censuses, ethnological surveys, and cartography.[28] Another possibility opened up by this approach relies more on the paths and shapes taken by the specific modes of inquiry associated with environmental history. Alongside heightened global concerns for the environment in times of increased insecurity, historical inquiries into environmental predicaments have taken new turns. The 1980s search into history, notably in the works of anthropologists, geographers, sociologists and political scientists, embraced and refined the concepts and tools of environmental studies. Paradoxically, as they developed the study of contemporary environmental problems, history and the exploration of long-term historical processes became the modes of inquiry. And as environmental and ecological research permeated the social science and humanities disciplines in the 1990s, the interdisciplinary rubric of political ecology made possible integrated studies that linked analyses of social change, environment, and development.[29]

For a long time, concerns for the environment targeted its degradation, which put the focus on the management of natural resources as well as on the policy priorities generated by state-manufactured development plans. Engagement with the formation and scope of the nation-state and international development policies were key points of departure for South Asian environmental history, and much attention has been given to the impact on the environment of the expanding colonial state. Despite intense study of the colonial state and the consequences of its expropriatory approach to natural resources, only lately has attention been brought to bear on the complex workings of power, at several levels of society, which have shaped actual and everyday forms of the polity, influenced actual resource control, and defined ownership. Most historical studies of colonial intervention in the nineteenth century have taken the role of the state in resource degradation for granted. This has meant that, at times, specific regimes of property, access, and resource-use have been left unproblematized.[30] We believe that the merging of political economy studies with postcolonial critical discussion of the nation-state may prove useful in bringing out the complex relationship between the experience of loss of access to physical and social landscapes (in both their material sense and in terms of values), and notions of lost identities. To the extent that the transformation of nature and polities in analyses that are sensitive to changes over time and space has been embraced within the field of environmental history, we now have a language and diagnostic tools for this project.

This development within the research field has paved the way for a broader understanding of historical inquiry. More than an inquiry into specific historical trajectories, events or discourses, environmental history has come to signify the use of historical explanation for present-day predicaments. In this respect, researchers working on South Asia have anticipated the more systematic incorporation of historical modes of inquiry and argument into environmental policy analysis in the various parts of the world that were made objects of development. Some have even, in line with Stephen Dovers, argued that environmental history must take urgent policy issues like culpability and relevance as its central concerns. They argue that history needs to provide explanations for the roots of, and reasons for, such things as institutions, consumption patterns, economic activities, settlement arrangements, and scientific approaches "relevant to particular environmental phenomena."[31] This means emphasizing the utility and immediate applicability of historical research with the intention of transforming historical findings into policy directives.

This is one example showing the crossroads between different disciplines, as well as where the research field of environmental history at large has come to transgress the boundaries of academic disciplines. Dovers has further suggested a prognostic agenda, in addition to the diagnostic mandate, i.e. an agenda to specify the conditions for global and local coexistence and stewardship, the need for these having been made more immediate by the spread of war, calamity, disease, and income disparities within and between nations.[32] However, within such an agenda the imminent risk is that present environmental policy concerns will structure not only the analytical frame of inquiry, but even shape research priorities—in terms of empirical focus and the formation of hypotheses for studies of the past. Such priorities have occasionally led to a scapegoat search for historical villains who disrupted an environmentally sustainable balance, and, in the course of this search, the so-often-targeted swidden cultivators have either been criminalized or idealized as Rousseauan noble savages.[33]

Yet, expansive visions can inspire cutting across disciplines and breaking new paths. Rather than extending the research focus to general policy assumptions, and claiming extensive applicability for the findings, recent work has, even more, argued the need for local histories and for integrating local, multifaceted realities with regional and world histories. The many studies critical of general development policies modeled on Western modernization trajectories have been followed by critical accounts of similarly extensive claims phrased by populist and eco-feminist analyses, with their often idealistic notions about primitive people, community, and women. Sarah Jewitt, for instance, argues that romantic notions of "traditional knowledge" and women's superior skills as managers of nature only work to conceal repressive social and gender structures. This "has tended to obscure [. . .] the political economy of factors underlying women's subordination, nature's degradation, and their interlinks." Place-based peoples have, so to speak, placed-based knowledges, which are dependent also on socially structuring relationships with gender divisions of labor and cultural restrictions on women's mobility.[34] Further gender-structured analysis sensitive to context is needed, not least in studies of subalternity and indigenous assertion where, even now, idealized dichotomies often structure the research.[35] Analyses that this recognition should prompt are already taking shape in South Asian scholarship. They are the product of hard cumulative work as well as intense debate in the relatively new but rapidly maturing field of environmental history. They range from river basin to tank irrigation studies, and from studies of vast biosphere reserves to community-based forest management, from research on poisoned wells to the pollution of major rivers and coastal fisheries.[36]

Kathleen Morrison's contribution to this volume illustrates this point very well. She alerts us to the long-standing history of exchange and interdependence between agriculturalists and hunter-gatherers. These relations were marked by a high degree of variability, with specific groups of people altering their strategies in relation to ecological, demographic, and political imperatives. Contemporary forager groups are best viewed as the outcome of historically generated, but not necessarily evolutionary, processes where cumulative impacts, events of unexpected intensity and power, and revolutionary outcomes followed no predictable paths. Certainly, then, such modern practitioners of simple agriculture are not cultural-evolutionary throwbacks. Further, political economy, agricultural ecology, and trade have to become central to the study of foragers. Morrison explores how foragers in the Western Ghats became involved in long-distance trade and shows how, as a result of market logic, their livelihoods became vulnerable to market demands as well as to political conflicts between states in Europe. The scope of such study is relevant also for the present time, for it suggests that polities are not to be understood in terms of cultural coherence over time, but in terms of enduring socio-economic integration over time and over space.

The lines drawn by trading houses and mercantile states with imperial ambitions or nineteenth-century empires have to be recognized and analyzed for their historical impact on the formation of nations and nationalities. As we also see in Urs Geiser's work on Pakistan, these lines are especially important for the way in which they shape variegated citizenship within nations.[37]

Morrison also notes an empirical pattern with implications for the understanding of long-term historical processes. She observes that forest people have always been integrated into larger political structures. In broad agreement with Sumit Guha, she notes that tribal polities were built and subsided in the hills along caste-Hindu ones and along Muslim states in the plains.[38] In the Western Ghats, with the increasing scope of political authority, the physical distance from the source of the product and the volume of stored goods increased, as did settlement nucleation and the status of landowning groups. In this process, people living off forest products specialized their trade and became exclusively forager-traders, dependent on economic fluctuations far outside their range of influence. Subsequently, upland economies and political ecologies changed. Such geographically grounded hierarchies, from coastal cities to riverine towns and to upland forest cultivators and gleaners, were built around caste and community hierarchies which were reinforced within these processes. Such political flux and ecological transformations have to be further situated within what Sanjay Subrahmanyam has called the historical self-consciousness that emerged in various non-European traditions. This happened as regional polities and successor states narrated these changes into accounts of empire and ethnonationalism, which often took the form of *sthala purana* in South India.[39] Local histories were frequently a record of the ways in which ruling elites consecrated their relations to lands claimed, and would include forms of religious enactment embodying these claims. Building temples, sacralizing nature in the vicinity of such construction, and narrating the wars of deities protecting and controlling the wilderness formed the substance of ethnonationalisms narrated in sthala purana.[40]

The significance of regionally specific polities in hill and forest areas, as well as sensitivity to historical time, become even more clear when Morrison's study is read with Gunnel Cederlöf's work on the Western Ghats. Compared to the Portuguese trading company's indirect influence on hill societies in the seventeenth century, the impact of the British East India Company in the nineteenth century on polities in the Western Ghats was deeper and transformative by way of extensive claims to land and resources, and via the physical presence of colonial administration in the Nilgiri Hills. The scale of the claims also changed in considerable ways. Both trading houses strove to ensure monopolistic status, but where the Portuguese claimed monopoly in specific goods—in the resource—the British claimed mono-poly over the totality of nature in the form of sovereign rule. All access to resources was now to be derived from the sovereign ruler and, thus, trading empires came to be political empires.

The colonial appropriation of nature in the Nilgiris followed several different paths. Cederlöf argues that, within the Company, there were contradictions in perceptions regarding the utility of space and nature. No single polity was at work or in agreement within the colonial administration with regard to the conquering of forest territories. The district administration argued forcefully for securing proprietary rights in land for all subjects, i.e. both for Europeans and for the pastoralist Toda community. In this way, the colonial administration there embodied the eighteenth-century merchants of the Company who secured profit and landed estates for themselves, even while it projected the British subjects' concern for the legitimacy of the English Common Law by which the liberties to property and security were to be ensured. In contrast, the Madras government intervened by administrative means and regulations to establish sovereign rule whereby all rights in land would be subordinated to the absolute rights of the ruler. Cederlöf argues that, in the process of formal codification, legal rights were shaped in relation to local conflicts, and local conditions had a deciding effect on their implementation. Ultimately, however, the pastoralists were alienated from both the material and social resources that had been manifest in nature. In its intricate elaboration of legal terminology, the strategies of the Madras government to get control over land resemble similar processes today—as is clear in Urs Geiser's study of the North West Frontier Province (NWFP). Geiser emphasizes, in particular, the political geography of the region, and how this interacts with the long institutional history of forest administration. In the process of drawing new administrative and economic boundaries in the landscapes, socio-political and religious geographies were trespassed. Therefore, Cederlöf argues, the process of establishing proprietary rights was one of exclusion in which rights were assigned on particularistic bases, differently for different communities.[41]

The regional specificity of the formation and the application of legal codes is significant in both Geiser's and Cederlöf's studies, which bring local histories to the center of the problematic. Götz Hoeppe's examination of the history of artisanal fishing and fisherfolk in Kerala visits the issue of local histories from a slightly different perspective. We know this quite well as the issue of local knowledge of natural resource management and local epistemologies of living-with-nature. Hoeppe brings out the ways in which knowledge is socially constructed, profoundly located in time and space, and, in the case of the Kerala fishermen, deeply entrenched in experiences of nature. In local epistemology, nature has bodily and gendered characteristics; the ocean is the "mother," and the flow of male rivers brings cool monsoon waters into intercourse with a hot female sea, which is beneficial for fish catches. When such seasonal variations are upset by technological interference, such as the damming of rivers, the consequences for the fishers are not merely economic: their lifeworld is violated. Given their place-based livelihood, the Kerala artisanal fishermen have not been physically displaced from their villages by state-led development projects. What Hoeppe describes is rather a displacement from a lifeworld whose meanings have changed over time. The question of being native to a place is often raised in the most intimate language of kinship extension. But this affinity between artisanal fisherfolk and the seas that support their livelihood is also constructed in ways that carry internationalist tones. Colonial, and subsequently national, developmental strategies clearly quantified and alienated ocean fisheries from their everyday community into national strategies of control and management. This situation resembles the experiences of the Paharis in Uttarakhand, where natural resources have been appropriated and utilized by states since the late nineteenth century, and, in the process, customary rights curtailed. In analyzing these historical trajectories, Antje Linkenbach contrasts the pragmatic with the cultural symbolism of nature. She reveals two different contexts in which nature became an issue and discursive point of reference, which happened when hill dwellers faced threats to their livelihood by environmental exploitation and natural disasters caused by denudation of the hills.

Vinita Damodaran notes a trend in East India in the eighteenth and nineteenth centuries similar to that described by Morrison for South India. During this period, the status of groups like the Mundas, Hos and Oraons declined on account of the encroachment by Indian, and later colonial, power on their lands and polities. In the course of their subsequent marginalization, resistance and cultural difference developed among them. However, where Morrison chooses to emphasize the integration of such groups into larger political entities, Damodaran highlights the complex ways in which these interactions generated an identity of difference. In a critical reading of arguments that appear to dismantle terms such as "tribe," "forest," and "indigenous" for the sake of disproving their historical authenticity—as has been done for example by Sumit Guha—Damodaran provides a bold argument about the nature of tribal difference in the context of multiple emerging forms of nationalism in colonial and postcolonial India which provoke the articulation of indigenous nations. Such categories and claims of indigeneity among these tribes are continuously salient also in the twentieth century. Here indigeneity refers to an affinity between landscape and culture that is identified, performed, and mobilized in claims for land rights threatened by processes of secular national development. It may be argued that as the nation-state was established in the period of high development, such regional assertions came to be seen as a threat to the nation-state project of political integration and, consequently, that the specific forms of regional resistance changed. Legislation that was shaped to suit the empire's needs for pacification, subjecthood, revenue, and resource management in the late nineteenth century came, over time, to be adjusted and used for national integration, citizenship, and control. In such ways, the shaping of regional identity relates both to landscapes and to polity.

The formation of villages and rural hierarchies in Chotanagpur in East India remains a vexed question, with both tribal and non-tribal peoples emerging as intermediaries and little kings in the twilight of the Mughal empire and before the consolidation of British rule.[42] In this way, not only Morrison, Cederlöf and Hoeppe, but also Damodaran, elaborate ways in which people located at the margins of empires realized and asserted means to sustain livelihood, territory, and identity. These four studies clearly show the necessity of avoiding general statements about "colonial rule" or the "colonial state" in regional analyses. For Morrison, colonial power implies Portuguese trading monopolies. Cederlöf's study discusses the establishment of colonial administration and control in the early nineteenth century. The people of Chotanagpur in Damodaran's contribution are confronted with the Empire when it reached its peak in the nineteenth century. And in Hoeppe's work colonial rule is the late British empire. This unevenly experienced and historically limited transformative change brought about by colonial rule in the process of state formation, which then argues the need to attend to regional and temporal variations, has also been elaborated by K. Sivaramakrishnan. His book structures an argument about forest management and environmental change in East India around the institutional changes and governmentality of the East India Company, in contrast to crown rule.[43]

We need to bring the elaboration of regionally specific patterns of environmental and political history back into the larger-scale consideration of empire and its various iterations. This is necessary in order to explore the relationship between region, nature, and nation. For we have set ourselves the task of looking at how nationalist sentiment is expressed in the formation of regional polities within the contested ground of affinities to nature. This requires a brief detour through the academic study of empire, which is older than the British Empire itself. Among British historians, Edward Gibbon's *The Decline and Fall of the Roman Empire* (1776–88), written in the time of the American Revolution, provided the tenor to a debate in the nineteenth century on the longevity and possible downfall of the British Empire. Historians in Victorian England, like Thomas Babington Macaulay and J.R. Seeley, answered the question with a firm belief in progress mediated by benevolent British imperial rule. Macaulay, however, was more arrogantly convinced of the Indian elite's need to mimic English culture, institutions, opinions and "intellect"; Seeley's concern was to see the "emancipation" of colonies within a "Greater Britain."[44] Empire and imperialism have since been the core questions within many empirical and theoretical inquiries, and the area of British imperial studies has provided a wealth of historiographies.[45]

A perspective which remains underdeveloped is a comparative history of the different European empires claiming territories and influence in South Asia. British imperial narratives of victory in the aftermath of the Napoleonic wars can fruitfully be contrasted with French imperial narratives of loss. Similarly, as French, British, Portuguese, Dutch, and other colonial powers were rooted in different parts of the world at different periods of time, also their visions of empire or rule in South Asia, as well as their production of "colonial knowledge" also differed. Considering these varying regional contexts and local histories of colonial experience, it is not farfetched to assume different discourses in Francophone and Portuguese South Asia. These would serve to counterpoint the Anglophone discourses that have completely dominated both political and academic debate since the eve of the British Empire on the subcontinent. There are debates on whether

"European knowledge" was produced by the establishment of colonial institutions on the Indian subcontinent, or whether a kind of long-term and stable common "European essence" of knowledge can be dated back to the medieval period within Europe. However, these debates leave out the possible influence of the heterogeneity of Europe's history on the nature and production of knowledge about the Orient. Such analyses will further help modify singular and essentialized conceptions of Europe in the sphere of ideologies and ideas.[46]

Lately, however, the study of empire has taken a new turn. Michael Hardt and Antonio Negri redefine the concept of "empire" to equate the global rule of capital within the era of globalization. They do not find "empire" a relevant term to denote either polity or the rule of colonial powers. These powers operated within the logic of imperialism and ultimately depended on the exercise of sovereignty by nation-states outside their own boundaries. However, Hardt and Negri argue, this does not make them empires. The ultimate significance of empire is the absence of nation-state sovereignty. Sovereignty itself has not disappeared but has rather moved into the sphere of the global, where it exercises a single logic of rule, which is empire. The distinctive features of empire, in Hardt and Negri's argument, is its lack of boundaries and physical power centers, its a-historic regime, ending in eternity, and its ability to create the world it inhabits by operating on all registers of the social order. Hardt and Negri go on to discuss the transition to "Empire," which they locate in the defeat of colonialism by the establishment of sovereign nation-states in the former colonies. However, this is explained as a delegated struggle, in that it established a bourgeoisie; the revolution was lost in "realism" and in the hierarchies of the world market, where all the dreams of autonomous sovereign rule were lost. The fate of the postcolonial nation-state is its subordination within the global order of capital. Hence, this use of the term empire becomes a way to discuss globalization in a different frame.[47]

So, what happens to analyses of South Asia from the eighteenth to the twentieth centuries if empire is ripped out of imperialism and made to denote the major characteristic of the postmodern order? Can we speak of ecological imperialism, or "green imperialism" (in the words of Richard Grove),[48] without speaking of an empire with a clear political core, claiming absolute sovereignty over nature? New theories of empire, like early writing on globalization, clearly underestimate the role of regional polities, patriotisms, and nation forms that emerged and sustained in, and through, the processes of global integration and subsumption that followed. In the present book, the studies of nineteenth- and twentieth-century India, relating to the Western Ghats and Chotanagpur, indicate how the long-distance connections and the forceful incorporation of diverse territories and peoples within the physical and political realms of the empire, were also structured and found legitimization in its discourse. As is evident in the Chotanagpur case, this discourse appears to have contributed to structuring also the political space at the margins of empire, where multiple ethnic nationalisms took shape. From the centre of these "margins" the encroachment of "colonial forces" into forest tracts may not be immediately identified as the presence of empire. The crucial difference is apparent in the colonial empire's extensive connections, its absolutist claims to power, its comparative lack of commitment to the needs of its subjects—who were assigned unequal subjecthood even as their politics and livelihoods were restructured. The ideological legitimization for this imperial expansion came to include the two faces of the eighteenth-century Enlightenment—those of liberalism and racism—without the marriage of which the ideological bases of the nineteenth-century empire would not have been sustained.[49]

The integration of liberal debates and principles of law with increasingly racial conceptions of people come out clearly in the elaboration of the Nilgiri situation within this volume. In its transition from a trading company to a political empire, the colonial administration appeared initially more preoccupied with the question of law, rather than with state power. By means of law, people and nature could both be subjected to colonial rule. Cederlöf contrasts two positions within the Company in the early nineteenth century. One focused the British subjects' exclusive rights in property in accordance with native custom, a position that found much support in the intellectual and political debates of the Scottish Enlightenment. The other focused the subjects' rights as being subordinate to the superior principle of the "public good," which can be described as a way of phrasing utilitarian ideas of government. The former position, emphasizing the value and utility of nature as defined by "aboriginal" livelihood and landscape use, had strong proponents in the district and local administrations of the South Indian forests. In deep conflict with district administrators, the Government of Madras argued for the public need as this was defined by the colonial government. Both positions rested on racial conceptions of people, and arguments based on ethnographic surveys were phrased either to include or exclude the pastoralist population from rights in nature.

Vinita Damodaran suggests an interesting shift in patterns of community and identity formation in the Munda community. The sustained attack on forests, and thereby on the livelihood of residents in these tracts, also produced by the end of the nineteenth century a pan-regional consciousness of difference and exploitation that came to be shared in the adivasi identity developed by various groups in the Jharkhand region (newly constituted in 2000 as the state of Jharkhand). The essays by Morrison and Damodaran also help us differentiate processes of economic integration that have linked hill tribal polities with plains economies and international trade flows on the one hand, and processes of political and cultural subsumption on the other. In the assertion of cultural and political autonomy, even while affirming control over natural resources and landscapes that evoke regional identities, the politics of indigenousness comes into its own. One may suggest that this occurs only when the nation-state form is clearly becoming hegemonic in its command over all manner of political community and collective memory. However, one may also extend Manuel Castells's perception of nationalisms in the postmodern era to apply also to identity formation in South Asian forest tracts under colonial rule. Nation-state formation has, for good reason, been mainly discussed in terms of the long history of struggles for freedom from colonial rule, emphasizing in the South Asian context the emergence of Hindus and Muslims as visible nations. However, in the words of Castells: "nationalism, and nations, have a life of their own, independent from statehood, albeit embedded in cultural constructs and political projects."[50] The role of nation formation at the margins of larger political processes and in conflict with emerging nation-states should not be underestimated.

III

The essays in this volume engage the question of reimagining the nation in the context of writing environmental history. This is a project of increasing salience, despite all the claims made on behalf of globalization, because, as Manuel Castells says, we live in the "age of nationalist resurgence, expressed both in the challenge to established nation-states, and in the widespread reconstruction of identity on the basis of nationality."[51] Such perspectives have not easily gained a hearing in research debates. Academic disciplinary divides have tended to separate inquiries into questions concerning institutions (including state formation) and identities (including subject formation). These divides are unable to grasp the tensions inherent in conditions of postcolonialism, where continuity and rupture, mimesis and repudiation, lived hybridity and the quest for authenticity are in constant conflict and correspondence. Recent research by postcolonial theorists has engaged with the question of nation and identities under colonial rule along these lines in useful ways. But it has still had little to say in relation to the manifestations of nations in nature. It is from within the field of environmental history that studies of ideas and representation are now increasingly brought into communication with a new materialism.[52]

Castells argues that nationalism needs to be reinvestigated from four fresh perspectives. First, contemporary nations may be entities independent of states. Second, nationalism had by the end of the twentieth century followed a wide range of cultural orientations and political projects which were inadequately understood as merely the working out of nineteenth-century European models. Third, scholars need to attend more to popular and other non-elite mobilizations that sustain contemporary nationalisms and are often reactions against elites. And, fourth, these current nationalisms are more likely to seek the defence of institutionalized cultures than the formation of states.[53] Such a socio-historical grounding of the study of nationalism not only offers the opportunity to combine material and symbolic treatments of the question, but also allows us to recognize that, even though "neoliberal global trends appear to have heightened the tenuousness of the coincidence of nation and state, they have also spurred national, supranational, and subnational state strategies [. . .] that seek to fortify this inherited framework."[54]

The work of anthropologists on nationalism contributes to the study of symbolic inequities that structure national citizenship in old and new nations that espouse multiculturalism, and uses the question of hybridity to trouble the relationship to autochthony which is so integral to the definition of national identity.[55] Interesting new directions thus emerge when anthropologists and historians of South Asia draw upon the ideas presented by Castells, when they turn to questions of nation, nationalism, and regional identity while dealing with issues of natural resource history, environmental politics, and nature conservation. This leads to an investigation of the "quasi-states" that new nationalisms, including ecological nationalisms, seek to create as they dismantle multinational states, assemble plurinational states, and participate in multilateral processes of state formation linking regional political formations to global governance—enacted through capital flows, migration, and international environmental regulations.

The study of nationalism in South Asia and elsewhere has often centered on political mobilizations wherein the nation around which mobilizations occurred has been taken for granted. This has been relatively easy for scholarship that assumed nations emerging out of political and economic integration within established territorial boundaries. Several culturalist critics of such ideas about nationalism, including John Pemberton, Benedict Anderson, and Ashis Nandy, have found the genesis of nationalist ideas in the lives and work of the intelligentsia—i.e. the urbane.[56] Such elite-centered historiography has been questioned by contributors to *Subaltern Studies*. But they too, curiously enough, have oriented their study of subaltern struggles to the national movement, if only to deny the participation of subaltern social movements in a unitarily defined freedom struggle.[57] Dipesh Chakrabarty critically addresses the longevity of an imperial historiography in which modernization, capitalism, and civilization were evolutionarily determined in transition narratives, carried on by generations of Indian nationalists.[58] Arguably, environmental history emerged within the confines of these dominant perspectives. Both in its early intimations, principally as a subtle undercurrent in agrarian history,[59] and later in self-confident and overt forms in forest and social movement history,[60] Indian scholarship on the environment was firmly established within the critique of colonialism, the nation-state, development, and the transitions to capitalism that engrossed a wider nationalist and postcolonial historiography.

The critique of historicism and evolutionary theories of history has in the hands of some practitioners of *Subaltern Studies* led to a critique of History itself. It is occasionally claimed that the entire academic discipline is a European-centered post-Enlightenment enterprise that regulates collective memory and produces forms of sanctioned, popular remembrance, favoring the nation as the preferred mode of political solidarity. However, as essays in this volume also show, social science and humanities research into environmental predicaments tends to prefer historical modes of knowing. In problematical ways, the sweeping indictment of historical consciousness that has emerged in the fold of poststructural scholarship has promoted a critique of essentialism in the writing of history from which it exempts itself. Further, by overestimating the power and reach of colonialism, the inner social dynamics reinforcing colonial power structures in South Asian societies, and the role of precolonial ideas and social formations in building colonial rule and sustaining or diminishing aspects of it, is underestimated.[61]

Recent work by Partha Chatterjee and Sudipta Kaviraj has, however, moved discussions in more intriguing directions. Nationalism—as a crucible for forging contrary visions of desirable prospects and a site for articulating identity politics—has now become a topic of inquiry.[62] One provocative contribution comes from Aloysius, who notes that India has become not a nation-state but in fact a powerful state-system comprising multiple warring communities. There is in India, he suggests, no nation.[63] In writing against the received wisdom of nationalist historiography, Aloysius distinguishes cultural nationalism from a political nationalism that he equates with the urge to democracy and full citizenship for all classes, castes, and religious groups in modern India. Aloysius finds indigenous roots for these democratic aspirations among dalits, adivasis, and religious minorities. Kaviraj, in his own way, remarks on something similar: he calls it unforced common sense, and notes the absence of plural cultural sensitivity in elite nationalism. This cultural failure gives the modern bureaucratic nation-state "vernacular feet of clay." State, capital, and community are present in both these very different analyses, but what is fascinating is their shared conclusion about the failure, or absence, of nation. For Aloysius it is a *political* failure resulting from the cultural hegemony of Gandhian and Nehruvian ideologies. For Kaviraj it is a *cultural* failure of cosmopolitan nationalism in the face of vernacular aspirations to nationhood.

These disagreements about the role played by cultural processes in the struggle for articulating nations in the Indian subcontinent actually serve as a productive tension that can be explored very fruitfully in environmental studies. Take the theme of tourism, the nation consumed, and the role specific regions play in shaping a national imagination. As Antje Linkenbach shows in her essay, the people who fought for a separate Uttarakhand and obtained the separate state of Uttaranchal simultaneously articulated their difference from the plains of Uttar Pradesh as Paharis—a regionalism mediated by geography—and underlined their place as citizens in the Indian nation who, among other things, were the guardians of a pan-Indian Hindu heritage of temples and watersheds of holy rivers. The convergence that has occurred between environmentalisms celebrating a more universal esthetic of pristine nature, and those colored by religious chauvinism (mainly Hindu versions) in North India is, in this regard, important to note.

The Vrindavana Forest Revival Project in Uttar Pradesh, started in 1991 by both environmental and religious groups, is illustrative. Vrindavana is seen as the birthplace of Krishna and, after the Ram Janmabhumi liberation campaign and the destruction of the Babri Mosque, the "liberation of

Krishna Janmabhumi" has become central to the agenda of Hindu conservatives—as Mukul Sharma points out. A fair held to honor the Kosi river was initiated in the early 1990s in Bihar to help control increasing land erosion and the river's seasonal change of course. This fair not only involved elaborate river worship by Brahmins, but also the drowning of a small goat as a mark of sacrifice.[64] Beyond this, the example of the protest against the construction of the Tehri Dam in Uttaranchal most clearly shows the convergence of environmentalisms that we have alluded to above. It also shows a common spirit of ecological nationalism inspired by very different cultural motivations and allegiances. Mukul Sharma has once again shown how issues of environmental and national security are conflated with Hindu sacred geography in the Western Himalaya of India:

> For the state and the pro-dam people, nation and nation-building has been intimately related to completing the construction of the dam. However, even for the environmentalists and the anti-dam activists, national security, national interest and national unity are no less important. Sunderlal Bahuguna and other prominent anti-dam activists have in their environmental discourse throughout emphasized water and forests as the basis of a safe and secure nation, free from outside threats.[65]

Even as they come together in the unusual coalitions constructed in postcolonial environmental movements,[66] the Rashtriya Swayamsevak Sangh (RSS) and Sunderlal Bahuguna represent two strands of an indigenist ecological nationalism that firmly locates itself in contrast both to metropolitan-secular forms of nature devotion (like those of aristocratic wildlife conservationists, for instance),[67] and the discourse of adivasi indigeneity discussed by several contributors to this volume. This discourse of indigeneity is, of course, rooted at once in a firm territorial alignment of cultural-ethnic identity and claims to citizenship, and hence to the right to livelihood, made possible only by participation in the idea of a constitutional Indian nation seen as being obliged to fulfill its directive principles.

A valuable distinction pertaining to state penetration into regional polities can be made by considering the differences between the relationship forged by empire and nation, respectively, with particular regions, especially those that ostensibly contained treasure troves of natural wealth. As Wolfgang Mey describes in his account of the Chittagong Hill Tracts, colonial intervention in the late nineteenth century was clearly driven by a growing interest in forests as economic resources. But colonial administrators in the Chittagong Hill Tracts (as elsewhere in tribal areas of Bengal) reacted in complex ways to the people and landscapes they came to know so well. A romantic appreciation of verdant lands and strong paternalist sentiment toward simple hill folk as well as the trades of shifting cultivation and nomadism combined to attenuate the worst consequences of resource exploitation. Simultaneously, such livelihoods were deemed primitive and improvident by some officers, and by others as the only possible method of cultivation in these tracts. Therefore, British civility and the ambiguous comfort of industrial society were evaluated, at times unfavorably, against the hill forest landscape.

As Willem van Schendel observed, colonial intervention in the Chittagong Hill Tracts was initially to create a safeguard against raids on British territory by Chin, Lushai, and Mizo people. Only when Bengali commercial interests intervened at the end of the nineteenth century was British control stepped up. Disguised as a measure to protect "tribal" rights, the Chittagong Hill Tracts became an administrative enclave where "reserved forests" under state control increased, swidden cultivation was combated, and migration strategies—which involved moving hill people within the region and encouraging Gurkhas and Santals to settle, while prohibiting Bengalis to do the same—worked to isolate the region and delimit peoples' means of livelihood.[68] In contrast, both the Pakistani nation and the Bangladeshi one that followed were more unremitting in their developmentalist and integrationist attack on hill peoples' difference. Mey explains the strategy of inclusion as a paternalistic negation of difference which denied hill peoples political representation on their own terms and banned their "indigenous knowledge" from feeding into development policies. Hence, the relationship between ruler and ruled within empire and nation-state expressed itself differently. While empire rested on the pacification and control of people, integration became an urgent issue for securing the integrity of the nation-state. As in the case of Kerala fisherfolk who felt a loss of power in the way they understood changes in the sea—dams in the east interfered with the regularity of the sea's roughening, bans on monsoonal trawling introduced new patterns in the sea's regularities—the hill people of Chittagong were violently displaced by metropolitan nationalist ideologies of development whereby dams and power plants resulted in the inundation of forty percent of cultivable lands in the hills. By the 1990s development in the Chittagong Hill Tracts was an enterprise led by the army. Ecological warfare—the destruction of forests to root out insurgents—was a staple of the development strategy.

Notions of community pose obstacles to national imaginations, and yet clearly serve as the building blocks for them. Investment in and ambivalence with regard to notions of community, especially regional or local forms of community, are the stuff of contested nature because the definition of nature has turned on defining the associated community. If the Bangladesh case illustrates the dismantling of communities in Chittagong, there are numerous examples from neighboring north-eastern India where a more ambiguous relationship to communities, considered relatively autochthonous to the area, was constructed with an Indian nation and its state forms.

Forest management in north-east India after Independence has long been described as exceptional because of the Sixth Schedule of the Indian Constitution, which grants control over almost all forests in the region to autonomous district councils, or to (as usually termed) "community control." This perception of ownership and management has often been taken for granted, and criticism is today directed at the communities for destroying forests via excessive felling. In his contribution to this volume, Bengt G. Karlsson questions the actual substance of "community" in "community forest" and argues that there is a rapid privatization of forests going on in the state of Meghalaya, even as communal institutions based on matrilineal land relations are breaking up. The political ecology of forests witnessed today is the close linking of movements for ethnic mobilization and political autonomy with the political discourse of indigenous peoples' rights and stewardship of nature. When the state intervened, via a Supreme Court order in 1996 which put a moratorium on the felling of trees as a means of conservation, and to stop the depletion of forests (this being a perception of the state of forests shared also in Meghalaya), discontent with the central government grew rapidly. The reason, Karlsson argues, was the state's inability to understand shifting cultivation and to consult peoples' experiences and skills in framing development policies.

As noted earlier, essentialized conceptions of people and communities have lately come under critical scrutiny.[69] Along these lines, Sarah Southwold-Llewellyn confronts idealized conceptions of community homogeneity from the perspective of conflicts over legal rights in land. She argues that the Pakistani state's ownership regimes in the NWFP, which are based on a reification of local legal land rights and which are an inheritance from the colonial government, have had unintended consequences. In the NWFP, patron–client relations and political factions have been reinforced, thus creating new arenas for conflict and identity formation. In particular, Southwold-Llewellyn analyzes the historical and contemporary ways in which Pukhtun identity is constructed by struggles over forest management. "Pukhtunwali" emerges in her account as both the naturalized set of beliefs within which relations are established and tested, and also the changing framework in which, through claims on lands and forests, relations with a Pakistani nation-state are negotiated.

Karlsson, in similar vein, problematizes the notion that people claiming tribal or indigenous-people identities either have the special skills and knowledge to manage resources, or utilize resources in an extensive way which, under increasing population pressures, imply a threat to sustainable management. Building on Tim Ingold's "dwelling perspective," where people are assumed to have a common, relational, understanding of themselves and their life-world, Karlsson concludes that indigenous peoples' closeness to nature—as they live in and from forests—"might translate into an increased ecological awareness and generate practices that aim at environmental conservation [. . .] Nature and nation are thus re-imagined as mutually constitutive." Karlsson's account of Meghalaya is edifying in that it reminds us of the continuing place-making that occurs when a socially constructed nature is the medium for struggles over livelihoods and identities. Patterns of migration and settlement uncovered in historical research may repudiate antique attachments to lands that are claimed by indigenous groups. But their prolonged cultivation and a recent history of intense dependence on these lands can produce a place attachment which is readily translated in processes of political mobilization into an ecological nationalism that is sharply ethnic in character.

In the modern multicultural nation, where liberal ideologies are dominant, indigenous subjects are called upon to perform—as Elizabeth Povinelli says—"an authentic difference in exchange for the good feelings of the nation and the reparative legislation of the state."[70] This performance calls for elaborate works of traditional recollection, and large acts of collective memory that substantiate an indigenous status (almost always built on a prior tribal status in colonial ethnology), which thereby assert unique and compelling claims to nature in the modern multicultural nation. Pierre Nora compares the role of memory and history in the negotiation of community identities, and refers to this acceleration as a consequence of democratization and the spread of mass-mediated technologies of communication. Nora observes that memory was once the legacy of what people knew intimately, but which has been supplanted by a thin film of current events.[71] We would supplement Nora's point by pointing out the powerful effects of development in postcolonial contexts like South Asia. Economic and social development, the chief enterprise and mission of the postcolonial state, contributed even more to this acceleration in conflicts over resources, and contingent struggles over identities. Development-related claims and reforms further hastened and widened the production of history—in the words of Teodor Shanin—as the story of progress.[72] Here, in a manner close to how Jharkhand identities were forged in the histories of dispossession and disarticulation from a lived experience of nature, Linkenbach asks us to rethink the history of similar events in Uttarakhand. Just as Bengt G. Karlsson's essays explores the potency of indigenous peoples' claims to authenticity in their lived experience of place, Linkenbach's provides a further connection between indigeneity and place-based identity located in landscapes and different polities. She shows that the people of the Western Himalayas, living now in the newly formed state of Uttaranchal, have consistently raised the issue of citizenship, rebelling against the differentiated and somewhat stultified form of citizenship in which they were placed by uneven development in Uttar Pradesh.

IV

Over the years, numerous migrations, voluntary and involuntary, have left traces and scars in memories of lost places. Some of these memories can be concrete and near physical, as in those that relate to the forced loss of lands, soils, trees, sacred places of worship, and ancestors' graves. Such displacement means the uprooting of place-based livelihoods, identities, and meaning. Such loss is immense. It is the loss of a life-world in which humans had a place; a world in which they were recognized, known, and possessed some control over their lives. Through generations, the place had gained its meaning by the actions of people living there and by relating to it. The meaning of loss here can be equated with the developmental state acting upon them while they become subject to the state's insensitive development projects. Other memories of loss are more immaterial. They carry an emotional affinity, as in the loss of the place of one's birth, from where one departed to study, marry, or earn; or as in the loss of a historical ancestral home of one's family or kin. The old village may have grown into the unrecognizable outskirts of a metropolitan town. Lone mountains or vast forests may have been invaded by tourists, exploited by transnational companies or become inaccessible by warfare. In the process of loss, landscapes and natures are easily fetishized. Their fauna gain symbolic value in the iconography of place remembrance or in the political process of reclaiming such places. Thereby, the place gains a special value via its absence.[73]

In claiming nationhood and celebrating the nation, nature is appropriated in order to manifest the legitimacy of claims. As mentioned at the outset, a distinction between metropolitan-secular nationalism and an indigenist regionalist appropriation of nature can be useful. The former builds on the distance in both geographical space and cultural difference which need to be bridged and overcome in the formation of the nation-state. (It is significant that, in the hour of Independence, the new Indian nation-state gathered under the emblem of the three lions of Ashoka's empire—the oldest earlier political unit that had incorporated the major part of the subcontinent.) In contrast, the indigenist articulation of nationalism builds on the notion of authenticity and of the physical attachment and historical memory of a specific place.

Seen from the perspective of the ruling elite, metropolitan-secular nationalism had one of its most evocative Indian spokesmen in Jawaharlal Nehru. Nehru lacked a lived experience of Kashmir, but he had a strong affinity and kinship attachment to that region. Describing his quest for and encounter with India's past, he wrote:

> I wandered over the Himalayas, which are closely connected with old myth and legend [...] my love of the mountains and my kinship with Kashmir drew me to them [...] the mighty rivers of India that flow from this great mountain barrier into the plains of India attracted me and reminded me of the innumerable phases of our history [...] the story of the Ganges, from her source to the sea, from old times to new, is the story of India's civilization and culture [...] in my own city of Allahabad or in Hardwar I would go to the great bathing festivals.[74]

Here and elsewhere Nehru gave words to the imagined landscape of the Indian nation of secular modernism. As David Arnold notes, an environmental imagery with strong cultural ingredients comes through in writings that construct a nature-mediated national and regional consciousness when generating anti-colonial sentiments—as in Rabindranath Tagore's work. Yet the romantic naturalism of the nation, often associated with the figure of the adivasi, was also contrasted with images of devastated nature as a reflection of India's state under British rule.[75] At the same time, in Nehru's years as prime minister, resources were directed at the immense transformation of this landscape in the name of stabilizing the modern Indian nation. By this contradictory way—portraying romantic visions of the landscape while transforming it profoundly—the colonial and postcolonial states converge in their relationship to nature. Evaluating the legacy of the Nehru years, environmental historians have led the charge against that period via metropolitan-secular nationalism and its ecologically disastrous manifestations in large dams, forest policy, industrial pollution, and nuclear proliferation.

Both in terms of high developmentalism and the use of forest policies for national integration along the vision of metropolitan-secular nationalists, there are remarkable similarities in the trends that we can find in postcolonial India and Pakistan. For instance, both countries have embarked on legislative reform in order to reflect a more aggressive nationalist agenda on forest law. In both cases the reform was initiated in the 1990s. This has also been a period when a democratic Indian polity and an authoritarian regime in Pakistan have both pushed forward on joint forest management schemes and devolution plans. Urs Geiser describes the international pressures on Pakistan forest management, but is also careful to point out the historical importance of colonial administration in the NWFP. As in India, the British recognized, in the northern regions of what became Pakistan, certain areas where the implementation of forest and revenue legislation had to follow patterns more sensitive to local arrangements. Sivaramakrishnan has elsewhere called these zones of anomaly. In these, national forest control was only extended formally in the 1970s.[76] The limited Raj that was established in Malakand was symptomatic of a wider policy of delicate dealings in tribal agencies across northern and eastern India. It took the abolition of princely states in 1969 and the subsequent extension of national (ex-colonial) forest law to the north-west provinces for a sustained nationalization of forests and peripheral regions to occur. The critique of these processes of political assimilation and suppression of ethnic and religious minorities—which at times have been cloaked in the discourse of scientific, natural resource management—has also been forceful in recent scholarly and popular writing. Reflecting on nationalistic images of the landscape, the contrast between imagined and managed landscapes has been immense.

Equally romantic in their nature devotion, many middle-class and largely urban environmental activists have voiced their concerns for conservation. However, they have also propagated a strategically essentialist, celebratory indigenism (inspired equally by Gandhian ideas and romantic primitivism). The identification and study of sacred groves in India, and their appropriation into a neo-romantic conservation discourse, is one of the most striking illustrations of this point. In the words of Madhav Gadgil who, in collaboration with an anthropologist has spent many years documenting these sacralized and thus protected landscapes in India, sacred groves are "ancient nature sanctuaries where all forms of living creatures are afforded protection through the grace of some deity."[77] In most instances the groves are associated with mother goddesses, fierce deities who have preserved old growth and endemic biodiversity. They are, by some, associated with popular Hinduism; by others claimed to be unrelated to the Hindu pantheon as specific adivasi religions. But even as ecologists, foresters, and some historians rush to adapt sacred groves to a particular account of human ecology, scholars of Indian religions have complicated the picture by asking a more fundamental question: what is the relationship between an Indic religion and a conservation ethic among its practitioners?[78] In a study specifically directed at discovering the shape, role, and politics of sacred groves, Rich Freeman finds "little correlation between the concerns and depictions of the modern environmentalist's models, and the actual local reasons for instituting and maintaining sacred groves."[79] He goes on to demonstrate the fluidity of both society and its natural environment in the recent historical period, challenging thereby what he describes as "neo-Hindu ecology."

Following the leads provided by Freeman's insightful socio-historical work, Claude Garcia and J.-P. Pascal provide a welcome ecological analysis of sacred forests in Coorg. We learn, as the theme of this essay has already indicated, that stories about sacred forests are stories about local history—sthala purana. Garcia and Pascal find that human pressure, be it direct (felling, extraction, grazing) or indirect (habitat loss, edge effects, etc.), shapes the nature and structure of sacred forests and leads them away from their natural dynamics. Garcia and Pascal have found that sacred forests have low densities, low woody biomass, and are vulnerable to colonization by light-demanding species adept at gap exploitation—often these are not endemic or rare. Disturbed, distributed as small fragments close to settlements, they certainly emerge as managed, and not virgin, forests. Garcia and Pascal impressively list the tremendous polysemy of the term sacred forest. These partially protected forests seem to provide a variety of functional services relating to religious needs, practical uses, and the formation of identity and political manifestations—again bringing us to local history.

As can be seen from the earlier discussion, nature remains, from the local to the national and global, a space for manifesting and celebrating political and cultural aspirations and asserting dominance. In Coorg, sacred forests are being re-sacralized by the majority Kodava community; some of the old cult places are being overshadowed by newly built temples and *pujaris* (priests) performing *pujas* (prayers) to a vegetarian god. Garcia and Pascal suggest that this is a way to restate the community's dominance over the landscape. This situation can be compared to similar processes in Meghalaya described by Karlsson, where a recent study has found that only one percent of the sacred forest area had a 100 percent canopy cover, and only 42 percent had more than 40 percent canopy cover. In the Khasi Hills, the urban elite among the Khasi majority community has begun to re-enchant sacred forests and revive traditional institutions to protect them, thus reinforcing Khasi "indigenous" identity. In this way, the Meghalaya and Coorg cases both reflect the material and symbolic commodification of nature. In Coorg, Garcia and Pascal note, the dominant Kodava community, in collaboration with the state forest department and local NGOs, has proposed to the Karnataka government a transfer of the management of sacred forests to village communities. The rules they have suggested are modeled on the Joint Forest Management Plan, thus politicizing the plan for communalist gains. This is one of the many versions of celebratory-indigenist nationalism that are the products of a rapid commodification of the environment.

In some ways the fetishization of nature as a commodity in the service of national development (the agenda articulated by metropolitan secularists) shaped the field in which rival visions imagined ecological refugees, as well as protest movements by peasants and adivasis, all of these being projected as seeking a pre-commodified world of life-in-nature which had been wrested from them. The rapid expansion of environmental NGOs coincided with the expansion of central state agencies, laws, and programs for environmental management and conservation—a mutually inspired growth that occurred from the early 1970s. In the national public sphere a discourse of heritage conservation grew, fueling, in the first instance, varieties of ethnonationalism. But if cultural and natural heritage were conflated in regional autonomy and adivasi rights movements in the 1970s and 1980s, the 1990s witnessed an alliance between these heritage movements and a new metropolitan nationalism around issues of intellectual property rights, biodiversity protection, and the disposal of hazardous wastes (cf. the recent despatch of shiploads of mercury from battery plants in South India for disposal in the United States, an effort of cooperation between the Indian state and Greenpeace).[80] A rising tide of hostility that threatens to uproot all "invasive species" is another manifestation of processes by which nature commodification and nationalism have now intersected in new ways that echo older struggles.[81] In short, while it is useful to think analytically of metropolitan-secular and ethno-regional forms of ecological nationalism, it would be a mistake to see these forms of nationalism as locked in implacable antagonism. It is more fruitful to view their mutual relation as one of creative tension; at times opposed, at times collusive.[82]

Programs like community forestry and participatory development introduce new and similar forces of conflict and realignment across South Asia, be it in Pakistan, Nepal, or India. In each of these countries historical similarities in social structure and organization have been overlaid with distinct processes of state formation in the twentieth century. Nepal's monarchy, influenced by international donors, was the first to introduce community forestry programs in the subcontinent. In the post-andolan or democratizing phase that has emerged in the 1990s, Nepal faces proliferating social conflict. Post-monarchic modern Nepali nationalism is vulnerable both to radical threat from Maoists and their view of the revolutionary state in Nepal, as well as from more ethnicized struggles over land that have been structured by decentralized development- and community-based conservation schemes.

The lower-level functionaries of the Pakistan forest department described by Sarah Southwold-Llewellyn also resemble, in their dilemmas, the forest guards and other field officials of conservation agencies being studied in a few cases in India and, of course, by Nina Bhatt in neighboring Nepal.[83] Through her account of wildlife wardens and park rangers we find that nationalism and nature are entwined in fascinating ways in the lives of staff in protected areas and community forests. Her research on the wildlife conservation enterprise in Nepal describes how a keen nationalism is cultivated among park rangers and other staff.

Park staff often perceive their situation as both like, and different from, that of soldiers. They are the defenders of the nation, not at its borders but within its territories. And the nation is narrated in stories about hardships endured for love of wildlife in difficult terrain and isolated postings far from home. One ranger evocatively recalled service in the Bardia National Park as consisting of long treks, sleeping in buffalo sheds, grinding corn, and losing all communication with the villages and towns left behind. As much as wilderness, the signposts memorializing this experience as one of national service include the traces of other livelihoods, necessarily marginalized and subject to civilizing forces in the creation and delineation of parks. A legendary game scout, whose chequered career includes a brief marriage to an American tourist, narrates his love for both wildlife and nation as follows: "Since I was twenty-five I worked for national parks—now even if a frog dies I feel bad [. . .] Guthi is the most difficult post [. . .] they send me there because [. . .] I know how to catch poachers [. . .] I have courage [. . .] I have to do my country's work."[84] In the setting of national parks, staff invoke themselves as stewards of nature and thereby of nation: "These repeated allusions to duty in the form of *desh prem* are crucial to community and bureaucratic character building. By using royals, who stand beyond and above the ordinary subject citizens, national park staff experiences nature as nationalistically indoctrinating."[85] One park ranger went so far as to claim that it was *nikunja* (parks) that contribute to *rastriya bikas* (national development).

V

Elaborations of the concept "ecological nationalism" build on the assumption that manifestations of political visions in nature and the formation of nations are mutually constitutive. This requires analyses that are empirically detailed, regionally specific, and which allow for heterogeneous and contradictory realities to be communicated within the research. Yet, placing the object of inquiry within the fields of political ecology and environmental history indicates, even necessitates, relational analyses of power and polity, and of the conditions of social and environmental change that have a historical grounding in processes of modernity and global capitalism. In this way, analyses of ecological nationalisms may work to further develop integrated studies of the two research fields.

As will be apparent to readers of the contributions to this volume, there are many ways in which the different varieties of nationalism are constructed and mediated by reference to the natural. We have found it useful to contrast a metropolitan-secular appropriation of nature and its celebration of the high-modern nation-state on the one hand, with an indigenist, ethno-regionalist reaction to the power and capacity of the state, or of global capital, to encroach on the natural and social environments of people on the other. Whereas the former may host numerous expressions legitimizing the nation-state project in the contested arena of nature, from the indigenist position the landscape becomes the place for contested identities.

In such manifestations, social forces and societal tensions are articulated as visions and claims to a place—in terms of belonging to a nation, or to a people, or via other such place-related community identifications. The legitimacy of the claims is often argued through the definition and deployment of symbols and iconographies of nature—landscapes, flora, and fauna—or through sacralized geographies. Likewise, the consolidation of political projects—from secular nation-states to regional claims of indigeneity—is often supported by ideologies and mobilizational strategies that rely on claiming nature in the service of collective histories. Therefore, the processes inherent in ecological nationalism involve both state formation and subject formation. These, in our view, require integrated analyses of both institutions and identities.

Ecological nationalisms are continuously generated in new spheres of political action. Some issues that have generated new waves of ecological nationalism include the controversies over intellectual property rights, genetically modified seeds for agricultural staples, international conflicts over patents and bioprospecting, toxic waste dumping, conservation and heritage tourism, and the disasters and hazards created by multinational corporations. These are all issues that necessarily target powerful interests, with which they clash in the process of national assertion. Taken collectively, these variegated processes, issues and conflicts point toward the relational character of analyses that seem to be required when studying ecological nationalism. Such questions promise to reward further inquiry along the lines outlined here. It is our hope that the central concept and related elaborations in this volume will spark more such inquiry.

NOTES

1. Figures as reported in *New Scientist*, vol. 177, no. 2384 (March 1, 2003), p. 4.
2. Roy 2004: 15.
3. See Klingensmith 2003 for a description of this project and its role in exemplifying the visions and contradictions of the Nehruvian phase of mega-development led by the national state.
4. As Anderson (1991: 204–5) points out, this mode of arguing the nation has been disseminated widely in the practice of writing history in modern times. It has thus been prevalent prior to the spread of explicitly environmental movements that reworked the idea of the nation in their service.

5. Ludden 2000: 254–5.

6. Grove 1997. The World Summit on Sustainable Development in South Africa constituted another high-profile venue for international scrutiny of the region's environment. For an interesting South Asian perspective on the summit and US efforts to undermine multilateralism in favor of bilateral private–public partnerships with nations willing to go with environmentally sound patterns of development, see Anju Sharma *et als* 2002: 25–33.

7. A fine ethnographic illustration of the ambivalence felt toward exotic plants is provided by Gold and Gujar 2001. As Sudipta Kaviraj (1992) reminds us, imagined regional affinities—vernacular nationalisms—that both built secular-metropolitan nationalism and the basis for its subsequent repudiation, are no less a product of recent colonial experiences than the derivative elite nationalisms exemplified by Moderates in the Indian National Congress. See also Jean and John Comaroff 2000 for a South African example of "naturing the nation."

8. Ludden 2000: 257.

9. Klingensmith 2003: 134–6.

10. Chatterjee 2001b: 403.

11. Gupta 2004: 275.

12. See, for instance, Baruah 2003.

13. Staff Reporter, "ABSU launches save Manas drive," *Sentinel*, September 19, 2003.

14. Deshpande 2004: 48–74.

15. We are indebted to Rosemary Coombe for pointing this out in her comments on a short version of this essay. As she further noted, the idea of ecological nationalism bears interesting resemblance to the cultural politics of livelihoods in Latin America as discussed in Escobar 1998, and Nash 2001.

16. See Coombe 2005 for more on this idea. We are, of course, grateful to her for alerting us to the emergent potential of the idea of ecological nationalism in the ongoing struggles of poor native peoples threatened with economic displacement and cultural degradation across the world.

17. This distinction is elaborated by Dobson 2000. For a discussion on ecologism and its eco-centric criticism of anthropocentric approaches to nature, see Smith 1999.

18. Anderson 1991; Spencer 1998: 43–68.

19. Hamilton 2002: 29.

20. One of the most interesting accounts of the characteristics and pathologies of the high-modernist nation-state remains Scott 1998.

21. As Mahesh Rangarajan points out in his comments on this essay, scholarship on nature politics in South Asia has been slow to develop a sophisticated discussion of the epistemological issues at stake. In contrast to other parts of the world (see Cronon 1995), this slowness may explain the allied slowness to explore links

between the politics of nature and competing nationalisms through which these politics become movements or struggles.

22. Subramanian 2003: 272.
23. Subramanian 2003: 283–4.
24. Ben-Habib 2002: 181.
25. In making these observations in the context of Europe, Hamilton notes that there has been a renaissance of ethno-territorial movements in the developed West, which not only belies the assumptions of modernization theorists but also shows such movements to be a common feature of developed and third world societies. See Hamilton 2002: 27, 31.
26. There is now a considerable literature on this process in respect of Europe and the USA. See, for instance, Schama 1995; Ferry 1995; Daniels 1993; Rackham 2001; Cronon 1991; Warren 1997; Jacoby 2001.
27. Sumit Guha 2003.
28. For accounts of the formation of colonial knowledge in these terms and the impact of these technologies of power on the formation of identities, notably nationalist sensibilities, see Dirks 2001; Edney 1997.
29. There is now a large literature defining and debating the development of political ecology. For our purpose it is sufficient to remember, in the words of a recent recapitulation, that political ecology refers to the processes by which "individuals, households, and communities possess or gain access to resources within a structured political economy," while also noting that "all forms of political economy have as their foundation the transformation of nature in social, historical, and culturally informed ways." See Peluso and Watts 2001: 5; Escobar 1999.
30. Some exceptions to these rather broad assertions would include Baker 2005; Mosse 2003; and Pratap 2000.
31. Dovers 2000: 138.
32. A valuable survey of these issues in the context of environmental decline and war in Africa is Fairhead 2001.
33. David Arnold and Ramachandra Guha (1995: 17–19) have pointed to the influence of the milieu and ideological traditions of the researcher on the work s/he does. They contrast the emphasis in the West on the loss of wilderness with the Gandhian criticism of consumerism and the urban civilization and its impact.
34. Jewitt 2002: 238–41.
35. See for example Madhu Sarin's work on joint forest management in Haryana. Sarin 1996.
36. See various contributions to Agrawal and Sivaramakrishnan 2000, and Sivaramakrishnan and Agrawal 2003.
37. Differentiated forms of citizenship that emerged in postcolonial nations of Asia are discussed with East Asian examples by Aihwa Ong (2000) in a way that is salient to our discussion here.
38. Sumit Guha 1999.

39. Subrahmanyam 2001: 186–219.

40. For the relationship of sthala purana to sacred geographies of the sort that are influential in ecological nationalisms based on religious identities, see Eck 1999. In his study of water-distribution systems and political power in pre-colonial and colonial Ramnad in South India, David Mosse (2003) develops an argument of the interconnection of the religious and military organization of the plains. He shows how water management and irrigation were tied into caste institutions, and how political interdependencies and legitimacy for social and political institutions were created by hydrological means. Protection of vulnerable livelihoods was secured according to decentralized principles whereby temples distributed status and symbols of legitimate power.

41. This argument has been further developed in Cederlöf 2002.
42. Thapar and Siddiqui 1991; Mohapatra 1991.
43. Sivaramakrishnan 1999.
44. Louis 1999: 3–10.
45. Cf. Stokes 1974; Bayly 1983; MacKenzie 1997.
46. Cf. Subrahmanyam 2002: 201.
47. Hardt and Negri 2000: i–xvii, 127, 132–4.
48. Grove 1995.
49. In the eighteenth-century debates on the role and end of the British Empire, the historian J.R. Seeley critically phrased the incompatibility of liberty and despotism within "Greater Britain" by questioning how such radically different policies as those of despotism in Asia and democracy in Australia could coexist. To Seeley, the Empire was organic and anyone British belonged to the same imperial nation. See further Louis 1999: 8–10.
50. Castells 1997: 29.
51. Castells 1997: 27.
52. This argument is developed further with examples from the politics of wildlife conservation in India, in Sivaramakrishnan 2004.
53. Castells 1997: 30–2.
54. Goswami 2002: 795.
55. A very interesting example of such work is Munasinghe 2002.
56. Anderson 1991; Pemberton 1994; Nandy 1990; and Nandy 2001.
57. Ludden 2001; Chaturvedi 2000.
58. Chakrabarty 2000: 267.
59. Whitcombe 1972; Ludden 1985.
60. R. Guha 1989; Baviskar 1995.
61. Sarkar 2000: 242; cf. Chakrabarty 2000, and Pandey 2001. Most recently these exchanges have led to a call for histories of struggle, and histories of ambivalence, contradictions, ironies, and tragedies, that are also part of the history of modernity.
62. Chatterjee 1993; Chatterjee 2002; Kaviraj 1984; Kaviraj 1992.

63. Aloysius 1999.
64. Sharma 2002: 26–30.
65. Sharma 2002: 28–9, Sharma 2001: 94–6.
66. A further discussion of such unusual coalitions and their relationship to the wider context of environmental politics in India is provided in Sivaramakrishnan 2002.
67. Rangarajan 1999.
68. van Schendel 1992a: 108–15.
69. Sundar and Jeffrey 1999: 37–40; Agrawal 1999: 92–108.
70. Povinelli 2002: 6.
71. Nora 1996.
72. Shanin 1997.
73. We are indebted to Michael Jackson, Copenhagen University, for inspiring us to these ideas.
74. Nehru 1999: 51.
75. Arnold 1996: 184–7. See also the fine work of Prasad (2003) on the role played by adivasis and tribes in the imagination of anticolonial nationalism associated with romantic anthropology, and subsequently forms of religious nationalism that demonize the same tribal communities for becoming obdurate and rights-demanding minorities standing in the way of national development projects.
76. See Sivaramakrishnan 1999, chapter two.
77. Gadgil 2001: 160.
78. For more on this point, see Sivaramakrishnan 2003.
79. Freeman 1999: 258.
80. Rai 2003.
81. In many of these novel environmental concerns, nationalism is manifest as nativism or autochthony. Nature may become "a fertile allegory for making people and objects strange, thus to forge critical new social and political distinctions." Jean and John Comaroff 2000: 8.
82. For more on this relationship, see Sivaramakrishnan 2003: 29.
83. For India, see Sudha Vasan 2002.
84. Bhatt 2002: 111.
85. Bhatt 2002: 286.

I
Regional Natures, Nation, and Empire

2

ENVIRONMENTAL HISTORY, THE SPICE TRADE, AND THE STATE IN SOUTH INDIA

Kathleen D. Morrison

IN CONTEMPORARY INDIA, BOTH OFFICIAL AND SELF-ASCRIBED IDEN-tities not only shape positions and possibilities in resource struggles, but also constitute real resources themselves. Among the poorest of India's poor, groups classified as "tribal," many of whom self-identify as *adivasi*, or original inhabitants, are eligible, along with other traditionally disadvantaged groups, to reserved positions in education and government service. Inclusion in these reserved categories has itself thus become an object of struggle. While some might see this development as both ironic and recent, it is in fact a contemporary example of a longer-term set of processes in South Asian history whereby complex and sometimes changing identities have been variably used as justifications for exploitation, mirrors for self-definition, and refuges from the larger society. The very existence of many of the distinctive named groups included in the broad and problematic "tribal" category itself speaks to past attempts, not only of exclusion and exploitation by outsiders, but also of definition and direction from within.

Sivaramakrishnan and Cederlöf, in their Introduction to this volume, define ecological nationalism as a space for cultural and political struggle for identity and livelihood, noting that in ecological nationalism competing perspectives are linked both to land (and its resources) and to claims of identity and authenticity, resources and identities being key terms in both

Portions of this essay were previously published as "Pepper in the Hills: Upland–Lowland Exchange and the Intensification of the Spice Trade," in Morrison and Junker, eds 2002. They are used here by permission of Cambridge University Press.

historical and contemporary struggles in India's western mountains. In these terms, the very existence (and persistence) of named, self-conscious upland "tribal" groups might be seen as a product of ecological nationalism—certainly there have been very diverse notions of what Sivaramakrishnan and Cederlöf call nature devotion in the development and enactment of nationalism in this region, including its smaller regional versions, Kaviraj's (1992) "vernacular nationalisms." I will examine some of these more local affinities (arguably cultural identities as much as nationalisms, in this case) and their intersections with larger political forces and players. In doing so, I add to the discussion a closer examination of the "ecological" side of ecological nationalism, where "nature" operates as more than simply an object of discourse, set of resources, or field of political contestation, where it is itself a player in the constitution of the lifeways, strategies, and even identities of human communities and individuals. This kind of environmental history takes the ecology in political ecology quite literally, stressing both interaction and interconnection in contingent human histories. Here an inclusive sense of ecology embraces both environments, many of these transformed by millennia of human action.

This essay describes the environmental and cultural history of the Western Ghats within the overall context of imperial expansion and incorporation, changes in agricultural production, and the oscillating history of long-distance and local exchange involving forest products. Integrating data from paleoecology, archeology and history, I track environmental, social, and political transformations in this region over the last two millennia, focusing on the period between the fifteenth and seventeenth centuries, when, I argue, many of the strategies available to South Indian hill peoples became more constrained, and when many of the basic contours of colonial and contemporary conflicts over forested areas were established. In this discussion of south-west India between the fifteenth and seventeenth centuries, a contingent history of imperial expansion and incorporation, changes in agricultural production and the histories of long-distance and local exchange involving forest products provide the context for a consideration of multiple, contesting "nationalisms," particularly those leading to the creation, maintenance, and sometimes loss of what are often also seen as fundamental cultural identities—those of small-scale "tribals" or hill peoples.

In South Asia, as elsewhere, the disciplinary gulf between the social and biological sciences has, to a large extent, obscured much of the complex imbrication between sociopolitics and landscape history, with the result that human–land relationships, if not simply ignored, are, conversely, typically seen as part of the essential "nature" of social groups rather than as the contingent products of long-term, mutually constitutive actions and interactions. Perhaps the best example of this tendency are the contemporary South Indian "tribal" groups, named identities,[1] who, in both scholarly and popular circles, are variously presumed to cohere on ethnic, caste, community, or even "racial" grounds, and who are often presumed to be the original inhabitants of this region (Morrison 2002a: 21–40). These groups tend to be seen as doubly "primitive," both aboriginal and simple. In this essay and elsewhere (Morrison 2002a), I argue that historically specific ecological, economic, and political relations have defined a range of sociocultural possibilities for residents of the South Indian uplands, and that far from exhibiting some essential "relation to nature," whether as hunter, farmer, pastoralist, or even bandit, upland groups have shown a great deal of flexibility and ingenuity in relating to both their mountain environment and to their neighbors.

Although the earliest inhabitants of South Asia subsisted solely by hunting wild animals and gathering wild plants, it is possible from the time of the first establishment of agriculture to document relations of exchange and interdependence between agriculturalists and hunting-and-gathering peoples. These relationships were marked by a high degree of variability and flexibility, with specific groups altering their strategies in relation to ecological, demographic, and political imperatives, such that it is difficult, and at times misleading, to use labels such as "hunter-gatherer" and "agriculturalist" as if they described an exclusive or stable strategy. I will be concerned here to trace some of the changes and possible changes in the organization of foraging/trading groups in south-western India coincident with the expansion[2] of the coastal spice trade and the increasing integration of this region into a world economy in the immediate precolonial and early colonial periods; that is, between about AD 1400 and 1700. Although the participation of South Indian "hill tribes" in regional and even international economics began much earlier than this (Morrison 2002a), I focus here on the early colonial and late precolonial organization of foraging and trading, and on some of the relationships of foragers with larger-scale political entities. In so doing I hope to illustrate the dynamic nature of these marginalized groups and the long-term evidence for economic integration and interdependence between foragers, peasant agriculturalists, states, and empires in this part of the world. This history illustrates the importance of the lived experiences of place in the construction of contemporary identities and resource contests, experiences doubly shaped by the human and natural worlds.

SOUTH-WEST COASTAL INDIA

The south-west coast of India is set apart from much of the rest of the peninsula by both physiography and climate. Bounded by the Indian Ocean on the west and the Western Ghats on the east, this region consists of mountain evergreen and semi-evergreen tropical forests dissected by well-watered alluvial valleys. The Ghats not only act as a rain shadow during the summer monsoon, ensuring a fairly high rainfall along their western slopes, but they also send down numerous small, navigable rivers to the coast. The Malabar coast, the primary locus of spice production in India, is largely contained within the modern state of Kerala, where backwater transport by boat is still very important for integrating the relatively dispersed population (Stein 1982: 120). Of the spices involved in expanding trade networks, the most important was pepper (*Piper nigrum*), indigenous to the region.

Further north, the Kanara and Konkan coasts boast a somewhat broader expanse of flat land between the coast and the mountains; this region is among the most productive rice-growing regions in India. These coasts are now divided between the modern states of Karnataka, Goa, and Kerala. Natural harbors are relatively rare all along the western coast, and most port cities were actually located slightly inland, along rivers. The Ghats, relatively steep on the western approach but more gently sloping on the east, are traversed by a number of natural passes, themselves called ghats, which rather strictly circumcise routes of movement from the coast across to the drier South Indian plateaus.

FOREST DWELLERS AND EXCHANGE:
THE WESTERN GHATS

In India today, a number of hill peoples or "tribes"[3] subsist in the Malabar Ghats and Nilgiri Hills (Hockings, ed. 1989: 1997) by hunting and collecting forest products for external markets, trading of those products, and sometimes also by wage labor. These groups include the Kadar, Paliyan, Karumba, and the Hill Pandaram (spellings and even names vary; these are from Morris 1982b; see Lee and Daly, eds 1999 for more ethnographic detail). Groups practising swidden agriculture, forest collecting, trading, and even some wet rice agriculture include the Nayadi, Kannikar, Muthuvan, and Urali Ulladan (Morris 1982b: 16–17), among others. In Sri Lanka the well-known Veddas (Brow 1978; Seligman and Seligman 1911) also consist of a number of different groups more or less integrated into the dominant Sinhalese and Tamil agricultural economy. Anthropologists and archeologists in South Asia helped create and now must contend with a tradition of research in which "tribals" are viewed as cultural-evolutionary fossils (e.g. "living stone age peoples"), useful as ideal types in the construction of generic hunter-gatherer models (cf. Fox 1969: 139–40) or as exemplars of the distant past (Morrison 2002b). More recently, anthropologists (e.g. Hockings 1985; Bird-David 1983; Bird-David 1992a; Morrison 2002b; Stiles 1993; Zagarell 1997) have begun to stress the lack of physical isolation of "tribal" groups from caste society and the time-depth of their integration with lowland agriculturalists. Many forest groups depend on lowland products, notably foodgrains, textiles, and iron, for their basic subsistence. Thus, exchange relations are not simply incidental, but provide staple food items and technologies.

Although the orthodox perception seems to be that contemporary foragers are descendants of an unbroken tradition dating back as far as the Mesolithic, some scholars have suggested alternative routes by which groups could have moved into specialized collecting and trading. Hockings, for example, considers the case of refugees from caste society—marginalized groups who move into the forests to take up new opportunities and/or to escape intolerable situations in their homeland (1980). Such movements are not unknown, and Hockings (1985) suggests more specifically that the Roman[4] market for pepper and cardamom may have opened up opportunities for marginal lowland groups. If this is correct, however, such groups may have also come into contact and perhaps competition with existing upland peoples.

Even if some upland groups represent refugees from the intensively cultivated lowlands, it is likely that other specialized forager-traders reliant on imported foodstuffs began as more generalized foragers and/or as swidden agriculturalists. Several key periods can be identified in the move toward specialized foraging. The first of these is the Early Historic, for which the rather sketchy evidence points to significant changes in the occupation history of the uplands—including the beginnings of large-scale modification of the vegetation—changes associated with good evidence for active networks of long-distance exchange. The second period, on which I focus here, is the sixteenth- and early-seventeenth century, a period in which the expanding spice trade and the concomitant expansion of lowland agriculture created both opportunity and constraint, a period when, even as new productive options opened, political and resource pressures combined to limit the subsistence flexibility of many hill peoples. In this latter period, we can document a transition toward specialized foraging, a move that may have been responsive to several factors. The first of these relates to the demands of the spice trade and other politically-based demands for forest produce. The second, more indirect but no less important, involves pressure on the forests from below created by expanding agriculture. Both the land-use "push" and the political "pull" or demand for produce from below forced foragers and forager/agriculturalists into an increasingly specialized (and increasingly marginalized) position as participants in a world market.

LONG-TERM OCCUPATIONAL HISTORY OF THE WESTERN GHATS

By the last few centuries BC, an extensive network of exchange stretched across the Indian Ocean, connecting, indirectly, the Mediterranean with East Asia (Morrison 1997). Forest products played a prominent role in this exchange, with peppercorns from the Malabar coast reported from an archeological context on the shore of the Red Sea and attested to in Chinese documents. Indo-Roman trade also included such forest products as sandalwood, ivory, ginger, cardamom, and myrobalan (*Terminalia chebula* and *T. bellirica*) (Morris 1982b: 15), as well as other woods, aromatics, and dyes (Ray 1986: 114). Finds of Roman coins are reported from both coastal and inland sites in south-west India and Mediterranean-made and inspired goods are found on both coasts (Nilakanta Sastri 1975: 135; and see Begley and DePuma 1991; Cimino 1994; Morrison 1997). In the corpus of Tamil Sangam poetry, dating to the first three or four centuries AD, there is mention of a coastal intra-Indian trade in pepper and honey (Nilakanta Sastri 1975: 110; Morris 1982b: 15), both forest products.

While some forest products may have been collected by lowland traders or agriculturalists, the degree of specialized knowledge involved and the dispersion and seasonal availability of such products suggest instead that they were collected by upland groups at least partially specialized toward the gathering and trading of forest produce. Preliminary work on the long-term occupational history of the Ghats suggests that intensive human use of these mountains may have begun quite late. In a review of archeological data from the Nilgiris, Noble (1989) concludes that these hills were not occupied prior to the first century AD. The earliest identifiable archeological remains consist of megaliths, most containing iron. Zagarell (1997) describes these megaliths in some detail, concluding that their forms and distributions show evidence of extensive, long-term relationships with surrounding polities and societies (and see Zagarell 1994). Although the dating of these features is uncertain, he generally accepts Leshnik's (1974) dates of the fourth through sixth centuries AD (Zagarell 1997: 29) for the majority of these burial/memorial features.

Another form of information on human use of the Ghat forests is provided by paleoenvironmental analyses that track, among other things, human impact on vegetation, soils, and landforms. Among the most important of these for the purposes of this essay are analyses of pollen data conducted by Caratini *et al.* (1990–1). These data derive from a pollen core taken from a buried sediment profile near Vazhavatta, in the Wayanad District of northern Kerala, at about 760 meters (2493 feet) elevation. This profile contains information on forest composition between about AD 200 and 700 (Caratini *et al.* 1990–1: 126). Although the climax vegetation of this area is wet evergreen forest, the landscape surrounding Caratini *et al.*'s Wayanad site is now under the permanent cultivation of wet rice, along with plantations of coffee and hevea. Pollen data indicate neither significant compositional change in the forest between the third and eighth centuries AD nor any indication of a regime of intensive agriculture. However, some pressure on the forest was noted in that *Pteridphyte* (fern) diversity declined steadily, a pattern they attribute to "a reduction in the forest on which the majority of ferns are dependent" (Caratini *et al.* 1990–1: 137). Further, taxa specific to forest openings or margins were common in the core, suggesting that clearing of the forest for cultivation had already been established.

A second paleoenvironmental study of the Ghat forests (540–600m above msl) near Bhatkal (Mariotti and Peterschmitt 1994), although limited in spatial scale, also provides powerful evidence for anthropogenic vegetation change by the first century AD. In this study, stable carbon isotope ratios on soil organic matter indicate destruction of the evergreen forest margins and creation of an anthropic savannah around the first few centuries BC/AD.

While this finding is in broad agreement with other studies reporting a near-universal pattern of savannah formation following earlier forest communities (see especially Archer 1990), unfortunately the limited spatial scope of this study (only a 350m long transect across the ecotone was analysed, Marriotti and Peterschmitt 1994: 475) makes it difficult to draw broad conclusions about the overall history of the Ghat forests.

Thus, there is good evidence to suggest at least small-scale occupation of the Ghat forests, of a nature sufficient to induce modest vegetation change, by the first few centuries AD. There is also limited though striking evidence for total destruction of some forest margins and the creation of an upland savannah, a more open vegetation form that may have been entirely artifactual, at the same time. This evidence does not, of course, mean that the Ghats were not used prior to the first century, nor does it necessarily indicate that these hills did not support small groups of mobile foragers prior to this time. Much more archeological research, in particular, needs to be carried out in this area before we can say that the lack of earlier archeological remains in the uplands represents definitive evidence for late colonization of the Ghats.

Thus, while it is not possible at present to precisely describe the mix of subsistence strategies employed by Ghat peoples before about AD 1800, there is sufficient evidence to indicate that swidden agriculture was practiced by many groups from about the first few centuries AD. For about the same time, textual and archeological sources indicate that Ghat forest products were involved in long-distance trade networks. It is difficult to say if the extraction of forest products at this time was carried out by specialists or if local farmers and subsistence foragers engaged in some collection for exchange; either way, the volume of forest produce involved was significant enough that some reorganization of production was undoubtedly already under way. It is certainly clear from contemporary indigenous texts that literate observers were not only aware of the existence of distinctive economies and lifeways apart from those of settled agriculture, but also had strategies for engaging with and avoiding those same peoples. I suggest here that relations of interdependence that were almost certainly in place by the first half of the first millennium AD formed partial frameworks for response to the increased pressures on forest dwellers in the later precolonial and early colonial periods. Understanding this later period requires consideration of political, ecological, and economic conditions in southern India; these are briefly sketched below.

COASTAL ENTREPÔTS AND INDIAN OCEAN TRADE: MALABAR AND KANARA

When the Portuguese first arrived on the south-west coast of India in AD 1498, the Malabar port city of Calicut was one of the most important trade centers in the region, largely as the result of its (not uncontested) political predominance over neighboring coastal polities. As the "first among equals," however, the ruler of Calicut, the Zamorin, was neither the ruler of an extensive territory nor was he able to control his coastal neighbors, including the independent states of Cochin to the south and Cannanore to the north (Bouchon 1988). Indeed, the extent of Calicut's direct political control did not include much of its forested, mountainous hinterland (Dale 1980: 15). Permanent settlement in the interior was sparse, and restricted largely to riverine areas. Building on a long tradition of local self-government in South India (Stein 1982; Frykenberg 1979), "chiefs" or other local leaders were often held accountable to larger-scale political entities for tribute, taxes, and control within their area of influence.

With the arrival of the Portuguese and the establishment of their trading empire along the coast (Bouchon 1988; Pearson 1981; Subrahmanyam 1993, 2001), Calicut's importance as a node in the regional exchange system was eclipsed by that of Goa (the seat of Portuguese power and one of their few territorial possessions) and, to a lesser extent, of Cochin. The position of Goa *vis-à-vis* the export and food-producing hinterlands of the west coast was, if anything, even more precarious than that of Calicut, underlining the importance of cheap coastal transportation in maintaining this network of interdependence in foodstuffs and export items. As noted, the Malabar coast was the primary locus of pepper gathering and production, as well as of many other forest products, including ginger, cardamom, honey and wax, various gums and resins, dyes and scented woods, and medicinal and poisonous plants (Morris 1982b).

Further north, the wider Kanara coast provided a large portion of the rice consumed further south in the Malabar region; much of the Kanara coast was under the control of the territorially extensive inland Vijayanagara empire. Goa lies even further north, on the Konkan coast, and not only imported Kanara rice (Mathew 1983; Subrahmanyam 1990) but also had to bring in pepper and other Malabar products up the coast for exchange. Similarly, other coastal cities such as Cannanore, Calicut, and Cochin also prospered commercially by the bulk storage and marketing of products neither manufactured on site nor procured in the immediate locality. Even discounting the important role such ports played in the redistribution of goods from further east and west, the local products, such as pepper, that they helped distribute came not from urban hinterlands, by and large, but from the Ghat uplands.

Understanding the role of the coastal entrepôt cities as both centers of consumption and as pivots in the larger sphere of exchange is important, inasmuch as increased demand for forest products in the late precolonial and early colonial periods cannot be dissociated from economic reorganization in the coastal lowlands. Lowland politics and economics ramified into the uplands, as discussed in more detail below. Most directly, the demand for pepper and other forest products and upland crops was accelerated by direct Portuguese purchases and forcible extractions as well as by ongoing extra-Portuguese trade. However, the pressure on the forests also had ramifications for lowland agriculturalists, ramifications involving changes in the organization of production and distribution of foodgrains in the lowlands, most notably of rice. Combined with increased exports of rice to coastal cities, changes in the organization of production must have been widespread in both uplands and lowlands.

Portuguese involvement in the movement of rice took three forms. The first was the demand for tribute, in order to supply Portuguese forts and settlements. These demands fell almost exclusively on the kingdoms of the Kanara coast,[5] particularly Honawar, Bhatkal, and Basrur (Subrahmanyam 1984: 445; Desai *et al.* 1981). The amount of rice involved was considerable; convoys of several hundred small ships, often under Portuguese guard (Pearson 1981: 77) sailed up the coast to Goa. In the 1570s and 1580s three to four convoys per year to Goa alone are reported (Pearson 1981: 77). The second form of Portuguese involvement stemmed from the cartaz, or pass system, for local as well as long-distance trade, so that no ocean transport whatsoever could officially take place without Portuguese approval and taxation. The third form of involvement in the rice trade may be seen as something of an unintended consequence to other forms of exchange and extraction, this being the escalation in demand for rice and other staples created by Portuguese extractions of pepper and similar products from the foothills and mountains of the Ghats. As discussed below, the shipment of staples to the forested interior was ultimately necessary to support the foragers and cultivators of spices, among others.

One striking effect of Portuguese involvement in southern India was the shift in the area around Goa from a grain surplus to a grain deficit. Before the arrival of the Portuguese and their efforts to shift the focus of trade from Calicut to Goa, rice was imported from the Goan hinterland and from "Vijayanagara" (Mathew 1983: 20, presumably this refers to the Konkan coast regions under Vijayanagara suzerainty) to Malabar cities. After the establishment of Portuguese Goa, the city became almost entirely dependent upon imported foodstuffs. The difference may not relate entirely to increased population in the cities, but rather to the severance of relations in the Portuguese period with the rural hinterland (Pearson 1981: 76–8). Numerous references to Goa's inability to feed itself exist in the literature (Subrahmanyam 1984: 434; Pearson 1981: 77), as indeed to the similar import of rice by precolonial Calicut (Danvers 1966: 85; Digby 1982: 147). Not all of Goa and the Malabar coast's foodstuffs came from the Kanara coast; a large portion also arrived from Bengal (Pearson 1981) and Orissa (Foster 1968: 26, 44) on the east coast. As I discuss below, the expansion and intensification of lowland agriculture had a significant contributing effect on changes in the opportunities of upland peoples.

EXPANSION AND INTENSIFICATION: UPLAND–LOWLAND LINKS

While it appears, then, that frameworks for exchange and economic interdependence were in place long before European involvement in South Asia, it is certainly the case that the scale of exchange underwent a rapid expansion in the early colonial period. Historians of both Europe and South Asia are in broad agreement that the volume of pepper, as well as of other products[6] such as ginger and cardamom, increased significantly in the sixteenth century. European pepper consumption doubled during the 1500s (Diffie and Winius 1977: 318; Boxer 1969: 59); Braudel (1972: 550) estimates that between 1554 and 1564 the flow of spices into the Mediterranean through the Red Sea route alone was of the order of 100 to 200,000 kilograms per year, most of it pepper. This quantity approximates that of the pre-Portuguese period, but does not include any of the spices brought around the Cape by the Portuguese at the height of their control. From the Indian perspective, Mathew (1983: 212–13) estimates that pepper production jumped 200 to 275 percent between 1515 and 1607. Wallerstein's contention (1974), then, that the impact of the increased pepper demand on Asia was "minimal" seems unrealistic at best, based perhaps on a notion of the importance of pepper to the average European rather than to foragers or to swidden cultivators (and see Chaudhuri 1985; Reid 1993a).

Luxury goods—items of relatively small size and high value, including most spices—moved from one end of the network to the other, while the movement of bulkier and more perishable goods formed smaller but sometimes still impressively large circuits within the larger system (Mathew 1983: 19). Although historical attention has traditionally been focused on the "small but trifling" (Wallerstein 1974) trade in high-value items, there has been an increasing awareness of the important role of more "utilitarian" trade goods, such as rice (Subrahmanyam 1984, 1990) and coarse cotton textiles (Ramaswamy 1985; Digby 1982). On the one hand, these two categories of trades good create distinct organizational problems and prospects for political control. European colonial powers such as the Portuguese in India adopted a program of regulation and taxation of the existing "country trade" (cf. J.H. Parry 1963), or local trade in utilitarian goods, in order to finance their costly involvement in the long-distance exchange of spices and other "luxury" goods. The colonial administration of the latter was organized quite differently—in the case of the Portuguese, the spice trade was considered to be the exclusive right of a centralized crown monopoly (Boxer 1969; Danvers 1966; Subrahmanyam 1993)—although certainly this represented more an ideal than a reality.

From the perspective of indigenous producers, however, distinctions between "luxuries" and "utilitarian" commodities and between the structure of international and interregional trade in each were largely academic. The productive demands placed on peasant agriculturalists, gatherers of forest products, and export-oriented swidden cultivators were all structured through networks of local power and authority. The expansion and restructuring of such demands promoted changes in the opportunities and strategies of different collectors and producers, and fostered relationships of economic interdependence that survive, in altered form, into the present. The structure of intensive wet rice agriculture was predicated on the existence of markets for surplus; the basic subsistence needs of specialized foragers and possibly swidden spice cultivators were met through the mobilization of this surplus. The implications of this accelerated demand for spices in India and beyond probably also meant an accelerated demand for rice and other subsistence goods that would have been felt by intensive agriculturalists as far afield as Java and Bengal.

If demands for forest products were on the rise in the sixteenth century, it is also the case that areas under forests were declining. Throughout the South, both inscriptional and archeological evidence from at least the tenth century AD has as a constant theme the expansion of agriculture at the expense of forests. The limited paleoenvironmental data that exist (Morrison 1994a) tend to confirm this pattern. In the Nilgiris, pressure on land was not simply the result of lowland agriculturalists clearing forests in the foothills. There, Hockings has documented the expansion of the Badagas ("northerners," Hockings 1980; and see Zagarell 2002) a refugee group supposedly fleeing the destruction of the Vijayanagara empire in the late sixteenth century. The Badagas were accommodated by various hill groups and, according to the soil evidence (von Lengerke and Blasco 1989: 44) established permanent fields about three or four hundred years ago. Thus, forest dwellers have come under increasing pressure as the result of local agricultural land-use practices as well as from demands for forest produce.

Pressure on forests was not entirely a byproduct of expanding agriculture, however. Vijayanagara kings as well as other rulers sometimes adopted specific policies of forest clearance for the express purpose of diminishing the potential threat forest dwellers posed to agriculture. In the *Amuktamalyada*, a sixteenth-century compilation of political maxims attributed to the expansionist Vijayanagara king Krishna Deva Raya, the clearance of forests is presented as the only way to control the activities of robbers (S. Guha 1999: 49). The text advises kings (Saraswati 1926: 65): "Increase the forests that are near your frontier fortresses (Gadi *desa*) and destroy all those which are in the middle of your territory. Then alone you will not have trouble from robbers." Deliberate forest removal, also advocated by later rulers, including the British (S. Guha 1999), probably rarely involved state-sponsored deforestation as that would have been extremely expensive and time-consuming, even if aided by fire. Instead, forests could be cleared and land claimed for agriculture through the labor of agriculturalists; from at least the tenth century, inscriptions note the existence of tax incentives for the clearance of forests and the establishment of new fields and new irrigation facilities such as reservoirs (e.g. Heitzman 1997). Land-clearance incentives are extremely common in the Vijayanagara period, accelerating in the sixteenth century (Morrison 1995).

THE TRADE IN FOREST PRODUCTS: STRUCTURES OF POLITICAL AUTHORITY BEYOND THE COAST

Throughout the massive expansion of the spice trade, connections between primary producers and collectors and colonial or indigenous governments benefiting from forest produce were generally indirect. Intermediate brokers or "secondary traders" (cf. Dunn 1975: 99) forged relations of dominance and indebtedness with forest peoples; these brokers then dealt with more proximate political authorities. The contractual system depended on keeping foragers constantly in debt and personally dependent on the broker, who also acted as the supplier of subsistence goods. Brokers were either independent entrepreneurs, or more often, it seems, agents or contractors of governments. Many precolonial South Indian polities used tax farmers as collectors rather than directly employing government functionaries (Sinopoli and Morrison 1996). These tax farmers bid for the privilege of collecting revenue and then had to recoup the cost of the bid through direct collections. Middleman broker positions may have been similarly contracted.

Describing the system somewhat later was Francis Buchanan, who in 1800 set out on a trip throughout southern India for the express purpose of describing the agriculture of the country, including the cultivation and preparation of the "valuable commodities" pepper, sandalwood, cardamom, and cotton (Buchanan 1988 (1806): ix–x). He described a contractual system in place between the Kadar and local authorities in the Anamalai Hills (southern Nilgiris). Buchanan explains (1988 (1806): 334, italics in the original):

> Here is a person called the *Malaya-pudy*, or *hill-village man*. He rents the exclusive privilege of collecting drugs in the hills south from *Ani-malaya*. These are collected for him by a hill people named *Cadar*, of who, among the hills two day's journey hence, there is a village of 13 houses. The renter has there a small house, to which he occasionally goes to receive the drugs the Cadar have collected and he brings them home on oxen. The men only work for him, and each daily receives in advance four *Puddies* of rice [. . .]

These "Cadar," Buchanan continued (1988 (1806): 338), "are a rude tribe inhabiting the hills in this neighborhood, and speaking dialect that differs only in accent from the Tamul. . . . They rear no domestic animals, nor cultivate anything whatever; but their clothing is as good as that of the neighboring peasantry." The renter obtained his concession from Tipu Sultan's government. Among the products collected were wild ginger and turmeric, honey and wax, several dyes and resins, and ivory. The wild pepper was said to be of bad quality. The renter was also noted to trade with several other groups, who provided cardamom, which was not cultivated. These other groups were said to practice (swidden) agriculture (1988 (1806): 336–7).

The Portuguese, too, used this system of intermediaries for obtaining forest products. Pepper, ginger, cardamom, and cinnamon (in Sri Lanka) were all procured via "native intermediaries of the Sudra caste" (Diffie and Winius 1977: 319). This label does not clearly identify the intermediaries, except to suggest that they were probably not tribal peoples, often considered outcastes. Goods were purchased by the Portuguese on fixed-price contracts with a go-between, much as they are today. The Portuguese did prefer, however, to induce local rulers to supply them with spices at an agreed-upon price (Bouchon 1988; Danvers 1966; Mathew 1983). Presumably, then, these rulers employed intermediaries. Pearson (1981: 28) notes that the Portuguese had no direct control over pepper-producing areas and thus were dependent upon coastal rajas and local merchants for their supplies. As an empirical pattern, then, we see with increasing scope of political authority an increasing physical distance from the source of the product, an increased concentration in stored goods, an increase in settlement nucleation, and an increase in the status of landholding groups. Along parts of the Kanara coastal strip, for example, Brahmins were the major landowners in the sixteenth and seventeenth centuries. Further inland, landholding was largely in the hands of the Bant, a "clean" Sudra caste (Subrahmanyam 1984: 439). Still further inland were the tribal swidden farmers and hunter-gatherers. This social ordering corresponded well with the pyramidal structure of power relations stretching from the forests to the inland riverine towns and to the coastal cities.

If this picture seems to be one of the exploitation of timid forest dwellers by outsiders— a picture not altogether inaccurate for some contemporary contexts—a closer historical look at political relations shows a more complex situation. As far back as we can trace, forest peoples have always been integrated in some way into larger political structures. Kings of the South Indian Chola empire, between the ninth and thirteenth centuries AD, demanded tribute in forest products from *nadus* (territorial units) located in the Ghats (Hockings 1985: 115; see also Stein 1982). R.G. Fox (1969:

144) cites early reports that the Kadar of Kerala made periodic visits to Tripura to carry tribute and to exchange "gathered" items, such as tame elephants, wild honey, cardamom, and other forest products for rice, iron, chillies, and opium.

Tribute could also be exacted through local leaders, rather than directly from producers or collectors, a method also used to collect taxes from agriculturalists. Morris (1982b: 23) describes a copper plate inscription describing a contract between the local king of Attingal and the Hill Pandaram, appointing the latter as "tenants" of the forest, in return for which the *muppan*, or chief, should bring certain forest products to the capital every year. At these visits, cloth and other "gifts" would be given. In this case the local king was subject in turn to the Raja of Travancore, to whom he had to pay tribute. Both Murthy's (1994) historical work on the Chenchus and S. Guha's (1999) study of the Kolis and Bhils of western India reveal not only potential independent bases of power of these groups, but also the intermittent establishment of independent polities, and the ongoing engagement of tribal leaders and warriors with lowland polities. Thus, although I outline here an account of the oppression and immiseration of some Ghat residents and their creation as specialized forager-traders, it is also the case that other upland peoples referred to as tribes were able to create for themselves positions of power and domination, especially as bandits preying on settled agriculturalists—the dacoits and criminal tribes of the British documents. Tribal kingdoms, if that is not a contradiction in terms, flourished in the interstices of Vijayanagara and, later, British, Mysore, and Maratha rule.

What, then were the effects of the expansion of the spice trade in and after the sixteenth century on "hill peoples" of the Ghats? Clearly, the effects were variable, but while it is clear that some tribals were able to restyle themselves as Rajputs and establish kingdoms, or at least elicit fear from lowlanders, many others became, in Sumit Guha's (1999) characterization, a landless proletariat. In trying to outline the processes by which this took place, it may be helpful to contextualize these political and economic dynamics with some ecological consideration of Ghat forest products.

ECOLOGICAL CONTEXTS: PEPPER AND CARDAMOM

Although the existence of a pepper trade was well established by at least the first century AD, pepper cultivation seems to have been rare until about the sixteenth century.[7] Here I briefly discuss the growing conditions of pepper and cardamom, two of the most important of the Ghat forest products. Black pepper is a perennial climbing plant cultivated in India today in monocrop plantations and in mixed areca nut palm/pepper associations. Pepper also still grows wild in the Ghat forests. It has a limited natural distribution, being confined to the Malabar region (Aiyer 1980: 269). It prospers in partly shaded locations from sea level to 1200 meters (4000 feet), and in areas with 152 cms (60 inches) or more of rain a year. Pepper does not do well in sandy or alluvial soils of the sort favored by coconut palms (Aiyer 1980: 270). Because pepper is a climbing vine, it requires standards to climb on; thus it is often intercropped with trees or trained onto poles. It begins to bear four years after planting (Aiyer 1980: 275).

Cultivation of pepper in mid-elevation, mixed-crop swidden field seems to be most appropriate for the requirements of the plant. Its drainage needs often result in its growth on hill slopes. In modern varieties, the harvest time falls between February and March (Aiyer 1980: 276), January to March in Sumatra (Hill 1969: 37), but wild strains usually have fruit at all stages of maturity on the vine at any given time. Thus, harvesting (or collecting) is an ongoing process. Harvesting involves cutting off branches of the plant-bearing ripe fruit, threshing the fruit from the vine, and about six days of sun-drying (Aiyer 1980: 277). Today pepper harvesting is done with the aid of ladders (as Buchanan also notes for the early seventeenth century: 1988 [1806]). The dangers of collecting are thus evocative of the dangers involved in honey collection among contemporary foraging groups such as the Hill Pandaram (Morris 1982b; see also Demmer 1997).

The scheduling demands of pepper cultivation, and particularly, of pepper collection, are of particular interest. According to Buchanan (1988 [1806]: 334), dry rice in the Anamalai region would have been harvested at about the same time as cultivated pepper. Thus there would have been conflict in scheduling and labor demands involved in these different activities. Subrahmanyam (1990: 66) notes that in later-sixteenth-century Portuguese Cochin, "an important point on the annual calendar was the arrival in March of the first pepper-laden boats from the mountains." Thus, demands of labor and demands of scheduling for grain production and pepper production (and even more for pepper collection) had to be balanced.

Cardamom (*Elettaria cardomom*) has a more limited range than pepper, occurring between 760 and 1525 meters (2500–5000 feet) in elevation (J.W. Parry 1962). Cardamom does not produce well in the lower, more deciduous Ghat forests, where leaf-fall has the effect of shortening the flowering season (Sahadevan 1965: 9). Cardamom prefers a slightly higher rainfall and cooler temperature range than pepper, as reflected in its occurrence at higher elevations. In addition, cardamom prefers a relatively deep shade (Aiyer 1980: 296), and while the depth of the soil is apparently not very important, the plants require "a well-developed vegetable mulch" (Sahadevan 1965: 10) like that found in the forest floor. Cardamom is today grown as a plantation crop, in mixed associations with areca and coffee, although Sahadevan (1965: 21) asserts that the actual cultivation of cardamom is not more than two hundred years old. Swidden plots containing cardamom are not unknown (Sahadevan 1965: 21); these may be placed along watercourses and in other damp situations. Wild stands are subject to varying degrees of management, as described by Aiyer (1980: 297):

> [...] in this the natural growth of cardamoms as an undergrowth in the favourable forest zones is aided in varying degrees by actual cultivation; the latter ranges from conditions where cardamom is wholly a forest product and practically grows under wild conditions, up to conditions where it approximates closely to systematic cultivation, except for the fact that it is a temporary and shifting one. Areas are abandoned and then allowed to revert to jungle after a few years of bearing and then a new area is taken up for similar cultivation.

Cardamom bears four to five years after sowing, and its harvest characteristics are similar to those of pepper. The picking of cardamom, is, however, an even more skilled task, since the joint must stay attached to the pod and the latter must be a precise stage of maturity. If the pods are picked too green, they will shrivel upon drying, if too ripe, they will shatter. Aiyer notes that the clumps of plants need to be visited every week to ten days in order to gather the ripe pods (Aiyer 1980: 302). Because the harvest season is more or less continuous, specialized indoor drying facilities are often necessary in order to properly dry the material during the rainy season (Aiyer 1980: 303; Sahadevan 1965: 18). Competition from elephants, birds, squirrels, and rats is also a problem (Aiyer 1980: 308).

CHANGING PATTERNS: ECONOMIC STRATEGIES AND RELATIONS OF POWER

By the beginning of the sixteenth century, then, there existed in upland south-west India a complex mosaic of economic practices which included swidden agriculture, gathering of forest products for trade with lowland groups, military service, and no doubt gathering and hunting for subsistence as well. There are hints of the presence of specialized foragers in inscriptions pre-dating European documents, but certainly by the time documentary sources become abundant from the sixteenth century onward, there are clear indications of the presence of named groups engaged in specialized collection of forest products for exchange, as well as subsistence activities that included agriculture, gathering, and hunting. There was at the same time a similarly wide range of political forms and ethnic/caste identities; although productive forms, political orders, and group identities do not map neatly onto one another, contests over land and resources as well as cultural and political legitimacy have always been key in their relationships.

Both the expansion of the spice trade and increasing pressure on forests from the sixteenth century on (accelerating thereafter) led to transformations in upland economies and political ecologies. Several different options may have been available to upland groups faced with pressures on land and demands for produce. One such option was, evidently, to begin producing rather than simply collecting pepper. Pepper growers, then, concentrated on their agricultural plots and the scheduling demands of those plots almost certainly limited the spatial scale of their gathering and hunting. Morris (1982b: 63) notes in this regard that the more sedentary Hill Pandaram who made a commitment to their swidden fields could make only daily rather than overnight foraging trips. It would be helpful to know how much of the pepper that made its way to the coast was cultivated and how much was simply collected; it seems reasonable to assume that both wild and cultivated pepper were in circulation, implying a variety of strategies for its procurement.

An alternative strategy available to groups with knowledge of forest resources would be to abandon cultivation as a major subsistence component and become specialized forager-traders, collecting forest products of the higher elevations, such as cardamom with its rather stringent scheduling demands for harvesting.[8] These groups would have had to abandon cultivation as a primary subsistence activity, becoming highly specialized forager-traders, collecting ginger, cardamom, and other forest products. Although this essay has concentrated on political and economic contexts and has not considered questions of the cultural integration of forager-traders with others (e.g. Bird-David 1983, 1992a, 1992b; Gardner 1985, 1991,

1993; Lee and Daly, eds 1999; and Hockings, ed. 1989: 1992), ethnographic descriptions of some South Indian foragers emphasize other kinds of specialist roles taken by upland hunter-gatherers, including sorcery and wage labor. It is difficult to say to what extent competition for land at lower elevations (where swidden plots of pepper were presumably appearing) would provide the "push" for the adoption of this strategy, and to what extent scheduling consideration would have come into play.

CONCLUSION

Despite the limited information now available on late-precolonial and early-colonial-period transformations of upland economic and social practices in southern India, it is possible to make some suggestions about the parameters of change. The picture that emerges seems to be one of increasing subsistence specialization and decreasing diversity of options available to particular people, although the overall level of both economic and social/political diversity certainly increased. Levels of interdependence between groups are high and power relations markedly unequal. It would be useful to be able to discuss patterns of ethnic, linguistic, and cultural differentiation or amalgamation, but there is at present little convincing information on these important topics, especially for earlier periods.

Perhaps the most important conclusion to be drawn from the empirical evidence presented here has to do with the historically constructed nature of forager-trader lifestyles. Far from being simple, timeless, denizens of the forest, South Indian forager-traders emerge as active, strategic agents working in the context of complex political worlds. The economic and political roles of South Asian foragers are, and have been, both variable and flexible. Within this range of strategies, specialized foraging for exchange—what Woodburn (1980) calls commercial foraging and R.G. Fox (1969) the role of "professional primitives"—is, however, a precarious one, ultimately dependent on long-distance rather than local exchange links, and on volatile world markets. In South India, the relations of domination and the precarious nature of forager-trader economies point to the marginality of their position, a problem that continues into the present (e.g. Baviskar 1995). This marginality is not, however, eternal. It has been created by a complex set of historical and ecological circumstances, only a few of which I have been able to sketch here.

Both the creation and maintenance of south-western Indian forager-trader identities appear to be related to their long histories of interconnection with lowland agriculturalists and states—histories of both cooperation and conflict. In the contested spaces of the Western Ghats, competing "nationalisms" involved a range of political forms: colonial empires, agrarian states, coastal trading entrepôts, merchant guilds, class- and caste-based agricultural groups, individual entrepreneurs, kin groups, and small-scale egalitarian societies. This complex world of power met an equally complex field of production. In the forests alone, people hunted for subsistence, trade, or sport, and grew, gathered, and processed plants for a similarly broad range of purposes. The forests also hosted traders, raiders, herders, rulers, mystics, teachers, and more. At the same time, the physical and biological environment of the Ghats was far from static, with overall forest loss and regeneration, changes in vegetation composition and distribution, and soil movement all contributing to changing ecological contexts. The connections between political forms, economic strategies, and ecological contexts were far from haphazard. Although some small upland groups were able to organize effective local polities or to threaten and intimidate their neighbors, most ultimately paid the price for their (at least partial) separation from the cultural forms and social mores of the lowlands in the coin of reduced power over their own subsistence options. At the same time, historical distinctions between lowland and upland groups, while not indexing anything like a "pristine state of nature" or indeed a lack of interaction and integration of hill peoples with those of the plains and beyond, do seem to reflect the success of these groups in creating and maintaining distinctive identities, identities which both then and now constituted bases for claims to resources and, thus, economic and cultural resources in themselves.

NOTES

1. Many of these groups consist of quite large numbers of people and are not in any real sense communities or co-residential groups.

2. Throughout this essay I use the terms expansion (in demand for pepper, for example) and "intensification" (in rice and pepper production, for example) rather loosely. It is worth noting, however, that this discussion is meant to help lay an empirical groundwork for a more explicitly theoretical consideration of the

process of intensification that includes foraging and trading as strategies of intensification and that takes into account power dynamics, including possible implications of the loss of diversity in subsistence options. Cf. Morrison 1994b, 1995, 1996.

3. The difficulties with such classifications as "tribe," "caste," and alternatives such as *adivasi* (a Hindi term for original dweller or indigenous person, cf. Baviskar 1995) are well discussed by Béteille 1998; see also Hardiman 1987b: 11–16).

4. Recent research on the Early Historic period in southern India, while continuing to emphasize the importance of regional and interregional exchange, would tend to de-emphasize the primary role of the Roman empire, stressing instead the great variety of trade connections at this time (e.g. Ray 1994).

5. With the fall of the capital city of the Vijayanagara empire in 1565, the empire was reorganized and reduced in size; these coastal areas seem to have shrugged off the sometimes nominal control they had formerly experienced. Nilakanta Sastri 1975; Sewell 1982 (1900).

6. These products would include cinnamon from Sri Lanka, cloves and other spices from the Moluccas, and many more. A more thoroughgoing analysis of the larger system of exchange from the points of view of collectors, extractors, and producers rather than solely traders and governments would certainly be desirable.

7. That pepper was indeed cultivated in the sixteenth century is clear. Although Marco Polo mentions the cultivation of both pepper and ginger in the Eli kingdom (the precursor to Cannanore) during the thirteenth century, it is doubtful that he actually witnessed it. The English traveler Ralph Fitch visited Cochin in 1589, where he noticed a group of people who seemed different from other Malabaris; they had bushy hair and held long bows and arrows. Of Cochin, Fisk wrote: "Heere groweth the pepper; and it springeth up by a tree or a pole, and is like our ivy berry . . . The pepper groweth in many parts of India, especially about Cochin; and much of it doth grow in the fields among the bushes without any labor, and when it is ripe they go and gather it. The shrubbe is like unto our ivy tree; and if it did not run about some tree or pole it wold fall down and rot. When they first gather it, it is greene; and then they lay it in the sun, and it becometh blacke." The unfamiliar appearance of a swidden field might well have seemed unplanned and unplanted to a European; this confusion may lie at the base of the persistent Portuguese notion that pepper cultivation required no labor. See Bouchon 1988: 3; Foster 1968: 45–6.

8. The Hill Pandaram today, for example, collect dammar, inja bark, honey, wax, and cardamom for export as well as hunting various game animals. These activities are, however, difficult for those with swidden plots to participate in. See Morris 1982b: 80.

3

THE TODA TIGER

Debates on Custom, Utility, and Rights in Nature, South India 1820–1843

Gunnel Cederlöf

It is beautiful to observe the agility with which they bound over the hills, shaking their black locks in the wind, and as conscious of liberty as the mountain deer, or any true-born Briton. They are remarkably frank in their deportment; and their entire freedom from Hindoo servility is very engaging to the Englishman, and cannot fail to remind him of the "bold peasantry" of a still dearer country.[1] (1829)

I learn that when stung with hunger they spring upon food with the eagerness of the tiger, when their appetite is sated, they doze away their hours in idleness or sleep, then they are an easy prey to the temptation of each wild and passionate impulse, and reckless in their manner of gratifying it. Their passions, wild and turbulent, have been prematurely kindled—their inborn sense of shame prematurely withered—they are imbruted—they are men without a God—they grope their way through a dark world, and know not of hereafter.[2] (1846)

THE EYES OF OUTSIDERS WERE CONTINUOUSLY AMAZED BY THE hilly landscape of the Nilgiris mountains in South India.[3] These outsiders were among the first Europeans to reach the plateau, about three decades after the British annexation of Mysore state in 1799. They took in its beauty, its promising climate, and its soils so perfectly rich and appropriate for British fruit and crops. And, just as perfectly, and as natural a part of this landscape, were its people: first and foremost the "herders," the Toda, who already, within ten years after the first brief interventions, had been surrounded by myths of their ancient origin and noble culture. When the Reverend

James Hough observed in 1829 their frank deportment—as the winds swept their hair—he thought of mountain deer running free and wild over fields. He thought them well proportioned and muscular, playful and easily amused, and freedom and liberty were words that came to his mind in connection with them. The wilderness of the landscape promised a healthy life, filled with opportunities.

Less than two decades later, in 1846, another observer writing for a Calcutta newspaper was equally struck by the wilderness of nature as he observed the Toda. There is, however, no trace of the encouraging absence of servility in this later report. On the contrary the absence of any sense of shame or of God, and unable to control their passions, the Toda are here portrayed as reckless tigers. Wilderness needs to be tamed or at least controlled. Both authors placed themselves as observers, spectators, distanced from the landscape, while nature itself engulfed the Toda—the mountain deer being as much a part of nature as the tiger.

During the two decades that span these two observations, the Nilgiris in the Western Ghats saw dramatic change in polity, man–land relationships, and systems of authority and rule. These were characteristic of the changeover from the East India Company (EIC) as an enterprise of traders to administrators and rulers of conquered territories. The establishment of British administration in the Nilgiri region was not physically violent, yet remarkably radical; and it revealed contradictions in the legal principles of colonial administration, and conflicts of interest within the British EIC. During this period, the existing legal and social order, which had legitimized access to and authority over resources, was eroded in favor of legal principles that were argued in contradictory ways by different sections of the colonial administration.

As has been copiously shown by Richard Grove, the transformation of scholarly thinking about nature and resource use from philosophy to science—not least in medicine and botany—had implications for the perception of threats to nature caused by human interference and the need for conservation. The tropics became both a field of study and experimental grounds for utilitarian projects to protect nature from extinction. Soon, however, colonial states made use of such policies to ensure economic gain and control over the population in colonized territories. These policies had far-reaching consequences for shifting cultivators and pastoralists.[4]

The importance of early natural sciences is evident in the implementation of colonial rule in the Nilgiris. But the main logic of events does not seem to lie in policies of conservation and their implications for colonial governance. In this essay, I want to draw attention to the centrality of law, the emerging idea of a national interest, and the principle of sovereign rule within the larger processes by which people in the Nilgiris lost control over their land. I also want to stress the importance of conflicting and strong interests within the EIC, in combination with local politics of resistance, for the course of events and prolonged conflicts over land settlement. In the ensuing legal disputes, principles of local custom and aboriginal right—that built on naturalistic visions and perceptions of the specificity of the landscape—collided with those of a national or public good and of sovereign rule.

When Europeans and Indians from the plains began locating themselves in the heartland of the Nilgiris in the early 1820s, in the place that came to be known as Ootacamund, their houses and roads as well as their ambitions and aspirations were engraved in the part of the hills which remained under Toda authority. The Toda were pastoralists who migrated seasonally with their buffaloes between small extended-family settlements. They bartered milk products for corn, forest products, and other necessities with Badaga, Curumba, Kota and Irula gleaners and cultivators. The socio-economic and cultural system of authority and exchange among these people appears to have been elaborate and well defined, judging from the somewhat stumbling descriptions made in reports and letters to the Revenue Department. The Toda were perceived as being in control and lords of the central part of the plateau, while, over time, slowly losing control of the surrounding areas to the Badaga shifting cultivators. However, the central portion of the plateau, into which Europeans and east Indians now moved, remained firm under Toda authority.

Irrespective of whether they argued for or against Toda rights in land, the members of the British administration depicted the Toda as exceptional and granted them special treatment as "herders." Only two communities came into question for land rights: first, the Toda; and later the Badaga. For the sake of clarity in tracing the establishment of legal codes for land relations, this essay privileges the settlement of land rights *vis-à-vis* the Toda.

Establishing British control over the Nilgiris turned into a lengthy process of negotiations, lasting more than two decades, from the 1820s to the 1840s. The Toda were actively influencing these negotiations, even though on uneven terms. However, this essay will discuss the competing legal norms for man–nature relationships that existed within the EIC itself, and how these came to influence the settlement of rights in nature. Two major contradictions were prominent in the debates: one focused on the subjects' exclusive rights according to native custom versus the subjects' rights subordinated to the superior principle of the "public good." The other focused on the value and utility of nature as defined by aboriginal livelihood and landscape use versus public need as defined by the colonial government. As a rule, proponents for aboriginal rights and the importance to respect native custom were found in the district and local administrations of the EIC, while the Madras government would argue strongly for utilizing nature and organizing the landscape according to the public good. Both positions rested on racial conceptions of people. The former used ethnological arguments to prove the Toda's aboriginality and lordship. Thereby, the Toda's absolute rights in land could be defended, and the racial argument was used in an inclusive way. The latter used ethnological arguments in an exclusive way, to prove Toda subordination and subjecthood to EIC rule. By this logic, the Toda would only be granted user rights under company sovereignty.

Within only a couple of years after their first visits, British officers and officials decided to stay permanently. From their enthusiastic letters, it seems they had found what they searched for: the finest land ever seen, bringing both Scotland and Switzerland to mind. The district collector, John Sullivan, was granted permission to enclose almost 2000 acres in 1822, which came to be a uniquely large individual landholding in the Nilgiris. In scale, rather than landholdings within India, the grant resembled estates in northern Britain, where wealthy merchants in the British EIC invested their profits. Such evidence of the early European encounter with the Nilgiri Hills is significant for its recollections of the familiar. But, more than this, the newcomers further reinforced landscapes that were familiar to them. Soon, orchards, rose hedges, and stone cottages began to climb the green hillsides, and rules for the hunting of wild game were established. The setting up of a sanatorium was supported by arguments in favor of medical topography, which was praised for working wonders with invalids; and European children were here said to be as healthy as any child in Britain. The Nilgiri was both an alien nature to be explored and conquered, and a well-known landscape that was perceived as full of reminders of sorely missed and highly idealized homelands in northern Europe.

Sullivan's holding was the first European settlement in what became Ootacamund, and he paid for it to the Toda living there. In his eyes, it was a purchase of property for money. In the following two decades, until the resolution of Toda rights and rules for land grants in the Nilgiris in 1843, debates ran high on how to define, or, rather, redefine access to and authority over land and natural resources. On the one hand there were district administrators and early ethnographers arguing for the absolute right of the Toda in the land; on the other there was the Government of Madras claiming sovereign rights over all subjects, Indian as well as European.[5]

The stories associated with Sullivan's "purchase" are varied, some even mythical, and already the great number of accounts suggests the sensitive nature of transfers of land, and of changes in authority and control. One oft-told story relates that Sullivan asked for land of the size of a sheepskin and, when measuring the land after closing the agreement, cut the sheepskin into a thin strip whereby he could claim an enormous piece of land. As noted by Paul Hockings, this tale has roots in Virgil's historical accounts, the ancient Roman poet and historian who described the means by which Dido acquired Carthage. Most likely, the tale made its way into the Nilgiris via Europeans arguing about the validity of Sullivan's land claims while referring to well-known ancient Roman history (which was part of any learned European's education).[6]

However, nowadays this story is told also in Toda settlements (or *munds*) in Ootacamund. It was with a slightly ironic smile that Pothili, son of Nanicane, who occasionally appears as a spokesperson for the Toda in the Nilgiris, referred to the sheepskin tale when narrating how they began losing land almost two hundred years earlier, as now they were in the midst of reclaiming land lost only one generation ago. At the same time, Sullivan is not known among the Toda as an impostor but as the champion of Toda rights, as the defender of the community before the EIC. In my conversation with Nanicane, the old man suddenly left for his house to fetch an old golden coin. He explained that this was the very coin that Sullivan had used to pay for the land he purchased. He said it had been passed on to him from his father, Tilipah, as a treasure of Kashmund. Nanicane had been recalling the places lost to the British, one by one—the land under St Stephen's Church, under the Ootacamund clubhouse, and so on—but, in contrast to those losses, Sullivan had paid for his land and Nanicane wanted me to see the coin. But as it turned out the coin was not to be found. Instead, Nanicane returned with two other coins that were carefully preserved as a heritage of the past among this Toda clan. Both coins looked old and important. One bore the portrait of Queen Victoria in relief, the other of Indira Gandhi, who, in my eyes, were two powerful rulers with far-reaching claims to state authority and intervention. The coin bearing Victoria's portrait had been minted to commemorate the Neelgherry Exhibition in Poona, 1875. This was one of several exhibitions where Toda culture and ritual ornaments were put on display in the form of exotica and photographs. In the 1880s, a group of Toda were even contracted for a circus to show them as "ethnological rarities" in Europe, Australia and North America, and came to be known as the "Travelled Toda." By then, the empire had firmly established its rule in the Nilgiri Hills and the Toda had become an object of curious investigation, exhibited far from the landscape in which they encountered outsiders more than half a century earlier.[7]

How then did mountain deer become a tiger? Iconic metaphors drawn from the animal world expressed the perceived essence of a people. Among some European visitors and officials, there was a strong notion that the Toda were threatened by extinction, either from the expanding Badaga villages or by European intrusion into their lands. In 1828 Sullivan advised against raising the taxes on Toda land, arguing "the desire to preserve and encourage a fine race which had almost become extinct." Just as he saw vulnerable *shola* forests in the region disappear because of the human need for fuel wood, so also the people, who were part of the same landscape, were under threat and in need of protection.[8] But when precisely did the perception of Todas "as liberal as true-born Britons" and resembling the bold peasantry of England change, making them appear as the "reckless tiger?"

ON ABSOLUTE RIGHTS FOR THE ABORIGINAL OR THE EIC

The relationship between people living in the Nilgiri Hills and the colonial administration changed dramatically in the years up until 1843. There were deep divisions within the colonial administration on how the relationship should be codified—as expressed, for example, in the conflicts between district and presidency administrations. In these conflicts the debates on the ruler–subject relationship dealt with the question of property. As an ideological principle, the right of personal security, liberty, and property were forcefully argued both in Britain and in British dominions overseas. Many considered the security of absolute property to be a birthright and legal debates were carefully observed. But in the actual administration of justice in Britain there were competing jurisdictions that recognized conflicting rights in the same property. There was a great discrepancy between the rationalist and liberal ideological arguments of principles, and the actual multifaceted realities of privileged access to land and resources. Robert Gordon argues that the limited sphere of absolute dominion rights in Britain was riddled with ambiguities and conflicts that disrupted any project to enforce a singular system of property rights. Needless to say, there was no single policy on property that could be brought from Britain and implemented in India.[9]

Within British India in the early nineteenth century, the competing principles of land and revenue settlement were argued either in terms of the Permanent Settlement—centering on the zemindar as the landholder and the revenue collector as an intermediary between the government and the tenants—or as *ryotwari*, entailing a direct relationship between government and the individual cultivator.[10] In the Madras Presidency, Governor Thomas Munro was a strong proponent of the ryotwari settlement and John Sullivan was one of his most loyal supporters. Their correspondence bears witness to their struggle to defend the ryotwari system against its critics. The system was modeled to ensure improved agriculture and provided district collectors with far-reaching judicial authority. It was argued to secure people from oppressive rulers; however, simultaneously, it tended to detach the implementation of law from civil control. To Munro, the legal system obstructed a successful operation of the ryotwari revenue system. Law was based on custom, which implied local difference and irregularity. The moment custom is codified, it ceases to be custom. Revenue assessment on the other hand required regularity, fixed categories, and general applicability: anything else would have been inefficient. In Britain, the law secured property. The fact that law in India was made for the sake of revenue was itself anomalous.[11] Munro's strong collector was well in line with Sullivan's ambitions in the Nilgiri Hills. However, in the Nilgiris the question was not so much a matter of revenue assessment as of land rights. The amount of revenue that could be assessed from the pastoralists and cultivators in the hills was never high during these years. It was an issue of absolute control of nature as property.[12]

The decades around the turn of the nineteenth century have in Indian history often been portrayed as seeing the introduction of private property in land, and stressing the importance of "private" and "individual" in contrast to "common" and "communal." These were also the peak years of enclosure in England, when many custom-based common rights disappeared and manorial wastelands were defined as private property. The mechanism for enclosure—the Private Acts that enabled enclosers to avoid negotiating with landless users of commons and thereby evade most compensation payments—was already established in the early eighteenth century. However, this became most useful in the 1790s, during the wars in Europe, when Parliament sensed the urgent need to cultivate wastelands. According to Jeanette Neeson, in this period a public argument developed in favor of enclosure of common lands in England, even when this caused local distress. In her work on common rights and enclosure, she has found that this was not a celebration of the individual above the community, but rather individual property rights became subordinate to the "national interest." Thereby, commoners, i.e. peasants exercising common or customary rights in land through gleaning and grazing, were accused of selfish individualism, of being thieves threatening the national interest.

This situation conforms with the many comments in Nilgiri reports about lazy Toda cattle-herders who sat watching buffaloes day in and day out, neither using land efficiently through cultivation nor contributing to government revenue—which was claimed to benefit all.[13] John Brewer and Susan Staves provide similar observations in their elaboration on property rights; they see property as necessarily relational, "conceivable only in the context of communities of people; property rights are rights 'against' other people, rights to exclude them from the use and enjoyment of the things owned."[14] Understanding the process of claiming absolute rights in land as a process of exclusion seems to be a useful way of approaching conflicts over land in the Nilgiris. These escalated in the 1830s and were defined to the advantage of the EIC in 1843.

During the 1820s, the Nilgiri region did not come particularly high on the Madras government's agenda, for it was remote and rather strenuous to reach. It was defined as a part of Coimbatore district even before the settlement of Europeans on the hills, and had come under the administration of Sullivan when he was made district collector in 1815. Sullivan, in fact, had to argue quite persistently in support of the place as the most appropriate location for a sanatorium to bring the government's attention to the prospects of exploiting the Nilgiris. The government's interest in the forests was at the time focused on the neighboring Malabar district on the western side of the mountain range. Settling land and revenue in these dense teak forests was crucial to ensure the availability of timber. Increasing demands from the navy and the Bombay docks heightened the pressure on the Malabar teak and legislation had been passed in 1805 that placed the forests of Malabar and Canara under the complete control of the Bombay government. As sovereignty of the forest was proclaimed, the influential jenmi landowners lost their absolute rights in land. Jenmi rights were permanent, heritable and saleable and the governor Thomas Munro, had argued in Parliament in favor of their rights in private property against the monopoly of the EIC. In a rhetorical statement, Munro questioned the moderation of the government who had promised "reasonable assistance" for getting hold of non-private timber, as "there can be no reasonable assistance where Government interferes; and this slight beginning with reasonable assistance has now grown into a wide and oppressive monopoly." The EIC had wanted to secure a stable supply of timber by way of a monopoly, while Munro argued that by re-establishing jenmi rights the free market would work as a regulator on the timber yield without destroying owners' trust in the government. Hence, the security of colonial rule would be guaranteed. These arguments in support of indigenous property rights and of free market forces against EIC monopolies would echo in the Nilgiris only a few years later.[15]

To secure the consent of people or, rather, of patrons in India was one of Munro's major concerns. The Toda were definitely not such patrons. However, in the conflicts of the 1830s that arose from European immigration into the Nilgiris, the highest board of the EIC, the Court of Directors, found reason to remind the Government of Madras of the importance of keeping up legal principles for the sake of securing subjects' confidence in a just government.[16] We must also keep in mind Munro's ideas of keeping the Bhils in West India under control—"a miserable race, poor and few in numbers." They were a people with substantial sovereignty, claiming kingship status, who raided the plains, and the British strove to pacify them. "I see no reason to expect disturbances from any of the native states now surrounded by our territory [. . .] The Bheels [. . .] well treated [. . .] will in a few years become as quiet as any of our other Indian subjects."[17]

Munro was a contemporary of Mountstuart Elphinstone and John Malcolm in India, and one among several middle- and upper-ranking Scots who made a career in the EIC. These three were particularly successful and reached high military rank, being appointed governors in Madras and Bombay. Historical research on the influence of Scots and the Scottish Enlightenment on the work of the EIC has recently taken a new turn. In her study of the influence of Scottish Enlightenment ideas on the thinking of Munro,

Elphinstone and Malcolm, Martha McLaren terms these three as an important and progressive leadership cadre that shared a Scottish school of thought on Indian government. She says their ideas were "a clearly articulated system of political economy on lines specified by Adam Smith, David Hume, and other Scottish writers."[18]

In contrast with the common characterization of British rule as an authoritarian, military state, McLaren argues that Munro, Elphinstone and Malcolm saw military rule as a necessary but temporary system of government.[19] It was only by securing the "good-will of the people" that the empire would survive. Despotism would inhibit economic growth, whereas growth would be ensured by giving a certain autonomy to the subject in the form of private property. The guiding idea of oriental despotism was indeed adopted by the colonial government, but it was eventually expected to be replaced by the idea of a European authoritarian monarchy. This position should not be mistaken for democracy, but it was a clear rejection of absolutism. In India as in Britain, there was to be a balance between authority and liberty, whereby liberty implied the protection of person and property from arbitrary absolute power by an enlightened, sovereign government, and authority rested on a bond of consent between the government and Indian elites as expressed in one of David Hume's "First Principles of Government."[20]

There are good reasons for asking if Munro's case illustrates the fact that principles of government need not reflect an implementation of such principles. McLaren's argument is made within the frames of intellectual history and focuses on *principles* of rule. David Washbrook's researches into the *implementation* of government policies arrive at a different conclusion. Washbrook stresses the pragmatism of the colonial government and points to a despotism made permanent when Munro centralized civil, military, and judicial powers in the hands of the sovereign (i.e. the EIC): "British-Indian law became less a tool of liberty than an instrument of despotism."[21]

Munro belonged to the generation of officers who were in the process of transforming their role from merchants into rulers. To perform their task they needed information. Unlike the Orientalists, who searched Hindu classical texts for knowledge of Indian society, colonial officers such as Munro searched for facts of actual polity, administration, and law in order to establish a functioning rule, thus diverging from classical Orientalists. But in contrast with Utilitarians, who argued for the function and effectiveness of law for the purpose of establishing a new social order—a perspective from which the multitude of local customs implied chaos—Munro searched for indigenous practice. To shape colonial administration according to traditions of the place was expected to be more comprehensible to Indians and thereby ensure stability under sovereign rule. McLaren notes that Munro turned to the "rough common sense empiricism" favored by Scottish moral philosophers. Jon Wilson correctly suggests that when officials searched for the "real state of things" it reflected a construction of the things that EIC officials found administratively useful. The means of finding information was inspired by the ethnological science that developed at the turn of the nineteenth century, wherein systematic description and the compilation of statistics implied statecraft.[22]

Interestingly, Neeladri Bhattacharya finds a similar logic in the colonial administration for a later period in Punjab. He contrasts the orientalists' ambition—of discovering the customs of India in their pure form and purged of the foreign influences and practices that had distorted their origin—with the Utilitarian positivists' disdain for tradition and custom. But none of these perspectives were applied in late-nineteenth-century Punjab. Bhattacharya finds the colonial administration's relationship with native traditions ambiguous and varied. The laws in colonial courts were based on the principles of common law, where custom was seen as embodied in practice. In that sense, law was contextual. But to establish custom as it existed in Punjab, the officials used surveys, civil code manuals, and case law. Their framework for interpreting custom was therefore founded in Victorian anthropology and Common Law theory rather than in Punjabi practice.[23]

Against this background it is not surprising to find that Munro's position on EIC monopoly and the free market was rather pragmatic. The market was expected to secure popular trust and at the same time regulate the timber trade. However, in 1813 Munro had argued quite the opposite. In a forceful statement in Parliament he defended EIC monopoly in the overseas trade. In Malabar, only a few years later, when Munro turned to criticize the monopoly, the issue was not so much about liberal ideas of trade but of securing the timber yield without a local revolt breaking out among the larger landlords. However, in the following decade Munro's plans came to nought. In 1824, only a year after the EIC monopoly in timber was banned, the collector of Malabar reported that there had been a rush to the market, which was cleared of timber felled for public purposes, leaving the government empty-handed. In 1840 the collector claimed that Munro's high opinion of owners' concerns for forest conservancy had been "utterly disproved by the last 17 years' experience" when large tracts had been clear-felled.[24]

So, at the time when Europeans first settled in the Nilgiris, when land settlement in the Western Ghats took much of the Madras government's time, it had also drawn attention away from the Nilgiri Hills. During most of Munro's governorship (1818–27), Sullivan was left quite undisturbed in the Nilgiris to administrate the land settlement by himself. Initially, there were only a handful of Europeans who chose to build houses in the hills. Documentation from the 1830s shows that the Toda did not seem to consider these early settlers as either intruders or as in any way interfering with their own authority over the land. Sullivan was one of only three individuals who had been permitted by the government to "enclose wateland." The vast majority of Europeans never applied to the government before erecting buildings and taking up trade in the hills. Their settlement in the Nilgiris appears only to have received the consent of Sullivan and the commander in charge of the military cantonment. But these permits had no relation to the Toda perception of European presence in their neighborhood which became even more evident by the fact that the Toda continued to pay revenue for land taken by Sullivan. These documents were only intended to secure proprietary rights from the government.

However, in 1827 the governorship passed to Stephen R. Lushington, who was hostile to all talk of Toda property rights. He considered such rights as a threat to government sovereignty. The following year a resolution regulated land transfers in the Nilgiris and, in 1829, Sullivan made an appeal to the government that echoed the logic of Munro's argument when he defended Toda rights and the integrity of the Nilgiris as a region: "I beg leave to remind the Board that these Hill people have rights. The Todavurs can show as clear a proprietary right to the soil, they now occupy, as can be produced by the Merassidars of Malabar and to a certain share of the produce of all land now cultivated, or that may be hereafter cultivated." Sullivan also took Munro's arguments a step further and argued that it was, in fact, the Toda who were the "Lords" of the Nilgiris, not the EIC. They would, of course, pay revenue to the government, yet the Toda predicament was not a question of revenue but of ownership. "Their exclusive proprietary rights to this [land] is not contested by any other class of natives. On the contrary, by the cultivating classes who occupy at least three fourths of the Neelgherries, they are considered as the ancient proprietors of the whole range [. . .]" However, the Lushington government was not impressed. They were keener on bringing this unruly district collector, with his own agenda, into line with the Madras government's principles of rule.[25]

These conflicts were among the first indications that polities in the hills had moved closer to those of the plains. In contrast with later histories of north-east India, where the hills became regions of difference, the South Indian hills were slowly integrated into the dominant administrative principles of the plains.[26]

RIGHTS OF CUSTOM OR FOR THE PUBLIC GOOD

Many of the most critical debates about absolute property rights versus government exclusive rights revolved around the question of custom. Within the EIC, from the district's administration in the Nilgiris to the Court of Directors, the arguments related in various ways to legal aspects (as in Common Law practices and the establishment of jurisdiction in the British territories) and to aspects of government in the exercise of control over territory and people. According to the English Common Law, a lord's absolute right in land as well as the tenants' right to use the commons were protected by the king. As the common rights were granted in return for labor services and rent, these rights were appendant to the land, and land could not be sold or bifurcated without them. Custom was thus deeply rooted in the legal discourse and common rights in Britain varied from place to place, depending on local history, locality, landscape, and nature. E.P. Thompson describes custom as "ambience," which is best understood via Bourdieu's term *habitus*: "[. . .] a lived environment comprised of practices, inherited expectations, rules which both determined limits to usages and disclosed possibilities, norms and sanctions both of law and neighborhood pressures." Viewed with this terminology, Sullivan's many Nilgiri reports are lengthy exercises toward establishing the habitus of the Nilgiris, and the Madras revenue board could not initially dismiss them as irrelevant: they had to take a debate on each issue.[27]

From the late eighteenth century, however, in the heyday of enclosure, the English courts increasingly decided against user rights derived from custom, for these stood in the way of "improvement." Much potentially rich land was laid waste unless laborers were made available to cultivate it. This could only be achieved if common rights were detached from land. Jeanette Neeson finds that critics of the commons wanted to develop the British nation and change the structure of rural England. In this agrarian transformation, "lazy commoners" were, in fact, people not available for farm labor and who were relatively independent of wages. Only the exclusive enjoyment of property could create a proletariat and ensure economic growth.[28]

A similar change is also visible in India, where the Madras government turned away from trying to disprove custom and toward subordinating custom to the superior principle of the "public good." By that logic, H.J. Chamier, secretary to the Madras government, criticized Sullivan for misrule under the duties of a magistrate, which included protecting the lives and properties of people from outrage. Sullivan had not ensured "the just protection of the Todawars and other classes of the people in the enjoyment of all the rights to which they are really entitled in the manner most conducive to the public good." In the Nilgiris, the government did not consider it conducive for large tracts of land to be under the control of people who had no interest in cultivation and thus unavailable for public purposes. Nor would it secure the enforcement of EIC sovereignty, defended by the British nation, which was supposed to protect Indian subjects from misrule under indigenous masters.[29]

There is no cause-and-effect relationship between the English legal debates and the settlement of rights in Indian forest tracts. What needs to be taken account of is the similarity of legal discourses in which customary rights could not be dismissed per se but could be disproved by reference to the potentially higher utility of nature for the benefit of the nation.

In a narrow sense, the debates on sovereignty and property in the Nilgiris reflect a transition within Company rule in the Madras Presidency where the government's attention began to shift from primarily targeting military security over dispersed areas to administrative consolidation and the rule of a sovereign government. This change cannot be equated with the administration of two different governors, even though Munro and Lushington quite clearly pursued different policies in the Nilgiris. Munro often explained the necessity of adjusting legislation and rule to local conditions and building on indigenous forms of government and land tenure, which was what Sullivan relied on. Consequently, Munro argued for each presidency acting for itself. No "fanciful theories founded on European models" were to be applied.[30] Lushington began diverting from this in an attempt to enforce a uniform polity in every part of the presidency.[31]

The difference in policy is clearly revealed in the exchange of arguments in the reports submitted to the Madras Board of Revenue from Sullivan and Chamier. Chamier discarded Sullivan's report as being just another of his "disquisitions filled with unsupported claims aimed at collision with public functionaries."[32] What Sullivan defended was the Toda birthright to their ancestral lands. These rights were prescriptive and should be respected, being founded in native custom. Also, Chamier argued for securing rights, but these rights were purposed to serve the "public good":

> It is universally acknowledged that the absolute property in the soil in India is vested in the Sovereign who is entitled to the rent and may transfer and assign it a right of occupying the cultivated lands, <u>on the condition of keeping up the cultivation so as to produce rent of revenue to the state</u> is allowed to the Ryots, but always subservient to and dependent upon the <u>absolute</u> proprietor.[33]

The voluminous correspondence on land conflicts in the Nilgiris reveals the contradictions within the EIC of perceptions on the utility of space and nature. No single polity was at work, nor was there agreement on the conquering of new forest territories. K. Sivaramakrishnan emphasizes such regional and local differences. He points to the specific conjunctures of historical trajectories of local histories, commercial interests, conflicting polities, forms of resistance, landscapes and natures, which all worked to give the colonial interaction its specific form. To this may be added the role of overarching interests and ideologies in which regional and local interests were politically played out. In the Nilgiris, in the actual application of principles, local conditions had a decisive effect on their implementation as well as their ultimate form. As I point out elsewhere, legally codified rights were shaped in relation to local conflicts. However, the principles argued within the EIC were rarely rooted in the locality, and the interests at force had large-scale, even global, ambitions. They were enacted on different arenas: locally in the Nilgiris, regionally in the political center of the presidency, and finally in the British Parliament. These were principles regarding the utility of nature, of rights seen as local custom or in the perspective of a larger nation, and of man–nature relationships.

ETHNOLOGY PROVING TODA SOVEREIGNTY AND SUBORDINATION

Many studies have observed that the ethnographic codification of people became part of legal and social transformations under colonial rule. Notions of caste, tribe, and clan were used to establish access to resources and exclusive rights in nature, as well as exclusion from these. Racially and socially structured questionnaires organized the censuses and revenue settlements. Ultimately, colonial interaction became racialized.[34]

In his disagreement with Sullivan in 1830, Chamier shaped his argument around a notion of the Toda as a people. His frustration with Sullivan's extensive communications with the government on the Toda issue is poorly concealed in the minute. These wandering herdsmen of the hills, he writes, have no reason for jealousy when strangers occupy a small portion of the land.

> These poor men are continually migrating from one part to another, have no fixed habitation, no settled rules of life, no written laws, no taste for agricultural pursuits, no population which presses on their means of subsistence, and no taxes which cannot be paid with the greatest ease; and if there is any class of people to whom a more free and enlarged intercourse with the inhabitants of the adjoining countries, and with settlers in their own, can be beneficial, it is surely those who will receive knowledge, clothing, and better supplies, in the place of ignorance, nakedness and discomfort.[35]

It was here, in the Revenue Board's communications in 1830, that the ethnography of the Nilgiris changed in a decisive way and arguments were phrased that would eventually disqualify the Toda from proprietary rights in land. In the document, Chamier redefined the Toda as a people distinguished by their unsettled trade and way of life. What Sullivan, Harkness, Hough and others had earlier described as the unique features of a lordly people were here defined as degrading. Several subsequent statements issued by the Revenue Board denied Toda lordship, and consequently their proprietary claims. These rudimentary ethnographical remarks were also immediately linked to government needs and to the public good, i.e. to the efficient land use of settled cultivation for revenue generation.[36] The situation may be phrased in Sivaramakrishnan's terminology as the making of a tribal place, but it might be even more correct to term it the remaking of a tribal place, since it had earlier been defined as uniquely different from the Indian plains in the romantic description of "herders". Now it began to be redefined in terms of perceptions of people, space, and rights. In both cases, the description was part of a process of racializing landscape.[37]

Clearly, this was the situation in the Nilgiris, even though such development was far from linear. The complexity of general principles and local adjustments may be exemplified by the settlement of land and revenue according to the ryotwari system.

In the Coimbatore district, where this revenue system was first tried out in the 1790s, the idea of giving titles to settled small farmers had to adjust to a situation where the dominant producers were cattle breeders. The *bhurty* or shifting system therefore reflected the existence of both shifting cultivation and pastoralism within the categories of revenue assessment. It allowed a cultivator to hold up to five times the amount of land than what was shown in his *patta* (the document showing the amount of land taxed to a particular holder). The *ayan* or grass allowance was a low-taxed piece of land not exceeding one-fifth of a person's holding. Grazing pattas denoted lands to which the holder had a preferential right. They were granted at one-fourth of the usual assessment and could be held until required for cultivation.[38]

The idea of keeping separate categories for shifting cultivation and pasturage was also applied in the Nilgiris. As late as 1842, the Board of Revenue warned the Malabar collector against changing the system since low-country practices were found unsuitable and premature for the hills. The board was "averse to sanctioning an innovation which would be very unpalatable, merely for the sake of effecting greater regularity of Revenue management." In the hills, sensitivity to local custom in law was thereby prioritized over the needs of regularity for the efficiency of the revenue system.[39]

However, the crucial question did not refer to revenue but to property and such exclusive rights in land were argued along racial lines—both by the early ethnographers and the Madras government. Henry Harkness's reports of 1832 came to be the most quoted of all ethnographies from the Nilgiris. Harkness was absorbed by the exotic; by dress and performance, living settlements, trades, cults, and ceremonies. He saw the Toda as a unique people, leading the natural life of a "hill tribe." As several before him, he concluded that they were the original inhabitants of the hills and Sullivan often quoted Harkness extensively. The early reports are remarkably positive. Hough's metaphor of the mountain deer is quite representative of these vivid descriptions.[40]

Sullivan had reason to quote Harkness as he saw immediate threats to the Toda. In 1831 a wealthy banker, William Rumbold, had forcibly purchased a large piece of land from the Toda of Kashmund by means of "persuasion" and blackmail. Simultaneously, the government had begun to investigate how best they could purchase exclusive rights to the land on which the military cantonment had been built in Ootacamund, the major part of which also belonged to Kashmund.[41] Many investigations were carried out and Sullivan, after having resigned as district collector, contributed with an extensive defense of Toda rights in 1835. In the following two years, conflicts between the government and the Toda in the central Nilgiris escalated and came to involve not only these two parties but also local strong men of neighboring regions and the Court of Directors. Part of the claims encroached not only on grazing lands and settlements but also on temple grounds, which had caused a major agitation among the Toda. In the end, the land claimed by the banker was returned to the Toda, while in 1840 the government purchased absolute rights to the cantonment land by payment of compensation to the Toda of Kashmund and Melgashmund.[42] To the Toda, the loss of land was more than loss of livelihood or loss of natural landscape. It was also the beginning of an alienation from social landscapes in which they held authority over land and resources and, further, an encroachment upon the sacred geographies of their place.

The Toda were, however, not mere victims passively awaiting their exclusion from land by legal confirmations of colonial conquest. During the period of open conflict they confronted civil servants and the government in many different ways. The relation between the two was highly uneven, but the documentation reveals that the Toda did not lack agency. On most occasions their means of resistance related to the legal sphere, which was simultaneously imposed and invented alongside the conflicts. Their protests were phrased in the form of petitions, depositions, by a refusal to appear for questioning, by delaying investigations via absenteeism, by a refusal to accept payment (or "compensation") for loss of land, by denying the validity of earlier agreements, by filing court cases, and so on. Since there was a conflict within the administration itself, a space had opened up where resistance could be expressed. Phrased differently, resistance was articulated in the discourse of the dominant. I have discussed a few of these conflicts in detail elsewhere and will concentrate here on the logic of the legal arguments.[43]

When conflicts over the government's and Rumbold's large land claims escalated in the 1830s, numerous reports of contradictory content were submitted to the Madras revenue board. The major part of these reports was built on inquiries and interviews with Todas and Badagas. The problem of understanding the existing norms appears at times to have been the result of surveys carried out in different locations. The Toda of Malnaud—a region where they were acknowledged to possess ultimate authority over land—and the Toda living in Khodanaud, where the Badagas occupied most of the land, need not have followed the same principles regarding land control.[44] But mostly, it seems, administrators ran into problems when they persistently searched for principles within a legal framework wherein exclusive possession was the ultimate norm. To put it more plainly, they wanted to find out from whom they could purchase ultimate rights to land, and such a person or group of persons does not seem to have been easily found.

George Drury, Collector of Coimbatore, and Daniel Eliott, Sub-collector of Malabar, came into conflict on the question if the Toda held land on an individual basis or as a common right. Drury had understood from the Toda of Khodanaud that each settlement or *mund* had its separate grounds, and that they did not consider themselves proprietors in common with Todas in other munds. Each family's rights were independent. In central Malnaud, he asserted, any Toda may sell the portion of the mund entered in his own patta, without reference to the Todas of the same mund. The man was, however, obliged to obtain the consent of his own family and relatives, and lands belonging to one mund were never transferred to people of another.[45]

Six months later Eliott made a particular inquiry into these conditions. He assembled all the Toda landholders who claimed rights in the cantonment lands, as also the Toda and Badaga *monigars* of Malnaud.[46]

> [. . .] they all agreed that in Malanaud, which they explained to be that part of Todanaud, the lands of which have always been retained in the exclusive possession of the Todas for pasturage, are the common property of the Todas of the Naud in general, and that neither the inhabitants of any Mund jointly, nor any individual Puttadar in it, can dispose of any portion of the Mund, without the consent of the inhabitants of all the other Munds in the Naud, or of all the Puttadars as the representations of the common proprietors, and that the Toda inhabitants of the other Nauds have no interest in the lands of Malnaud.[47]

Eliott disputed Sullivan's position as well, this time on the issue of *gudu*, the gift exchanged between people of different communities and, in particular, between the Badaga shifting cultivators and the Toda. In a long minute, Sullivan reiterated his claims to the Toda's exclusive proprietary right to the lands of Malnaud, this being acknowledged by all other inhabitants of the Nilgiris. In this capacity, "[. . .] they derive an annual income from the land which both by the Burgher and the Todawars is called Goodoo."[48]

According to Sullivan, gudu was a right according to *mamool*, or custom, which was claimed to have existed "since time immemorial." This was measured as a portion of grain from the lands cultivated and annually given to the Toda, who controlled the land, but both Todas and Badagas had explained to Collector Drury that they considered the contribution as applicable in the first instance for religious purposes. The Badaga gave gudu to the Toda, "to whom their deference was due by prescription, from having conceded to their ancestors, the privilege of cultivating lands," since they did not want to risk their protection against the sorceries of other tribes. From Sullivan's and Drury's reports it can be concluded that this was a gift that affirmed social relations in a complex system of economic, social, political and ritual interrelationships.[49]

By 1842 all such social and cultural logic had disappeared from government communications. Instead, the economic principles of ownership had become the guiding norm. Fascination with the Toda as a unique people had been exchanged for descriptions of them as "a pastoral half nomad tribe, unacquainted with agriculture," and as people not differing from those of the plains. Their claims to lordship were considered unfounded and Sullivan's comparisons between the Toda rights and those of the landlords of Malabar were thought nonsense.[50] The governor's instructions for the Regulation on Toda rights, which was being drafted, were clear:

> [The collector should arrange . . .] the payment of an annual sum in compensation for the space from which the Todas have been excluded in Ootacamund and likewise for the lands without the cantonment but he directs that this disbursement be distinctly made as "<u>compensation</u>," and that the terms "quit rent", "Goodoo" or other words of similar import be carefully avoided.[51]

When the Toda finally accepted exchanging cantonment land for compensation payment, they also consented to a substitution of the term "compensation" for the term "goodoo." And in a stroke this locally specific right was rooted out of the legal text. But it remains unclear whether the Toda knew or bothered about the legal implications of this exchange of terminology.[52] Less than a year later, Toda claims to authority weakened even further while the EIC simultaneously strengthened its control. The Court of Directors remarked that the Toda could only dispose of such rights as they themselves possessed. And, explained the court, since they were only pasturing herds, their only right was pasturage. The Badagas' only right was stated as "occupation." This meant that if land had been bought from either of such people for the purpose of cultivation, such purchase would only be valid if disposed of by public auction. This was a decisive step to ensure the EIC's sovereign rights in land, while people's access to nature was reduced to usage.[53]

When the "Rights of the Todawars" were finally codified in 1843, the Toda were acknowledged as having the privilege of "immemorial occupation," i.e. they had lived on the land as far back as anyone could remember and had utilized its resources. Their authority over the region, expressed in the socio-economic and cultural system of exchange, which had regulated land control and access in the Nilgiris, could not be combined with the intention of the Regulation and was subsequently disregarded. Likewise, all surveys that had brought forth information from the Toda about the exact extent of their claims were ignored, and the giving of gudu was considered "unexplained" since "whether these donations are made from superstitious motives, or with the object of inducing the Toda to refrain from molesting them, or as an acknowledgement of their proprietary right in the land, has never been satisfactorily ascertained." The Toda could, by all means, carry on their trade as pastoralists as long as they paid the grazing tax and, more importantly, as long as they did not "bar the progress of improvement or hinder the application of the land to more useful and valuable purposes." But the Board of Revenue did not foresee the need to expropriate their lands in the immediate future since they expected the Toda to become influenced by more settled habits and thereby receive a permanent hold on the land. To further inspire the Toda to change their trade, the payment of compensation for land lost was to be made through an addition to the assessment. The capital would then be invested by the government to yield an annual income from which money could be forwarded to Todas who wanted to take up agriculture.[54]

A few years later, the Calcutta *Oriental Christian Spectator*'s correspondent reported on the Toda "tiger," wild and "imbruted", following his passions through a dark world, recklessly gratifying his needs, and dozing idly when sated. The image of the Toda in the 1840s was far from that of the bold and free peasants of Britain which had characterized their representation only twenty years earlier. In the Nilgiris, the English peasantry were no longer accepted as a valid model for the subjects of sovereign, colonial rule. It was not even a question of accepting lordship under the Sovereign, a relationship in which the "lords" would have to abide by the rules while a sovereign ruler had exclusive right to set the rules. However, lordship as a model would have implied also the rights of the lord to authority over tenants and laborers. But the Madras government sought exclusive and immediate control over nature and people, without intermediate lords, or a social class equivalent to zamindars, not only in the Nilgiris but in all territories of the Madras Presidency. The British nation was to assure security and prosperity of "the public," according to the guiding principle of the 1840s. Therefore, the legal processes that established such control inevitably resulted in the dismantling of Toda authority.

These arguments brought the notion of a "nation" and "public" into the debates. It is important to note that discussions did not center on the question of "state," but of law and how to legally secure the interests of the colonial government. As these interests were attached to a place, they were also shaped in relation to the landscape and people of that place. Thus, nature was perceived from the perspective of the colonial administrator with his vision of a progressive and fundamental transformation of resource use. People were identified in essentialized, delimited ethnographical categories that, in turn, fixed them to the idea of the Nilgiri landscape. Studies of late-nineteenth-century and twentieth-century Nilgiris give ample evidence of how the idea of the Toda herder penetrated government regulations, anthropological investigations, and even self-perceptions of the "Nilgiri Todas." In the process, the imprints of both British and Indian nation formation have been engraved in Nilgiri natures and ecologies. In the 1840s, when the Toda did not conform to the idea of the entrepreneurial subject as settled cultivators, they were no longer seen as being "free from servility" but "wild" and "reckless." They were now to be domesticated by the project of establishing and consolidating British sovereign rule. In the Nilgiris, the prime tool of the government was law, and the arguments here all centered on nature.

NOTES

1. Hough 1829: 64–5. The Reverend James Hough was a chaplain on the Madras establishment.

2. *Calcutta Oriental Christian Spectator*, September 29, 1846, "From our Correspondents, Ootacamund."

3. This essay has benefited greatly from comments by David Arnold, Jeanette Neeson, Pamela Price, Mahesh Rangarajan, C.R. Sathyanarayanan, Rolf Thorstendahl and David Washbrook, as well as from my affiliations as a fellow at the Swedish Collegium of Advanced Study in the Social Sciences, Uppsala University; and Queen Elizabeth House, Oxford University. The essay is part of a larger research

project funded by the Bank of Sweden Tercentenary Foundation and the Swedish International Development Cooperation Agency (Sida/SAREC).

4. Grove 1995, "Introduction."

5. Oriental and India Office Collections, hereafter OIOC, Madras Revenue Proceedings, September 17, 1822, no. 15, 2422–3.

6. Hockings 1989: 336.

7. Meeting with Pothili and Nanicane in Kashmund, Nilgiri Hills, November 2001. See also Sutton 2002: 67 for a discussion on the display of "Toda tribal culture" in exhibitions and museums at the end of the nineteenth century.

8. OIOC, Madras Board of Revenue Proceedings, October 23, 1828: To the Board of Revenue, from John Sullivan, para 14.

9. In the process of the English enclosure, customary usage could be extinguished from Common Law by the Court of Common Pleas. In spite of this, usage could still be claimed as a local right by custom of a manor or village. Gordon 1996: 95–7, 104; Thompson 1993: 143; Lieberman 1996: 144–7.

10. Baker 1984: 56–62; McLaren 2001: 72–3.

11. I am indebted to David Washbrook for a discussion of this issue.

12. OIOC, Thomas Munro Collection, box 75, 1820, Mr. Fullarton's Plan. Stein 1989: chap. 3; Washbrook 1999: 407; Cederlöf 2002.

13. Neeson 1993: 19, 44.

14. Brewer and Staves, 1996: 3.

15. Thomas Munro (1761–1827), lieutenant-colonel and superintending the Ceded Districts until 1807, in England 1807–14. Jenmi, *jemnum*: sovereign proprietary right in land. Parliamentary Papers, Session 1812, vol. 7, *Fifth Select Committee*, App. 23, Extracts from Reports Respecting Land Tenures and Assessments, in Malabar, Para 179. Gleig 1830, vol. 2, app. XI, *Minute on Monopoly of Timber at Malabar, 6.12.1822*, paras 3, 4 and 15. Kumar 1982: 221–4.

16. OIOC, Madras Despatches, Madras Revenue Department, April 10, 1839, para 49.

17. Gleig 1830, vol. 2: 51–2; Hardiman 1994: 106–12; Skaria 1999: 135, 155.

18. See further John MacKenzie 1993: 714–39, for a discussion of the Scottish role in the British Empire; and Bryant 1985: 22–41, for a study of the Scots in eighteenth-century India. McLaren 2001: 79.

19. To see British rule during the late-eighteenth and early-nineteenth century as a military state is argued, among others, by Douglas Peers and David Washbrook. Peers 1995: 44–6; Washbrook 1999: 404–8. Burton Stein notes that two-thirds of the more than two hundred minutes written by Thomas Munro between the years 1820 and 1824 were on military matters. Stein 1989: 252.

20. McLaren 1993: 470–1, 2001: 182–8; Thompson 1991 (1963): 86–7; Wilson 2000: 80, 103–5; Wootton 1996: 606.

21. Washbrook 1999: 407; see also Stein 1989: 106.

22. David Ludden defines this position as empirical orientalism. Bhattacharya 1996: 22–4; McLaren 2001: 235–7; Ludden 1993; Pels 1999: 85–6, 88–90; Wilson 2000: 75.

23. Bhattacharya 1996: 24–7, 48–9.

24. Gleig 1830, vol. 1, *Memorandum on Opening the Trade with India to the Outports*, February 1, 1813: 386–7, 390; Gleig 1830, vol. 2, app. XI, *Minute on Monopoly of Timber at Malabar*, December 6, 1822, particularly para 15; OIOC, Madras Board of Revenue Proceedings, July 27, 1840, app. A, para 6; Grove 1995: 399, 417–19; Rangarajan 1996: 20–2; Stokes 1959: 39; Washbrook 1999: 402–3.

25. OIOC, Madras Despatches, October 26, 1831: 1159–62; OIOC, Madras Board of Revenue Proceedings, October 23, 1828, To the Board of Revenue from John Sullivan, Collector, October 11, 1828, para 5 and 9; OIOC, Madras Revenue Consultations, February 1, 1830, To BR from John Sullivan, para 19.

26. See, for example, the contributions by Karlsson and Mey in this volume.

27. Peluso and Vandergeest discuss this as "customary practices." Peluso and Vandergeest 2001: 791–2; Thompson 1991: 102.

28. Neeson 1993: 22–34.

29. OIOC, Board's Collections, April 7, 1826, Parts of Sir John Malcolm's Instructions OIOC, Madras Revenue Consultations, March 1, 1830, to the Board of Revenue from H.J. Chamier.

30. Munro's opinion to build on old, indigenous forms of administration and his argument that ryotwari was closer to native revenue systems should, however, not be taken as indicative of an ambition to secure native rights against the EIC. As Burton Stein argues for the settlement of the Kanara district, "Munro constructed a history in order to justify a level of revenue assessment... which could be collected without promoting opposition from its ancient, dominant landholders." In strong opposition to the permanent settlement of Bengal, Munro claimed the right of the Madras Presidency to act independently. Stein 1989: 71.

31. Gleig 1830, vol. 3: 320; Stein 1989: 289–90.

32. OIOC, Madras Revenue Consultations, March 1, 1830, to the Board of Revenue from H.J. Chamier.

33. Ibid. Emphasis in the original.

34. Bhattacharya 1996; Susan Bayly 1999; Peluso and Vandergeest 2001; Cederlöf 2002.

35. Ibid.

36. In several communications it was noted that they were unable to produce written documents to prove their land claims—remarks thought of as absurd by John Sullivan since the Toda language had no written script. OIOC, Madras Revenue Consultations, March 1, 1830, to Board of Revenue from H.J. Chamier; OIOC, Board's Collections, February 16, 1836, State of the Todawars on the Neilgherry Hills, Mr Sullivan's Minute, para 41.

37. Sivaramakrishnan 1999: 83–7; Peluso and Vandergeest 2001: 792.

38. Francis 1908: 268–9; Cederlöf 1997: 45–6.
39. OIOC, Madras Board of Revenue Proceedings, November 10, 1842, para 1.
40. OIOC, Madras Board of Revenue Proceedings, January 3, 1828, pp. 324–5, letter from J. Sullivan to Board of Revenue October 2, 1827; OIOC, Board's Collections, February 16, 1836, State of the Todawars on the Neilgherry Hills. Harkness 1832: 7–8; Keys 1812: xlviii; Macpherson 1820: lviii; Ward 1821: lxxiii.
41. See further Cederlöf 2006.
42. The term "payment" was avoided as it would indicate a seller or an owner of land. To use "compensation" was meant to imply the "loss of usufruct." In Tamil, the names of the munds are Kandelmund and Manjakalmund. OIOC, Madras Board of Revenue Proceedings, March 23 1837, from Binny & Co. to Chief Secr. to Government, and August 3, 1840, from H.V. Conolly to Secr. to the Board of Revenue, Kararnamah between the Toda of ten munds and the Government of Madras.
43. Cederlöf 2002 and 2006.
44. The Badaga were claimed as being in possession of two divisions, Todanaud and Khondanaud, while Malnaud was exclusively Toda land. OIOC, Board's Collections, February 16, 1836, State of the Todawars on the Neilgherry Hills, Mr. Sullivan's Minute, para 50.
45. George Dominico Drury, Collector of Coimbatore District 1833–1841. OIOC, Board's Collections, State of the Todawars on the Neilgherry Hills, Extract of Revenue Consultations, October 6, 1835.
46. The lowest-level government official who represented a link between the colonial administration and an individual locality.
47. OIOC, Madras Revenue Proceedings, December 27, 1836, no. 43, Memorandum for the Consideration of the Board of Revenue, Daniel Eliott, Sub. Coll., Malabar.
48. OIOC, Board's Collections, February 16, 1836, State of the Todawars on the Neilgherry Hills, Mr. Sullivan's Minute, para 26.
49. Ibid., para 30.
50. OIOC, Madras Board of Revenue Proceedings, October 17, 1842, Extract from the Minutes of Consultation September 17, 1842, From the Secr. to the Board of Revenue, para 4.
51. Ibid., para 5. Emphasis in the original.
52. OIOC, Madras Board of Revenue Proceedings, January 9, 1843, from H.V. Conolly to Secretary to the Board of Revenue.
53. OIOC, Madras Board of Revenue Proceedings, December 14, 1843, para 20.
54. OIOC, Madras Despatches, Fort St George Revenue Department, June 21, 1843, no. 13 of 1843, Rights of the Todawars, and Rules for Grants of Land on the Neilgherries, para 3; OIOC, Madras Board of Revenue Proceedings, October 17, 1842, Extract from the Minutes of Consultation, September 17, 1842, from the Secretary to the Board of Revenue, para 6.

4

CONTESTED FORESTS IN NORTH-WEST PAKISTAN

The Bureaucracy between the "Ecological," the "National," and the Realities of a Nation's Frontier

Urs Geiser

SETTING THE SCENE

TODAY, THE FORESTS OF THE NORTH WEST FRONTIER PROVINCE (NWFP) of Pakistan are at great risk. A survey in the late 1990s projected that "[using] relevant growth parameters on demand and supply developments and excluding areas that are inaccessible for any wood supply (25 percent of the total forest area) the total forest stock that existed in 1995 would be completely consumed sometime between the years 2015 and 2025" (PFRI 2000; for similar statements see Ahmed and Mahmood 1998).

Efforts to halt this forest destruction are ongoing. A key agent in the search for sustainable forest management is the NWFP Department of Forestry, Fisheries and Wildlife (DFFW). The DFFW is supported in its efforts, and advised and financed by, a range of bilateral and multilateral donors. Around 1995 the DFFW—i.e. the forest bureaucracy—and its donors embarked on a wide-ranging forest sector reform process, this being considered a key requirement to secure sustainable resource use. A new forest policy was enacted in August 1999, a new forest act drafted, and a number of related rules are presently under preparation (for details, see Geiser 2000; Suleri 2001). In a nutshell, the key components of this reform process are:

(i) strengthening the DFFW staff and its competence, and (ii) the adoption of peoples' participation, or community participation, in forest management.

An example of the first is that the DFFW would not only be in charge of 17 percent of land in the province, i.e. demarcated forest lands, but would influence 65 per cent if one includes all "non-cultivable land." The latter is argued for ecological reasons: "Since the small and fragmented natural resource base [the forests] of NWFP cannot be effectively protected and sustainably managed in isolation, therefore these resources would be managed as an integral part of the ecological system of which they are part," which is to say forests, along with other land use types, including watershed areas, rangelands, etc. (GoNWFP 1999: 6).

Having identified illicit timber removal and excessive local demand for firewood and grazing as the key problems (i.e. the blame falls on local people), the new forest policy calls for a new participatory approach to involve such people:

> All these factors together have rendered the current authoritative top down protection and management of forests unsustainable and a need has arisen for making serious efforts to obtain the participation of the relevant stakeholders in the management of our forests in ways appropriate to the circumstances of each forest. To ensure the sustainable management of forests under radically different circumstances than a century ago, the local people must be enrolled as the principal bulwark against the tide of forest depletion (GoNWFP 2002: 3).

Participation, though, is to take place within frame conditions defined by the DFFW. Looking closer at the Draft Forest Act, one finds that forest committees are to be under the strict control of the forest bureaucracy which can, for example, abolish these committees.

The present reform process is challenged from many quarters. The Sarhad Awami Forestry Ittehad (SAFI), a platform of organizations engaged in challenging the Forest Department's handling of the process, states that forestry laws and institutions "reflect the colonial form of governance. These laws and institutional structures were meant to increase the government's income, depriving people of their rights on natural resources, and suppressing the people's aspirations through centralization of bureaucratic powers"

(SAFI 2000: 1). For SAFI, the present state of forests is proof enough of the inadequacy of the forest bureaucracy, and the present reform is thought by them to reproduce and even reinforce old structures.

The military too challenges the role and authority of the bureaucracy. On October 12, 1999, the Nawaz Sharif government was ousted by a military coup led by General Musharraf. On October 17, the chief executive (i.e. General Musharraf) addressed the nation and announced a seven-point programme; Point Six reads: "Devolution of power to the grass roots level" (NRB 1999). And already, by August 14, 2001, the new local government system was in place—at least de jure. Among others things, the new system prescribes that the forest bureaucracy be subordinated to the newly established district governments—in order to increase accountability and, as a consequence, improve ecological conditions. This attempt, though, would break the present DFFW's hierarchical and centralized command structure.

In sum, forests in the NWFP represent a highly contested arena with many stakeholders involved in heated debates and struggles on how to reorganize technical forest management procedures and institutional arrangements—the issues mentioned are only a few aspects of these conflicts. Projects are trying to experiment with joint forest management; experts draw up the details of rules and regulations, i.e. the organizational proposals for the watershed-based new forest management. This reform process has been going seven or eight years—and *very little has actually changed.*

Can a journey into (environmental) history help us understand, or grasp at least some of the underlying (structural) dynamics of these struggles, and especially why so little changes?[1] And can such understanding emerge by focusing on—and linking—notions such as *ecological* and the *national*?

THE ARGUMENT

For this journey into environmental history, my argument focuses on the NWFP's Malakand Division (very important in relation to forests) and takes as a starting point the peculiar political geography of this region. Until late 1969 the region now called Malakand Division was not formally part of Pakistan but was governed under three princely states, i.e. Chitral, Dir and Swat, as well as the Kalam Tribal Agency under the Wali of Swat. Pakistan's laws were extended to Malakand only around 1973. Earlier, this region was not even formally part of the territory occupied by the British Indian empire. After the annexation of Punjab in 1849, up to independence in 1947, the British territory included the plains of Peshawar and the hills of Hazara, but not the fertile valleys and forested mountains of Malakand (see Maps 1 and 2).

A second starting point is the region's peculiar institutional history. The forest bureaucracy in what is now called the NWFP is much older than the state of Pakistan. It emerged during the British colonial period and consolidated its internal structures and external power over time. It survived the collapse of empire and continued—unchanged and untouched—in the new state of Pakistan.

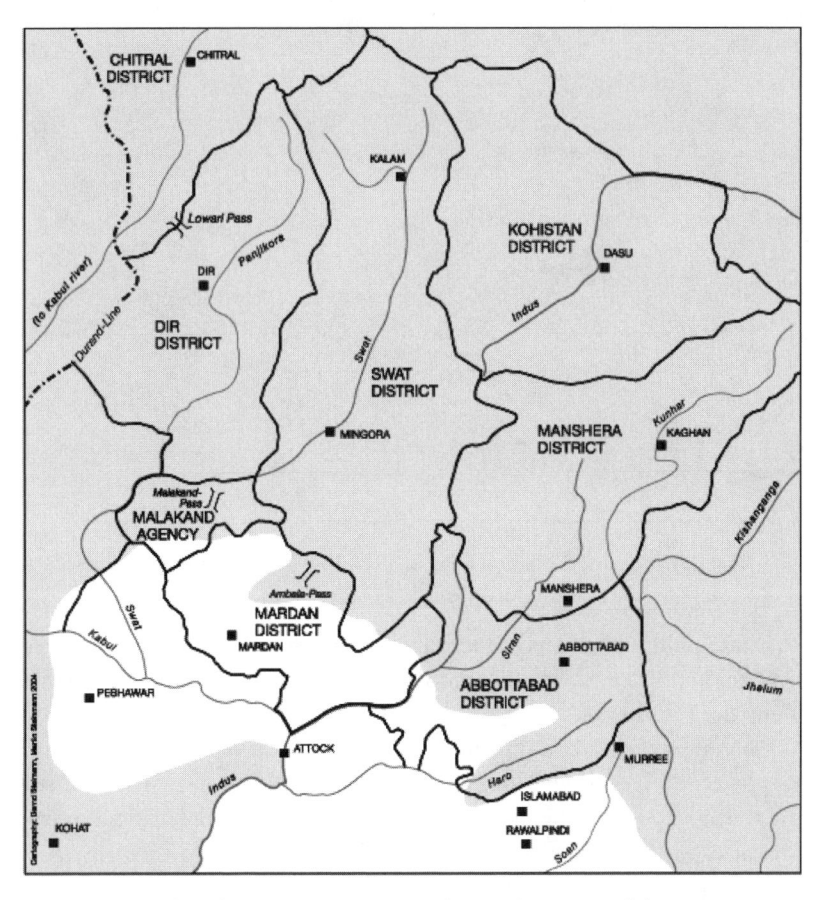

Map 1: The administrative set-up in the northern part of the NWFP after 1969 (grey: mountains; the districts of Swat, Dir, Chitral, and the Malakand Agency are forming the Malakand Division).

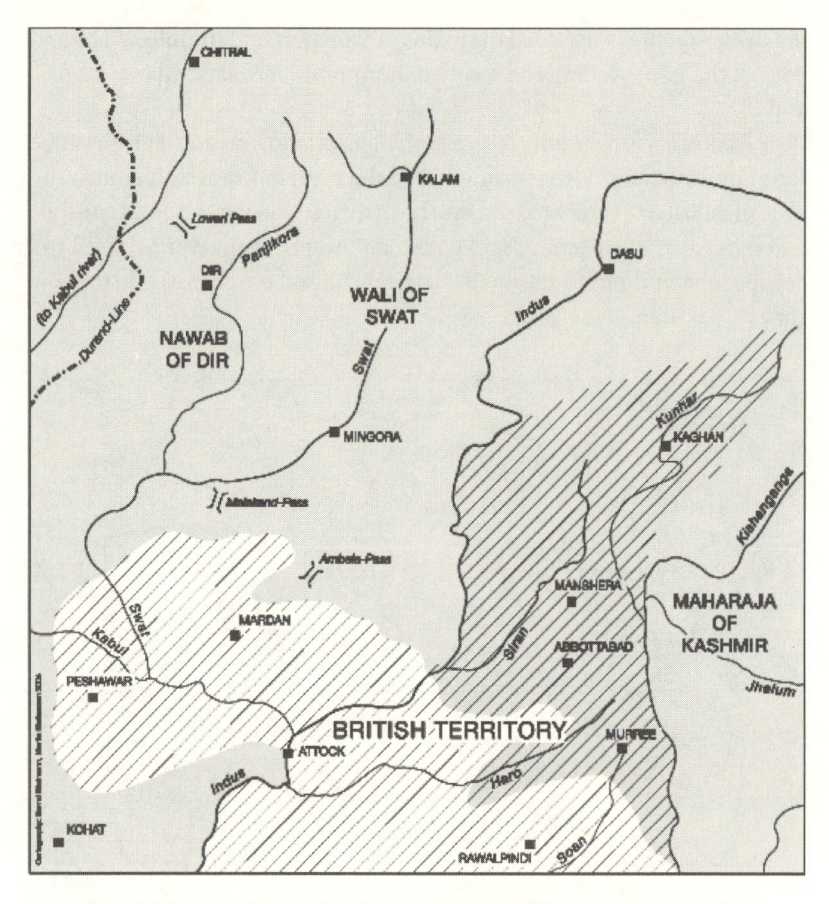

Map 2: The spatial situation from 1849 to 1947 (grey area: mountains; lines: British territory).

These points offer a possible way of contextualizing today's struggles over the forests in Malakand, and provoke the sketching of a hypothesis along the lines below.

The forest bureaucracy in the NWFP is—institutionally—very strong. Its power emerges partly from the construction and strategic use of three discourses: the forest bureaucracy's *ecological discourse* emphasizes the ecological importance of forests and the need for their scientific management—skills available with the forest bureaucracy alone. Second, the *discourse of "the national" or "the national interest"* constructs the purpose and gives legitimacy: the scientific management of forests is done by the forest bureaucracy in the name of the public or the people—earlier the people of the

British empire, then the people of the new nation. As a recent official document puts it: "These renewable resources of the Province are being managed by the NWFP Forest Department for the benefit of the local communities, provincial government, national economy and the international community at large" (GoNWFP 2002: 4f). But the forest bureaucracy in Malakand is—on the ground—very weak. Its rules and regulations (derived from scientific forestry) are rarely implemented, and actual forest management practices take place outside the control of the bureaucracy (see the article by Sarah Southwold in this volume). This fact is tackled by deploying a third discourse, i.e. a *discourse of justifying non-implementation*. People in this region at the frontier of the empire, and then the nation state, always resisted—and still resist—the role of the forest bureaucracy. But, the discourse suggests, *in spite of all these difficulties, the bureaucracy is prepared to continue its mission*. Resistance is described as caused by unawareness, and thus the need for change is argued, for example, by a strategy of "[enrolling] the local people [...] as the principal bulwark against the tide of forest depletion."

The hypothesis is in short that today's circumstances are not so "radically different [...] than a century ago." The forest bureaucracy was positioned, and continues to position itself, between "the ecological" and "the national" (or the nation's interest); it uses both notions as (flexible) discourses to justify and reproduce its structures, mandates and practices. But as these structures, mandates and practices fail, it is the fault of the unaware people "out there," not the forest bureaucracy. And environmental history indicates that a real forest reform process would indeed need to question the prevailing practices and routines of the forest bureaucracy shaped by these discourses.

THE BEGINNINGS OF
THE ECOLOGICAL DISCOURSE

In Upper India, but little attention was paid to the forests by the British during this period. The ruthless methods of exploitation, burning and grazing, which had been in force for centuries, continued unchecked. The question of opening out the hill forests of the Punjab and of affording them some measure of protection was receiving some attention in the middle of the century, but no attempts of this nature had been commenced in the North-West Provinces or in Bengal. (Stebbing, 1926, vol. 1: 66)

With these words, Stebbing introduces the colonial encounter with the area "beyond our North West Provinces"—an area almost unknown to the colonizers when the British annexed Punjab in 1849. Some travelers visited the area and reported it to be a "wild and lawless territory," but also that a "considerable amount of timber came down the Indus, Swat and Kabul rivers" and was seen stored with traders in Peshawar and Attock (Stebbing 1926, vol. 1: 464).

After the annexation of Punjab, British territory included the plains of Peshawar and the hills of Murree and Hazara (see Map 2). First documentation of British activities in Hazara relate to Col. J. Abbott, who was asked to supply timber from Kaghan in 1852 but failed to do so on account of problems with floating timber down the river.

But British redefinition of forest management started quickly now. Within the controlled territory, first rules were written for Hazara in 1855, and draft rules were published in late 1856 for Murree (Stebbing 1926, vol. 1: 274). These rules declared forests and "shrubs of spontaneous growth" as the property of government. They were available for the villagers "as far as required," by setting a permit and after paying fees. "Proprietors" of forests were to receive one-eighth of what they received prior to the annexation,[2] "under the condition of their co-operating with the officers of Government in enforcing the rules. The remainder of the fund is intended to pay for the cost of surveillance, and to provide means for reproduction of trees" (Stebbing 1926, vol. 1: 275).

The "Trans-Indus Region" (our Malakand Division), however, was outside direct British control, and almost no data were available. Therefore, in November 1861, Cleghorn, who became Conservator of Forests in the Madras Presidency in 1856, was sent to the Punjab to report on the forests of the Western Himalayas (Stebbing 1926: vol. 1: 275) and to ascertain supply possibilities. He visited the valleys of the Giri, Pabur, Tons, Sutlej, Beas, Ravi, Chenab and Jhelum, toured Kaghan, Hazara and the Murree Hills in 1863. But he also collected information available on the Trans-Indus areas, i.e. "on the timber procurable from the Indus, Swat and Kabul rivers." Stebbing describes Cleghorn's report, published in 1864, with words full of pride:

[the report shows] in the most striking manner the lines upon which British administration, even in the wild frontier districts, was now being carried on; and with what devotion and self-sacrifice the British officials were throwing their whole hearts into ameliorating the condition of the people and bringing so far as possible order and the pax Britannica into regions which had known no orderly regime through the centuries.[3] (Stebbing 1926:, vol. 1: 448)

According to Cleghorn, the only study available for Swat was by Captain Raverty (published in 1862), "based upon the narrative of a native of Kandahar." This account of an account describes the lower hills as being treeless and the higher hills well stocked with deodar. When felling trees, locals had to pay fees to their Khans. According to this report, timber trade beyond the area using the river Swat was in the hands of only one man, i.e. Papa Mea, head of the Kakakhel Sayeds, "a fair-dealing old man, somewhat stubborn and difficult to manage, but frank and independent [. . .] fine qualities which often exist, amongst so much that is treacherous and bad, in these border tribesmen" (Stebbing 1926, vol. 1: 467).

Cleghorn saw much timber coming "within our territories" down the Indus river from outside the "British sphere of control," from "unknown areas." Supplies, though, were not sufficient: "It has been realized, however, that the supplies would at best be very irregular, since they entirely depended on the wants of the people in the hills who would only take the trouble to send down timber [. . .] in any quantity when their need for money or supplies became urgent, or when it suited them. It was considered, however, that the trade was capable of great extension" (Stebbing 1926, vol. 1: 466). The British tested the deodar timber and found the one from the Indus the best, followed by Swat, and then Kabul. Cleghorn thus recommended increasing supplies through the Indus and Swat rivers: "He makes no allusion, however, to the harmful effect on the forests of these rivers and on their catchment areas, even though they were outside our frontier, of the totally uncontrolled methods of felling by which the trade was to be carried on, and the danger to the water level of these rivers which eventually flowed through British territory which must ensue therefrom" (Stebbing 1926, vol. 1: 471).

Thus, by the late 1860s, we find a situation in which the Trans-Indus region was outside British control, but not of British desires. While the British were able to extract timber in Kaghan and Murree, they depended on locals for supplies from Malakand. These locals were portrayed as wild and unreliable, and their way of forest treatment as wasteful. Additional ecological notions are now entering the arguments: Most forests being in the hills, but outside British control, the British were in need not only of timber, but of water too especially for agriculture. This called urgently for something to be done; or in the words of Stebbing:

> This history of the Punjab Forests at this period will have clearly indicated that many of the Civil Officers, Commissioners, Deputy Commissioners and their Assistants, had commenced to fully appreciate the necessity of introducing conservancy into forest areas with the object of putting an end to wasteful and uncontrolled exploitation and the unchecked grazing and firing by the native population [. . .] The new spirit and gradual awakening to a full understanding of the position was to result during the next sixty years in a remarkable piece of work, no less than the conservation of what remained of the forests of the country, their extension and great improvement and in the building up of an effective administration, a work due to the close interworking and co-operation between the civil and forest officials. (1926, vol. 1: 481)

By the late 1860s, the ecological discourse is in full swing to justify the increasing aspirations of the forest bureaucracy over the Trans-Indus region. What was now required was the legal cover, and a strengthened bureaucracy to work with.

THE DISCOURSE OF "THE NATIONAL INTEREST"

British aspirations to control the Trans-Indus zone were clear by 1865, not only to ensure timber supplies for present needs but also to secure future delivery, it being difficult to forecast requirements. An intensive debate emerged within the colonial administration on how to ensure such future supplies. While some favored the use of upland forests such as those in Malakand, others wanted to put management emphasis on the remaining forests in the plains (Rukhs); again others were interested in completely exploiting these forests, including their roots, in order to convert the land for agricultural use (ensuring more revenue). In August 1863, Brandis and Cleghorn contributed a joint memorandum to this discussion and arrived at the conclusion that "the hill forests are not likely to be more than self-supporting, and occasionally from physical obstructions, uncertainty of floods, etc., the outlay may exceed the proceeds." They therefore recommended maintaining the disputed lands in the plains for forestry, "for the yield of a regular surplus revenue," including the raising of plantations. The colonial government first accepted this proposal, but soon reversed the decision. Thus, British desires for the upland forests were enhanced, and as they had to supply timber in spite of the fact that costs would be high, this necessitated a strict control over the hill areas, and the devising of cost-effective means of extraction.

Blaming the natives—i.e. the ecological discourse—was part of the wider argument to justify emphasis on hill forests. Stebbing, for example, writes: "[Amongst] the population, speaking generally, the value of the forests and the necessity of their conservancy had received no recognition" (1926, vol. 1: 521). But a new dimension now starts to emerge, i.e. the direct translation of these claims into the need for strict colonial control over forests in the name of the public, and thus the construction of a new discourse, centering around the public will, or more generally the *national* interest. Informative in this regard is the despatch by the Governor-General in Council to the Secretary of State in London, dated November 1, 1862:

> In the first place we may express our belief, that under *no conceivable circumstances it is possible that personal interests can be made compatible with public interests* in the working of forests, otherwise than under a system of such stringent supervision as would, in fact, reduce those working under it to the position of mere agents of the administration. The length of time required for maturing a growth of timber is so great that no individual can have a personal interest in doing more than realizing the largest possible present amount from any forest tract of which he may get possession. In fact, timber is produced of which no man can expect to get more than one crop in his lifetime, and the sooner and more completely he realizes it the better.
>
> The moral or social restraints that are likely to operate to prevent such a course are most especially wanting in India, whether we deal with natives of the country or European settlers. Therefore, we think that the idea of giving a proprietary right in forest to any individual should be abandoned, as the possession of such a right is almost certain to lead to the destruction of the forest; *personal interests, in short, under existing conditions and in this respect, are not only incompatible with public interests, but they are absolutely antagonistic* [. . .] We consider also that all Government forests should be strictly set apart, and made unalienable; of course, where private rights already exist [. . .] they must be respected, though it might be good policy to extinguish such rights on equitable terms, whenever it be found possible to do so. (quoted in Stebbing 1926, vol. 1: 526f, my emphasis)

To operationalize this intention of taking forests into colonial control, excellent personnel and a well-functioning forest bureaucracy are required:

> Organisation to be of real and permanent value must not be essentially, or even mainly, dependent on extraordinary personal acquirements or activity; the *machinery should be such as will work with average men under the direction of the best of their class.* And this is peculiarly the case as regards the administration of forests. Results will be so long in coming, and ruin is so easily and so immediately brought about by the neglect of first principles by a single individual, that as little as possible should be left open to the local executive authorities in this respect.[4] (Quoted in Stebbing 1926, vol. 1: 30; my emphasis)

London is full of praise for the proposal, and even amplifies the tenor of the debate by linking it to international developments: "Most countries of the world have suffered from similar neglect; and the results have shown themselves, not only in the dearth and consequent high price of timber, but very often in the deterioration of climate, and in the barrenness of land formerly culturable, if not fertile, situated at the base of hills, when these have been stripped of the forests which clothed them, condensed the vapours into rain, and gave protection to the country below them" (quoted in Stebbing 1926, vol. 1: 531).

As an intended consequence, Brandis became the first Inspector General of Forests in India in 1864, and forest administrations were started or strengthened in the provinces. Dr J.L. Stewart became first Conservator of Forests in Punjab in 1864 (Stebbing 1926, vol. 2: 255). In 1865, the Indian Forest Act was published, and a series of rules (for marking, demarcation of forests, etc.) released. To achieve *esprit de corps* within the bureaucracy, a dense net of internal rules and regulations was developed.

Thus, by the end of the 1860s the forest bureaucracy—or "machinery"—was able to justify its existence by making use of the second discourse, i.e. the need for strict forest control in the name of the public, or, for that matter, in the name of the wider colonial (and later national) interests.

THE NEED FOR A DISCOURSE
TO JUSTIFY NON-IMPLEMENTATION

The mission to supply timber from the Trans-Indus region—justified by the needs of "the ecological" on the one hand, and "the public interest" on the other, was now in a position to start full swing. Initial enthusiasm, though, soon faded as implementation was slow. Explanations for the non-achievement of targets were needed and were found in the unwillingness of natives to realize the benefits of the new era: "the people with their Oriental conservatism and apathy had to be gradually weaned from their old methods of utilising—wastefully utilising—the forests and educated to a recognition of the fact that the work being carried out was *in their true interests*" (Stebbing 1926, vol. 2: 462, my emphasis).

Implementation difficulties were also explained by suggesting the Forest Act was not strict enough, e.g. in dealing with pre-annexation claims to forest ownership and use rights in forest resources. Therefore, a new Forest Act appeared in 1878, allowing the constitution of reserved and protected forests. The act also clarified procedures for forest settlement, i.e. their demarcation and legal declaration.[5] These new rules of the game (North 1990) were complemented by new organizational arrangements. On November 9, 1901, the NWFP was created by separating Hazara, Peshawar, Kohat, and some Trans-Indus *tehsils* of Dera Ismail Khan and Bannu district from Punjab. Forest services within the new province were consolidated and a Conservator of Forests appointed. For some time, he remained under the Chief Conservator of Forests of Punjab Province. In September 1935, the provincial forest cadre was placed under NWFP administration, completing the separation of the NWFP from Punjab.

In the Trans-Indus area, though, all these institutions and institutional arrangements were not applicable, as it was "outside our territory." And general relations between the British and the tribals of these regions were not all that good—thus making the mission even more difficult.[6] For a closer look at these developments, the following section focuses on the Swat region of Malakand. The main sources of information are the annual reports of the NWFP Forest Department. General history reports that, in the fifteenth century, Youzufzai Pathans had to leave Afghanistan and eventually settle in the Swat valley, driving the then local population toward Hazara (Sultan-I-Rome 1999: 4). In the period following, up to the early twentieth century, they lived in "tribal fashion," like other groups in this north-west region. A Swat historian portrays the Swat-Youzufzais as maintaining their independence not only during Mughal India, but also from the British after they established rule over Punjab in 1849: "Swat not only remained independent but also became an harbour of refuge for outlaws and opponents of the colonial rulers and a centre of anti-British sentiments" (Sultan-I-Rome 1999: 5).

Sultan-I-Rome (1999) proposes that in order to resist the growing British challenge, the Youzufzais of Swat agreed in 1915 on a common leader and Abdul Jabbar Shah became the first "king" of what became the Swat state. In 1917 his rival, Miangul Abdul Wadud, became Bacha of Swat and rigorously started to consolidate the new state at the northern fringe of the British NWFP. Over time, Swat state extended its control into Buner and Indus Kohistan. In 1926, Abdul Wadud was recognized by the British as the Wali of Swat. He governed Swat state up to 1949, and this period is described by many local authors as a time during which the Wali developed Swat into a peaceful and prosperous region.

During these decades, already established lines of arguments regarding the Trans-Indus forests—now often called the "Trans-Frontier forests"— can be found in the reports of the NWFP Forest Department, e.g. to *deplore the overexploitation* and denudation of the forests by the natives; to lament the *negative ecological consequences* of local practices; to maintain the proposition that *better forest management* can be achieved by writing and implementing working plans; and to argue the need for further strengthening of the forest administration.

One hurdle was the lack of knowledge on the forests in the Trans-Indus region. Little seems to have been added since Cleghorn, and the urgency for "conservancy" (calling for such knowledge) is again and again repeated (in fact since the 1850s); for example:

> As observed by the Chief Conservator the preservation of forest cover in the upper basins of the Indus and its tributaries is not only of vital economic concern to the people, but has intimate reactions on the Peshawar canals, and on the vast Indus irrigation projects of the Punjab and Bombay. For political and other reasons it has not been possible for the problems of forest administration in the Trans-Indus terrain to assume a practical shape until the expiry of half a century from the date of the initiation of such measures in the remainder of north western India. The enquiries made during the past few years demonstrate, however, not only the importance of securing control without further delay, but the possibility in certain tracts of obtaining revenue by exploitation or by import duties.[7] (Report for 1926-7)

Relief came through the Inspector General of Forests, who visited Peshawar in March 1927, sanctioning the means necessary for getting more information. Mr Parnell, Conservator of Forests, was deputed to Peshawar for the period May to November 1927 to study the Trans-Indus area and provide a report. Parnell's analysis is fully in line with the mainstream perception, and so is his recommendation—to intensively work the forests of Swat.

However, to implement Parnell's recommendations, new staff would be required (Report for 1927-8). Finally, in April 1930, an additional post of Conservator of Forests was sanctioned, and filled in April 1931. A new Peshawar Forest Division was created in October 1930. This division also included the areas beyond British territory which were now divided into three ranges, all with headquarters outside the actual ranges—or better, with headquarters inside British territory. Swat and Kabul River Range had their headquarters at Nowshera; Indus River Range at Tarbela; and the Cherat–Buner Border Range at Mardan. The working plan by Khan Sahib Malik Allah Yar Khan for the deodar forests of Swat State was completed in 1928 and approved on January 1, 1931 (Reports from 1927–8 to 1931–2).

These developments again aroused enthusiasm among the forest officials and were experienced as a success and breakthrough: the Forest Department now "virtually crossed the Indus river" (Champion and Osmaston 1962: 397). The Annual Report for 1925-6 claims: "These facts [...] are an indication of the rising interest and initiative displayed by individual Political Officers in the forests in their districts. Such a welcome spirit, apart from the interests of the forest owners [...] appear to call for some definite forest policy in these areas, however simple or rudimentary."

And the 1926-7 Report states:

> The year under review [...] is likely to prove a landmark in the history of forest development in the North West Frontier Province. It is the object of this Administration to initiate measures to check the further denudation of the existing forests in the catchment areas of the Indus and its great western tributaries, in so far as they lie within political control, and to build up fuel reserves in and around the Peshawar Valley to meet the ever-growing pressure of a dense population on inadequate fuel resources. (Report for 1926–7)

In Swat, working plan implementation started as planned, and "the work was undertaken and trees were sold to the firm of Spedding, Dinga Singh & Co" (Report for 1930–1). However, things developed less easily. Timber prices seem to have fallen, and thus also the interest of Spedding & Co., forcing the Forest Department to reduce expenditures (Report for 1931–2), and *local co-operation was not forthcoming*: "[like] the ordinary husbandman, the forest husbandman has to ward off many foes" (Report for 1931–2). The main foes were the natives, and in report after report the damage done by "man" is deplored.

In Swat, the Wali accepted allowing timber cutting under British control in the "Export Felling Series" (there was also a "Local Felling Series" to cater to the Wali's needs). Champion and Osmaston (1962: 395) describe the practical arrangements such that the forests "belonged" to the Wali of Swat but were under the technical control of the Forest Department. "For all revenue and expenditure the Wali was responsible, but there were certain items of expenditure—viz. pay, allowances, etc., of the establishment employed by the Forest Department—which the Government met and subsequently recovered in the form of duty levied on the timber exported into British India." But only a few trees were cut, and all other working plan prescriptions were not implemented:

> It is to be noted with regret that it was not found possible to carry out the main prescriptions of the Swat Kohistan working plan [. . .] There was not much head way made with the carrying out of other prescriptions of the plan such as those relating to thinnings which could not be carried out as no one was willing to buy thinnings trees nor did the Wali find himself able to utilise them. In fact no fellings were made beyond the removal of 204 trees from the local felling series by the Wali for his State requirements. Preliminary demarcation of the forests also met with opposition from the villagers and was completed in a Swab area with some difficulty. The years' experience has shown that it will not be possible to successfully work this plan unless there is a complete co-operation between all the parties concerned including the Wali and his subjects. (Report for 1931–2)

The Report for 1935–6 states a few years later: "Since 1931, when a proper working plan was introduced, very little progress has been made with other working plan prescriptions. No forest demarcation has been done because the Wali objects to spending money in this way; no thinning can be done till a market can be found for small plots, and only 50 acres of forest have so far been re-sown on account of opposition from the local villagers." The construction of forest boundary pillars and sowings "prescribed by the Working Plan have both been postponed owing to strong objection on the part of the villagers" (Report for 1934–5). In addition, it is understood that "uncontrolled" (from the point of view of the British) fellings occurred.

The Wali of Swat continued to refuse to follow the working plan for demarcation, sowings, etc. Justifying working pan failure, the Report for 1937–8 explains: "It must, however, be remembered that this tract has not been under control for many years, and *it is necessary to proceed with caution when introducing measures of forest conservancy so as not to antagonise the local people* [emphasis mine]." And the Report for 1938–9 laments that "All work on natural regeneration has been neglected, as the State will not undertake the collection and burning of debris, being unable to persuade the villagers to do this work even on payment. *Efforts, however, must not be slackened in pressing up on the State, the absolute necessity of this work on which rests the future existence of the forests* [emphasis mine]."

In 1947 Pakistan became independent. The NWFP continued as an administrative and political unit, and so did the relations between this province and the Trans-Indus region, which continued to exist as princely states. And generally, the NWFP Forest Department had little to say on the ground—before as well as after Pakistan's independence:

> Forest Acts are not applicable to the Frontier States and forest offence cases are dealt with by the State Authorities according to their own rules and regulations. Besides the control over felling for local use is ever used by State Officials without the cognisance of the Forest Department. It is only in the case of export of timber that the Forest Department comes to picture. Due to the loose control and in tempo of development in Dir State, the forests have been damaged considerably. (Report for 1963–4)

Abdul Wadud retired in December 1949 and his son Jahanzeb became the new Wali of Swat. Little harvesting is reported "due to lack of labour which came generally every year from Kashmir State [. . .] in which disturbances had occurred," and (as usual), all other prescriptions were not carried out (Report for 1948–9). Forest control seems to have been far from expectations: "[the] unauthorized export of timber from Kalam or unworked forests of Usha Valley by various agencies of the Swat State *is to be discouraged in the interest of forest conservancy*" (Report for 1949–50; emphasis mine). In 1959 the Swat working plan expired, and the felling cycle was now repeated; other things were not in need of extension "because the state authorities do not like to spend anything on the improvement of the forests" (Report for 1959–60). The annual reports continue to report on difficulties with implementation and, among other things, blame the sort of "dual control," i.e. the parallel existence of a NWFP Forest Department system, and the systems of the princely states (Report for 1964–5).

Over more than a century, thus, the discourse justifying non-implementation was used, reproduced, and never questioned by the NWFP forest bureaucracy. But by 1969, finally, the forest bureaucracy saw an opportunity, abandoning this discourse and completing its mission.

COMPLETING THE MISSION?

In 1969 the Pakistan government abolished the special status of princely states and merged Swat, including Kalam, Dir, and Chitral into Malakand Division, adding the Malakand Agency.[8] The present section focuses on Swat, and especially its northern tehsil of Kalam, or Swat Kohistan. With the merger, the administration, and thus the forest bureaucracy, was now able to directly operate in the region—which of course gave rise to new hopes.

In September 1972 the Government of NWFP declared in a preliminary statement that all forests situated in the former state of Swat were now the property of government, subject to a payment of 15 percent of their income as royalty to the local right holders (Khattak 1987). In May 1974, the Forest Act of 1927 was formally extended to Swat and Kalam. This (colonial) act is the revision of the Indian Forest Act of 1878. Champion and Osmaston (1962: 23f), comparing the 1927 act with the 1878 act, write that the "changes were small and consisted mainly in redrafting the previous act and its amendments"—as a matter of fact, then, the colonial law of 1878 was applied to a "new territory" a hundred years later, and this, it appears, in the same spirit as a century earlier!

Based on the 1927 act, all forest land in Chitral, Dir, Swat, and Kalam was declared as protected forests. On December 22, 1975, the Pakistan government declared all trees within protected forests as reserved and prohibited the removal of any forest produce and breaking up or clearing of land in such forests. On December 24, 1975, the Government of NWFP issued rules for the management of forests.

A meeting of the NWFP cabinet held under the chairmanship of the prime minister of Pakistan on November 10, 1976 reiterated that the forests would be supervised and controlled by the government, "60 percent share from the income would be earmarked for the people while 40 percent would be earmarked for Government for bearing expenses of maintenance and development of forest" (Khattak 1987).

This regulation was approved on March 14, 1977, and its implementation is under way—actually even today. Through the land settlement programme, the boundaries of government-owned forests are to be determined, as well as the nature and extent of local people's rights (again, this process is the very same as that during the colonial period, when annexing new territories). Only after completion of this land settlement programme can the forests actually be declared and notified as protected; the relevant section, Section 29 of the Forest Act 1927, reads: "No such notification shall be made unless the nature and extent of the rights of Government and of private persons in or over the forest land or wasteland comprised therein have been inquired into and recorded at a survey of settlement" (Khattak 1987). The legal situation of the forests in Malakand by the late 1980s is thus described by Khattak (1987) as: "Government has declared them as Protected Forests, pending inquiry and record of rights of individuals or communities, Government still must carry out the due process required by law." And this process has not been completed even today.

The forest bureaucracy's mission, thus, is still not complete. The Forest Department, though, continues its practice of working plan preparation and approval as mandated by the nation of Pakistan, and also continues (or has to continue) to justify non-implementation (mainly by blaming locals) while maintaining the urgent need for action on account of ecological reasons—and this remains the arena within which forest sector "reform" is taking place today.

DISCUSSION

The argument proposed here states that today's circumstances are not so different from those a century ago. The forest bureaucracy positioned itself, and continues to, between the "ecological" and the "national;" it uses both notions as (flexible) discourses to justify and reproduce its structures, mandates, and practices. And because its mandates and practices fail, this is attributed to unaware people "out there;" in spite of this, the forest bureaucracy is prepared to continue its mission.

These brief glimpses of the environmental history of the region indicate the persistence of discourses and related practices. The most obvious are the references to the ecological damage of unscientific forestry; those made in the 1860s are almost the same as the ones made today. This first discourse constructs an image of the Trans-Indus region required by the second discourse, which legitimizes strict control by the bureaucracy in the name of the wider public.

What is astonishing is that the familiar periodizing of history seems not to fit with any analysis of the forest bureaucracy. Browsing though the annual reports of the NWFP Forest Department in the provincial archives at Peshawar, and reading through successive reports for the 1940s and early 1950s, one fails to discern that Pakistan has changed from a colony of the British Empire to an independent modern nation state. The reports continue to be structured along the same proforma, and the statements on the ecological importance of forests, or the problems faced in the field, are the same prior to and after Pakistan's independence. The bureaucracy remains; what changes is merely the name of the entity providing legitimacy: The justification for the forest bureaucracy as caretaker of forest resources in the name of the public—or in the name of the people—is basically the same during colonial and postcolonial times.

Here, one is reminded of recent statements by Harriss (Fuller and Harriss 2000) recalling the need to distinguish between the "state system" ("the cluster of institutions of political and executive control and their key personnel;" Fuller and Harriss 2000: 3) and the "state idea." The state—or the idea of the nation for that matter—should not be reified, but seen as an "illusionary general interest" (Miliband, quoted in Fuller and Harriss 2000: 3), as "a backstage institutionalization of political power behind the on-stage agencies of government" (Abrams, quoted in Fuller and Harriss 2000: 3), and "the idea of the state [must be analyzed] as an ideological power" (Abrams, quoted in Fuller and Harriss 2000: 4). In other words, in addition to "a state-system in Miliband's sense," there is also "a state-idea, projected, purveyed and variously believed in different societies at different times." It is important to "study the relationship among the state-system and the state-idea, and other forms of power" (Fuller and Harriss 2000: 4, quoting Abrams).

Our forest bureaucracy fits well with this understanding, as part of a powerful state system. The bureaucracy's appeal to the general interest, and it being mandated by the wider public, can then clearly be read as part of a state-idea—which is a powerful idea because "of its political strength as a mythic or ideological construct" (Mitchell, quoted in Fuller and Harriss

2000: 3). It provides, to use Abrams's notion, the backstage for the frontstage performance of the forest bureaucracy.

Consequently, this calls for a reversal of the statement made in the introduction to this volume, i.e. that "nationalism is a parasite that 'preys upon other ideologies, forming new amalgams suitable for use by political entrepreneurs.' " For the case of the NWFP forest bureaucracy, it is this bureaucracy that is the parasite preying on ideological notions of "nationalism"—be it the interests of the public under the colonial empire, or the interests of the people in the modern state.

A key insight that environmental history suggests for contemporary policy debates, though, is the third discourse, i.e. the explanation of failure or non-implementation of plans at field level—again statements that show not much difference over the last 140 years. The to-be-completed mission of scientific forestry in the Trans-Indus region became and becomes a reason, sufficient in itself, for the existence of the forest bureaucracy. This strategic use of non-implementation (specifically of working plans, these being the key tool of the forest bureaucracy) shows parallels to present-day forms of intervention by donor-supported development projects. Here too, implementation problems (as realized through so-called project evaluations) occur, but seldom lead to the halting of an intervention. Long and van der Ploeg even state that:

> Since it is seldom the case that evaluations question the whole idea of planned intervention and the rationality of planning, it is usually the farmers, environmental factors or the mysteries of distant commodity markets that are blamed for failure, not the package or the activities of the agency itself. In this way evaluation comes to play a useful role in confirming the self-fulfilling prophecy that interventionist policies are indeed viable and ideologically sound [. . .] (Long and van der Ploeg 1989: 235)

As such evaluations are "an important factor in the systematic production of ideologies legitimating the role of intervening agencies and thus also the implied power relations between these agencies and target groups [. . .] *One could even argue that a certain degree of "failure" is strategic in the reproduction of intervention itself*" (my emphasis).

In sum, the three discourses outlined in this essay are today as powerful as they were at the time of their production. Their persistence, however, does not yet explain their durability and permanence. That would require further (Foucauldian) analysis. But key ingredients are, most likely, the internal rules and regulations—legitimized by the three discourses—that strictly ensure rigid reproduction of the "machinery." In the past, as today, rules such as the ACR (Annual Confidential Report) condition the acting of personnel *vis-à-vis* the bureaucracy—not necessarily, though, with regard to their actual practices in the field. At field level, the discourses and ideologies of the bureaucracy often give "room for manoeuvre" and allow flexible interpretation in the light of local conditions and personal needs.

In spite of these obvious requirements for further probing, the environmental history of the forest bureaucracy of the NWFP strongly suggests that a contemporary forestry reform process would, first of all, require a radical questioning of the role played by the DFFW, and especially its century-old discourses that relate to—and interlink—the "ecological" and the "national": discourses of being mandated, of being caretakers of the forests, of being scientifically equipped for forest conservation, being entitled to educate the rural people, and of explaining away implementation difficulties. In addition, international donors' partial acceptance and reproduction of some of these discourses too needs critical reflection.[9] Only then can new grounds for re-imagining "sustainable" forest resource use emerge.

NOTES

1. The analysis of the colonial past is expected to give hints for an understanding of the present; e.g. Nichols 2001: iv: "Because the legacy of the imperial system in place by 1900 shaped inequities that continued to be experienced decades after the formal end of the colonial era, this history offers an insight for those concerned with twentieth-century issues of colonialism, nationalism, and social justice." See also the statement in the introduction to this volume regarding the need for environmental history to have "explanatory power." The present essay is an attempt to show the operations of these propositions.

2. Stebbing does not provide information on the situation in these mountains prior to the annexation. A detailed understanding of these social relations would, though, be important to position the British practices.

3. In the late 1980s, senior DFFW staff described their activities in Swat and Swat Kohistan with very similar words.

4. The team leader of a donor-supported project that intended to support peoples' involvement in forestry stated in 1999 that the Forest Department resisted these reforms, having "psychological barriers" and a deeply rooted *esprit de corps*. They feared losing authority and control over valuable forest resources: "[The FD's]

perception of 'participation' is still based on paternalistic and dirigistic patterns prevailing in the forest administration, which together with the 'vested interests' of [the FD], are instrumental to control and manipulate local community" (my emphasis).

5. The act applied to all of colonial India except places where the earlier rules were allowed to continue. One such place was Hazara.

6. For the conflicting nature of the relations between the British and "their" territory, and the people "outside" British territory, see Nichols 2001: 172–91.

7. For the attempts to use import duties as strategic means, see Geiser 2002.

8. Various reasons and developments led to this merger; for details, see Sultan-I-Rome 1999.

9. Taking these insights gained through environmental history into account, the new NWFP forest policy enacted in 1999 appears to have been written more or less outside the forest bureaucracy, as it reproduces recent international language on the need for participatory forest management. The new Draft NWFP Forest Act, however, is closer to the thinking of the DFFW—and as such reproduces much of the three discourses described herein. They become most obvious, though, at the level of the recent draft rules. For details, see Geiser 2002.

II
Competing Nationalisms

5

INDIGENOUS FORESTS

Rights, Discourses, and Resistance in Chotanagpur, 1860–2002

Vinita Damodaran

THE WAYS IN WHICH VARIOUS ETHNIC AND NATIONAL GROUPS living in and impinging on the Chotanagpur plateau perceived and used the landscape to further their economic ends and symbolic causes is relatively under-researched. In this essay I explore the plateau as an economic, ethnic, anthropologic, religious, and ecological terrain, and look at the ways in which landscape was molded, defined, and used. In doing so I examine the interactions between colonial forestry and constructions of indigeneity, and between Jesuit missions and Ho radicalization. Finally, I unfold the historical relationship between sacralization of the landscape by local communities and the explosion of emotions guiding contemporary ethnic autonomy movements in the region.

It is important to note, in this context, that some current revisionism in environmental history and ecological anthropology has been focused on dismantling such long-established terms as "tribe," "forest," "indigenous," and others. The revisionist argument—that earlier ethnographers and colonial administrators had mistakenly thought "tribes" were static entities—urges the researcher to look for the ways and moments in which enduring notions of distinct tribes are constructed and lived. This search, however, also risks supporting the idea that the claims of indigenous people for autonomy must have no theoretical legitimacy or historical validity.[1] Work on ethnicity in other contexts has effectively argued that ethnicity and ethnic ideologies are historically contingent creations. For example, while it may be true that the Chakmas of the Chittagong Hill Tracts were by no means the first people to enter these regions—in fact they were only one of a succession of immigrant cultures following the Arakanese and Tripurans into the area—today Chakma identity is firmly linked to the hill tracts where they have sought to develop an "indigenous" model of state, society, and culture.[2] Elsewhere in India, as Hardiman argues, the term *adivasi* relates to a particular historical development: that of subjugation during the nineteenth century of a wide variety of communities, which, before colonial rule, had remained free or relatively free from control by outsiders. The experience generated a spirit of resistance which incorporated a "consciousness" of the adivasi against the "outsider." As Hardiman notes, the term was used by political activists in Chotanagpur in the 1930s, with the aim of forging a new sense of identity among different "tribal" peoples, a tactic that has had considerable success.[3] James Bodley has recently observed that the revisionist assault on the "noble savage" and the wilderness idea has come at the historical moment when global culture's unsustainable cultural imperative of perpetual capital accumulation is "reducing the earth's stocks of water, soil, forests and fisheries to dangerously low levels."[4] Similarly as notions of indigeneity and customary rights come in for revisionist attack, the marginalization and proletarianization of many forest-based communities and their traditional livelihoods gain pace all over the world.

FORESTS, DEFORESTATION, AND FOREST RESERVES

The forested landscape of Chotanagpur provided the material background to colonial and nationalist debates on notions of indigeneity. A "tribal" way of life was seen to be one intimately linked with the forested environment. That the landscape may have been imagined in various ways within colonial discourse as wild, remote, pristine, and so on has been the subject of much research in recent times. Agrawal and Sivaramakrishnan have usefully argued that the separation of woodlands from the surrounding agrarian environment allowed colonial foresters to "construct a forest landscape removing it from the world of agrarian relations."[5] However, in referring to the constructed nature of all landscapes, some research takes on a postmodern stance, providing a narrow and restricted reading of the writings of colonial administrators, travelers, and explorers. We now know that far from being proponents of an all-embracing "Orientalist" prejudice,

Europeans until the nineteenth century frequently approached Asia, Africa and the Americas in many different ways, describing the new world in minute detail and often with sympathy. Given this, the argument that there is a marked tendency in colonial reports to overdraw the relationship between the forest and local communities, in order to construct the forest as a "naturalized" environment alone, ignoring local practices and thus to consistently misread the landscape, does not stand up to critical scrutiny. In understanding what constituted the forested landscape, the explorer and colonial administrator were forced to contend with indigenous knowledge and ideas of place. That these knowledges were accumulated as a result of careful observation and study, often relying on indigenous ideas, is not in doubt.[6]

The importance of the forest economy to many local communities of the region in the nineteenth century should also not be underestimated. The question of wild food abundance is one that has been debated on extensively, in the literature elsewhere, though not so much for South Asia. The hypothesis that foraging humans could never have lived in tropical forests completely on wild foods is widely debated.[7] Those that appeared to do so relied heavily on cultivated foods. However, the extent of foraging foods in the diet is an indicator of the importance of forests to the local economy. In the case of Chotanagpur, one can argue from the evidence in colonial reports, and by writers such as Valentine Ball,[8] that foraging was an important part of the diet of communities such as the Hos of Singhbhum in the late nineteenth century, and well into the twentieth century. In an anthropological study conducted in two villages in the Saranda forest division in the 1970s, Michael Yorke noted that the economy of the forest-based Hos was heavily dependent on collecting. The one household in Dubil village that was capable of growing all its cereal requirements collected many other carbohydrate foods, such as tubers, from the forest, and also marketed large quantities of forest produce, such as rope grass, *bachom* or *sawai* grass, and broom grass.[9]

Some work on Indian forest history adopts the Leach–Fairhead thesis,[10] where it is argued, in the context of Guinea, that the Kissidougou landscape is currently filling up with rather than being emptied of forests, and that the notion of linear change with regard to deforestation and agricultural intensification is unhelpful. In this story, social groups in Guinea carefully planted trees in a hitherto denuded landscape. While it is useful to retain a critical perspective, and to be wary of either romanticizing or indicting indigenous peoples and their attitudes to the environment, it is much harder to dismiss the very real evidence of ecological change and deforestation taking place in India all through the colonial period. One is not making the case here for a pristine environmental past. Clearly, people's engagement with the forest in multiple ways saw the creation of a human landscape, one that was ever changing, with past forests giving way to settlements, shifting agricultural practices, and the altering of boundaries between villages and forest. Nature was not "out there" but was a lived relationship for local communities. However, only a much more detailed environmental history of the locality will allow us to piece together these rich and complex stories.

The discourse of scientific forestry was no more accepting of indigenous ideas of conservation than the earlier ethics of exploitation had been. This has to be seen as a mechanistic science where nature, the human body, and animals could be described, repaired, and controlled—as could the parts of a machine—by a separate human mind acting by rational laws. In Carolyn Merchant's words, the scientific worldview—within which the debates on scientific forestry were embedded—saw the "world as dead and inert, manipulable from outside and exploitable for profits [. . .] living animate nature died [. . .] increasingly capital and the market assumed the organic attributes of growth [. . .] nature, women and wage labourers were set on a path as human resources for the modern world system."[11] In this view the domination of women and nature was inherent in the market economy's use of both as resources. Subsistence production, oriented toward the reproduction of daily life, was disrupted by this new development discourse, which had a particularly negative impact on women's subsistence, such subsistence being specifically linked to the forest.

That the dominant trend in the colonial period in Chotanagpur was one of deforestation is not surprising given the fact that the landscape that evolved under colonial rule clearly expressed British attempts to dominate the forest, and mineral and water sources, in the interest of production and profit. One can argue that it was redefined in these terms through the "masculine" discourse of scientific forestry. In the process it threatened the small and relatively autonomous economies of "tribal" communities,[12] with catastrophic effects on the subsistence ethic of all groups, particularly women.[13]

The forests were, in the early part of the nineteenth century, primarily regarded as a resource. The policy of the colonial rulers was to extend cultivation at the expense of forest tracts and to exterminate all wild and dangerous game. The rewards offered by the state to destroy tigers effectively decimated them. By the mid nineteenth century the effects of deforestation were already beginning to be felt. In Purulia town, H. Ricketts noted the total absence of trees, in 1855, around Chaibasa in Singhbhum.[14] In the Santhal Parganas, E.G. Man reported in the 1860s that where elephants and rhinos were abundant as late as the 1830s and 1840s, "now the latter are extinct and of the former but three are left."[15] Vermin eradication was central to early colonial policy in the forested areas of Bengal in a bid to making forested areas more habitable, and to tame the wild.[16] In Ranchi, the district gazetteer recorded the unchecked destruction of forests in the district in the latter half of the nineteenth century.[17] Dr Schlich reported in 1885 that "in a general way it may be said that the Hazaribagh and Ranchi plateau now contain comparatively little forest."

One report concluded that the average net decrease in the area under jungle in fourteen villages was 11 percent within a period of twenty-five years, in this case due to reclamation.[18] The major cause of the destruction of jungles in most districts was the sale or lease of the forest to contractors for the supply of railway sleepers: large areas of forest were destroyed to supply the necessary timber. The forests of Singhbhum were subject to heavy fellings, and it was reported in 1898 that "selection fellings for the supply of broad gauge sleepers from trees over 6½ feet girth amounted to over 20921 trees at the average of 10.4 sleepers per tree." These fellings were reported to have greatly impoverished the forests.[19] Singhbhum was a district with the largest proportion of forest in the 1880s and with over 80 percent of its population still "tribal." This was now threatened. An attempt was launched in the 1880s to acquire all private forests with a view to exploiting timber even in remote areas. The private forests in Dumka subdivision were thus acquired, as were those in Parasnath and Gobindpur, which were seen as particularly valuable, for they lay between the railway and the Grand Trunk Road.[20] A recent study of land use changes in Chotanagpur has concluded that most of the shift in land use took place prior to 1890.[21]

To combat extensive deforestation, the government and the forest department embarked on a wholesale program of forest reservation. However, the growth of a forest policy in India was extraordinarily slow and, for the most part of the eighteenth century, the whole policy of the government was to extend agriculture and destroy forests. It was only by the early nineteenth century that increased demands on the forests were viewed with sufficient gravity, and efforts made to conserve them. Even then, the seriousness of the situation was not recognized and, though a forest conservancy system was established in some provinces, it was not till much later that it rose above the level of revenue administration.[22] By the late nineteenth century the emergence of the discipline of scientific forestry had led to a systematic program of forest management derived from German and French continental systems, where the principles of minimum diversity, sustained yield, and the balance sheet held sway. As Ravi Rajan notes, "by the end of the nineteenth century this utilitarian conservation sentiment became a development ideology in its own right."[23] However, it is important to note Sivaramakrishnan's qualification that the conflicted constitution of scientific forestry limited the homogenization of state resource control.[24]

It is of course important in this context not to see Chotanagpur as a monolithic whole but to look at interregional variations in colonial policy, indigenous responses, and the effect on resource use and the environment. The destruction of the local forest environment had a greater impact in the context of increasing landlordism in rural Chotanagpur. The northern districts had begun to be heavily overrun by Hindu immigrants before the advent of the British. The pace of change increased under colonial rule, and even the southern districts began to feel threatened. The Mundas in Ranchi, for example, had managed to hold on to their traditional (*khuntkhatti*) tenures in the face of outsider landlord encroachment. By the time of census operations in 1881, the original indigenous population in the districts of Palamau and Hazaribagh was only 36 percent and 34 percent, while in the remoter districts of Ranchi and Hazaribagh it was at 74 percent and 75 percent. In the northern districts of Palamau and Hazaribagh and in the Santhal Parganas, increasing subinfeudation and the growing spread of debt bondage were the main grievance of the peasantry. In areas such as Palganj estate, the *mahajans*, who had taken control of the estate, were exploiting the jungles pitilessly, and ripe and unripe timbers were being cut indiscriminately. The result was that "nothing or very little was left for tenants to claim their customary rights in these jungles."[25] The report went on to note that the landlords, *thikadars*, and mahajans were fast acquiring all the best lands, and tenants were increasingly becoming landless, making the subdivision more vulnerable to famine.

In the Santhal Parganas great distress was caused by grasping and rapacious mahajans, along with hereditary bondage, the unparalleled corruption of the police, and the impossibility of redress in the courts. In certain districts, as in Barbhum, the invasion of the pargana by a powerful English company, bent on destroying the rights of the Ghatwals or Bhumij khuntkhattidars, gave rise to much disturbance. These settler rights, all across

Chotanagpur, were to be challenged by colonial courts and superior land interests.

One settlement report recorded: "But it is common experience in Chotanagpur that the aboriginals are ruined by their incapacity to state their claims intelligently." Clearly, the discursive framework in which they had to operate disadvantaged indigenous people. This situation was to intensify in the twentieth century.

In many places the landlord and the state battled with each other to secure large areas of jungle land, extinguishing the traditional common rights of the people.[26] In Ranchi district, several landlords looked upon the jungles as a providential asset to be exploited for payment of debt.[27] They were prevented from fully exploiting this asset only by difficulties of communication, so that the more remote jungles survived. However, most of the latter were taken over by the state for forest reserves under its rigorous policy of forest conservation. By the 1890s the total area of reserved forest in Chotanagpur was 5839 sq. miles. Of these, over 5431 sq. miles were closed against grazing. In 1894 all state lands within the five districts of Chotanagpur division were declared protected forest, further controlling hitherto unclassed forests. Where patches of jungle survived the grip of both state and landlords, the spread of the railway system aided the process of their destruction. The opening up of the Purulia–Ranchi railway and the main Bengal–Nagpur line, fringing the southern portion of Gumla subdivision, led eventually to the total deforestation of this hitherto untouched region.[28]

The difficulties forest reserves posed for local people is indicated in Valentine Ball's comments in 1870. He records the great distress of people in Hazaribagh and Palamau, caused by forest reserves. He notes that:

> [. . .] the people living on the edge of forest reserves have complained to me of the great hardship caused to them by being shut out of the forest, which had previously afforded them a means of livelihood, or at least of collecting certain jungle products, the sale of which has enabled them to supplement their other means of subsistence. They said that if their cattle strayed across the boundary, the *chuprasi* in charge of the forest was down upon them at once, and they had either to bribe him or accompany him to the magistrates court forty miles off, to answer the charge.[29]

Women bore the brunt of this ecological crisis as primary collectors of forest produce and their hardship, recorded by Ball, was to go unredressed by colonial conservation policy, which was even more determined to conserve the remaining forest and demarcate rigid boundaries.

LINKED TO THE FOREST? THE SYMBOLISM OF THE LANDSCAPE AND PAST READINGS OF IT

It was in this context, and given a growing sense of injustice, that the landscape of Chotanagpur became a symbolic terrain for definitions of Chotanagpuri identity: identities were transformed in the context of this rapid ecological and cultural change.[30] It must be noted here that "landscape" is a complex concept. As Cosgrove argues, it can be seen as a "socio-historical construct," a way of seeing projected onto the land, which has its own techniques and which articulates a particular way of experiencing a relationship with nature. It can be argued, in similar fashion, that the landscape of Chotanagpur has been reclaimed and reconstituted in defining Chotanagpuri identity.[31] Sahlins has noted, in the context of Hawaii, that "the landscape and its legends inscribe a criticism of the existing regime. In the current jargon, the landscape is text. Places and names evoke an alternate society older, truer and more directly related to the people." In this way the landscapes of Chotanagpur were organized by stories and legends of conquest and through memories of better times. The revisionist point that the forest connection of tribal communities has been overdrawn needs therefore to be re-examined.

In the context of Amazonia, Peter Gow shows how the Bayo Urubanka river was lived as a human landscape by local native peoples through a multiplicity of engagements with the forest and the river, with each other in acts of generosity, in narration and in encounter with the dead and with spirits.[32] In similar fashion, the landscapes of Chotanagpur were lived as a human landscape in the past. The original forests were spread out over thousands of square miles, especially in the districts of Hazaribagh, Singhbhum, Palamau, and Ranchi, all of which had large forest areas. Local rulers had tended to preserve the forest for military reasons and, as Walter Hamilton noted in 1820, in several parts of Chotanagpur the woods had been forested with great care by rajas as a protection against external invasion. The trees were mainly either moist deciduous or dry deciduous, and the whole division had a rich growth of *sal* (*Shorea robusta*).

In the valleys, especially in sheltered situations, the principal companions of the sal were the *asan* (*Terminalia tomentosa*), *gambhar*, *kend* and *simal*. The *mahua* tree (*Bassia latifolia*) was common throughout Chotanagpur and was very important to the local economy. In the villages, better fruit-bearing trees grew: the *jamun* (*Eugenia jambolina*), *karanj* (*Ponamia glabra*), *tetar* (*Tamarindus indica*), *bael* (*Aegle marmegos*), jackfruit (*Autocarpus integrifolia*), *pipal* (*Ficus bengalensis*). Many other forest shrubs and trees yielded fruit and afforded valuable food supplements in years of scarcity. Slacke, in his report on settlement operations in Chotanagpur estate in 1882, enumerated 21 species of seeds and the fruits of 45 uncultivated trees which were used as food, in addition to 34 trees the leaves of which were used as vegetables, and 18 species of edible roots. He also gives the names of 97 forest products used as medicines, 28 used as oil and gums, 17 used as dyes, and 33 creepers or barks of trees used as rope fiber. The length of these lists gives us some indication of the economic value of the jungles to the local inhabitants. Valentine Ball noted in the 1860s that several of the communities were heavily dependent on jungle products. For example, the Keriahs of the Jolhari hills, who were not settled agriculturalists, relied on the jungle for a supply of fruits, leaves, and roots. This they supplemented with rice, procured from lowland agricultural communities by trading jungle products such as honey, lac, sal seeds and leaves, and *tusser* cocoons.[33]

Settlement reports note that most of the communities, even the settled agricultural ones, and particularly the women of these communities, had a highly sophisticated technical knowledge of their jungles. The Hos of Singhbhum, for example, had names for all the common plants as well as those of financial importance to them, and, like the forest Mundas, were well versed in the edible properties of plants. The Birhors, in the extreme east of Singhbhum, were a wandering community who lived by snaring monkeys and by collecting the fiber of the *Bauhinia vahlii* creeper.[34] The forest environment, and a knowledge of it, were thus of critical importance to the local people, particularly *vis-à-vis* their diet. This importance was paralleled by an equal significance in terms of belief; and the two were not truly separable. Chotanagpur folk taxonomy was completely embedded in and mediated by the local cultural order.

Munda understandings of the landscape and its productivity seem to have encompassed conceptual links between women and forests. Every Munda village, for example, had its own particular spirits whose duty it was to look after the crops. These spirits were known as *bongas*, a generic name for spirits as well as for the power and force of mountains, hills, forests, trees, rivers, houses, and the village. One such spirit, known as Desawali, played a large part in Munda festivals connected with cultivation. The home of this presiding deity was the *sarna* or sacred grove, a little path of jungle that, when all else had been cleared for cultivation, was left as a refuge where the gods might live apart. At all seasons of the year offerings were made in the sarna, for on the favor of the Desawali depended the success or failure of the crops. Among the Hos, the religious and symbolic community incorporated the forest in various ways. The twofold division of the landscape into tame *(hatu)* and wild *(buru)* represented the ongoing attempt of the communities to pacify and live with the forest (buru), and its spirits *(burubongako)*.[35] As Yorke notes, religious boundaries ensured important notions of community. All the springs, hills, and large forest trees left standing in the village after clearing still harbored spirits against which the protection of the village spirit was necessary. All animals and plants were divided into those that were domesticated, and hence of the village, and those that were wild, and hence belonged to the forest.[36]

Propitiating female spirits of the grove was done mainly by men, women being excluded. The sacrifice began by sacrificing fowl before a rough image of mud or stone. At night, villagers returned home with sal blossoms and marched to the beating of drums and the blowing of horns, with much dancing along the way. The following morning the women, decked with sal blossoms, carried baskets filled with these same blossoms, which they placed over the door of very house for luck. The festivals of the sacred grove were very important for the settled agricultural communities of Chotanagpur and emphasized the importance of the forest and its flowering seasons in the ritual life of these communities. The forest was central to human life and the forest and the village together made up a spiritual and moral entity. It was to be protected and preserved and people respected it. Clearly, a symbiotic relationship prevailed between the people and the landscape in Chotanagpur.[37] Such symbiosis is not always found in forest communities. In one study of the Mende of Sierra Leone conducted in 1980, the forest was found to be regarded as opposing mankind and as an obstacle to human progress; the Mende believing that the bush contained innumerable dangers, including evil spirits, and that it constantly threatened farms.[38] The Chotanagpuris, on the other hand, tended to experience the forest and village as part of each other, the one being the life force for the other's continuing existence. An interesting study of the Nayakas of South India argues for a similar cosmic economy of sharing.[39] The Nayakas converse, dance, sing, and even share cigarettes with the spirits of the forest, which they invoke with shamanistic experience.

What can be forcefully argued here is that Chotanagpuri understandings of the landscape, their stories of nature, and their lived history were to differ radically from the perceptions of nature and the land among colonial scientists and policy-makers, and later from those of modernizing nationalist elite. To say this is not to romanticize indigenous people and their relationship to nature. In his reply to Obeysekere, Sahlins has noted that the postmodern attack on the notion of a bounded and coherent culture has occurred at the very moment when groups such as the Maoris, Tibetans, and Australian aborigines around the world "all speak of their culture using that word or some other equivalent, as a value worthy of respect, commitment and defence." He argues that no good history can be written without regard for "ideas, actions and ontologies that are not and never were our own."[40] To the Chotanagpuris, therefore, the landscape was an important context for their ritual and customary traditions. The destruction of forests that was to occur as a result of colonial intervention, in the nineteenth century and later, was to change this relationship between the people and their environment. However, the memory of landscape lived on and became a repository of Chotanagpur's nostalgic past, to be revived in complex oppositional contexts.[41]

It can be argued that the despoliation of the forested landscape and the transformation of the peoples' relationship with their environment in Chotanagpur in the nineteenth century was a powerful memory revived in periods of cultural resistance. In the latter half of the twentieth century, this resulted in specific cultural images of the landscape being evoked through ritual festivals of the sacred grove, emerging also as a factor in protest. Images of the landscape have long played a role in cultural resistance in other regions. For example, as Daniels notes, the "ethnic nationalism fuelling the dissolution of the Soviet Union was codified by pictorial images of independent homelands."[42] Resistance may have been fanned by memory of better times in a less despoiled setting. These memories were present in the "landscape of their current servitude." In the context of Chotanagpur, the "remembered landscape" was to fuel a long cycle of protest.[43]

THE POLITICS OF MARGINALITY AND THE CONSTRUCTION OF INDIGENEITY

All through the nineteenth century, the local communities of Chotanagpur sought to protest against growing cultural and physical incursions into their lives. Beginning with the unrest in Tamar in 1816 and the Munda rebellion in 1832, disaffection continued through the mutiny of 1857, and the last decades of the nineteenth century saw unrest in almost every district of Chotanagpur. W.J. Allen, who made an extensive tour of Singhbhum in

1861, noted "that the love of freedom was the general characteristic of the wild and hilly country of the savage Kols and Santhals."[44] The Birsa Munda uprising in the 1890s was the culmination of this period of rebellion.

British forest reservation laws had long proved irksome to the Mundas, and, in the context of the degradation of their forest environment, as well as exploitation by Hindu moneylenders and a modernizing colonial state, they rose in protest. Perhaps it was through the mapping of the notion of the *diku* or outsider in these resistance movements that a new sense of community was renegotiated and a radical consciousness began to emerge. The resistance movements of the latter half of the nineteenth century were critical to this growing consciousness.

By the twentieth century there was thus an established tradition of protest in the region. In 1915, British reports began to mention the Tana Bhagat disturbances among the Oraons in Ranchi district. This movement, which had strong religious overtones, aimed to redress local grievances against zamindars and traders. The Oraons were apparently enjoined by divine command to "give up superstitious practices and animal sacrifices," to "stop eating meat and drinking liquor," to "cease ploughing their fields," and to withdraw their field labor from non-adivasi landowners.[45] One of the movement's leaders, Sibu Oraon, had been reported as distributing leaflets to the effect that zamindari raj had come to an end, that it was no longer necessary to pay rent or *chaukidari* tax, that the Marwaris were selling cloth very dear and should be turned out, their cloth burnt, and the bones of Muhammadans be broken because they killed cows.[46] The movement had a large following and was said to resemble Birsa Munda's uprising of 1895. By the 1920s the Tana Bhagat movement had acquired "disturbing" links with the Congress movement in the rest of Bihar. Gandhi's non-cooperation struggle resulted in renewed agitation in Chotanagpur, and protesters intensified their demands for low rents, restoration of rights to the jungle, and abolition of forced labor.[47] The restriction of access to forests and fresh water fisheries resulted in a wave of protest among the Oraons, Mundas, and Santhals in the 1920s and 1930s in Midnapur, Bankura, Singhbhum, and the rest of Chotanagpur. Many of these were fueled by memories of better times, by stories of their fathers' times—when all jungles were free and all *bandhs* open to the general public.[48]

When they lost their lands and forest to the dikus, the local community refused to recognize the loss as legitimate. William Archer, a colonial official of the time, records the ceremonial taking possession of villages by Tana

Bhagats, the planting of the Tana Bhagat flag in the village, and the reallocation of land among followers. He recorded that to the question, "Where are your title deeds?" the Bhagats replied, "The answer is: my spade, my axe, my ploughshare are my title deeds [. . .] ploughing is the writing of the golden pen on golden land." To the argument, "your lands have been auctioned for arrears of rent and purchased by another," the reply was, "when a man buys a mat he rolls it up and takes it away, similarly, unless the purchaser has rolled up my land and taken it away, how can he be said to have purchased them?"[49] This is like native readings of the landscape in Amazonia. As Peter Gow notes, the native people of that region were implicated in the landscape through moving around in it and leaving traces on it. It was a lived space and no piece of paper in a far-off government office determined who owned what could transform the people's own complex relationship with the land.[50]

The Tana Bhagat movement is interesting because its Oraon followers adopted vegetarianism and an austere lifestyle and incorporated other Gandhian symbols in an attempt to strengthen their hands against landlords. It can be argued that the movement's appropriation of the symbols of the national movement helped promote a feeling of solidarity with a wider struggle against an oppressor state. Gandhi was also understood in terms of the people's own religious consciousness. The Chotanagpuri world was filled with divine and semi-divine beings, and Gandhi was considered a divine force of this type, with powers to mediate between the local communities and nature. [51] While some of the prescriptions of the movement, mainly the move to vegetarianism, can be characterized as an internalization of a caste ideology, the striving for a higher status is not an unambiguous one. Even while there was an acceptance of some of the principles of Hindu religion, the attack on Hindu landlords and local oppressors was clear and striking. With hindsight it is clear that the people of Chotanagpur were beginning to produce their own brand of culture and modernity.

MODERNITY AND ITS DISCONTENTS

The second decade of the twentieth century saw the development of a modern political idiom which sought to arrest the marginalization of local communities. The concept of adivasi now begins to come into use. It is interesting to examine the changing notions of this term over this period. In the beginning, a pan-adivasi identity was also asserted under the

Chotanagpur Unnati Samaj, which was started in 1915. The leaders of this organization were mainly Christian converts, English-educated students belonging to the Munda and Oraon tribes, and they embodied an inter denominational unity of the missions for political purposes.[52] At times, however, the Samaj tended toward sectarian behavior against non-"tribal" autochthones.

Rising adivasi consciousness was given an impetus by the activities of Christian missionaries and by colonial writings which categorized people into essentialized tribal identities with fixed boundaries.[53] Hoffman's *Encyclopaedia Mundarica* and other early missionary writings on the tribes of Chotanagpur helped in part to construct their identities as distinct from those of plains Hindus and helped distinguish between different tribal groups: the Hos, Oraons, and Birhors, for example. The romanticization of tribes also continued to be part of the stereotype and, it was claimed, the government was responsible for the decay of an authentic "tribal" culture within which "in ancient times they had no kings and were kept together by their conferences. The fields they cleared were their own and their whole land belonged to them."[54]

The link between tribes and territory had been established in the nineteenth century through the many tribal rebellions over land and the special administrative status accorded to Chotanagpur.[55] This claim to territory was reformulated in the period after the Second World War, once the discourse of indigenous rights began to be politically articulated in the modern period via the issue of a separate state. In 1937 the Unnati Samaj was reorganized as the Adivasi Mahasabha and, for the first time, raised the question of a separate Jharkhand state. We see here also, for the first time, usage of the term "adivasi" in a political context. The immediate cause of the formation of the Mahasabha was the experience of the first elections held in 1937 under the Government of India Act of 1935. The Congress swept the polls and there was a growing realization among educated tribals that, unless they organized themselves, the Congress would hold sway in Chotanagpur, as elsewhere. It was felt that the Congress had little to offer the indigenous inhabitants of Chotanagpur and was a party of dikus (foreigners). This provided the impetus for some Christian and non-Christian tribals to join forces under the Adivasi Mahasabha, which continued its efforts to forge a pan-tribal identity. It also opened up its membership to non-adivasis of that region, although it must be remembered that the strict distinction between tribals and non-tribals in the popular mind crystallized only years after the announcement of the Scheduled Tribes list in 1936. In its manifesto in 1937, the Sabha emphasized above all unity among different "tribal" groups. This emphasis on unity was in keeping with a growing understanding that only a broad movement would strengthen the hands of the Sabha *vis-à-vis* the state. Its expressed objectives were to be the improvement of the economic and political status of adivasis in Chotanagpur.[56] The party was opposed to the Congress in this period and was seen as loyalist by the British. It therefore remained outside the mainstream of nationalist politics.[57] This attitude of the adivasi leadership to the Congress in this period was in part because the Congress was seen as a party of dikus which had little respect for "tribal" tradition and culture. In the 1940s the party gained new support for its movement from the Muslim League, which hoped to establish a corridor through Chotanagpur to link it with East Pakistan. The nature of the relationship between the Congress and the Adivasi Mahasabha can be gauged by the violence which erupted during the elections in 1946. In these elections fights broke out in the region between the Adivasi Mahasabha and the Congress at various polling stations. In Kunti district, five adivasis were killed and several injured in the violence, generating widespread condemnation.[58] A renewed period of mistrust and hostility between the Congress and the Adivasi Mahasabha followed.

Events in the preceding period had resulted in ethnic arguments based on the notion of a separate tribal identity losing its force in favor of regionalism, as the Jharkhand Party began to embrace the discourse of Western modernity. In 1950 the Adivasi Mahasabha was wound up to form the Jharkhand Party, which gradually changed its policy *vis-à-vis* the Congress. The party then had to broaden its base and attempted to enlist more non-Scheduled-Tribe members. By the 1950s it was clear that ethnicity alone could not be the basis of a political dialogue in Chotanagpur. The census of 1951 showed that tribals had become a minority in Chotanagpur. The party was therefore thrown open, at least in principle (as embodied in its constitution), to all Chotanagpuris. A significant transition from ethnicity to regionalism now emerged as the formative factor in the movement. This is not to say that ethnic arguments lost their force but only that the Jharkhand Party saw it as politically tactful to air more regionally-based arguments. Notions of ethnicity had to be reconstituted in different historical moments. The history of cultural contact with the plains peoples, migration both to and from Chotanagpur, and growing inequality were challenging the notions of a pure adivasi identity. Many of the more recent migrants into Chotanagpur were in fact poor low-caste plains Hindus. It was felt that the new Jharkhand parties had to contend with this change by abandoning the old political language.

The foremost ideologue of the Jharkhand Party in the 1950s was a Western-educated Munda, Jaipal Singh. He had been active in the Adivasi Mahasabha and epitomized the new breed of leadership, which was Western-educated, Christian, and had an urban outlook. As a charismatic leader, he had a large following. [59] Under his leadership the concept of Jharkhand was enlarged to include all the regions that once formed the Chotanagpur administrative division.[60] The party had decided it would use constitutional means to achieve its goal. That the policy worked is clear, for the popularity of the party in the 1950s rapidly increased. It swept the polls both in 1952 and 1957, emerging as the major political organization in the Chotanagpur/Santhal Parganas area. The 1957 elections then saw it extend its influence into Orissa, where it captured five seats. It displayed remarkable unity, and thousands of people turned up at party meetings to show support. However, despite this show of strength, in the mid-1950s the States Reorganization Committee turned down the plea for a separate Jharkhand state.[61]

By the late 1950s the party entered a period of decline. At the leadership level, there was a growing split between Christian and non-Christian adivasis on account of the former controlling high party positions. There was also a growing realization among the people that the party had failed to deliver the goods. It did not have any concrete agrarian program and the leadership was drawn from the high strata of tribal society, that is, mainly from Mundas and Mankis (village headmen) in many parts, and from among the Manjhi and educated Christians from the Munda and Oraon areas. As agrarian conditions continued to deteriorate, new measures were needed to remedy widespread impoverishment but the party organization was too weak, and it had no radical program. [62] Eventually, the search for funds led it into dealing with the hated diku class of exploiters. In 1962 the party accepted as member an ex-zamindar of Chotanagpur and appointed a secretary from the moneylending community. By 1962 the Congress, with its program of *garibi hatao*, actually seemed to be more in tune with mass demands to end poverty. Support for the Congress correspondingly increased with the decline of the Jharkhand Party. In the 1962 elections the Jharkhand Party was reduced to twenty seats in the Bihar assembly and it appeared that it could no longer maintain itself as a viable political organization. The merger of the Jharkhand Party with the Congress was thus a natural corollary to these events. Jaipal Singh accepted a portfolio in the Bihar cabinet and many of his supporters never forgot this betrayal.[63] The merger signaled the end of the Jharkhand Party as a party of the people and effectively outlawed the radical stream.

A period of dissent followed, with grassroots activists struggling to build a political base. A radicalization of politics was inevitable, given the increased exploitation of the Chotanagpuri communities under the Congress regime. Indeed, Congress policy toward tribal areas in the post-Independence period had totally alienated the adivasis. After 1947, the "isolationist" thinking of the colonial rulers was heavily criticized by the nationalist state which was wedded, as its imperial precursors had been, to the ideology of development.[64] The report of the Scheduled Tribes Commissioner, known as the Dhebar Report, on the Indian state's policy toward tribals, argued that the British policy of isolating them had resulted in their exploitation.[65] Professor Ghurye, a long-time critic of British rule, voiced this change in thinking when he stated that "the policy of protecting the so-called aborigines through the constitutional expedient of excluded areas or partially excluded areas evoked a protest from politically conscious Indians and was resented by many of them."[66] In a conscious attempt to move away from the British policy toward the tribes, the new policy was unashamedly assimilationist, its professed aim being to draw the tribes into the mainstream of Indian political culture. The consequences of such a policy were predictably disastrous and fueled more tension in the region.[67]

The Government of Bihar pushed ahead with a massive exploitation of the forest and mineral wealth of the region while maintaining in its official "tribal" policies that "tribals" should be allowed to develop according to their own genius. After the 1950s, thousands of acres of adivasi land were lost to new industries. The cities of Ranchi, Dhanbad, and Jamshedpur continued to grow rapidly through an ever-increasing in-migration of non-adivasi dikus. By 1961 there were already half a million migrants in Dhanbad and Singhbhum. There was also an extensive loss of land through sales by adivasis to non-adivasis, not only for business purposes but for residential buildings.[68] The result was an increasing "de-tribalization," with communities such as the Bauris becoming de-Scheduled on account of their developing into coalminers. The 1971 census disclosed an alarming state of affairs. The percentage of Scheduled Tribes in the population of the districts of tribal Bihar had fallen sharply in the decade from 1961: in Ranchi from 61.61 to 58.08, in Singhbhum from 47.31 to 46.12 and in the Santhal Parganas from 38.24 to 36.22. This was not only due to the slow growth rate of the adivasi population, which was in fact among the lowest in India, but the influx of people from other parts of Bihar. In this period, struggles to halt these dramatic changes developed under a new leadership and resulted in the creation of political organizations like the Birsa Seva Dal and the Jharkhand Mukti Morcha (JMM). The new political extremism was reflected most clearly in the formation, in 1973, of the JMM, whose object was to form a separate Jharkhand state, end the exploitation of "tribals" by "non-tribals," and secure preferential treatment for "sons of the soil" in the matter of employment. Under the aegis of this organization, adivasi consciousness acquired a new political orientation. They led large-scale movements of protest to regain tribal lands in the 1960s and 1970s. In 1968, a movement among the Santhals in the Santhal Parganas followed, and resulted in, among other things, the Santhals forcibly harvesting standing crops on lands illegally occupied by moneylenders. The period 1967–74 also saw many struggles under the aegis of the JMM to recover alienated lands from moneylenders and rich peasants in Chotanagpur, amounting to a renewed assertion of strength in a people long exploited.[69]

A history of this period of obvious exploitation can help us understand the nature of the counterdiscourse of local people in Chotanagpur. Faced with economic and political marginalization, the adivasi leadership in Bihar under the Jharkhand Party first sought to assert its political views by emphasizing a broad convergence of interests with other non-adivasi groups. In a region where the adivasi/non-adivasi distinction had been blurred through decades of migration and where the poorer parts of the Hindu migrant population were as badly off as their adivasi brethren, it would have been politically inept to emphasize only an adivasi identity. However, the constitutional policy followed by the Jharkhand Party through its embracing the language of modernity and the lack of a radical program in the countryside soon resulted in its decline and ultimate merger with the Congress in 1963.[70] That this happened with disastrous consequences for the adivasi people's struggle in the 1960s is evident from the attempts made in the later 1960s and 1970s to evolve new independent political organizations to meet popular demands and, specifically the emergence of the JMM. The JMM was to attempt a successful cultural revival in the 1970s and 1980s and revive the image of the Jharkhand people as the inheritors of their ancestral lands and forests. A new and interesting period in the struggle of what was increasingly seen as the "indigenous people" of Jharkhand, against an oppressive state, had begun.[71] It was in this context and given a growing sense of adivasi consciousness that the landscape of Chotanagpur became a symbolic terrain for definitions of Chotanagpuri identity.

JAL, JANGAL, JAMMEEN: THE DISCOURSE OF THE INDIGENOUS FOREST

The JMM gave particular emphasis to a cultural revival of adivasi rituals relating to the land and signaled the revival of the *sahrul puja*. This "festival of the sacred grove," which was traditionally confined to the villages, now became a grand political event in urban centers, and was accompanied by large processions, drum beating and dancing, with large crowds lining the streets.[72] In the context of a despoiled landscape, the ritual harked back to the days of an idyllic environmental past, and can be seen as a selective use of memory. The memory of a pristine environmental past is linked here to the solution of contemporary political and economic problems. Given the ecological degradation in Chotanagpur today and the poor state of its village sacred groves—often left with only one tree—this ritual has taken on enormous symbolic significance. It evokes a particular image of the landscape as "older, truer and more directly related to the people" and was used to revive memories of better times as well as criticize the inequities of the current regime. It symbolized a flamboyant assertion of "tribal" identity and strength, and can be compared to the Ramanavami or Moharrum processions,[73] demonstrating militancy.[74] The puja thus became a highly visible, elaborate, and ritualized culture of public celebration involving both performers and crowds in a collective act articulating the special relationship of Chotanagpuri peoples with nature, and asserting their rights as true custodians of their lands and forests.[75] It is possible to argue, in this context—as Paul Gilroy does when he describes the performance of black expressive cultures—that these performances were an attempt to transform the relationship "between the performers and the crowd in dialogic rituals so that spectators acquired the active role of participants in collective processes which are sometimes cathartic and which may symbolize or even create a community."[76]

This reinvention of "tribal" traditions happened, as James Clifford notes, in a complex oppositional context where indigenous populations were threatened by forces of progress and modernity. In-migration had changed the character of Chotanagpur society and, by the late nineteenth century, it was a society that could not really be categorized as predominantly adivasi. Hobsbawm and Ranger have pointed to ways in which nationalist mythologies were historically contingent creations, as was ethnic and tribal identity.[77] An understanding of ethnic symbols and myths is thus invaluable for our study. Elements of adivasi self-government were also revived or reinvented. The Biasi (assembly) in the Santhal Parganas today functions as a court without fees or pleaders and deals out simple justice. Traditions of collective farming, and the preservation of jungles, pastures, and common land began to be asserted more forcefully, while common grain pools were encouraged. The attitude of the JMM toward non-adivasis, however, was still ambivalent. While the concept of diku is central to the notions of adivasi identity and solidarity, the Jharkhand parties began to realize that they could not sustain an appeal based on ethnicity alone.[78] Many of the low-caste migrants who arrived in the region in the nineteenth century felt that they had as much a right to be in Chotanagpur as the adivasis. Any political program for Jharkhand therefore had to include these groups, and the Jharkhand parties were therefore, only partly constituted by ethnic meanings and groupings.

The attitude toward dikus in this period is important to our understanding of how the adivasis conceptualize themselves and others. Moreover, the concept of diku itself is important, for it amounts to a form of boundary maintenance. By mapping the named category of diku we can, perhaps, uncover the vocabulary of group differences in the region. What groups call themselves and what they call others is related, of course, both to a language of esteem and a language of insult. Names, as Manning Nash has noted, condense the relevant cultural information into handy social and psychological packages for easy self- and other identification.[79] The notion of diku has not been a stagnant one in Jharkhand. In the nineteenth and early twentieth centuries, as we have seen, there were already clear notions of difference between dikus and tribal groups. The diku was clearly seen as a recent immigrant and as an outsider and exploiter who seized tribal lands. In more recent times, while the diku was still seen as the outsider who took all the government jobs, the boundary differences between dikus and non-dikus began to blur. An adivasi identity was emphasized, but boundary mechanisms were breached with ease. A more regional identity was taking over, based on secondary cultural markers, that is, on a shared history of exploitation, a territorial boundary, and a shared culture among adivasi groups. The last is important because, although there was a growing understanding that the future of non-tribals was assured in the envisaged state of Jharkhand, the parties continued to lay importance on "tribal" culture. The appeal to voters was made on grounds of a common economic and cultural predicament. Ethnicity continued to have force in Jharkhand to the extent that it was a politically powerful argument against the way in which state and national political arenas were structured in favor of dominant outsider groups.[80] Thus, although the parties emphasized a regional identity, ethnic arguments continued to be aired at the popular level. [81] The flag of the Jharkhand Party was green in colour, deliberately to emphasize the common cultural and ecological heritage of all Jharkhandi adivasis, while the election symbol was a *sismandi* (a particular kind of fowl sacrificed to a bonga). The JMM flag had the traditional weapons of bow and arrow as symbols of tribal resurgence. [82] Diku culture, it was argued, showed little respect for any of these symbols. But there is little doubt that a homogeneous adivasi identity can no longer be asserted—given the history of the region and the impact of the long history of low-caste Hindu migration—even though ethnicity continued to rear its head in different guises.[83]

The Jharkhand parties also attempted, in this period, to attack the relatively careless attitude of the Bihar state government with regard to environmental issues in Chotanagpur. One of the most widespread movements in the area has in recent times been motivated against attempts by the Forest Development Corporation to replace sal with *sagwan* (teak), since the latter is more valuable as wood in the market. This has grave consequences for the lifestyle of local people. As we have seen, sal products have been useful to them in various ways. In 1978, resistance to the planting of teak was sparked when the forest department undertook to plant teak in 2000 hectares of sal forest. A strong popular belief developed that nothing grew under teak, and particularly not the grass roots and tubers on which the local wildlife and people subsisted. It was also alleged that since elephants did not eat teak leaves, they would be forced to seek food in areas where crops grew, thus increasing their depredations. Agitators also argued that fruit-bearing trees were being cut to establish teak nurseries, thus depriving tribals of a source of food.[84]

A detailed analysis of the forest *andolan* in Singhbhum district had been provided by Father Matthew Areeparampil, a Jesuit priest who has been working among the Hos for many years and who was actively involved in defending them in court.[85] (It can even be argued that Jesuit mission activity in this region fired local protest.) He noted that:

> [...] the immediate cause for this sudden outburst were certain actions of the government which the tribals felt were detrimental to their interests. In 1973 the government nationalised the kendu leaves trade. In 1976 it took over the *sal* leaves trade and in 1978 all the Minor Non-Forest Produce (MNFP) was taken over by the government. In 1975 the Forest Development Corporation was formed and a total area of 1.92 lakh hectares were leased out to the corporations for purposes of clear felling and planting high yielding varieties like teak.

The first major incident of the uprising against these actions took place at Simdega on August 4, 1978, when police fired at a crowd of adivasis killing one person. As the andolan progressed, the forest issue came to acquire greater prominence. Forest officials were assaulted on a large scale and, as part of the direct action program in support of the movement for a separate state, 2000 adivasis from the forest areas of Chakradharpur, Sonua, Goilkera, and Bandgaon took part with their bow and arrows in this demonstration. Areeparampil notes that the *jungle katai andolan* was started at the same time at places where trees had been felled in forest areas to create fields.

The initial phase of the movement included sixty-seven villages in the Karaikela area. The movement also attempted to reclaim lands which had *sasandiri* (burial stones) of their ancestors, this serving as evidence that these lands once belonged to them. The resistance to teak plantation specifically targeted teak nurseries and, at Searing, several huts, a pump set, and all the teak saplings were destroyed. In October eleven teak nurseries were destroyed in the Sonua and Goilkera areas, causing considerable loss to the corporation. The *Singhbhum Ekta* newspaper described the reasons for the movement in the following manner: "the planting of teak after cutting the natural forests is against the interests of the adivasis. Adivasi life depends very much on the produce of the forest like *mahua, kusum, karanj* etc [...] in many areas."

The Bihar administration reacted by intensifying repression. Section 144 of the Criminal Procedure Code was imposed throughout the forest areas on November 2, 1978. The next day, the subdivisional officer and his party severely beat up several adivasis including women, at the Goilkera market.

Further shooting followed in Serengda and Goilkera, killing five adivasis. On November 5, leaders of the Jharkhand Party, N.E. Horo, Haricharan Sinku, and Sohanlal Aneja, were arrested. However, the andolan was to come more firmly in the grip of the JMM as the Jharkhand Party gradually distanced itself from it. As the political leadership wavered the jungle andolan spread to other areas and continued to gain momentum until it climaxed in the Gua firings. Here a peaceful demonstration of adivasis was fired on by the Bihar military police. Fifty-nine rounds were fired and three adivasis killed outright. What followed was indescribable.

When the injured adivasis were brought into hospital, "they were surrounded within the hospital, assaulted, and shot dead. To quote the official version, 9 rounds were shot, killing 9 adivasis within the hospital." As the hospital staff cowered, the "dead bodies remained there until darkness and the blood until the next day." The police in south-west Singhbhum district had moved at the behest of local politicians, mine owners, and timber contractors to arrest 4100 tribals and non-tribals for unlawfully cutting trees.[86] The morcha was driven underground, only to emerge again in new guises and locations.[87] In the context of a state-declared scarcity, and with famine stalking the land, the resistance of the Singhbhum adivasis was laudable, and there is little doubt that the movement for a separate Jharkhand state was renewed and intensified during this period.

In recent years many ethnic movements have legitimized their claims by reference to a global environmentalism.[88] This involves arguing that local people are the best stewards of the landscape and have best claims to control it. The discourse of the rights of indigenous peoples to their forest was an important part of the struggle of the Jharkhand parties. In the late 1960s and 1970s, the Birsa Seva Dal, Bihar Prant Hul Jharkhand Party, and the Jharkhand Mukti Morcha were set up to contest what they saw as the tyranny of developmentalism, both within and outside the parliamentary area. These organizations participated in elections, even as their activists infiltrated and cropped diku lands, sabotaged local transport lines, and organized new forest satyagrahas. [89] There is also now a renewed attempt to preserve the sacred groves of adivasis and a growing protest against dam-building, as at Koel Karo. The effort to prevent the flooding of tribal lands and groves under this project has generated widespread support. The main outcry seems to be directed against the destruction of sacred groves where the gods are said to reside. Over the years they have been successful in stalling the project, indicating the power of collective resistance.[90]

By the mid 1980s a full-fledged adivasi movement was under way to claim as their own lands and forests expropriated by outsiders and by the state. The attack on forest lands held in reserved forest areas, inaugurated in Singhbhum, soon spread to other areas in neighboring Ranchi where, under the auspices of the Jharkhand parties, large areas in the protected forest zones came to be legitimate targets of struggle.[91] As the forest department fought back, attacks on forest guards and the burning of forest department rest houses in the Saranda forest area became a regular feature of the protest. Slogans such as *jal, jangal, jameen* (water, forest, land), and the movement for securing "indigenous" rights, had come to acquire a new significance. In Singhbhum alone 4000 acres of forest were illegally cut. Areeparampil has provided an analysis of both the strong and weak points of the jungle katao andolan.

He argues, I believe rightly, that this was a important new phase in the history of the movement at a time when it became truly popular, with wide participation by all groups, including women. However, it was plagued with problems, not the least being the ambiguous support of traditional Jharkhand leaders to the movement. There was also little support for the movement from the plains adivasis and non-adivasis. Furthermore, the large-scale looting of forests that followed mainly benefited contractors, timber merchants, and corrupt politicians, and in Porahat a raid in the 1980s unearthed timber worth a million rupees in several saw mills and timber godowns.[92] It is interesting to note in this context that a trend toward ecological vandalism had been noted by settlement officers in Ranchi in the latter half of the nineteenth century, caused by fear of forest settlements and the imminent seizure of forest land by the state. We can note a similar process here, but one that has markedly intensified given the inroads of the forest department, in cahoots with timber contractors and middlemen, in the post-Independence period. The extreme reaction of local communities to these excesses by the state and timber contractors was thus to be expected. Often their reactions caused a further denudation of the forest cover.

One effect of the movement has been a marked deterioration in the lifestyles of local villagers in the Porahat and Chaibasa areas of Singhbhum, the region of my case study. A widespread denudation of the hills has resulted in many protected forest areas here. In local memory, hills that had been as recently forested as ten years ago were stripped bare of foliage. Local communities bartered their forest resources in the provincial towns and, in 1997 for example, columns of bicycle poachers could be seen weaving their way down from the hills, laden with wood.[93] In Purnea village in central

Singhbhum, village women complained of the extensive distances they had to walk to collect fuel. Interestingly, a reaction to this phase of the struggle is currently taking place in Singhbhum district. In this case, a local conservation movement invoking perceived age-old conservation values among local people has developed in several villages, actively encouraged by local Jesuits. Here the hardship of villages like Purnea, affected by uncontrolled local forest-cutting, have forced villages such as Basakuti, Thakurugutu, and Gutuhatu, to name only a few, to voluntarily take up the conservation of local forests and limit access to them in order to preserve fuel and other wood resources for the future.

The phase of environmental vandalism that occurred in Jharkhand in the 1980s and 1990s leads one to a reassessment of "indigenous" forest rights. It also leads one to question whether local people should have the right to freely pursue traditional practices or to develop their lands, especially when the exercise of these rights has implications that conflict with environmental values. This is an issue currently being debated globally.[94] The debate has been particularly controversial where threats to the survival of endangered species is involved. It has been noted in the context of American Indians that the traditional subsistence conservationist practices of indigenous people have not really led to sound modern environmentalism.[95] Furthermore, the granting of land rights to indigenous people in the American Indian context has repeatedly led to their not returning to traditional subsistence practices, but rather to "develop" their lands without respect for the environment.

In the case of Chotanagpur, while one cannot deny that traditional indigenous practice incorporated valuable environmentalist lessons, as we have seen the terrible toll on the land—associated with state intervention and capitalist interests in the colonial and postcolonial period—has resulted in these communities demanding the return of their forests, not necessarily to develop them sustainably, as in the past, but in order to harvest them, often uneconomically, in order that they not lose out to commercial interests. Very often, they have been abetted in this process by commercial interests. Meanwhile contractors, timber merchants, and corrupt politicians have used the cloak of the popular movement of the jungle katao andolan to loot forests.

In an interesting article, Roy Perrett has argued that conflicts between indigenous rights and environmental interests can be seen as conflicts between local and global justice. He argues that it is unlikely that (given the history of injustice) local people are going to give way when the exercise of their land rights happens to conflict with environmentalist values. Using the discourse of rights and Amartya Sen's capability approach,[96] he goes on to submit a theoretical model of freedom, rights, justice, and equality where full moral weight is given to the notion of indigenous rights while allowing for an overriding of these rights in order to respect some more basic right, such as the right to be well nourished and disease-free. In the case of Chotanagpur, the value of these debates lies in the framing of policy where local communities have a stake in protecting their environmental resources. Examples of what may happen when trees rather than local people become the objects of conservation have been provided in many accounts.[97] New policy departures need to be evolved that will prove effective in extending the lifespan of the world's remaining forests, and in countering the formidable interests of those exploiting them for short-term gain. Co-management of resources and joint forest management have been seen as the way forward. Only individual case studies will show the extent of participation, or show the ways in which definitions of "community" have in fact strengthened certain hierarchies in society.[98] The local conservation movement under way in some villages in Singhbhum is an example of community forest management operating without the approval of the forest department. The major fear of the local people, engaged in managing their local forest by hiring their own forest guards, is that their stake in the forests will be lost in a changed political climate.[99]

The cultural struggle for indigenous rights being waged in many parts of contemporary India must be seen, I think, as essentially a movement directed toward transforming the balance of power in the region. In Gramscian terms, it may be seen as a struggle for hegemony in the cultural and political arena. In rejecting terms such as *jangli* that form part of a discourse that aids compliance toward forms of economic and political domination, by forcefully claiming indigenous status and rejecting the notions of backwardness and inferiority in comparison with plains Hindus, adivasi leaders in the twentieth century attempted to secure political advantage in the colonial and postcolonial period. In the process, claims about the inherent originality or purity of adivasi culture were made, while the history of acculturation with the dominant Hindu culture was pushed aside. It is in this moment of struggle against dominant values and the narratives of the state, as Homi Bhabha notes, that the "meanings and symbols of culture are appropriated, translated, rehistoricized and read anew."[100]

It seems very likely that ethnicity will increasingly dominate Indian politics. As the discourse of the nation-state in India becomes increasingly undemocratic, ethnic politics seeks to express itself more forcefully. Moreover, while regarding ethnicity as a process, there is little doubt that, with the creation of the new states of Jharkhand, Uttarakhand, and so on, ethnic arguments in India have already come into their own. But these continue to tread a complicated path.[101] The original demand for Jharkhand included the tribal areas of West Bengal, Orissa, and Madhya Pradesh. These were left out of the new state, and indigenous groups became a minority in Jharkhand.[102] It has been argued that the division of the indigenous people of Jharkhand allows national elites to continue exploiting its rich natural resources.[103] The struggle is far from over. The extraordinary attempts of the Jharkhand government to award indigenous land claims on the basis of colonial documentation dating back to the 1920s must be seen in this context. More surprising is the limited success achieved by the Bharatiya Janata Party (BJP) to co-opt adivasis. This has included a determined effort on the part of the Hindutva brigade to Hinduize tribals, in the process dropping the word adivasi from the lexicon and substituting it with *vanvasi* or forest dweller. This can be seen as a move to deny "indigenous" status to tribals: that status runs contrary to the Hindutva notion that the Aryans are the original indigenous people of India. The attempt to ban cow slaughter and conversion to Christianity is part of the determined effort to "return tribals to the Hindu fold." The right-wing agenda to co-opt these groups indicates the ways in which the term "indigenous" remains highly contested.

The recognition of the invented nature of many traditions and the notion of the constructed nature of culture and ethnicity allows us to approach these complex developments meaningfully through a historical lens. What emerges then are the links between culture and power: culture as a form of power and domination, especially when it masks itself as a "national" culture. Culture also as a medium in which power is both constituted and resisted; one is thinking here of political separatist movements in a global context which use the notion of a separate ethnic identity to challenge the notion of a homogeneous national culture. Instances of dramatic resistance to cultural hegemony and the power of a particular class or group or Western capitalism shows also that culture need not always be on the side of power. Examples of indigenous peoples movements, such as the Jharkhand movement, demonstrate this.

In conclusion, one might state that, given the history of the Jharkhand movement, claims to an "authentic indigeneity" cannot be so easily dismissed by revisionist writers.[104] Dirks, Eley, and Ortner have usefully argued the political significance of these categories for subordinate and marginalized groups seeking to contest the power of hegemonic formations, whether constituted within academic disciplines, institutional fields, or at the level of whole societies. They note: "if otherness is a category that must always be suspected, nevertheless it may facilitate our attempts to listen to the voices of anthropologist informants and colonised subalterns."[105] The fact that the term adivasi, with its connotation of autochthonous power, has found most favor with these communities, is of great significance. It can be seen as a way of creating alternative power structures and of being outside the narratives of the Indian nation-state. As Skaria puts it, "being adivasi or indigenous is about the shared experience of the loss of the forests, the alienation of land, repeated displacements since independence in the name of development, and much more."[106] The most recent furore over the recommencing of work on the Koel Karo project indicates that this threat continues in the new state of Jharkhand. The debate over the damming of the Narmada has highlighted the question of indigenous rights. Approximately 37,000 hectares of land and 152,000 people are scheduled to be displaced by the reservoir. Secondary displacement will add many more to these numbers raising the total to a million.[107] While it is true that hill adivasis are only a third of the number ultimately affected, their plight has been highlighted by reference to global environmentalism. In this, the activists of the Narmada Bachao Andolan have been helped by the contemporary political prominence of the issue of indigenous rights and the international shift in attitudes toward indigenous people since the Second World War. A recent Indian Supreme Court decision to give the green signal to the construction of the Sardar Sarovar dam indicates the new determination of the national and power elites to harness resources at any cost. It continues to show that adivasi lives are not as valuable.[108]

A reassessment of the post-1865 period, in particular, will need to take into account the local traditions and transforming historical developments that have led gradually to the emergence of the identity of the adivasi. In the absence of such an analysis, the argument made by writers such as Sumit Guha, that invocations of indigeneity can only have explosive consequences, simply ignores, wholesale, the real and extant politics of such identity formations in India.[109] Embracing the identity of indigenous or adivasi must be seen in political terms. Given the effects of economic exploitation, political disenfranchisement, social manipulation, and ideological domination on the cultural formation of minority subjects and discourses, a redefinition of the subject position of tribes, and an exploration of its strengths and weaknesses, as of the affirmations and negations of the term adivasi itself, was inevitable.[110] In this context, it becomes useful to see contemporary adivasi culture and the assertion of indigenous rights, in many parts of India today, as a form of continuing political struggle, albeit one deeply connected with a critical global environmental predicament.

NOTES

1. For work in this vein, see, for example, Sumit Guha 1999. Here Guha argues for well-integrated local communities, with forest folk engaging extensively in trade in eighteenth-century western India, rendering the idea of "isolated" Bhil tribes invalid. See my review of this book in Damodaran 2000. See also Judith Whitehead, who notes that much of Guha's data for this comes from Khandesh, because that supports his thesis, while elsewhere, even just 50 km west in Rajpipla, the large majority of Bhils were primarily swidden cultivators engaged in a variety of subsistence-oriented practices. Personal communication, January 27, 2001, and Whitehead 2002.

2. van Schendel 1995.
3. Hardiman 1987: 15.
4. Bodley 1997.
5. Agrawal and Sivaramakrishnan 2001: 2.
6. Grove, 1998: 187–236.
7. See T.N. Headland and R.C. Bailey, *Human Foragers in Tropical Rainforests*, cited in Headland 1997: 608.
8. Ball 1985.
9. Yorke 1976: 50–1.
10. See Leach and Fairhead 1996.
11. Merchant 1992: 44.
12. For an interesting study on the redefinition of the landscape in America under the plantation economy, see Stewart 1991.
13. See Damodaran 2002.
14. Ricketts 1855: 2–3.
15. Man 1983.
16. Sivaramakrishnan 1998: 27.

17. *Ranchi District Gazetteer* 1917: 121. See also "Forests of Chotanagpur," 1884: 890–1.

18. Reid 1912: 129.

19. *Annual Progress Report of the Forest Administration in Bengal* 1898.

20. *Forest Administration Report for Bengal 1882–83*, 1897: 223.

21. The expansion of arable land increased after the mid-nineteenth century and 80–95 percent of the optimal geographical limit to cultivation was reached between 1900 and 1910. In Palamau district alone, approximately 100,000 ha. of forest were cleared for the specific purpose of cotton production between 1860 and 1910. As can be seen from the Table below, woodlands in Chotanagpur declined by 201,450 hectares in the period 1870–90, or approximately by over 11 percent. This was a large decrease, with dramatic changes of lifestyle for the people affected.

Table 1: Forest and Woodland Changes in Chotanagpur 1870–90 (Hectares)

Chotanagpur plateau	1870	1890
Dhanbad	10,382	9,794
Hazaribagh	316,408	306,495
Palamau	555,413	530,025
Ranchi	344,317	338,749
Santhal Parganas	308,138	177,577
Singhbhum	274,258	244,826
Total	**1,808,916**	**1,607,466**

Source: Richards *et al.* 1985: 699–732

22. See Ribbentrop 1899. It was only in the 1840s that Alexander Gibson was appointed as a regular forest conservator by Bombay Presidency, for conservation reasons. By this time the Company had been made aware of the possible hazards of deforestation, which was mainly that it might cause rainfall changes, leading to drought and famine. Gibson's appointment was followed by the appointment of Hugh Cleghorn as conservator in Madras. Gibson reported the serious consequences which the destruction of forests was having upon the water supply, leading to erosion of the hills and the silting of rivers, creeks, and harbors. Both these officers strongly advocated that the government claim and exercise proprietary rights to all forests which were not proved to be private property, and that a stricter conservatory control be immediately instituted, restricting shifting cultivation to the hills.

23. See Rajan 1998: 351.

24. Sivaramakrishnan 1999: 3.

25. Report of the Rent Settlement Officer, Giridih subdivision, 1939.

26. Under Company rule, the question of common rights was never raised, let alone understood. Under the Permanent Settlement of Bengal, all such rights had been transferred to the landlord under the terms of the *Fard Rewaz Jungle*, to enable such lands to be taxed. The landlords then proceeded wherever they could to extinguish local rights to common property resources, which included forest and grazing lands and fish tanks, and began to charge peasants for the privilege of using them. All through the latter half of the eighteenth century and the early nineteenth, landlords set about privatizing large areas of common land in Bihar. Aided by a blind colonial state, common rights were negated in several parts of the region. In Hazaribagh district, the English managers of the Dhanwar and Dorander estates, for example, between 1864 and 1900, set themselves firmly against peasant customary claims to trees. Such developments were common in several villages. Rather late in the day, in 1914, settlement reports underlined the importance of recognizing these customary rights, pointing out that hitherto tenancy law in Chotanagpur had ignored their existence: "fifteen years ago the very talk of customary rights would have been poophooed by the civil courts." See *Final Report on Survey and Settlement Operations in the District of Hazaribagh,1917.*

27. *Final Report on the Survey and Settlement Operations in the District of Ranchi,*1912.

28. Ibid.

29. Ball 1985: 649.

30. As Steve Daniels notes (and this is certainly true both of ethnic and national identities): "Identities are often defined by legends and landscapes, by stories of golden ages, enduring traditions, heroic deeds and dramatic destinies located in ancient or promised homelands with hallowed sites and scenery. The symbolic activation of time and space often drawing on religious sentiment gives shape to the imagined community of the nation." Daniels 1993: 5.

31. For similar writings on history, landscape and identity, see Lowenthal 1991.

32. Gow 1995; see also similar studies elsewhere: Thomas *et al.* 2001: 570.

33. Ball 1985; Haines 1910.

34. See S.C. Roy 1925 for a fascinating empirical study of the Birhors.

35. Yorke 1976: 53.

36. Ibid.

37. It could be argued, as R. Freeman has done for Malabar, South India, that perceptions of the forest differ according to one's class position. In Malabar, he argues, for the elites of settled agricultural regimes "the forest becomes a symbolic repository for the demonic, antinomian, antisocial of all those lower castes and tribals with whom the higher castes were dependently but ambivalently tied." See R. Freeman 1994: 27.

38. See Leach 1992: 57–76. For similar views, see Ellen 1993: 140.

39. See Bird-David 1992: 25–34.
40. Sahlins 1995.
41. Simon Schama has noted that "Landscapes are culture before they are nature; constructs of the imagination projected onto wood, water and rock [. . .] once a certain idea of the landscape, a myth, a vision establishes itself in an actual place, it has a peculiar way of muddling categories, of making metaphors more real than their referents; of becoming in fact part of the scenery." Schama 1995: 61.
42. Daniels 1993: 7.
43. See Sahlins 1992 for the idea of the remembered landscape.
44. Home Public 150–2, September 26, 1861, quoted in Kumar 1991: 87.
45. S.C. Roy 1972: 251.
46. Extract from the confidential diary of the S.P. Ranchi 1919, Political Special/1919.
47. Report of the Commissioner of Chotanagpur, May 12, 1921, Political Special/1921.
48. Poffenberger 1985: 348.
49. Archer Collection, MSS eur 236/1.
50. Gow 1995.
51. In Gujarat, the Devi movement of the tribals developed similar links with the national movement. Hardiman 1987b: 168–76.
52. See "Tribal Autonomy Movements in Chotanagpur," in K.S. Singh 1983.
53. One can argue with some reservation, recorded above, as the Comaroffs do in the context of the Tswana, that "the long conversations with missionaries had set the terms of the encounter that sought to make Africans through their everyday dress, agriculture, architecture and so on, through formal education [. . .] the various ways in which culture shown by the churchmen took root in the social terrain of the Tswana to be reinvented or reified into ethnic tradition [. . .] Some to be creatively transformed, some to be creatively redeployed to talk back to the whites, parts of the evangelical message . . . giving rise to novel forms of consciousness and action." See Comaroff 1991: 288.
54. See Hoffman 1906: 2390–401, on customary rights.
55. Dalton 1872: 3.
56. See *Chotanagpur Unnati Samaj ki Varshik Mahasabha ka Report aur Chotanagpur Adivasi Sabha ka Uthpathi* 1937: 1–14.
57. Political Special, April 25, 1946.
58. See *Indian Nation*, March 8, 1946, and *Sentinel*, March 10, 1946.
59. Interview with Cornelius Ekka Ranchi, April 1992. Ekka remembers going to Jaipal Singh's meeting in 1945, where there was a crowd of nearly 50,000 people.
60. At an adivasi meeting in Pathkudua in 1948, the slogans raised included "*Chotanagpur, Santhal Pargana ki jai, adibasi ki jai, Jharkhand le ke rahenge.*" That

the integrity of the Chotanagpur plateau was a major issue for Jaipal Singh and his associates came up in the debates leading up to the reorganization of states. The Kharsawan firing, wherein the Orissa government attempted in 1948 to gain control of the princely state of Kharsawan and many peaceful adivasi demonstrators were killed, brought home the fact that the spoils of the Chotanagpur plateau were subject to division by successor states in the newly independent India, whose policies were no different from those of the colonial rulers.

61. The party fought in the 1952 general election, the first in free India, and won 32 seats out of 325, becoming the major opposition party in the legislature. It demonstrated an impressive show of strength before the States Reorganization Committee (SRC) when the latter visited the area in 1955. However, the SRC did not recommend separate statehood, the main reason being the lack of viability of the area as a linguistic unit. In the general election in 1957, the party once again became the leading opposition party, with 28 seats in the legislative assembly of Bihar.

62. See K.S. Singh 1983: 7.

63. Interview with Jharkhand Party leader N.E. Horo, Ranchi, April 1992.

64. Verrier Elwin noted that at the time "there was endless talk of tribal development." Elwin 1964: 299.

65. For details of these views, see Corbridge 1986.

66. Ghurye 1943: 293.

67. This was not just confined to Bihar, for, as Christoph von Fürer Haimendorf has noted, a massive invasion of tribal land by outsiders occurred all over India, specifically after 1947. See Christoph von Fürer Haimendorf 1989: 39.

68. See Weiner 1978: 165.

69. For details see R.N. Maharaj and K.G. Iyer, "Agrarian Movement in Dhanbad," in Sen Gupta 1982.

70. The merger was declared illegal shortly afterwards and the Jharkhand Party was revived. It still retained some of its constitutional tactics. In a memorandum sent to Indira Gandhi in 1973, the party demanded rectification of the mistake committed by the SRC in 1950 and noted. "We want peace with justice. We want the government and the parliament to consider this demand with justice and fairplay [. . .] we do not want a situation to develop which would breed bitterness, strife, violence [. . .] our demand is one of the oldest in the country which involves people who have suffered thousands of years. It deserves immediate consideration on merit." See a memorandum by the Jharkhand Party submitted to the prime minister of India, March 12, 1973 (personal copy).

71. As Ram Dayal Munda notes, "a period of self search followed the direct action movement of 1978 and after its brutal repression by the government an all-inclusive effort with better planning was launched. This included a series of seminars, symposia, workshops and orientation classes all over the Jharkhand region. At the same time, Ranchi University opened the department of tribal and regional

languages to promote teaching and research on the languages, literature and cultures of the Jharkhand region." Ram Dayal Munda and Bisheshwar Kesari Prasad, "Recent Developments in the Jharkhand Movement," in Munda and Mullick 2003: 216.

72. I was told on a visit to Ranchi town in 1992 that the scale of the sahrul puja I had witnessed there was a new phenomenon, an "invention of tradition" (in Hobsbawm's terms). As James Clifford notes, "throughout the world indigenous populations have had to reckon with the forces of 'progress' and 'national' unification. The results have been both destructive and inventive. Many traditions, languages, cosmologies and values are lost, some literally murdered but much has been invented and revived in complex oppositional contexts." See Clifford 1988: 16.

73. Celebrations of the Hindu religious festival of Ramnavami and the Muslim festival of Muharram were often used to assert the strength of these communities in urban areas, and sometimes resulted in communal rioting.

74. A reassertion of traditional cultural practices is an intrinsic element of the economy and political struggles of third world peoples. For many minorities, culture is not a mere superstructure; all too often, in an ironic twist of Sartrean phenomenology, the physical survival of the minority depends on its cultural variable. As Arif Dirlik argues, cultural struggle is an essential counterpart to political and economic struggle. See, Dirlik 1987: 13–50.

75. Some scholars studying "festive culture" have interpreted rituals as manifestations of an evolving folk culture, creating meaning and helping people to cope with an alien world, and as instruments for the promotion of group solidarity as well as public assertions of group power and demands. See Conzen 1989: 46.

76. Gilroy 1987: 214.

77. Hobsbawm and Ranger 1992; Vail 1989.

78. Whereas in 1872, 51.38 percent of Chotanagpuris were classified by the British as aboriginals and semi-aboriginals, by 1971 only 30.14 percent of the region's population belonged to the Scheduled Tribes in Bihar. See *Census of India, 1971.*

79. Nash 1989: 9.

80. Recent scholarship in the field argues, quite convincingly, that ethnicity, i.e. belonging and being perceived by others as belonging to an ethnic group, is an invention. Ethnic groups are part of the historical process and, though they may pretend to be eternal and essential, they are usually of recent origin and eminently pliable and unstable. They thus constantly change and redefine themselves. See Sollors 1989; Ericksen 1993.

81. As Nash notes, "Ethnicity is a resource in political economic and cultural struggle [...] When economic ends are sought (opportunity, wealth and income redistribution or claims to ownership of a national patrimony) the ethnic group may approximate a political class and exhibit a form of class struggle powered by an ethnic ideology, not a false consciousness but often a true appreciation of the existing state of economic affairs." Nash 1989: 127.

82. P.C. Hembram, "Return to the Sacred Grove," in K.S. Singh 1983: 89.

83. Homi Bhabha has emphasized the "hybrid moment of political change where ideas and forms are rearticulated; where there is a negotiation between gender and class where each formation encounters the displaced." He argues that agents of political change are discontinuous, divided subjects caught in conflicting interests and identities. See Bhabha 1995.

84. Ibid.: 20.

85. See Writ Petition no. 371–5 of 1983 in the matter of *Matthew Areeparampil and Others* versus *State of Bihar and Others* (personal copy). Father Matthew Areeparampil died recently. His death is a serious loss to scholars of India.

86. A.K. Roy 1980: 1123.

87. See A.K. Roy 1979: 46–7.

88. For an interesting discussion of this in India, see Panjuli 1998: 186–217.

89. See K.S. Singh 1983: 14–21.

90. The recent efforts of the BJP-led government to recommence work on the project was met with stubborn resistance, resulting in the death of ten adivasis in police firings. A recent People's Union of Civil Liberties (PUCL) bulletin, signed by Thomas Kochery, M.G. Sanjay, and Medha Patkar notes that this recommencing of the project is "indicative of the fact that in these heydays of globalization and liberalization, the government and power elites of the tribal states of Jharkhand and Chhattisgarh are preparing for mortgaging the forests and rights of tribals for the sake of national and multi-national capital." See http://www.pucl.org/reports/Bihar/2001tapkara-pr.htm

91. Areeparampil 1984: 143–86.

92. Ibid.

93. Field notes 1997–8 in Ranchi and Singhbhum districts.

94. Perrett 1998: 377–91.

95. Ibid.

96. Sen's capability approach rests on the notion of developing people's basic capabilities to achieve functionings they have reason to value. These functionings can vary from elementary ones (like being well nourished and disease-free) to rather complex achievements like having self-respect and being able to take part in the life of the community. See Amartya Sen, *Inequality Reexamined*, cited in Perrett 1998: 386–9.

97. See Sato's account of the Karen people living in "ambiguous lands" in buffer zones between areas designated for forest conservation and farming, in "People In Between: Conversion and Conservation in Forest Lands in Thailand." See also Cohen's depiction of the upland Akha populations of the Laos People's Democratic Republic, who have been shifted to settlements on lower slopes and incorporated into lowland commercial Tai agriculture as an important, opium-addicted wage labor force, in "Resettlement, Opium and LabourDdependence: Akha-Tai

Relations in Northern Laos." These articles are in *Development and Change*, vol. 31, no 1, January 2000, pp. 179–200.

98. Sundar 2000: 255–79.

99. That this is not an ill-judged fear can be seen from the examples that Gadgil and Guha cite in Uttara Kannada, which had its own systems of forest management. This involved keeping a watchman and regulating the harvest. These village councils were given formal recognition in 1926 and continued until the 1960s, when they were disbanded by the Karnataka forest department. The timber rights were then passed on to a local timber contractor. See Gadgil and Guha 1992: 41.

100. Bhabha 1995: 37.

101. This is not to argue that the politics of the new state will be radically different from the state of Bihar. Corruption continues to plague the new state, and the former central government's alliance of the BJP and the Samata Party was bogged down by controversies. The threat posed by the ultra left MCC (Maoist Coordination Committee) in attacking small zamindaris has proved a major irritant to the new state in the period leading up to December 2001, and continues. The NDA alliance was seen to soft pedal on the "indigenous" issue. To counter this allegation, the Marandi government, in 2001, took up the cudgels in favor of "indigenes" by a "domicile" policy for clerical government jobs, causing outrage among settled Biharis. The police firing in Ranchi, where five people were killed, was witness to this. The fact remains that the indigenous population in the current state of Jharkhand comprises less than 30 percent. Any policy for ousting "outsiders" or redistributing resources can only be painful and bloody. At the same time, the right-wing agenda under the BJP to co-opt these communities was fraught with difficulties. It remains to be seen how the state of Jharkhand will fare in relation to its impoverished communities.

102. See Munda and Mullick 2003: xvi.

103. The attempt to recommence work on the Koel Karo project is indicative of this. See PUCL bulletin cited in note 90.

104. See writers like S. Guha 1999.

105. Dirks, Eley, and Ortner 1994: 38.

106. Skaria 1999: 281.

107. Baviskar 1995: 200.

108. See examples of this in P. Sainath's reporting of the environmental consequences of Netrahat firing range in Gumla. Sainath 1996.

109. See S. Guha 1999, Afterword.

110. See also Abdul, Mohammed, and Lloyd 1987: 11–12.

6

NATURE AND POLITICS

The Case of Uttarakhand, North India

Antje Linkenbach

IN BOTH POPULAR AND ACADEMIC WRITING, REPRESENTATIONS OF the Central Himalayan region of Uttarakhand often take nature as a significant point of reference.[1] Yet nature is also portrayed in very different ways. Some historical and religious texts, as also tourist guides, evoke the image of a consecrated land, highlighting the religious significance of Uttarakhand for the whole of India. Uttarakhand is painted as a region blessed with sacred and beautiful nature. Its high and densely forested mountain ranges, with their snowy peaks, are the abode of gods. And human beings are said here to find salvation by visiting the *tirthas* of the holy rivers Ganga and Yamuna and their tributaries, which rise from its glaciers and descend to the plains. Other representations, primarily those concentrating on national economics and development, appreciate the natural environment of Uttarakhand as a possible source of wealth, immensely useful in the process of national progress and development. Jawaharlal Nehru himself, in a speech in 1947, praised the Himalayan mountains as "an amazing source of power, probably the biggest source anywhere in the world—this Himalayan range, with its rivers, minerals and other resources" (Bright n.d.: 454). A third image, also prevalent in development discourse, depicts the mountainous landscape of Uttarakhand as a natural barrier, responsible for the remoteness of land and people. Most parts of Uttarakhand are deemed marginal, inhabited by a largely backward population which follows a simple subsistence-oriented way of life. Only a few urban areas in the Himalayan foothills are regarded as somewhat advanced and able to catch up with life in the plains.

In my essay, I discuss nature as a central dimension, but instead of looking at it from an observer's point of view I want to focus on the way in which local inhabitants themselves relate to nature in their diverse forms of praxis and interpretation, representation and/or imagination. In particular, I want to show the way in which nature in Uttarakhand, in its distinct and particular form, has become a major and explicit point of reference for the local population, both in their imaginaries of the future and development, and in their framework of identity construction. Further, I attempt to illustrate the way in which this process is linked to the evolution of a political consciousness among hill residents. To fully understand the crucial role of nature as an element of identification and politicization it is, however, necessary to first explore its role as an implicitly given environment, appropriated in the everyday life of Uttarakhand's hill dwellers.

The environmental history of Uttarakhand has since the late nineteenth century been marked by the increasing interest of the state (in its different historical manifestations as princely, colonial and national state) in appropriating and exploiting the natural resources of the region, especially the forests, and thereby curtailing the customary rights of local inhabitants to control, manage, and use them for their own benefit. But there is another side to this coin, where the history of deprivation has to be supplemented by a history of protest, pointing to a tradition of resistance mainly directed against the restrictive forest laws and forest policies of the state.[2] In particular, the Chipko movement of the 1970s has to be seen as a key event and turning point in the environmental history of the region. Not only did Chipko stop certain exploitative practices and alter state policies, it seems also to have been largely responsible for a more general political awakening of local inhabitants, at least in the core regions of the movement. In its aftermath, discourses of (sustainable) development came into being in Uttarakhand, entangling the local and the translocal (national, global), and discussing autonomous and self-defined ways of coping with the modern constellation. The recent and successful struggle for a separate state within the Indian union further strengthened the self-confidence of hill people (Paharis), who see themselves as distinct from plains people.

The twofold history of deprivation and protest provides the context in which the relation of Paharis to nature became increasingly reflexive and explicit. To illuminate how an understanding of nature as local resource and object of protection accompanies the development of a particular political self-understanding (self-consciousness), I will focus on two important protest movements in the recent history of Uttarakhand: the Chipko movement and the movement for political autonomy. As regards the first case, the process of ecological consciousness and political awakening of the local population—i.e. the question of ecology, forest rights, and citizenship—will be discussed. As regards the second, emphasis will be laid on the role of nature as an explicit point of reference in the cultural construction of identity and the relation between region and nation.

But before I turn to these, I want to give an idea of how nature functions as a given environment in the everyday life-world of hill dwellers, implicitly constructed and appropriated in the course of their cultural practices. I take the example of people's relation to the forest, which I explored in my field research in the Rawain region of western Garhwal (see also Linkenbach 1998 and forthcoming).[3]

VILLAGERS AND FOREST IN UTTARAKHAND: MULTIPLE FORMS OF RELATIONSHIP

In the Central Himalayan region of Uttarakhand a close relationship between humans and forests seems to have existed for long. Forests, as a culturally significant and multidimensionally appropriated space, are meaningful in everyday religious, social, and economic life. Especially from an economic point of view, common access to local forests as well as management and use of these are essential in the reproduction of the agro-sylvo-pastoral lifestyle of villagers.

In the perception of the local people, a forest is the land outside the inhabited and cultivated area, covered with trees and shrubs of different varieties, in varying density. Whereas fields and cultivated places are distinguished by name, the forest is simply *jangal* or *vana*, remaining without a special denotation. But certain places in the jungle—clearings used as grazing grounds, *bugyals* (high-altitude meadows), crossroads, peaks, and sacred places around a temple—are more clearly named, indicating a greater closeness and significance. Hence, the forest seems to be meaningful not as a concept or as an abstract idea but as sometimes the particular forest people are surrounded by, which they appropriate in their everyday life and to which they refer as "our forest," *hamara jangal*.[4] One can analytically distinguish different dimensions of appropriation: besides being a space of economic and symbolic appropriation, the forest is a space of gender-related activities and—as a recent phenomenon—of recreation.

The forest is also of course a setting for subsistence activities. As far as production and reproduction are concerned the hill economy depends on the forest, which provides fuel, fodder (leaves, pasture), fiber and fertilizer (dry leaves). In certain communities, herbs for medical purposes are collected as well as wild vegetables, and mushrooms. Local timber is used for house construction and agricultural instruments. The forest is frequented by men, women, and children of all status groups,[5] regularly used paths and cattle tracks run through it, and temporarily used stables (*chanis*) have been constructed at certain spots. As long as hill people had control over local forests, they cared about their regeneration—by collectively extinguishing forest fires, using lopping techniques that allowed trees to regain their foliage, and limiting the clearing of forest land for cultivation. Such economic use was interrelated with symbolic practices. Villagers, for example, said that even a couple of years back they would ask the local deities for permission and make them offerings before felling a tree. However, care for the local environment has very obviously declined with the state management of forests.[6] Additionally, villagers continuously try at present to extend the agricultural area for cash crop cultivation—which has become the main source of income in the region—by encroaching on forest land.

Peoples' relation to the forest in the context of subsistence production seems always to have been characterized by a certain ambivalence and tension: a pragmatic, instrumental attitude combines with a preservative one, primarily rooted in social responsibility and respect toward the forest. But whereas these two attitudes were formerly somehow balanced, instrumental action has now gained greater importance, which means increasingly objectifying nature.

In the village in which I conducted my main fieldwork, a number of places in and at the edges of the forest are of particular symbolic significance for the local inhabitants and constitute a kind of religious landscape. The important landmarks are the forest temples of the local deities. Three main local gods are worshiped in the region. Each god occupies a village temple, but two of them, Baukhanaga and Ludeshwara, own an additional temple, located each on a thickly wooded hilltop amidst the jungle. The forest temple is only used once a year on the occasion of the *mela*, the annual fair visited by thousands of people from the surrounding region. Local Brahmins say the deities would prefer to stay there permanently, but because they need daily worship *(puja)* performed by a Brahmin priest, they (are forced to) live in the village. The forested hilltops, so the Brahmins say, are the favorite abodes of the gods because they are clean and calm—just the opposite of the village, regarded as dirty and noisy. The high altitude is especially associated with purity and calmness, the forest only providing additional quality.

In the case of Ludeshwara-*devta*, a strong relationship between ritual and politics finds symbolic expression in the forest area. A stone platform, located in front of the forest temple of Ludeshwara, was traditionally used as a seat by the local *thokdar* (the political representative of the Raja of Tehri Garhwal), who also functioned as "minister" (*wazir*) of the deity.[7] In the region of the former princely state of Tehri Garhwal, political networks were dependent on religious identification (Galey 1990). When acting as wazir of the local deity and when occupying the platform in front of the forest temple, the thokdar claimed his political rights, these being mediated through his religious authority.

A connection also exists between the cult of the Pandavas and the forest. Pandavas—the heroes of the great *Mahabharata*—are worshiped as divine ancestors by the Rajput clans in west Garhwal.[8] The forest seems to be the space to which the Pandavas have a special affinity and over which they exert control. Villagers believe that it is only the Pandavas who can protect the village and its inhabitants from certain negative powers that inhabit the forest and threaten the community.

The forest is a space linked with gods, spirits (helpful and dangerous), and divine ancestors, and therefore has a strong symbolic significance. Human beings not only have to share the jungle with non-humans, the forest is also a space where humans are dependent on the guidance and benevolence of supra-natural beings, and so interact with them. The symbolic power of the forest also plays a constitutive role for the political and social integration of the community as it is an important space for maintaining and strengthening collective memory and identity.

Remarkable differences exist between the way village men and village women relate to the forest in their everyday practices, attitudes, and concepts. Especially for women, forests are an ambivalent space—providing certain liberties but holding many dangers as well.

In the villages of western Garhwal, human action and behavior can be differentiated by demarcating a "front" and a "back" region.[9] Front region refers to a space with strong normative control, where people try to behave according to dominant social norms and role expectations; whereas in the back region these norms are temporarily repealed. An important back region for men is the tea stall ("hotel"), where they can sit and talk, drink and smoke. For women there is no such opportunity for retreat within the village, they are always watched by the elders. Therefore they enjoy working in the forest, collecting firewood or dry leaves to use as litter. They usually start toward the forest in groups, talking, joking, laughing, and singing. On the way, during and after work, they rest, smoke *bidis* and eat some groundnuts or roasted rice if these are available. Songs and talk are often provocative and teasing. Difficulties with husbands and mothers-in-law are freely communicated to female friends in the forest. Apart from being a space of the heavy work that women have to carry out in the jungle, the forest seems to be a space of secrecy, joy, and relaxation where, for a limited span, women can disappear from the sight of other village people and behave more freely.[10]

However, the forest is not always a benign space. Women and girls are especially threatened by wild animals and evil spirits that dwell and roam in the forest. Women and girls are more easily mentally affected, possessed, or even killed by evil female spirits (*matri*). Therefore they are enjoined against staying in the jungle at night and are also meant to avoid dense forests.

Certain activities related to the forest are carried out exclusively by men. The most obvious male activity in the forest is hunting. Even though hunting without a license is prohibited today, as it has been since 1929 in the former Tehri state (Rawat 1989: 123), the practice is alive and at least a few men who possess or have access to guns go for a hunt sporadically. Successful hunters were and still are highly respected persons about whom their co-villagers talk with pride. Now, as earlier, hunting is a good opportunity to obtain meat, even as it carries on the Kshatriya tradition: by hunting men can prove themselves true Rajputs.

Experiencing a landscape primarily for its esthetic qualities is uncommon among villagers. This does not imply that they are unable to appreciate scenic beauty, but nature's beauty is overdetermined by its role in everyday life as well as in their religious conceptions. An alternative perspective has been developing only recently: a few younger and educated people, born in villages but studying or living and working in local small market towns or in the district capital, have started enjoying forests and mountains for vacation and recreation. Individual young men or even girls (mostly college students) go trekking and mountaineering; young, married, well-off couples on a visit to the girl's home may spend some hours walking and picnicking in the forest, accompanied by friends and relatives. For such people, nature has become detached from their everyday life, they have developed a more distanced (and explicit) relation to it. They also often display a certain awareness of ecological issues and talk in a more sophisticated language, arguing for forest conservation and against the felling of trees.

In the aftermath of the Chipko *andolan*, "ecology" was much discussed in all parts of the hills, and ideas and practices of forest conservation disseminated. How far did this ecological discourse affect the everyday relation of villagers in west Garhwal to their forest?

Villagers of Rawain look proudly back at a tradition of forest protest directed against the monopolization and closing of forests in the time of the Rajas of Tehri Garhwal, which culminated in the Dhandak of Rawain 1929/30. This protest movement, which demanded the re-establishment of customary rights for the local population, came to a violent end when the military was directed by officials to shoot at villagers who assembled at Tilari Maidan (in the upper Yamuna valley) to seek a compromise with the ruler. A number of people were killed, varying from 17 to 200 in the different records. In 1968 a declaration of forest rights prepared by Gandhian activists (and by some called the first document of the Chipko movement) was presented to the public at Tilari. This event was meant to honor victims of the former struggle and simultaneously construct a continuity of forest protest. Afterward, only one or two demonstrations were organized in the Yamuna valley; the main Chipko activities emerged in eastern Garhwal and Kumaon, in areas where Gandhian activists had settled and large-scale commercial felling had happened. Despite the historical roots of protest, the inhabitants of Rawain were not involved in the Chipko movement and did not even show any substantial interest in it. For the majority of them, the Chipko andolan remained a distant event which did not influence their everyday life. Only after the formal success of the movement did villagers become affected by Chipko events. They now came under the obligation to adopt the rules and regulations passed by an ecologically minded forest legislation and policy, and were forced to cope with the hegemonic claim of the environmental discourse. With nature and forest becoming an explicit issue of debate, Rawain villagers also took a position and developed their own ideas and projects for life improvement and social advancement (see Linkenbach, forthcoming).

THE CHIPKO MOVEMENT: FOREST RIGHTS, ECOLOGY, AND CITIZENSHIP

None of the numerous publications on the Chipko andolan can be regarded as an authentic account of the movement. This movement has been instrumentalized by various academic and political interests, and sometimes glorified. Different and competing constructions of Chipko have all selected, arranged, and interpreted the information from varying perspectives. These constructions, based on implicit social concepts of agency and gender, follow a particular interpretation of the imaginary element inherent in Chipko activities: they unfold a particular interpretation of the visions and concepts of the social actors regarding their future, relating to ideas of "development" and life improvement as well as to the role of nature and the forest. All constructions, for example, refer to Chipko as an organized social movement which spread all over Uttarakhand, and all assume that what they identify as the ideals and targets of Chipko represent the view of local inhabitants in general, which involves largely neglecting (sub-)regional and social differences. One can distinguish the three most common modes of representing the Chipko andolan: first, as a peasant movement (S. Guha 1989); second, as an ecological movement (Bandyopadhyay and Shiva 1987a and 1987b; Bahuguna 1987); third, as an ecofeminist or women's movement (Shiva 1988; Mies and Shiva 1993; also Agarwal *et al.* 1982).[11] All authors agree that Chipko was rooted in the Gandhian tradition, and some authors lay particular emphasis on this fact (Berndt 1987; Weber 1988). All accounts stress the ecological content of the movement and/or postulate a general shift from economic interests, which triggered the activities, toward ecological considerations.

To privilege the ecological thus actually leads to a somehow inappropriate picture of the Chipko andolan. My research among villagers and activists in east Garhwal suggests that the Chipko struggle cannot be reduced to a single or dominant target: it certainly does not represent a coherent or unambiguous movement which has united the places and people of Uttarakhand. Instead, it should be seen as a set of (partially related) campaigns which took place in particular localities at a particular time, these being guided by different persons. The Chipko andolan was in fact very dependent on the leadership and the involvement of Gandhian activists, but it also owed a lot to members of the Communist Party of India (CPI), which had succeeded in closely linking the social, economic, political, and ecological dimensions. Despite other representations, the Chipko struggle in its quintessence has to be acknowledged as a movement of village men and women to regain the right to control and manage their forest—a right which includes the protection as well as use of forests within the traditional subsistence economy, as a source of income. When discussing the Chipko movement, one has also to take into consideration its internal dynamics. In the course of the struggle, contradictions and tensions arose between different leaders and activists, based on different perspectives of the role of ecology and forest protection, and linked to larger concepts of local development and the relation between humans and the forest. Two main paradigmatically opposed concepts exist, represented by the two central figures of the movement: Chandi Prasad Bhatt and Sunderlal Bahuguna.

Chandi Prasad Bhatt arrived at the conclusion that human beings are a constituent element of nature, enjoying the same right of existence as its other manifestations. But he felt that this perspective is constantly challenged and complains: "The use of the word 'environment' often brings out various shades of meaning. The word is used to describe rivers, forests, mountains and so on, but very often human beings are missed out" (Bhatt 1987: 2). The traditional practices within rural subsistence economy are, according to Bhatt, the best way of maintaining the equilibrium between men and nature. Yet, he also believes in the dynamics of the man–nature relation and states that meanwhile, this equilibrium has come under threat, the most fundamental change here having resulted from the monopolization of forests by the state, and from their large-scale commercial use. The integration of the previously distant Himalayan regions into the market economy, together with the increasing needs of its population, have further added to the erosion of a self-sufficient way of life. Forms of local knowledge and traditional production practices can no longer cope with modern requirements. To meet the new challenges, both have to be transformed and enlarged by deploying knowledge and methods deriving from other contexts, and by altering one's attitude toward nature, which is now basically perceived as an economic resource. At the outset, Bhatt, together with a group of activists, was engaged in establishing village industries to generate income in the region. However, after the formal success of the Chipko movement and the ban on green felling in the higher altitudes of the Himalayan ranges, he started to implement local afforestation programs and turned to the even broader strategy of eco-development.

Sunderlal Bahuguna's concept of "life improvement" has also undergone major changes. From a position which demanded the use of forest resources in the process of local development (showing some proximity with Bhatt's ideas) he shifted to a concept which can be described as "deep ecology."[12] This aims to seek a new harmony with nature—seen as the "other subject"—by replenishing nature and rejecting modern technology. Bahuguna vigorously propagates the idea of "tree-farming," which becomes the key issue in his vision of an alternative concept of development and a new socio-economic order (Bahuguna 1990). Development—as he understands it—should satisfy the basic needs of human beings (oxygen, water, food, clothing, shelter) and should not be oriented to the accumulation of wealth which, in the long term, will result in the destruction of nature. "Ecology is permanent economy," is the leitmotif and basic principle of Bahuguna's thought. As against Bhatt's ideas, Bahuguna's vision does not translate into practical work on a broader basis.

In the present context I do not want to focus on the different strands of the Chipko movement,[13] yet I do want to throw light on the fact that in the course of the movement nature became an explicit subject of discourse. Nature—more specifically forests—turned into an issue when hill dwellers faced two major threats: first, environmental exploitation by outsiders, which increasingly deprived them of their basis of livelihood; second, natural hazards and disasters (like the Alakananda flood in 1970), which were seen as a result of hill denudation. Such incidents have largely disrupted their earlier traditional way of life. Fighting against destructive practices and their sources, however, marks only one dimension. The Chipko protest was equally linked to the emergence of local debates on the importance of the forest cover for the Himalayan ecosystem (and its importance for the plains as well), and on future prospects and sustainable development in the hills. Leaders and activists as well as village men and women started to think about environmentally sound projects of life improvement, and the ways in which nature and natural resources can support this process.

The process of nature becoming an explicit dimension is paralleled by another development: the evolution of political awareness. To fight against the exploitation of forests, sanctioned by the state in the name of national interest, requires reflecting on the role and function of the state within society. Engaging in local development on the basis of sustainable forest use made it necessary for people to evaluate the environmental and developmental politics of the state and its administrative implementation in the region. In short, hill people involved in these enterprises necessarily had to learn to take an explicit political stand. By this means the Chipko movement initiated a processes of politicization culminating in the emergence of a local "public sphere" (in German: *Öffentlichkeit*) and the formation of a "critical publicity" (in German: *kritische Publizität*), which, according to Habermas, has to be seen as its core principle (Habermas 1989). Especially in the heartlands of Chipko, a discursive culture started to spread, involving a whole network of villages and individuals, including intellectuals, teachers, and journalists. According to Habermas, Öffentlichkeit is not deployed to rule, but to control those who are in power, to negotiate rules and regulations of political and social life, and, under certain circumstances, initiate change. In the words of Albert O. Hirschman (1970), the public sphere is "the place of voice rather than of loyalty." In Chipko's core areas, villagers have become increasingly vigilant and alert (*jagrat*), and sensitive to forms of exploitation, injustice, marginalization, inappropriate planning and corruption. They have learned to claim their legitimate rights against the federal and central states—not as petitioners (subjects, subalterns), but as equally entitled citizens. They have also started to formulate concepts of local development and the vision of a self-determined future.

More recent events have proved the political awareness of Paharis. They take up current problems and often react with collective action: localized movements arose against the construction of the Tehri dam, against the selling of alcohol, and for local employment in Kumaon. People complain against the felling of forests and the extraction of forest produce by the "forest mafia." Bhotiyas in eastern Garhwal, living in the buffer zone of the Nanda Devi Biosphere Reserve, have started taking a position against what they call a one-sided ecologically minded policy that severely restricts their use of forests for individual and communal needs (see also Mitra 1993).

Although Habermas's theory of public sphere is relevant to Uttarakhand, one has to take into account the fact that publicity in Uttarakhand seems to be less institutionalized. Therefore it is useful to bring in Partha's concept of "political society," a concept which he thinks more adequate to non-Western conditions and a developing modernity. Chatterjee (1998, 2001a) wants to restrict the term "civil society" to a context which resembles the classical occidental, where "publicity" is constituted in the shape of free associations, salons, coffee-houses, etc. He asks: What about the rest of society which lives outside "civil society?" How can these people interact with the state, how can they bring in their interests? And he introduces another notion, namely "political society." Although the term may lack conceptual clarity as of now, it is meant to describe another form of mediation which allows the integration of large parts of the population into the larger critical discourse. Central for the concept of political society are political parties, but the notion includes less formalized institutions as well: social movements, NGOs, voluntary organizations. Political society takes into account that, in India, individuals and communities of different social background, coming from different regions, urban as well as rural, have increasingly started to articulate their grievances and voice their demands. Chatterjee takes this process of the "democratization of democracy" as characteristic of contemporary India. And, in my opinion, Uttarakhand provides an outstanding example of this.

THE CULTURAL CONSTRUCTION OF IDENTITY AND THE RELATION BETWEEN REGION AND NATION

Identity formation became a central issue over the struggle for a separate hill state, in which large parts of the population were actively involved during the years 1994–6.[14] Of special importance in the present context is the fact that the Uttarakhand movement was neither a separatist (secessionist) nor an ethnicist movement, and that it was not based on exclusively regionalist arguments. Rather, identities of hill residents oscillate between difference and belonging: regional as well as national identities and solidarities—emerging or being affirmed (intensified) during the struggle—are intensely linked, fashioning a particular form of "patriotism,"[15] which is essentially grounded in various ways of culturally constructing nature.

Identity formation in Uttarakhand refers basically to territorial, cultural and religious aspects and I want to give a brief overview of the multiple and complementary ways of defining oneself or one's community.[16] Generally, men and women present themselves as belonging to a particular locality or village (in the case of women this is usually the *mait*, the parents' house). They lay emphasis on the fact that it is their birthplace (*janmbhumi, matribhumi*), the place where the family has long resided. They feel deeply rooted in the local community, which is said to be characterized by solidarity and "brotherhood." Other rationales given for the sense of belonging to a particular village are the assumed purity of surrounding nature (forest, water, air), rights of ownership over land, and the right to use the commons. "All things are ours" (*hamara hai*), people say with pride. In certain parts of Uttarakhand, another strong element of identification is a small sub-regional unit or territory defined primarily by historical and cultural bonds. Residents of Rawain, for example, identify themselves as "Rawaltas" and refer to the particularity of marriage customs (brideprice, polyandry, polygyny), festivals (e.g. a local Diwali), and especially the tradition of resistance (the *dhandak* of Rawain).

The majority of villagers express a strong feeling of being Garhwali or Kumaoni, which also includes mutual distancing. People mention linguistic variation as a main element of intra-Pahari distinction, but they also see major differences in ways of living (*rahan-sahan*), i.e. eating and drinking habits, ways of dressing, carrying loads, and religious festivals. History, education, and advancement are also markers of difference, but they seem less important in the process of identity construction (Kumaonis are said to be more educated as well as more developed in relation to infrastructure, industry, and tourism).

Despite this sense of difference, the concept of being a Pahari normally includes both Garhwalis and Kumaonis.[17] Pahari identity is enacted when people try to distance themselves from the inhabitants of the plains (*maidani log, deshi log*). Residents of Garhwal and Kumaon describe themselves as honest, sincere, and frank (*seedha aur sacché admi*), who value brotherhood, truth, helpfulness, and a sense of community. These exclusively Pahari qualities contrast with the characteristics that are used to describe plains people: they are all said to be thieves (*gundé*), and to be dishonest, untrustworthy, and greedy. And if dishonesty is sometimes to be found in the hills, people are convinced that this is only because bad elements from the plains have negatively influenced hill dwellers. Apparently, nature and environment symbolize and mirror the character of human beings. Villagers made the following comparison: whereas in the hills the weather is cool, the air and water fresh, and peace and freedom (*shanti, swatantrata*) reign, the plains suffer from pollution, heat, mosquitoes, and dirt, and life there is characterized by frantic activity. Pahari people have no wealth but there is no real poverty either; in the plains many are hugely rich but even more are poor and haven't enough to live on.

Villagers from the hills do admit that life in the plains has its advantages—thus slightly correcting the dominating negative image. An important advantage in the plains is greater economic and infrastructural development, resulting in greater mobility and job opportunities. The number and quality of schools and universities allow an incomparably better education for young people of both sexes. Generally speaking, in the plains men and women have a plurality of life options; they can live a life of comfort, with less exhausting work.

Expressing a regional identity as Pahari (or Uttarakhandi) is often explicitly and strongly associated with the idea of being Indian. One of my respondents stressed that she considered herself Uttarakhandi but was also proud to be Bharatvarshi—because India has set a positive example in the cultural, moral, and ethical arena. P. Kumar and E. Mawdsley came across the same phenomenon: both mention that certain slogans raised in favor of the new state combine the region with the nation.[18]

Basically, the argued religious and spiritual quality of the region, evolving from a particular natural environment, is responsible for hill people's ambiguous stance on difference and belonging. High-caste Paharis—nearly 78 percent, and this the vast majority of the hill population—recognize theirs as a region of pan-Indian religious significance: the holy rivers Yamuna and Ganga rise in the Garhwal Himalayas and important pilgrimage centers are located in their upper catchment areas. The temples of Jageshwar in Kumaon, too, attract pilgrims from the whole country. The landscape of the Central Himalayas has always been a retreat for the faithful and the ascetic. People of Uttarakhand worship the main Hindu gods and goddesses, besides their local deities; biannually, they stage the story of Rama and Sita, the *Ramayana*, in a Hindi or local Pahari version. Central episodes of the *Mahabharata* are said to have taken place in the hills, and, in Pandavalila or Pandavanrtya, scenes from the epic are enacted.

Whereas elements of belonging are indicated by Rajputs (often claiming descent from clans in Rajasthan and Gujarat) and immigrant Brahmins, people of all status groups point to differences which distinguish them and their region from the larger part of India.[19] Besides mentioning their language, their cultural and religious traditions, they refer to nature as the main feature of distinction. The very landscape that is sacred and meaningful in the pan-Indian context also helps Paharis to establish a particular territorial identity. The hills are geographically and ecologically set apart from the mainland, they are rich in natural resources such as forest and water, they provide pure air. As a *dharmic* land, the hills are responsible for the religiosity and the honesty of the inhabitants; they provide a morally pure space.[20]

To summarize: the Garhwal and Kumaon Himalayas are perceived as core areas of Hindu India by the majority of their inhabitants, and the regional identity of (high-caste) Paharis suggests a "patriotic" dimension. By demanding their own state they asked to be recognized and respected in their particularity—*because* they are, and not *despite being* a genuine part of the whole. There seems to be some evidence that high-caste patriotism in Uttarakhand is not free from a Hindu nationalist tinge.[21] Besides equating India with Hinduism, and constructing Himalayan nature as a Hindu landscape, Paharis have evolved an anti-Muslim rhetoric.[22] Stereotypes about Muslim character and behavior are frequent, coinciding with expressions of the fear of being cut off from the main part of India by a "Muslim belt" (the districts of Bijnor and Muzzaffarnagar). Though it has never been explicitly voiced, a hidden motive among high-caste Paharis in their struggle for a separate state could have been their desire to be "purified" of a contaminating Muslim influence.

CONCLUSION

In the last few decades, nature in Uttarakhand has ceased to be an implicitly given environment which is appropriated in multiple ways by local residents within their everyday life. It has, rather, become an explicit point of reference in their discursive practices and imaginaries. Today, hill residents refer to nature chiefly in two contexts.

First, nature has become an issue in the pragmatics of life. With traditional modes of existence losing their self-evident character, with nature coming under threat as a result of the destructive practices of state agencies and industry, the role and significance of nature have to be defined afresh. By taking up the example of the forest, I have tried to show that new and complementary perspectives have emerged on the forest, and, together with existing perspectives, these constitute a diverse field of perceptions defining the various attitudes and practices of local and translocal actors. The range of perceptions can be best grasped with the notions of "provider forest," protection forest, and "forest as capital asset" (or commodity).[23] These perspectives on (and uses of) the forest are often contested and the important question is how to balance them regionally, as also at the national level.

After the formation of the new state, other elements of nature—water, minerals, and landscape—became a topic of debate as well. The prevalent question is whether, or in which way and to what extent, natural resources can be used in a non-destructive and sustainable way in the general effort to consolidate state finances as well as support local advancement and life improvement. The evolution of ecological consciousness as well as political awareness among the people of Uttarakhand has been closely linked to the existence of an (exploitative) external opponent—in the form of industrial capital and the neighboring state of Uttar Pradesh (UP). After the foundation of the autonomous hill state, the opponent (UP) has been formally omitted and people have started to use nature and natural resources for the development of their own new state. But, for this reason, the danger of weakening the critical discourse crops up. At this juncture, "political society," which was strengthened during the autonomy movement, and which has brought forth visions of a new political culture and morality in Uttarakhand, has to play its role. It must continue to be vigilant and closely investi-gate industrial and state politics as well as development decisions.

Second, nature has become explicit in the context of cultural symbolism. As topographical space and landscape, nature is quoted to symbolize individual virtues as well as communal qualities, so becoming a conscious element in the process of identity construction. The sacredness and purity of Himalayan nature are said to be reflected in the (assumed) morality of the Pahari community, thus drawing strong boundaries against the (dishonest) people of the plains. Yet, by referring to its translocal religious significance, Himalayan nature is equally potent in justifying Pahari identity as being part of the larger whole—understood largely as Bharat or Hindu India. By making their "Hinduized" nature a symbol of Pahari community and identity, Paharis simultaneously reach the level of current nationalist imaginaries.

NOTES

1. Uttarakhand (literally meaning "land in the north") comprises the two regions of Garhwal and Kumaon. Since November 9, 2000 these regions form the new state of Uttaranchal, which was carved out of the state of Uttar Pradesh. Apparently, the old and widely known name Uttarakhand would have been preferred as the state name by the local population.

2. For Uttarakhand's history of forestry and history of protest, see R. Guha 1983a and 1983b, and 1989; Pant n.d. [1922]; A. Pathak 1994; S. Pathak 1991 and 1998; Rawat 1991 and 1992a and 1992b; Saklani 1987; Tucker 1982.

3. Field research was conducted between 1993 and 1996 in western Garhwal (Rawain, district Uttarkashi) and in Eastern Garhwal (District Chamoli); here I worked with villagers in the vicinity of Gopeshwar, and with Bhotiya communities in the Nanda Devi region.

4. Additionally, the forest is always a shared space: no community enjoys exclusive rights and access. It is primarily shared with other human beings (those of one's own village, as well as from neighboring villages), who use and appropriate certain parts of the jungle. It is also shared with non-human beings—animals, gods (devtas), evil spirits (matri, bhutas), normally occupying those parts of the forest which are more dense and remote, and located at higher altitudes. The forest also has to be "shared" with paramount political institutions that claim access to it, and which control and regulate the local appropriation.

5. Approximately 78 percent of the population of Uttarakhand is of high-caste origin (Rajputs and Brahmins), followed by 17 percent Scheduled Castes, 3 percent tribals, and 2 percent members of Other Backward Classes (OBC).

6. I do not intend to romanticize earlier forms of common property resource management (Das 2000); I only want to indicate that individual and collective responsibility for natural resources has existed in parts of western Garhwal, at least to a certain extent.

7. The function of wazir is still existent. A wazir (usually a Rajput) has to look after the finances of the deity. He is also responsible for the organization of the god's journeys (*yatra*) and in former times was expected to accompany the deity.

8. In the area of Bangan, between the rivers Tons and Pabar, an epic tradition of rendering the *Mahabharata* is still alive and the *Mahabharata* is here sung by specialists. Zoller 1994, 1996. In other parts of the region, different forms of Pandavalila, dramatic performances from the life of the five Pandava brothers and their wife Draupadi, are celebrated. Sax 2002. The less elaborate form seems to be the Pandava Nrtya (dance of the Pandavas), mostly short performances which can be seen on several occasions all round the year. In these, certain villagers are possessed by individual brothers of the Pandavas (Arjuna and Bhima, preferably) or by their common wife, Draupadi. In my area of research Harijans are involved in Pandava performances. They are possessed by what are called *bana* devtas, mostly interpreted as deities linked with or symbolizing the arrow (bana). Bana devtas are the *shakti* (power) of the Pandavas, with whom they build a symbiotic unity. Members of the Scheduled Castes in Garhwal call themselves Harijans; their consciousness of being "Dalit" is emerging only now.

9. This distinction was first made by Erving Goffman. Anthony Giddens connects the spatial and social separation of "back" and "front" regions to practical consciousness and the operation of normative sanctions. Giddens 1979: 207.

10. For the behavior of women in the forest, see also Krengel 1989. As a back region, the forest also provides security and protection in times of conflict. It is recorded that, during the reign of Narendra Shah (Raja of Tehri, 1919–46) village people who were accused of offenses against forest laws withdrew into the safety of the jungle when persecuted by the king's officials. During my research in the 1990s young men disappeared several times into the jungle for a couple of days, after

serious quarrels. In each case, they returned silently after the issue had been calmed, after which nobody openly discussed the matter again.

11. Whether Chipko can be interpreted as a women's movement is controversial. See especially K. Sharma n.d.; S. Jain 1984; B. Agarwal 1991, who have argued against such an interpretation.

12. I refer to M.W. Lewis 1992 who has categorized existing forms of radical environmental ethics into "deep ecologies," views from the classical left, and ecofeminism. See also Guha 2000; Guha and Martinez-Alier 1998.

13. The concepts (philosophies) of Bahuguna and Bhatt are much more complex than presented here. For a detailed discussion, see Linkenbach forthcoming.

14. For detailed accounts of the movement, see Pradeep Kumar 2000; Linkenbach 2002a; Mawdsley 1996 and 1997.

15. I use "patriotism" in C.A. Bayly's sense. In his view the term describes a "sense of loyalty to place and institutions which bound some Indians, even in the immediate precolonial period, to their regional homelands." Bayly 1998: vii.

16. Every person embraces a plurality of identities and it is an important aspect of his/her "self" (i.e. his/her remaining the same person) to be able to "manage" and to enact them according to contexts. Sökefeld 1999: 424.

17. The identity of a Pahari is very different from that of an Uttarakhandi. The Uttarakhandi identity is a new, political identity, mainly embraced by people who were intellectually and practically strongly involved in the autonomy struggle. Members of the Bania, Jain, and Punjabi communities who have migrated to the hills and work in small-scale business regard themselves as Uttarakhandi. Not rooted in the region and for a long time enjoying only a limited sense of belonging, they seem to have been helped, by the autonomy struggle for separate statehood, to gain a positive regional identity.

18. *Bharat desh rahey akandh, le kar rahenge Uttarakhand*—Long live united India, we shall get Uttarakhand! *Jai Bharat, Jai Uttarakhand*—Viva India, viva Uttarakhand. See Pradeep Kumar 2000: 104; Mawdsley 1997: 2230.

19. Harijans in western Garhwal construct their regional identity with special reference to the Himalayan landscape as a place of mythical events. Harijans largely participate in the social and religious life and are in particular involved in the cult of the Pandavas (see note 8).

20. Nature also plays a role in constructing regional historiography. In the work of Rai Pati Ram Bahadur the conditions of nature are correlated with qualities of rule and conditions of life in the different historical periods. Bahadur 1992 (1916); Linkenbach 2002b.

21. The hill regions of Garhwal and Kumaon have been a stronghold of the Bharatiya Janata Party (BJP). In the Lok Sabha elections of 2004, three seats out of five were won by the BJP in Uttaranchal.

22. Mukul Sharma has argued that environmental myths and Hindu-nationalist constructions of landscape have entered the language of social movements, especially in Uttaranchal. He also says the anti-Tehri dam movement has recently invoked popular stereotypes of the Muslim community. Sharma 2002.

23. The distinction between these perspectives was made by Franz Heske, a German forester employed as forest adviser in the years 1929/30 by Narendra Shah, then Raja of Tehri Garhwal. Heske used the German notions of "Schutzwald," "Ertragswald," and "Versorgungswald." Heske 1931.

7

INDIGENOUS NATURES

Forest and Community Dynamics in Meghalaya, North-East India

Bengt G. Karlsson

THIS ESSAY REVOLVES AROUND THE POLITICS OF INDIGENOUSNESS and nature in India.[1] More precisely, it relates to the struggle over forests and land in Meghalaya, a small hill state of almost two million people situated in the north-eastern region. The majority of people in Meghalaya consist of so-called tribal or indigenous peoples (85 percent), the main ones being Khasi, Jaintia, and Garo (groups that also give names to the three main areas, Khasi Hills, Jaintia Hills and Garo Hills).[2] In the literature, these three communities are perhaps best known for their matrilineal kinship system where descent is traced through the female line and land rights—which we will be particularly concerned with here—are held by the woman. My point of departure is a book by the anthropologist A.C. Sinha on the environmental history of the eastern Himalayan region. Sinha, who lives in Shillong (the capital of Meghalaya), begins his study thus:

> It all started with the occasional observations on the tree cover around the highway between Shillong to Gauhati during the last fifteen years. Slowly and slowly, hills turned naked, trees have become fewer, scattered and younger: thickets have replaced the clumps of trees and settlements have sprung up all around. During the dry days one comes across even clouds of dust. From nowhere a new problem of drinking water in the abode of clouds—Meghalaya—has been added to the list of the urgent issues which are to be attended. Then, one is startled on the paradoxical expression: "the wet desert

of Cherrapunji." The Government Forest Officials claim not to be responsible for the alleged rape of forests as they hardly control an appreciable acreage of the forests. It is the community, represented by the district council, which controls and manages the extensive forests as per constitutional provisions. Elsewhere [in India] the environmentalists are articulating the issue as a conflict between the state control and community interests, and demanding the forest to be given back to the community as they were in the hands of local communities in the pre-colonial days. Is it so that the community control has led to destruction of forests in this region?[3]

As Sinha rightly argues, the situation in the north-eastern hill areas differs greatly from that in mainland India. The bulk of the forests are, as pointed out, formally in the hands of communities, under the control of the so-called autonomous district councils (hereafter district councils), rather than with the forest department, as elsewhere in India. In Meghalaya only about four percent of the total area constitutes reserved forests and protected areas (national parks and sanctuaries) under the forest department. In India as a whole, the same areas under forest department control come up to about a quarter of the geographical area of the country.

In any case, what does the north-eastern experience tell us? Sinha has a straightforward answer: "community control over the forest resources has completely failed to safeguard the forests."[4] If this is correct, it certainly has important implications for the larger debate about conservation and forest management in India and other parts of the third world, where concerned scholars, aid donors, and environmental organizations are advocating community involvement as the best way of protecting the remaining forests. Are they all heading in the wrong direction? Are communities, in this case indigenous people, as bad or even worse than state departments in managing forests in a sustainable fashion?

Before beginning to answer such questions, one needs to ask what "community control" implies and what sort of community involvement we are actually talking about in the north-eastern case. As recent literature on conservation and resource management in South Asia has pointed out, the notion of "community" is deeply problematic and in need of serious unpacking.[5] What this critique points to is that much of the development discourse on "joint forest management," "eco-development" and the like is based on rather naïve perceptions of communities as small-scale, homogeneous territorial units (the self-evident atoms of rural polities). Agrawal and Gibson rightly argue that such understandings fail to take into account differences within communities; differences that indeed "affect resource management outcomes."[6] As they put it, communities thus need to be reconceptualized as "complex entities containing individuals differentiated by status, political and economic power, religion, and social prestige, and intentions."[7] And here we must also stress differences based on gender.[8] Such reconceptualization allows a critical scrutiny of existing structures of dominance that tend to disappear or are played down by populist understandings of "community" as the embodiment of grassroots democracy, solidarity and equity.[9] Sinha is not unaware that the term community can conceal internal differences, and he raises the question of who is controlling the forest in the name of "communal control." But he does not really engage the question seriously and, as mentioned, sticks to his main conclusion that community forest management has proved disastrous in northeast India.

At the outset, I would argue that the whole idea that lands and resources in Meghalaya are in the hands of communities is seriously misleading. Even if, for example, forests are under the jurisdiction of the district councils, de facto ownership and control are to a large extent with private persons, lineages, or clans. There are community and village forests, but these seem today to make up a rather nominal part of the total forest lands in the state. The word "seem" is important here. The simple fact is that nobody really knows. No comprehensive land survey has been conducted, and, as most landholdings lacks formal registration, actual ownership and forms of management are unclear, to say the least. There have been several attempts by the state to carry out cadastral surveys, but—as I have been told over and over again in meetings with forest officers and other government servants—because of popular resistance all such attempts have proven futile. It appears that opposition to the mapping and registration of land is the result of a fear that this will lead to taxation and other forms of government interference.[10] It is also argued that politicians and influential persons with an interest in keeping landholdings away from public scrutiny have instigated or misled people toward such a stand.[11] Be that as it may, what nevertheless seems to have taken place is a far-reaching privatization of land at the expense of earlier "communal" institutions of land management that were a part of swidden or *jhum* cultivation. I will come back to this point, that landownership is highly complicated and suffers great variation in different parts of Meghalaya. In general, however, it could be argued that we have a bifurcated set-up of, on the one hand, the erosion of community-based institutions in relation to land and resource management, and, on the other, a very significant development of private ownership of land and the subsequent exploitation of forest and other natural resources. The sociologist Julius L. R. Marak, claims that the transfer of clan land (so-called A'king land) into private holdings has gone so far in the Garo Hills that the entire system of traditional land management is at risk.[12] In the Khasi Hills a similar process of converting communal or so-called Ri Raid land into private land goes on. This, among other things, has created a new and growing section of landless people in Khasi society.[13]

Coming back to the issue of deforestation, then, it is important to stress that this has taken place in a situation of multiple and changing property regimes, with the increased influence of private ownership. Communities have in fact little say in the management of forests, and thus it is hardly justifiable to blame communities for the destruction of forests in Meghalaya. The district councils are entitled, under special forest acts,[14] to manage and control all forests in their respective areas, but they have for various reasons abstained from or failed to take this responsibility. Timber has been one of the main sources of revenues for the district councils, thus apparently making them less inclined to regulate the felling of trees.[15]

In this essay I explore a number of issues concerning conflicting interests and uses of the forest in Meghalaya. I hope to show that the politics of nature is intrinsically linked to ethnic mobilization and aspirations for increased political autonomy; and these aspirations or struggles are increasingly being framed in terms of indigenous peoples' rights and their stewardship of nature.

ETHNIC HOMELANDS

An experienced ecologist in charge of an international development program in community resource management told me during a field tour in the Garo Hills that the rise of militancy in the area over the past ten years had to a large extent to do with mistaken government development policies. The dominant strategy of the state during the past few decades has been to encourage permanent cultivation as a substitute for shifting cultivation.[16] As more and more lands have been converted into tree plantations, tea gardens, orange groves, and other forms of permanent cash crop cultivation, there is now an acute shortage of land for shifting cultivation.

The new plantations have not been able to generate a sufficient alternative income for people, due among other things to poor market linkages. Shifting or jhum cultivation—as it is known in most parts of the north-eastern hills—thus remains the main form of livelihood for the majority. Less land implies the shortening of fallow cycles, and as a result a decreased return, alongside increased soil degradation and other detrimental environmental effects, all leading to a severe ecological crisis in the Garo Hills. As the population has increased over this period, the situation has deteriorated even further. The final blow to livelihood in the hills was the Supreme Court order of 1996, which, as I will later discuss, put a moratorium on the felling of trees. The ecologist argued the need to check the alarming rate of deforestation, but again suggested that the state failed to act in ways that resonated with the needs and aspirations of local people. The state, he further argued, had *never* understood shifting cultivation, and had never bothered consulting or taking people's knowledge and skills into consideration in the framing of policies and development programs. Because of this, most development initiatives had failed, and the state has lost credibility among the population at large. This has bred discontent, particularly among the young, whom the insurgency outfits have been able to recruit.[17]

There are certainly other stories to be told when explaining the emergence of violent separatism and militancy in the Garo Hills,[18] but I think the above account captures some crucial insights worth pursuing. The forest is the backbone of livelihood in the Garo Hills, as well as in other parts of Meghalaya, and loss of control over this vital resource is bound to have serious repercussions. The colonial policy of establishing forest reserves at the turn of the twentieth century led to a massive uproar in these hills and is commonly regarded as the first spark of modern political organization among the Garos,[19] even as the beginning of Garo nationalism.[20] The leader of the movement, Sonaram R. Sangma, is invoked today by the political party Garo National Council (GNC), as well as by the outlawed militant outfit A'chik National Volunteers' Council (ANVC), to support their claim for a separate Garoland. It is hard to tell the extent to which Garos today share such aspirations for an ethnic homeland. The GNC has, for example, during its long existence, never been able to generate much electoral support.[21] Yet there is strong dissatisfaction with the present system of governance, most believing it has failed to improve economic and social conditions in the Garo Hills. Poor healthcare, lack of education facilities, pathetic roads, and a general underdevelopment of the physical infrastructure are commonly highlighted. Similar failures of state-run development are also cited for north-east India in general. This, as the political scientist Sanjib Baruah argues, has created a deeply felt notion among the public that the region's underdevelopment is the consequence of a persisting colonial relationship with "mainland" India. Baruah describes this in the case of Assam:

> The question of Assam's claim to its resources has been a persistent theme in the politics of Assamese subnationalism. There is probably no other area where the political demands of separatist militants are more continuous with mainstream Assamese social discourse than the issue of Assam's economic underdevelopment and what is described either as the "neglect" of Assam by New Delhi or as a colonial relationship.[22]

Baruah describes how financial flows or development funds, channeled from the central government to the state governments, are commonly perceived as mainly enriching contractors and license holders who work hand in glove with corrupt politicians. Such people are unconcerned with the long-term development of the region. This, he argues, creates a fertile soil for organizations speaking of the need for increased autonomy or self-determination.[23]

Compared to other parts of India, tribal communities in the north-east enjoying provisions under the Indian constitution's Sixth Schedule are often seen as being in a favorable position. As the sociologist Virginius Xaxa puts it, such peoples of the north-east "exercise some power over their territory," a scenario "just the opposite in other parts of tribal India."[24] Yet, even if this can in general be said to be correct, it is interesting that more or less all tribal or indigenous peoples in the north-east speak of their lack of control over land and resources, and thus argue for increased "self-determination." Autonomy movements have thus dominated the political scene in north-east India even since Independence. In many cases, such movements have turned into armed struggles, the most well-known cases being the five-decades-long Naga assertion for sovereignty.

To accommodate such aspirations, after Independence the Indian government adopted constitutional provisions under its Sixth Schedule for the creation of autonomous district councils in the hill areas of the then undivided Assam. These councils were given relatively far-reaching self-governing powers, and above all jurisdiction over land, forests (except reserved forests) and natural resources, all to be managed in accordance with customary law. This was done in the name of allowing "tribal peoples" to manage their own affairs and maintain their culture and traditions without outside interference. The Sixth Schedule builds to a large extent on the previous colonial policy of a special administration of areas defined as "excluded" or "partly excluded," areas where outsiders needed special permission to enter, where general Indian laws do not apply, and where only the local people may own land. The district council is nevertheless a modern institution based on political parties and an elected leadership, and this undermines the powers of traditional chiefs and headmen. District councils have, for example, the right to appoint and suspend chiefs.[25] As the Sixth Schedule failed to appease the sentiments of many hill peoples, the Naga leaders rejected it straightaway; the central government later opted for the creation of union territories and new states, and north-east India today comprises seven separate states. Meghalaya, as one of them, came into being as a full-fledged state in 1972.[26] It was earlier regarded as the peaceful exception in north-east India. Now, with two active armed organizations—namely the Hynniewtrep National Liberation Council (HNLC) which is fighting for a separate state for the Khasis and Jaintias (or the Hynniewtrep people);[27] and the earlier mentioned ANVC which is struggling for a separate Garoland; not to mention various other external insurgency groups seeking refuge in the state—the culture of political violence has increasingly come to pervade civil society.[28]

A significant development during the 1990s was that self-determination demands in north-east India were increasingly articulated in terms of "indigenousness," or in the global language of indigenous rights.[29] Speaking at the United Nations Working Group of Indigenous Populations in Geneva, 1994, P. K. Debbarma and Apam Muivah state that "indigenous peoples" in north-east India are "losing control over their land" and that they are being "systematically marginalized." They assert that they, the indigenous peoples, are "nationalities" with "right to self-determination."[30] This is echoed in other statements. For example, in the resolution of a meeting by various tribal organizations in north-east India, it was claimed that the right to self-determination is a "prerequisite" for their very survival as people. It is stated here that indigenous peoples' way of land management is not respected and that the region's natural resources are being exploited by outsiders in the name of development and nation-building. According to the resolution, indigenous peoples are capable of safeguarding their "land and forest without any state/central intervention."[31] Expressed in a less direct way, but nevertheless sharing the same sense of insecurity in relation to control over land and resources, well-known member of the Indian Parliament,

Professor G.G. Swell, said (in relation to a Khasi celebration of the United Nations Year of Indigenous Peoples in 1993): "we share with the rest of the world's indigenous peoples our critical dependence on our land and vulnerability. Take away the land from us and we can easily be swamped, uprooted and dispersed."[32]

Similarly, in a newspaper article,[33] the former president of the Khasi Students' Union (KSU), Paul Lyngdoh,[34] places the Khasi demand for self-determination in the context of universal indigenous peoples' rights. He points out that the Indian government has not recognized India's tribal communities as "indigenous peoples." To him this seems part of a strategy to deny these communities their "inalienable right" to self-determination or self-governance, a right that, as he points out, is approved by the United Nations' Declaration on Rights of Indigenous Peoples (Article 3, of the Draft Declaration). Lyngdoh points to the twenty-five Khasi native states that remained "semi-independent" up to Indian Independence and, it is claimed, formally and legally never joined the Indian union.[35] Rather than in the present system of district councils, Lyngdoh puts his hope in a remodeled and modernized form of the traditional governing bodies among the Khasis.[36]

There are also attempts by the leaders of these traditional political bodies to assert themselves and take a more active role in the public life of the state. The Syiem (king) of Hima Mylliem (one of the Khasi states), namely Laborious Manik S. Syiem, has been leading an initiative to get constitutional protection for the rights of the Khasi states and their traditional institutions. He and other syiems in the Federation of Khasi states urged the National Commission for Review of the Constitution to rectify the degradation of customary laws that followed the establishment of district councils, arguing that these politically elected bodies were granted powers that superseded the traditional dorbars (durbars) of the Khasi states.[37] For these leaders it is a question of upholding ancient Khasi democracy against the onslaught of an imposed, alien Western democratic system followed by mainland India.[38] In the cultural sphere, the organization Seng Khasi pursues a similar cause, mainly focusing on the revival and preservation of a traditional Khasi religion and customs. This organization, which has been around for more than hundred years, now has increased public support and has gained renewed interest for itself within the younger generation.[39]

For an outsider, this talk about political, economic, and cultural marginalization might come as a surprise in a state like Meghalaya, which is actually dominated by the three mentioned communities, i.e. Khasis, Jaintias, and Garos. All the political leaders in the state come, for example, from these communities, and as much as 80 percent of government jobs are reserved for them. There is a land transfer act of 1971 (with several later amendments) that restricts all sale of land to non-tribals. Land sale transactions need to be approved by the dorbars or village councils, again protecting local people against unwanted land deeds or the sort of land alienation that has taken place in most other parts of tribal India.[40] This indeed might confirm Xaxa's view, cited earlier, that tribal peoples in the north-east have at least some control over their territories. This notwithstanding, people feel they are being dominated by "outsiders" (by the *dkhar*, as people from the plains are referred to in the Khasi Hills). In the build-up to the 2003 elections for the Meghalaya state assembly, two livelihood issues stood out in the media as being of particular public importance. The first was the incumbent government's proposal to amend the Land Transfer Act to allow eight additional tribal groups—for example, the Hajongs, Rabhas, Koch, and Karbis—to buy land in the state.[41] The second issue was the long-standing conflict relating to uranium mining in West Khasi Hill district. This conflict was a strong popular reaction that developed from the mining process initiated by the Uranium Corporation of India, a Government of India undertaking. This corporation announced its determination to go ahead with the project.

In the first case, the debate has largely centred on the question of who is to be recognized as falling within the "indigenous tribes" of Meghalaya, and subsequently whether any tribal community other than the Khasis, Jaintias, and Garos should be entitled to such status. A large number of political and social organizations in the Khasi Hills have strongly objected to the proposed amendment, saying that such a move will put genuine indigenous communities at the risk of being ousted from their own homelands.[42] The act itself, however, does not make any reference to "indigenous tribes," but is built rather on the two categories "tribal" and "non-tribal." The purpose of the act, as it states it, is "to regulate transfer of land in Meghalaya for the protection of the interests of the Scheduled Tribes therein." No land should be transferred from a tribal to a non-tribal. The act further defines "tribal," as "a person belonging to any of the Scheduled Tribes pertaining to Meghalaya" (as specified in the Constitution Order of 1950). Many of the shortlisted tribes, as far as I can see, are already covered by the act. Without going further into the details of the matter, what interests me here is the apparent heat that any land issue generates. This points to the sense of insecurity—the lack of "ontological security"[43]—as expressed in Swell's 1993 speech, when referring to the Khasi "vulnerability" and the risk of their being "swamped, uprooted and dispersed." In the case of the uranium mining, the debates relate to the apparent health risks and environmental hazards involved. In addition, subsequently, there is the question of who will derive the benefits and royalties from the mining. The understandable fear is that local people have to bear the environmental costs while the profits accrue elsewhere.[44] Similar arguments are also put forth in the debate around plans to tap the hydroelectric potential of the state, i.e. that resources are floating out of the state, leaving local people as poor as ever. But the most controversial issue during the last few years concerns control over the forest, triggered by the Supreme Court intervention to halt deforestation by imposing a so-called "timber ban."

THE "TIMBER BAN"

During my first stay in Meghalaya in early 2000, I landed in the middle of the "timber-ban" controversy. The ban was on everyone's lips and most of the people I talked to in Shillong described it as yet another example of New Delhi's insensitive exercise of power. I was invited to take part in a one-day workshop on the timber ban, arranged in one of the nicer hotels in Shillong. Influential persons from all walks of life participated: senior representatives of the state government, forest department officials, development organizations, researchers, journalists, and civil society groups. All, except the forest department officer (in charge of monitoring the Supreme Court's order), condemned the timber ban. The forest officer claimed it was in fact not a ban but rather a temporal moratorium on timber operations until approved working plans had been established. Nobody took notice of this point, and "ban" was what everyone else seemed to accept as the most relevant term. The minister of finance said the loss of revenue from timber was ruining the state's finances, not to speak of loss of employment as, for example, almost the entire sawmill industry had closed down. A Catholic nun running a boarding school said they were no longer getting students from rural areas, and she urged in a most emotional way that, for the sake of children, the timber ban had to go. Tiplut Nongbri, a sociologist from Jawaharlal Nehru University in Delhi (originally from Shillong) described the severe consequences the ban had on women's lives, and she questioned the legal basis of the Supreme Court order, saying it violated the autonomy of tribal communities under the Sixth Schedule.[45] One of the organizers, Dev Nathan, a political scientist working at the Centre for International Forestry Research in Indonesia, spoke of the serious environmental consequences of the ban: people had started making charcoal out of valuable timber, begun selling the bark of standing tress, or converting woodlands into *jhum* fields as trees no longer had any market value. The ban was thus not only "anti-people," but also "anti-environment." Nathan ended by questioning the very rationale of the Supreme Court's intervention. Quoting the forest department's latest forest assessment, he said Meghalaya had a forest cover of as much as 69.8 percent of the state's total geographical area. And, as he pointed out, this figure was based on data derived from satellite images. The National Forest Policy recommendation for hill areas was, he said, a 66 percent forest cover, this being less than Meghalaya's. Why then should the people of Meghalaya be penalized or "banned," he asked rhetorically.[46]

The Supreme Court intervention derived from a lawsuit in the early 1990s by a private person against the Indian union, alleging state failure to control logging.[47] The case concerned, initially, Tamil Nadu, and later, because of a reported large-scale loss of forests, north-east India was also included.[48] The Supreme Court order of December 1996 states that "all ongoing activity in any Forest [. . .] without prior approval of the Central Government, must cease forthwith" (Paragraph 1). The court's additional order of January 1998, similarly, speaks of the suspension of timber operations and other wood-based industries until the concerned state governments had developed working plans approved by the central government.

In a critical scrutiny of the order, Nongbri draws particular attention to two things. First, as indicated above, that the Supreme Court order bypasses the Sixth Schedule in which the autonomous district councils are given full jurisdiction over all forests, except those declared reserved and protected areas. In the name of forest conservation, the Supreme Court now entrusts power over all forests—as stated in the order, "irrespective of ownership and classification thereof"—to the forest department or the state through the requirement of approved working plans. Second, the usage of the term "forest" in the Supreme Court order fails to take into account the particular situation of the north-eastern region where shifting cultivation is still the dominant form of agriculture. As Nongbri points out, the Khasis have a most intricate system of ownership and management of land, and above all there is no "clear-cut separation between land and forests." People of course do conceptually make a distinction between land and forest (and have different terms for the two), but as the very nature of shifting cultivation is such that trees and bushes reclaim land that has been cultivated, the boundary between the two is constantly blurred or in flux. The Supreme Court does not take these very basic features into consideration and, by stating that the order should apply to "all forests," it in fact imposes centralized state control over most of the lands and resources that people depend on for their livelihood. The relative autonomy and freedom that tribal communities in the north-east previously enjoyed has thus seriously been constrained. To Nongbri this is not an accident but "symptomatic of the state's attitude to the rights of indigenous people.". The underlying assumption, which she questions, is that state institutions rather than tribal people are best suited to conserve or manage nature in a sustainable fashion. Deforestation has to be checked, but, according to her, more sophisticated measures are needed that, above all, differentiate between subsistence farmers' use of the forest and outside contractors' large-scale timber extraction (Nongbri 2001: 1895–7).

Prior to the ban there was pressure from within the state, advocating radical measures to control the timber trade and thus protect the forests. The otherwise stern promoters of indigenous self-rule, the KSU in 1996 filed a public interest litigation in the Guwahati High Court urging a ten-year moratorium on logging as well as the closure of all saw and veneer mills. According to the KSU, forests were virtually being wiped out in the state. Hundreds of trucks were daily carrying loads of timber down to the plains, and the timber trade was mainly in the hands of contractors from outside the state.[49] The KSU thus came out as supporters of the ban and had to take a lot of criticism for this by the public. Some claim that the timber contractors and, above all, the lobby group Meghalaya Land and Forest Owners' Association, were the most vocal protesters. It is nevertheless clear that the ban changed in a stroke the life of a large group of people who were dependent on the timber trade. The journalist Sanat K. Chakraborty, in a study of the effects of the ban in the Western Khasi Hills, describes a sudden collapse of the timber-driven local economy, putting not only timber traders and daily workers out of business, but also all those who made a living out of ancillary services (tea-stall wallahs, road-garage owners, shopkeepers, truckers, etc.). This naturally created large discontent and an outcry against the Supreme Court intervention. But in the midst of all this, Chakraborty still found those who spoke in favor of the ban, calling it a "blessing in disguise."[50]

When I got back to Shillong two years later, the issue had settled considerably and I found public opinion less critical of the ban. The view now was that it was, after all, an inevitable step, and the timber trade would have come to an end sooner or later as there would be no more trees to cut. The critique focused more now on how the whole thing was carried out, pointing to the lack of back-up plans and measures to provide alternative means of survival for those hardest hit. It was also argued that illegal trade in timber still flourished and that trees were increasingly being converted to charcoal. A more comprehensive and participatory environmental strategy should have foreseen and taken these into consideration.

There were also now temporary relaxations of the ban, allowing the controlled felling of trees in areas under "working schemes," approved by the Ministry of Environment and Forests. In future, the forest wings of the district councils were supposed to take a much more active role in developing regular working plans, register land and monitoring—together with the state forest department—all forest-related activities in areas under their jurisdiction. But considering the lack of trained staff, and technical equipment as well as financial resources in the district council, it is hard to see how this will happen.[51]

But again, staff and resources are evidently not in themselves a guarantee for successful forest management. The forest department, while the second biggest government department in Meghalaya, has only direct control over a small portion of forests in the state. In spite of this, the department was found incapable or rather directly responsible for the devastation of two reserved forests—described as undisturbed "high forests" of immense ecological value—in the Garo Hills. After reports of rampant illegal logging in these forests during the 1990s an independent inquiry commission was set up in 1996 to look into the matter. According to the findings of the commission, approximately 45,000 trees had been illegally cut inside the reserves.[52] The commission pointed to a "systemic collapse" of the forest administration as the main factor responsible for the illegal felling. As the commission report states: "[T]he responsibility for this state of affairs is to be shared by all officers of the Forest Department in the entire chain of command."[53] The High Powered Committee for the North Eastern Region, set up to monitor the implementation of the Supreme Court order, has been equally outspoken, saying that "forest and other government officers and the politicians" in collusion with "mill owners and forests contractors" are responsible for large-scale illegal felling in north-east India.[54] So, even if the forest department has been more successful in preserving other reserved forests in Meghalaya, the example here shows it would be a mistake to think that transferring more forest to the state administration is the answer.[55] Taking a step back: was the Supreme Court ban called for at all, considering the alleged forest cover of the state is supposed to be 69.8 percent of total land?

READING NATURE

Meghalaya prides itself for its richness in flora and fauna, one of the "world's hot-spots of biodiversity," as is often pointed out in official gatherings.[56] The budding tourism industry also uses the "lavish nature" of Meghalaya as its main selling point. Forests and wildlife are indeed plentiful, but I think that anyone who travels extensively through the state would have serious doubts about the correctness of the stated forest cover as close to 70 percent. Barren hills, grasslands, and highly degraded forests are most common in the state. In the larger debate about the state of affairs of the world's forests, opinions differ greatly. Are the forests really being lost in such an alarming fashion, as one is made to believe through, for example, mass media reports on tropical deforestation? How much forest is there, and further, what kinds of forests are lost and what remains? Questions like these are subjects for debate, and, indeed, have proved hard to answer. Even with the help of recent techniques such as satellite imaging, great uncertainties remain.[57] The Principal Chief Conservator of Forests in Meghalaya, Balvinder Singh, confirms the figure of 69.8 percent forest cover. When I met him, he showed me the Indian State Forest Report of 1999,[58] and emphasized the correctness of the figure.[59] This report also contains color forest maps for each state, extracted via satellite images. In the case of Meghalaya, the map is largely light greenish, meaning that most of the state is covered by "open forests." Dark green areas, denoting "dense forests," are relatively few and more limited in size. These areas are concentrated mainly in the Garo Hills and the bordering Western Khasi Hills. To the east, on the Central Khasi Hills plateau and large parts of the Jaintia Hills, the map is mostly white, denoting "non-forest" areas. Put in numbers, the report assesses the total forest cover at roughly 16,000 sq. km, or 69.8 percent of the total geographical area. Of these forests, about 6000 sq. km are classified as "dense forest" and 10,000 sq. km as "open forest." The report notices an increase of dense forest and a slight total loss of forest (compared to the assement two years earlier). Shifting cultivation is said to have caused the loss. Logging is not mentioned. The overall impression, however, is that things are under control, and that there is no cause for alarm. In view of this, the Supreme Court intervention seems questionable, particularly considering that it targets the timber trade and not shifting cultivation, which is held to be the main threat to the forest.

Let us look a bit closer at the issue. In the report, "forest cover" means "all lands with a tree canopy density of more than 10 percent;" open forest 10–40 percent; and dense forest 40 percent canopy density and above.[60] As open forest is the most prevalent, it appears crucial to discover more about exactly what kind of forest comes under this category. The report mentions the difficulty of satellite assessments in differentiating between forests and "bushy vegetation" or plantations such as those of tea and coffee.[61] In Meghalaya there are large areas with various types of plantations, and further jhum land that, after being quickly cultivated, is covered by bamboo, bushes, and other "secondary vegetation." The question that arises is: to what extent are such types of vegetation registered as (open) forest.

The Meghalaya state homepage gives a much more modest assessment of the forest. Of the total area of the state, which is 22,429 sq. km, only 8514 sq. km are said to be forests.[62] This would give a 38 percent forest cover. There is no information on how this estimate is reached, or how the term "forest" is used. Other reports also confirm substantially lower forest cover than the State of Forests Report. A senior officer at the Ministry of Environment and Forests told me jokingly that it would be more correct to talk about a 69.8 percent vegetation cover. A retired chief conservator of forests states that the forest cover was around 70 percent prior to Independence, and that it was down to about 44 percent in the early 1990s.[63] To be sure, different understandings of what makes a forest, or forest cover, are at play here. Forest is certainly not a neutral or self-evident category. The history of forest management teaches us that the entire exercise of mapping and measuring forests has at least as much to do with political and administrative concerns, as with biological and ecological methods of classifying forests.[64] It could be argued that reading nature and interpreting environmental change is always a question of one's perspective or interest.[65] But even if the forest cover, type of forest, and rate of deforestation remain disputed, one can at least assume that if logging has had such an enormous importance—which all seem to agree on for Meghalaya—there must have been a sizeable out-take of timber. This also takes us back to the words of Sinha, and his observation that the forests of Meghalaya are diminishing day by day, causing serious environmental damage such as shortages of water and soil erosion. Is this what is actually happening in the state? Many claim that this is the case.

The noted ecologist P. S. Ramakrishnan describes the general situation in north-east India in the early 1990s as follows:

> Large-scale timber extraction has been carried out in this region during the last few decades. In fact, a substantial part of the timber needs of the country is met from the north-east. The secondary damage done to the forest due to the falling trees during timber harvest, destroying everything else in their path, is also substantial.[66]

When the forest is cleared of trees, various exotic and native seeds take over, often creating a bald grass landscape where trees cannot regenerate in their natural way. This, he argues further, in its turn narrows the land available for jhum cultivation, and adds pressure to an agricultural system already under great stress with population increase.[67] Ramakrishnan has carried out extensive research on shifting cultivation in north-east India (and Meghalaya in particular). He describes a drastic shortening of the jhum cycle from an earlier sustainable interval of twenty years or more, down to the present-day cycle of four to five years (in some areas even less). According to him, a ten-year cycle could be made both economically and ecologically viable, but below that shifting cultivation starts degrading the ecosystem.[68] In his analysis, the large-scale extraction of timber, together with an increasingly unsustainable jhum cultivation, creates a vicious circle that severely affects water flow and soil fertility. In extreme cases, degradation of the forest ecosystem can lead to "total desertification," which too has taken place in large areas of the Western Khasi Hills.[69]

There are certainly those who will refute this type of eco-crisis scenario. In the contemporary literature on forests and deforestation, a number of researchers have started to question such gloomy accounts in which, first of all, large-scale losses of tropical forest are taken at face value, and as a corollary it is assumed that deforestation always triggers negative spirals of ecological destruction.[70] Even if their warnings against jumping to hasty conclusions about the burgeoning ecosystem breakdown should be taken seriously, some researchers have clearly taken this argument too far and subsumed all accounts of serious environmental disturbance under the rubric of ideologically motivated "alarmist discourses," or as just "myths."[71] Sinha, as we saw, alludes to the "wet desert of Cherrapunji," ironically capturing the ecological crises caused by the "rape of forests" in Meghalaya. Cherrapunji, known to have the highest annual rainfall in the world (some say the second highest), has indeed an acute drinking-water problem, but this has little to do with the depletion of forests over the last two decades or so. This part of the Khasi Hills has a history of iron smelting that long predates the colonial period, and this industry certainly taxed forest resources in a major way. As P. R. Gurdon says in his influential monograph, *The Khasis*,[72] there has been a substantial production and export of iron from the Khasi Hills. But the industry was substantially reduced in the latter part of the nineteenth century, as cheap imports from England became available on the market, and, more importantly, because of a lack of trees for charcoal (which is required in large quantities for iron smelting).[73] During his excursions in the Khasi Hills in the mid-nineteenth century, Joseph Dalton Hooker, famous botanist and close friend of Charles Darwin, found the "Cherra plateau" almost completely bare ("there is not a tree and scarcely a scrub to be seen").[74] A.J.M. Mills, officiating judge sent on deputation to the Khasi Hills in 1853, makes similar comments: "Cherra is one of the most barren spots I have ever seen."[75] Recent research on the Cherrapunji plateau also confirms that there has been no significant change of forest cover over the last 150 years.[76] What is happening in the area, however, is the significant out-take of coal and limestone which may explain the burgeoning drinking-water problem there. But taking Meghalaya as a whole, I would still hold that though the Supreme Court's attempt to stop logging can be criticized on many grounds, the ecological rationale behind it does seem to be justified.

The forests in Meghalaya (along with protected areas) commonly held to be the best preserved and richest in biodiversity are "sacred forests" or "sacred groves." The state has a large number of such forests that cover altogether as much as five percent of the total geographical area. Most of these are located in the Khasi Hills and have become a source of great pride. When I mentioned the fact that I work on forest issues, the immediate question most people in Shillong asked was whether I had visited the Mawphlang sacred forest situated some 20 km outside the town. Most travel sites on the Internet highlight these sacred forests as one of the main attractions of the state. Some of these forests also stand out as green islands under a strict community management regime; others, however, have lost most of their tree cover. A recent inventory found that only about one percent of the sacred forest area was "undisturbed," i.e. with a 100 percent canopy cover, and that 42 percent was "dense," with more than 40 percent canopy cover. The remaining areas were either "sparse" (with 10–40 percent canopy cover) or "open" (with less than 10 percent canopy cover). According to the research team carrying out the investigation, the situation is deteriorating daily and calls for urgent preservation measures.[77] A main reason for the degradation of sacred forests is said to be Khasi conversions to Christianity and the subsequent loss for them of the sanctity of these forests. However, sacred forests seem to be increasingly appreciated by the urban elite, not least as a valuable part of their cultural heritage and as an important aspect of their present identity as people who are "indigenous." There have also been attempts to re-enchant sacred forests and revive the traditional institutions that protect them.[78]

INDIGENOUS NATURES

The notion of indigenous peoples is intertwined with questions concerning nature or the environment. It is more or less universally claimed by indigenous peoples today that they have a particular relationship with nature, and thus a particularly close attachment to the land and territories they inhabit. This relationship is often cast in terms of deep ecological knowledge as well as an ethical–religious worldview of respect for life or, as it were, all of Creation ("Mother Earth").[79] To be sure, this claim is of great political significance to the global movement of indigenous peoples, giving a moral justification to their struggle for rights to ancestral lands, forests, and natural resources. Environmental stewardship, it is argued, is thus best vested with indigenous peoples as they have the required knowledge and ethos. And there is certainly fairly widespread popular support for the indigenous cause which draws on similar types of ideas.[80]

But alongside this discourse a more critical view of indigenous rights has also gained momentum. Summed up under labels such as "green primitivism" or "the noble ecological savage," it is argued in such discourse that indigenous peoples' closeness to nature, or their ecological wisdom, is nothing but a myth. If this argument once had some critical edge to it—say in the mid-1980s when Roy Ellen published his provocative and pioneering article "What Black Elk Left Unsaid: On the Illusionary Images of Green Primitivism,"[81]—it is by now a rather well-established fact that small-scale societies of hunter-gatherers, pastoralists, and shifting cultivators can also pursue unsustainable livelihood strategies, and thus in the long run cause environmental degradation or permanently change the natural landscape. There is no doubt that forests and other ecosystems that might popularly appear pristine or truly "natural" have in fact often evolved in relation to human practices. We are, in other words, in most cases encountering "hybrid natures" marked or manipulated by human beings.[82] "Nature," as the historian William Cronon puts it, "is not nearly so natural as it seems."[83] In a similar way, people inhabiting these places are no longer thought of as self-contained or timeless beings who have always lived in pristine natural bliss. In fact, most anthropologists today agree that people in even the remotest places are part of larger social, economic, and political networks that shape their ways of living and thinking. Cultures and knowledge are thus products of contact and travel, and, as such, constantly evolving or in the making.[84]

But what does this imply for indigenous peoples' claim that their culture and way of life is closely tuned to nature and, as such, intrinsically bound to their ancestral lands? Is this mere political ideology, and thus a strategic use of "myth" to get control over (disputed) lands and resources?[85] To be sure, many researchers today seem to think this is so. It is certainly important to question popular simplifications and pursue critical inquiry into these matters. Yet disclosing the "illusion" of green primitivism is, at least academically, a straw man today. There seems in fact to be some political motivation behind the promotion of a counterimage, namely indigenous people being as bad or as good as anyone else in preserving the environment. A book by the historian Sumit Guha, *Environment and Ethnicity in India, 1200–1991* (1999), is an example of this perspective. Guha sets out in this book to reconstruct the history of forest communities, and his main objective is to dispute what he considers the dominant theme in popular and academic writings, whereby forest dwellers or "tribals" in India are portrayed as pristine people living in "timeless harmony with nature."[86] Guha stresses, quite rightly, that these communities have not been cut off from the larger world, and that the forests they inhabit are not at all pristine jungles, but rather, to a large extent, environments infested with human history. But in his anxiety to show that the lifeways of forest people such as the Bhils and Gonds have been shaped by their participation in a regional political economy, Guha seems to completely eschew the possibility that these people may have developed knowledges and understandings of nature that significantly differ from those of the majority population in the plains. It is as if he can only conceive of two opposing lines of reasoning: forest communities are either "relic populations" living in "relic forests" without outside contact; or, alternatively, populations fully integrated into larger polities and cultures.

Guha goes to great length to try proving the latter, and his analysis seems to become disturbingly one-sided. His readings of the historical sources appear driven by the explicit aim of disputing claims of indigeneity that, according to him, would have "explosive consequences."[87] Contesting these communities' closeness to nature thus becomes a way of contesting their assertion of rights as indigenous peoples or *adivasis* (original dwellers). Guha describes such assertions to be the handiwork of "international experts" who classify tribal communities as indigenous "quite regardless of their actual histories."[88] He leaves no room for subaltern agency, nor for claims to an indigenous status that is part of a self-chosen identity, or part of a forest community's contemporary struggle for survival.[89]

Above all, what seems lacking in Guha's account, as Vinita Damodaran points out in a review of his book, is an engagement with forest communities' own "understandings of landscape, their stories of nature, [and] their lived histories."[90] Such engagement might reveal that forest communities' old relationships with their landscape have developed into "sophisticated knowledge of the jungle environment."[91] "To say this," to quote Damodaran again, "is not to romanticize these communities and their relationship to nature."[92] Tim Ingold, a leading scholar within ecological anthropology, offers a useful opening here. He has, for some time now, argued for what he calls a "dwelling perspective;" a perspective that situates the human being in an "active engagement with the constituents of his or her surroundings." He focuses on "skills" that develop through the "performance of particular tasks."[93] Ingold's work concerns mainly hunter-gatherer and pastoralist communities, people who are today often defined as indigenous people, and here he identifies a common "relational" understanding of them and their life-world. For indigenous people, he writes, "it is in their relationships with the land, in their very business of dwelling, that their history unfolds. Both the land and the living beings who inhabit it are caught up in the same, ongoing historical process."[94]

This might come out as a confirmation of present-day claims by indigenous peoples' movements of them being one with nature and with their ancestral land. In a way, yes; but Ingold also takes a critical stance *vis-à-vis* contemporary assertions of indigenousness. To him, the whole notion of indigenous peoples has come to be based on a mistaken "genealogical model" that emphasizes descent instead of active dwelling. Being indigenous has thus primarily become a question of whether people are descendants of some original inhabitants, and further that such descent supposedly endows such people with certain cultural traits regardless of their present livelihood.[95] It is *how you live* and not *who your ancestors are* that determines your relatedness to nature, he argues. To him, then, a settler born and raised in the countryside becomes more attuned to the land than urbanized or displaced persons in the tribal diaspora.

Even if Ingold's perspective on the indigenous peoples' movement is deeply problematic—not taking into account that it is a political mobilization stemming from the experience of losing their lands and traditional livelihoods[96]—I still find his perspective useful in thinking beyond green primitivism or the noble ecological savage impasse. In its most basic form, the Ingoldian dwelling perspective teaches us that, for example, people who live in and by the forest acquire skills and perceptions of the environment that differ from those possessed by people living under other circumstances. And as "enskillment" is an ongoing process of learning through active engagement with one's surroundings, these skills and perceptions change as life circumstances change.

Let us here take the example of shifting cultivation, which, as mentioned (particularly in the Garo Hills), serves as the basis of peoples' livelihood in rural areas. Following Ingold, it can be argued that this type of dwelling has great bearing on peoples' way of being-in-the-world, and thus on how they relate to the environment. Shifting cultivators, such as the Garos, of necessity acquire specialized knowledge of the particular hill environment they inhabit. In recent times, their stained reputation of shifting or swidden cultivators, and thus as being among the main destroyers of precious tropical forests, has also been re-evaluated. Contemporary research shows, for example, that shifting cultivation maintains a diversified forest ecosystem and aids the regeneration of forests, and further that shifting cultivation requires "in-depth knowledge of the environment and a high degree of managerial skill to succeed."[97] But it is equally stressed that, under contemporary circumstances, shifting cultivation is becoming more and more unsustainable in many parts of the world. The reasons for this are the well-known problems of increasing population, as well as competition from loggers, settlers, industries, and wildlife interests, resulting in the scarcity of swidden land and ever shorter fallow circles: in other words, the very process we have observed in Meghalaya.[98] To such external pressures, one has of course to add peoples' own aspirations for a "modern" life and all the material goods of a consumer society. Such aspirations generate new forms of dwelling that can certainly be described as less green.

The timber trade is an example of such an avenue of fast cash earnings. Although the commercial out-take of timber has been going on in a relatively large-scale manner since the colonial period, the big boom came in the 1970s and 1980s. In the forests under the district councils, the timber deals were, as mentioned, made between private landowners and timber merchants without the involvement of the "community" or of the state forest authorities. The Supreme Court order has now changed this, vesting ultimate power and control with the state, i.e. the forest department and the Ministry of Environment and Forests. This takes us back to the burgeoning discourse of indigenousness. Besides asserting indigenous peoples' rights of self-determination, this discourse emphasizes collective rights in land and natural resources, favoring traditional community land management systems as an alternative to private and state ownership regimes. It is not the case that indigenous activists urge a wholesale return to how things were in earlier days, but rather a learning from these to create new institutions for governance and community management of land and natural resources.

Some commentators see this turn to the "past" as a reactionary move that might undermine democratic rights and, for example, the rights of women.[99] Indeed it may. But it can equally be stressed that the transnational indigenous movement offers a new political space for women's voices. However naïve this might appear, I would argue that the insistence on indigenous peoples' closeness to nature might translate into an increased ecological awareness and generate practices that facilitate environmental conservation. The Khasis' increased interest in preserving their sacred forests is such an example. Through assertions of indigenousness, the issues of political self-determination and environmental sustainability can be seen to merge. Nature and nation can, thus, be reimagined as mutually constitutive.

NOTES

1. Earlier versions of this text have been presented at the South Asia Workshop at the University of Chicago; later at the University of Washington seminar series "Whose Nature;" at Queen Elizabeth House, Oxford University; and, finally, at my own Department of Cultural Anthropology and Ethnology, Uppsala University. Comments and critique at all these locations have certainly been helpful, and I am

grateful to all those who generously contributed. Gunnel Cederlöf and K. Sivaramakrishnan have done a great job as critical and engaging editors, and my main thanks go to them. Thanks also to Linda Chhakchhuak and Sanat Chakraborty for supplying me with valuable documents and critical insights relating to the ethnic and natural landscape of Meghalaya. This essay is part of an ongoing research project entitled "Claims and Rights: Power and Negotiations over Nature in India—An Anthropological and Historical Study," funded by the Bank of Sweden Tercentenary Foundation.

2. The Garos also call themselves A'chic, and those living in Bangladesh are known as Mande. See Burling 1997a.

3. Sinha 1993: 7.

4. Ibid.: 10.

5. See, for example, the two recent collections of articles, Sundar and Jeffrey 1999; and Agrawal and Sivaramakrishnan 2000.

6. Agrawal and Gibson 2001: 7.

7. Ibid.: 1.

8. For a larger discussion on gender and community resource management, see for example, Bina Agarwal 1997, and, in the case of Meghalaya, Tiplut Nongbri 2003.

9. Such realization need not, however, translate into a cynical dismissal of all claims to "community" as a site of bonds of solidarity and action that cannot be reduced to the pursuit of self-interest. Cf. Partha Chatterjee's notion of a still unfolding "narrative of community." Chatterjee 1993: chapter 11.

10. A senior officer from the Ministry of Environment and Forests, Government of India, told me for example that they have not been able to get local people to participate in their forest surveys due to the popular belief that this would open up the forest department's takeover of their forests. Personal communication, November 2002.

11. See Laungaramsri 2001 for a discussion on how communities can make use of land and resource mapping—"counter-mapping" as she calls it—to claim rights vis-à-vis the state and other powerful interests.

12. Marak 2000: 185–6. M.C. Goswami and D.N. Majumdar observed already in the 1970s a tendency toward private ownership of land in the Garo Hills (1972: chapter 6). P.C. Kar's (1982) study of one Garo village also confirms these findings; and further, Robbins Burling (1997b), who recently revisited the area in which he conducted field research in the 1950s, finding that most land had been privatized. As Bina Agarwal (1994: 154–68) suggests, the privatization of community land in the Garo Hills has also had important repercussions for women, above all leading to a weakening of their rights in land.

13. The sociologist A.K. Nongkynrih is working on the increasing problem of landlessness in Khasi society, which, as he claims, is mainly an effect of powerful

individuals acquiring earlier clan land. Personal communication, January 2000. In a study of twelve villages, in an area called Khatar Shnong, he found that as much as 57 percent were landless. Nongkynrih 2002a: 50. Regarding land management, Nongkynrih further found, in a micro study of one village, that all lands (agricultural, forest, and residential) were private holdings (so-called Ri Kynti land), but that most households owned land (out of 65 households, 54 owned land). Nongkynrih 2002b: 110, 114–15.

14. These acts are collectively known as the "Management and Control of Forests Act, 1958," initially one for the Garo Hills autonomous district council, and one for the United Khasi–Jaintia autonomous district council. The latter was later bifurcated into two district councils, whereby the Jaintia Hills also got its own forest act. The contents of these acts are more or less the same. There have also been some later amendments to these acts.

15. The district councils used to auction their check gates to private persons (the highest bidders), who were then authorized to collect toll fees from timber trucks. See "First Report by the High Powered Committee for the North Eastern Region," May 1, 1997, pp. 13–14.

16. See Malik 2003 for a more elaborate account on the historical trajectory of jhum or shifting cultivation in the Garo Hills.

17. This is a summary of a longer conversation in November 2002.

18. Sajal Nag argues, in a recent book on separatist movements in north-east India, that insurgency outfits like the ANVC were the creation of the Naga underground organization NSCN(IM), i.e. that the latter has "sown" the "seeds of insurgency in the peaceful hills of Meghalaya." By creating new front organizations in different parts of north-east India, NSCN(IM) could generate more income and create "acute turbulence in the region." Nag 2002: 299–300. That such links exist, alongside the supply of weapons and logistics, has also been pointed out by other commentators and seems most likely. But this again is not a sufficient explanation. For seeds to grow they have to be planted in fertile soil.

19. See, for example, Majumdar 1982: 206; and M.S. Sangma 1981: 40.

20. I deal with this movement in my paper, "Having Rights in the Forest: The Coming of a New Property Regime in the Garo Hills, Northeast India," presented at the International Conference on the Environmental History of Asia, December 2002, New Delhi.

21. I thank Erik de Maaker for reminding me of this.

22. Baruah 1999: 206.

23. Ibid.: 207.

24. Xaxa 1999: 3595.

25. Gassah 1998: 7.

26. For further details on the Sixth Schedule and a discussion on the formation of new states, see Chaube 1973; and Baruah 1999.

27. The Khasis and Jaintias are often described as belonging to the same people, with only minor differences in language and other cultural practices. But as they inhabit distinct territories and their historical trajectories differ, people are commonly identified, and to a large extent identify themselves, as being separate peoples/ethnic groups/nations.

28. The local newspapers carry daily reports on killings, kidnappings, extortion and other unlawful activities that are attributed to insurgency groups.

29. See Karlsson 2001 and 2003.

30. From an intervention at the 12th Session of the UN Working Group of Indigenous Populations, July 25–29, 1994, Geneva.

31. Quoted from "Statement and Resolutions" by the North-East Indigenous and Tribal Peoples Forum, Guwahati: 1994, 1, 3.

32. Khasi National Celebration Committee, 1994: Introduction.

33. "Khasi States' Inclusion in District Council a Mockery," article in *The Sentinel*, December 22, 2001.

34. Paul Lyngdoh is now leader of the newly established political party Khun Hynniewtrep National Awakening Movement, consisting to a large extent of former members of the Khasi Students' Union.

35. The inclusion or merger of the Khasi states with the Indian union is a matter that has several times come up in interviews and conversations with Khasi people in Shillong. The commonly voiced opinion is that injustice was done to the Khasis in the process. For a historical account of these events, see Giri 1998: chapter 8.

36. For a similar argument, see John F. Kharshiing, "6th Schedule Irrelevant, District Councils a Threat to Traditional Institutions," *The Sentinel*, December 20, 2001.

37. A similar initiative is also taken by the Nokmas, village "headmen," in the Garo Hills. The newly established Nokma Council is seeking constitutional recognition of the traditional political institutions related to the A'king Nokma and his Council of Elders, institutions that, they claim, have been curtailed by the district councils. See "Memorandum Seeking Constitutional Recognition and Protection of the Traditional Institutions of the Garo Race," submitted by Drafting Committee Council of Nokmas (n.d.).

38. See "Memorandum of the Dorbar of the Rulers of the Khasi States submitted to the Honourable Chairman National Commission for Review of the Working of the Constitution," July 22, 2000, and press release, Syiem Hima Mylliem in Dorbar, Shillong, November 24, 2000. See further, "Khasi Democracy—An Unwritten Constitution," unpublished document by Laborious Manik S. Syiem, Shillong, June 15, 2001.

39. Interview with the Seng Khasi President Mr M.F. Blah and his wife Mrs Kong Sweetymon Rynjah, renowned authorities on Khasi customs, December 2002.

40. In, for example, the Garo Hills, the Nokma or the village headman has to give a "no objection certificate" before any land transaction can take place.

41. The Meghalaya Transfer of Land (Regulation) Act, 1971.

42. The local English newspapers *Meghalaya Guardian* and *Shillong Times*, as well as the north-eastern section of *The Telegraph* and *Asian Age*, carried a large number of articles on the issue during the months of November and December 2002. For example, "Land Transfer Act to be Amended," *Shillong Times*, November 13; "Govt. Decision to Amend Land Transfer Act Draws Flak," *Shillong Times*, November 14; "Uproar over Khonglam Land Plan," *Telegraph*, November 15; "SSSS Opposes Govt. Move to Amend the State Land Act," *Meghalaya Guardian*, November 26; "Lapang for Land Rights Only to Genuine Tribals," *Asian Age*, December 21; "Govt. Justifies Move to Amend Land Transfer Act," *Shillong Times*, December 21; and so on.

43. Giddens 1991.

44. Representatives of the Uranium Corporation of India Limited claim that the fear of health risks among the public is due to misinformation. See, for example, *Shillong Times*, November 13 and 14, 2002.

45. Nongbri's paper, "Timber Ban in North-East India: Effects on Livelihood and Gender," was later published in *Economic and Political Weekly*, May 26, 2001.

46. The paper Nathan presented, "Timber in Meghalaya," is also published in *Economic and Political Weekly*, January 22, 2000.

47. "Writ Petition (Civil) No. 202 of 1995, *T.N. Godavarman Thirumulkpad* versus *Union of India*, the Supreme Court of India.

48. It is not entirely clear to me how the extension of the Supreme Court case took place (see further "Logjam," *Down to Earth*, March 15, 2002).

49. Nongbri 2001: 1895–7. Personal communication, former KSU president Paul Lyngdoh, December 2002.

50. See the unpublished report, "When the Bubble Bursts: Impact of the Supreme Court Ban on Logging in Meghalaya, Especially in the West Khasi Hills," by Sanat K. Chakraborty 2000.

51. The forest officers of the Khasi district council have bluntly told me that they are fumbling in the dark. They lack the most basic information, about, for example, how much forest there is, what kinds of forest there are, and under what type of ownership these forests exist. All the resources are with the state forest department, even though the councils are supposed to manage the bulk of the forests in the state (personal communication, December 2002).

52. Rangan Dutta, "Report on the One Man Commission of Enquiry on the Alleged Large Scale Felling of Trees in the Reserved Forests under Dainadubi Forest Range of East Garo Hills District, Meghalaya," Shillong, January 31, 1997: 107–8.

53. Ibid.: 50–60.

54. See "Second Report of the High Powered Committee for the North-Eastern Region," July 12, 1997, paragraph 5.7.

55. Similar examples are reported from all over India, see, for example, my earlier work on forest issues in North Bengal: Karlsson 2000.

56. In a workshop on biodiversity at St Mary's College in Shillong, inaugurated by the chief minister, several of the speeches referred to Meghalaya, and the northeast in general, as one of the "world's biodiversity hot-spots" (November 2002).

57. Even among those who celebrate the use of remote satellite images in accessing environmental change and, as in this case, changes in forest cover, the many problems and uncertainties are acknowledged. At almost every step of processing the satellite images, the researcher needs to filter the information through his or her own categories and interpretation. There is, further, a whole set of practical problems: for example, getting clear shots without clouds, smoke, dust, or topographic shadows. Just differentiating between forests and water surfaces can be extremely difficult. To verify the data derived from satellite images, it is essential to conduct field observations on the ground, which is commonly not done. See, for example, Echavarnia 1998; O'Brien 1998.

58. *State of Forest Report* (1999), Forest Survey of India, Government of India, Dehradun.

59. Interview with Mr B. Singh, November 2002.

60. *Forest Report*, paragraph 1.3.

61. Ibid.: paragraph 1.2.5.

62. www.meghalaya.nic.in/natural-resources/forest.htm

63. Quoted from an unpublished report, "Meghalaya Eco-Resource Development Project—1994," Government of India, by F. Suchiang, former chief conservator of forests, Meghalaya: 21–2, 77.

64. The anthropologists Nancy Lee Peluso and Peter Vandergeest use the term "political forest" in a study on colonial forestry in Southeast Asia to emphasize that we are dealing with land that states declare as forest on political grounds rather than as a "biological or universal category." Peluso and Vandergeest 2001: 766.

65. Piers Blaikie and Harold Brookfield argue, in their classical study *Land Degradation and Society*, that it is critical to realize there are always "competing social definitions of land degradation," and that, for example, deforestation does not necessarily "constitute degradation in a social sense." Blaikie and Brookfield 1987: 6, 17.

66. Ramakrishnan 1992: 3.

67. Ibid.: 386–7.

68. Ibid.: 44.

69. Ibid.: 59, 373.

70. The anthropologists James Fairhead and Melissa Leach argue, in the case of Western Africa, that the alarmist discourse on depletion of the tropical rain forests is "hugely exaggerated." Fairhead and Leach 1998: xiv. Forest is lost, but not to the extent claimed. The type of forest lost is also different from the commonly mourned

destruction of rain forests. On the basis of different types of historical material, they claim that in some areas there has even been an increase in forest cover, ibid., 1998. In the same spirit, Jack D. Ives and Bruno Messerli argue against "the widely supported prediction that the Himalayan region is inevitably drifting into a situation of environmental supercrises and collapse." Ibid., 1998: xvii. Their particular critique relates to the taken-for-granted relationship and supposed causal linkages between population increase, deforestation, soil erosion, and water shortage and floods. Ibid.: 8–9.

71. A good example of this is Vasant K. Saberwal's "Environmental Alarm and Institutionalized Conservation in Himachal Pradesh, 1865–1994," wherein he goes so far as to claim that there is no scientific evidence to back up the "popular" idea that deforestation can lead to different types of environmental degradation (such as water shortage, soil erosion, or floods). The "alarmist degradation discourse," he argues, is purely ideologically or politically motivated (Saberwal 2000: 69, 79).

72. Gurdon 1906: 57–9.

73. The historian Amalendu Guha claims that iron smelting has been going on in the Khasi Hills from at least the thirteenth century. A. Guha 1991: 35. In the first Forest Report for the Province of Assam from 1875, it is also mentioned that iron production was going on at a limited scale in the western Khasi Hills, and that the widespread use of charcoal in the industry had caused "denudation of forests" in the area. *Progress Report of Forest Administration in the Province of Assam, for the years 1874–75*: 7.

74. Hooker 1854: 277.

75. Mills 1995 1853: 2.

76. Paper presented by the geographer Prokop Pawel, based on the findings of an Indo-Polish research project on long-term environmental changes in Cherrapunji, at a workshop on mountain environments held at the North-Eastern Hill University, Shillong, November 14–15, 2002.

77. Tiwari, Barik and Tripathi 1999.

78. The folklorist and poet Desmond L. Kharmawphlang initiated, in the early 1990s, such an initiative to regenerate sacred groves in the Khyrim Syiemship, with financial support from Europe.

79. In the case of the Khasis, see Mawrie 2001.

80. See Brosius 2000.

81. Ellen 1986.

82. I borrow this term from Arturo Escobar 1999.

83. Cronon 1996: 25.

84. Clifford 1997.

85. I thank Mikael Kurkiala for this point.

86. Guha 1999: 21.

87. Ibid.: 203.

88. Ibid.: 4.
89. See further Damodaran in this volume.
90. Damodaran 2000: 4.
91. Ibid.: 5.
92. Ibid.: 4.
93. Ingold 2000: 5.
94. Ibid.: 139.
95. Ibid.: 150–1.
96. Nathan Porath (2000: 176), aptly describes such lost indigenous territories as "landscapes of dispossession," calling these "areas of land which, although fraught with meaning for its inhabitants, have been expropriated and transformed by other politically defined groups." And, as he rightly points out, "indigenous landscapes" are commonly associated with experiences of dispossession. Ibid.
97. Warner 1991: 2; Chandran 1998.
98. For a recent overview of the marginalization of shifting cultivation in the north-eastern hill region, see Choudhury and Sundriyal 2002.
99. Cf. Sundar 1997: 261–2.

8

SACRED FORESTS OF KODAGU

Ecological Value and Social Role

Claude A. Garcia and J.-P. Pascal

SACRED FORESTS ARE PATCHES OF FOREST THAT EITHER BELONG to a temple or are said to shelter a god or spirit revered by the local inhabitants. Such sacred places can be found all over South and South East Asia, Africa, Latin America and are also mentioned in the classical Greek and Latin writings (Juhé-Beaulaton and Roussel 1992; Chandran and Hughes 2000).

In India, scientists and managers alike have taken a keen interest in such forests, since it is felt that they represent a unique and invaluable traditional conservation institution. Could it not be possible, through the practice of instituting and maintaining sacred groves, to involve local communities in the conservation of forest biodiversity (Kushalappa and Bhagwat 2001)? Reported from all over the country (Malhotra, Chatterjee *et al.* 2001), sacred forests are as present in the Indian landscape as in the literature (see Malhotra, Gokhale *et al.* 2001 for a good overview).

Gadgil and Vartak (1975) were probably the first Indian scientists to highlight the ecological and cultural value of such forests. Because of the absence of human disturbance, they are described as the last and only remnants of the original forests within their area. As such, their value for the conservation of local and regional biodiversity is firmly established. This point of view has been accepted to the point of becoming paradigmatic (see Ramakrishnan, Saxena *et al.* 1998; Chandran and Hughes 2000; Ghosh 2001; Kushalappa and Bhagwat 2001 for examples). Apart from a few works, sacred groves are mostly described as *"vegetation in its climax formation, and probably the only representation of forest in near virgin condition"* (emphasis added; Vartak and Gadgil 1981).

Interestingly, the main challenges to this paradigm have come not from the natural sciences, but from the sociological and anthropological field (Freeman 1994; Kalam 1996; Jeffrey 1998).

Either way there are few ecological studies that give hard evidence of such a scenario. The aim of this essay is to (a) revisit this widely accepted refrain, providing evidence that this image does not fit the reality in the field; and (b) explore reasons for this gap between discourse and reality, and the way this positive and romanticized image of sacred forests is instrumentalized in a struggle for identity and dominance within the cultural and political landscape to which they belong. If sacred forests and their traditional management techniques are to teach us anything in the field of conservation biology, and since there are conflicts over the control and management of such forests on grounds of their biodiversity and ecological value, a sound assessment of such value is needed.

To provide a case study, we will focus on an area known for the strength and richness of this tradition: Kodagu district, in the state of Karnataka. In a climatically homogeneous zone, we will compare the structure and floristic composition of all the sacred forests (larger than 1 ha) with that of the nearest natural forest—the reserve forest owned and managed by the Karnataka forest department—in this case the Brahmagiri Wildlife Sanctuary.

STUDY AREA AND LANDSCAPE DYNAMICS

Kodagu District

The district of Kodagu (75°25'–76°14' E and 12°15'–12°45' N) lies on the summit and eastern slopes of the Western Ghats (Figure 1). The barrier formed by the Ghats, which blocks the landward progress of the monsoon rains, causes a sharp decline in the rainfall pattern in this district. The annual rainfall goes from over 5000 mm/year on the western side to less than 800 mm toward the Mysore plateau, in the east (Figure 2). This, added to the length of the dry season and the altitude gradient, shapes the vegetation cover of the district (Pascal 1988). The vegetation types have been described and mapped by Pascal (Pascal 1982 ; Pascal 1986; Pascal 1988).

The forest cover in Kodagu district is high: 46 percent of total land area. Of this 46 percent, 30 percent comprises reserve forests, forming a belt at the periphery of the district. Central Kodagu (the so-called coffee belt) harbors only 16 percent of the forest cover. The remaining part of the

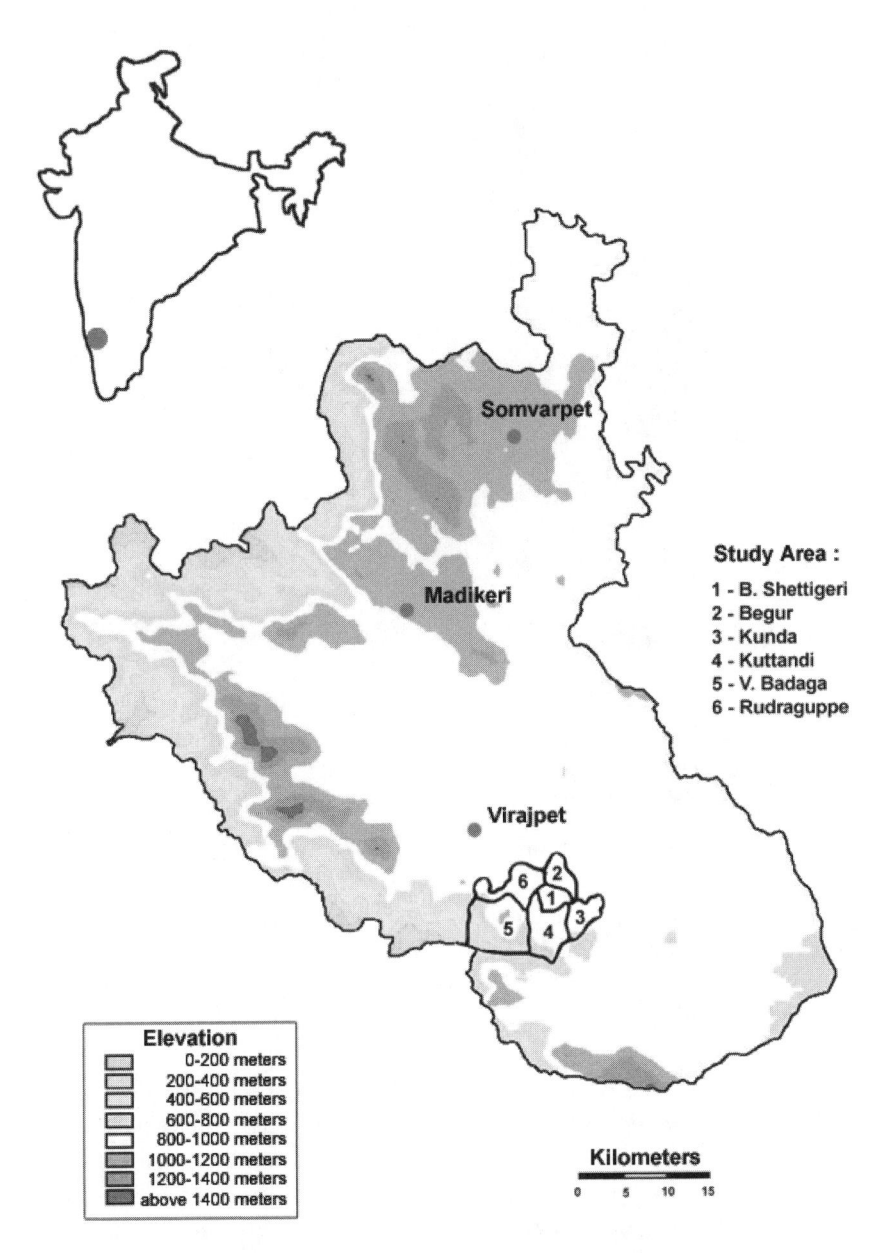

Fig. 1: Kodagu District Physical Map and Location of the Study Area (Source: French Institute, Pondicherry)

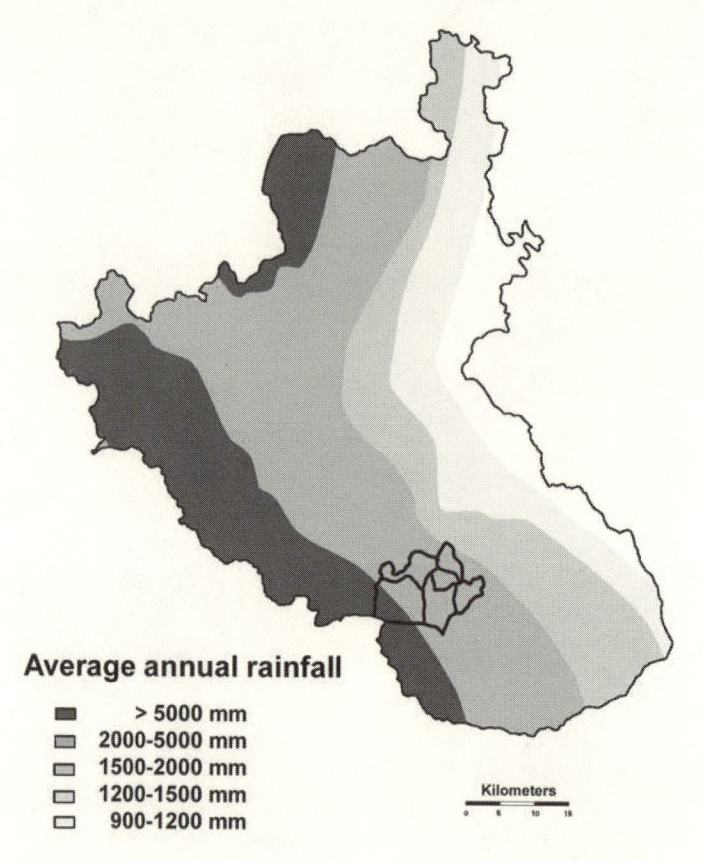

Average annual rainfall
- ■ > 5000 mm
- ▨ 2000-5000 mm
- ▧ 1500-2000 mm
- ▦ 1200-1500 mm
- □ 900-1200 mm

Fig. 2: Rainfall Gradient (Source: French Institute, Pondicherry)

landscape is agricultural land, essentially coffee estates that cover 29 percent of the total area of the district (Ramakrishnan et al. 2000). One of the peculiarities of Kodagu is the cultivation of coffee under tree shade. This is needed to avoid loss of coffee floral buds during the dry season, before the pre-monsoon rains. Initially consisting of pre-existing, local species, this tree cover is now undergoing massive change. Exotic species like the silver oak (*Grevillea robusta*) are replacing the native trees and are preferred since they are fast growing and can be harvested without a permit from the state forest department. Moreover, the development of irrigation facilities and hardy varieties of coffee allow the planters to remove the tree shade entirely for better yields (Kushalappa, personal communication).

Hence, large scale landscape transformation is expected in the years to come, in the form of loss of tree cover as well as a strong depletion of biodiversity. The centre of the district will see the more drastic changes, while the periphery—especially the western side—may remain relatively untouched because it holds a belt of reserved forest and wild life sanctuaries under the protection of the Forest Department.

Study Area

There are at least 1214 sacred forests, or *devarakadus* as they are known locally, in Kodagu (Kalam 1996). They are small: 70 percent are less than one hectare (Kushalappa and Bhagwat 2001) and cover 0.6 percent of the total area of the district, and almost 2 percent of the forested area. Most of them are located in the central coffee belt. We selected a homogeneous zone for the different climatic factors and vegetation cover Figures 2 and 3. It covers six villages in the south-western part of the district (Figure 1), and is located in the Mesua-Palaquium wet evergreen forest subtype (Pascal 1988).

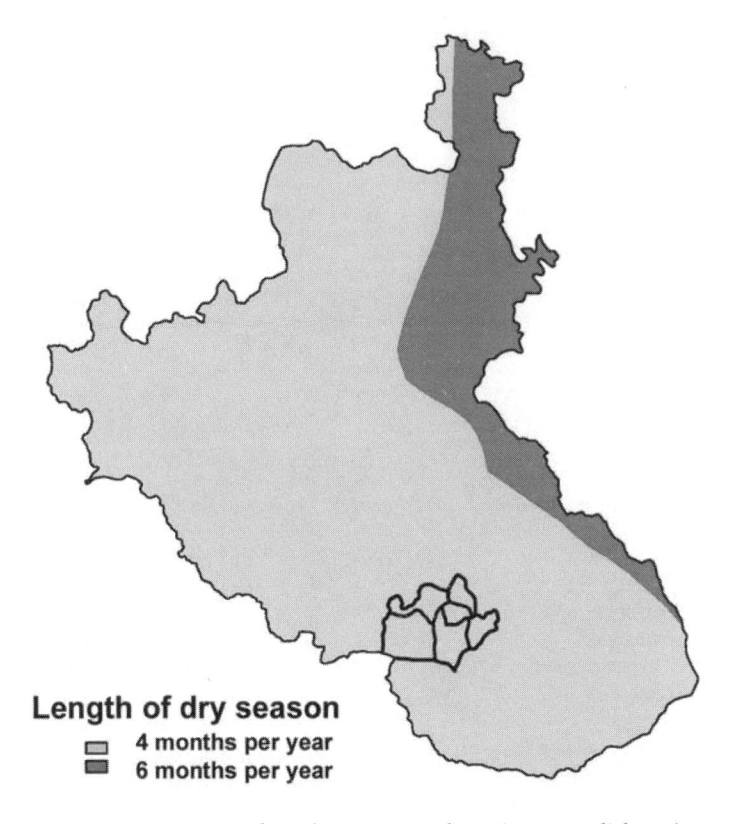

Length of dry season
▭ 4 months per year
▬ 6 months per year

Fig. 3: Dry-season Gradient (Source: French Institute, Pondicherry)

Fieldwork, ecological surveys and interviews were done between October 2000 and May 2002.

Sacred Forests: According to the Karnataka forest department, there are thirty-two devarakadus in the study zone. All sacred forests with an area over 1 hectare were inspected (Table I). The minimum area was fixed to ensure that edge effects would not be predominant over forest dynamics. Sacred Forest 5 had been converted into a coffee estate some twenty years ago, and is therefore excluded from the ecological assessment.[1] A similar situation occurred with Forest 9, even if the conversion process left a small clump of trees untouched.[2]

Natural Forest: Part of the BWS, the closest natural forest, comes into our study zone. This sanctuary (181 km^2) is contiguous with the Aralam Wildlife Sanctuary in the neighboring state of Kerala (Ahmed 2001). Even if it was selectively logged under British rule and later, the structure and species composition of the forest are still close enough to the undisturbed type so as to provide a good reference (Kushalappa: personal communication). Two patches of 4 hectares each were selected, away from the border of the sanctuary, to avoid edge disturbances.

Table I: List of Forests Surveyed. The ID is given according to the size of the fragment

ID	Name	Area (ha.)	Village	Land Use
1.	Kaadele Aiyappa Yane Kaali	1.024	B-Shettigeri	Devarakadu
2.	Aiyappa	1.032	Begur	Devarakadu
3.	Vishnu Murti	1.088	V-Badaga	Devarakadu
4.	Badu Maadu Aiyappa	1.228	B-Shettigeri	Devarakadu
5.	Hole[1]	1.36	Kuttandi	Devarakadu
6.	Kundachappa	1.388	Kuttandi	Devarakadu
7.	Kaakemani Aiyappa	1.564	B-Shettigeri	Devarakadu
8.	Kaadu Motte Bhagavathi	1.592	Kuttandi	Devarakadu
9.	Holeri Bhagavathi and Aiyappa[2]	1.72	Kuttandi	Devarakadu
10.	Nerche	2.044	Kuttandi	Devarakadu
11.	Bhadrakali Nalkeri	2.048	V-Badaga	Devarakadu
12.	Kappemani Aiyappa	2.304	Kunda	Devarakadu
13.	Kaadilerappa	3.148	Kuttandi	Devarakadu
14.	Kare Kunda Aiyappa	3.376	Kuttandi	Devarakadu
15.	Karpa Aiyappa	11.104	Rudraguppe	Devarakadu
16.	Peggri Aiyappa	11.972	Rudraguppe	Devarakadu
17.	Brahmagiri Wildlife Sanctuary 1	–	V-Badaga	Reserve forest
18.	Brahmagiri Wildlife Sanctuary 2	–	V-Badaga	Reserve forest

METHODOLOGY

Ecological Characterization

Given the controversial subject of study, a particular effort was made to ensure that the data gathered was statistically significant. A battery of structural and botanical indexes (density, basal area, richness, etc.) has been used to describe these forests. All indexes are sample-size sensitive. Only when the sample reaches a minimum size can the results be considered significant. This evolution can be monitored. When it is not stabilized, the sampling must be completed. This led us to complete the data set when the initial sampling proved insufficient. Fieldwork was conducted in three steps.

Step I: The entire area of every sacred forest was systematically covered with 5x5m quadrats laid every 10, 15 or 20 meters, depending on the size of the fragment. In every quadrat, we recorded the girth, height, and species of all the trees with girth at breast height (gbh) ≥ 30 cm (breast height = 1.30m above ground). The species identification was based on vegetative characters (Pascal and Ramesh 1987). When in doubt, specimens were collected, deposited, and identified in the herbarium of the French Institute of Pondicherry. Height measurements were made using graduated pipes up to 7 meters and through visual estimation (with a Blum-Leiss dendrometer to provide corrections) above that. Every trace of human activity inside the quadrat was recorded: presence of a path, cut stems, humus removal, etc. A total of 703 plots (1.75 hectares) were measured.

Step II: This is identical to the first one. The only difference is the size of the quadrats and their spacing: 10x10m quadrats laid every 10 meters. It was specifically carried out in the two BWS patches. A total of 197 quadrats (1.97 ha) were inspected.

Step III: This was used to complete the data set in the sacred forests when Step I proved insufficient (sample size was too small). An exhaustive inventory of the fragment was then carried out. The same measures of species, girth, and height were recorded. This does not provide data on human activity. It was applied to Forests 1, 2, 3, 4, 6, 7, 8, 10, 11, 12, and 13.

Stakeholders and Representations

We interviewed a sample of the neighboring inhabitants (coffee estate laborers, coffee planters, farmers), as well as stakeholders outside the study zone (political or community leaders, journalists, forest department officials), using semi-structured interviews. The discussions were carried out in English when possible, otherwise in Kannara or Kodava, with the assistance of a translator. The six villages were so surveyed, the first contact being always made with temple committees, then with inhabitants, depending on their availability. Complementary data was gathered on site, whenever we met someone inside the forests. The sample is heavily skewed on a gender basis: few women were willing to talk with us on the subject. In total, 45 interviews of 2 to 6 hours each were made.

Whenever the interviews are quoted, the first number specifies the village where the interview took place (1 to 6 for the villages, 7 for out-zone interviews), the second number marks the chronological order of the interviews at that location. The quotes are edited for grammatical correction, without further modification.

ECOLOGICAL CHARACTERIZATION

The results describe the structure (1) and the species composition (2) of sacred forests as compared to natural forests. Those are only the salient features. A more detailed study can be found in Garcia 2003.

Forest Structure

Traces of the history of a forest can be found deep in its structure. Events that shape the canopy, giving it its present shape, leave marks and scars that can be read with reasonable confidence. It is thus possible to find out if (as is claimed) sacred forests are patches of undisturbed forest. Of the many indexes used to analyse forest structure, we shall retain density and basal area.

Density: This means the number of trees per hectare. Figure 4 gives the average tree density per quadrat (+ 95 percent confidence interval) for sacred forests and the BWS. Sacred forests as a group (all forests pooled together) have a density half of that of a natural forest. A low density can mean either a clear forest (thicket or tree savannah) or an old and closed one, with a deficit of young trees. Hence, it doesn't necessarily mean that there is less biomass in sacred forests. Since density alone can be misleading, it is often associated with the measure of the basal area.

Basal Area: Its value is equal to the ratio of woody sections per unit of area, all stems above 30 cm gbh considered. Figure 5 gives the average basal

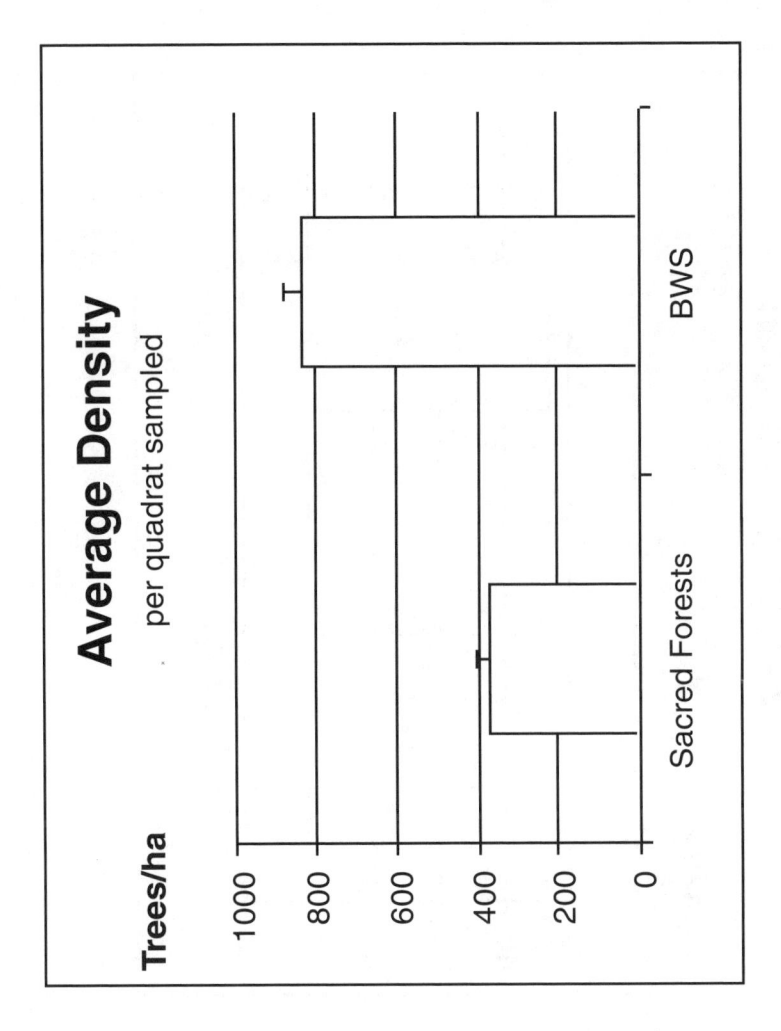

Fig. 4: Average Density per Quadrat. The error bars show the 95 percent confidence interval.

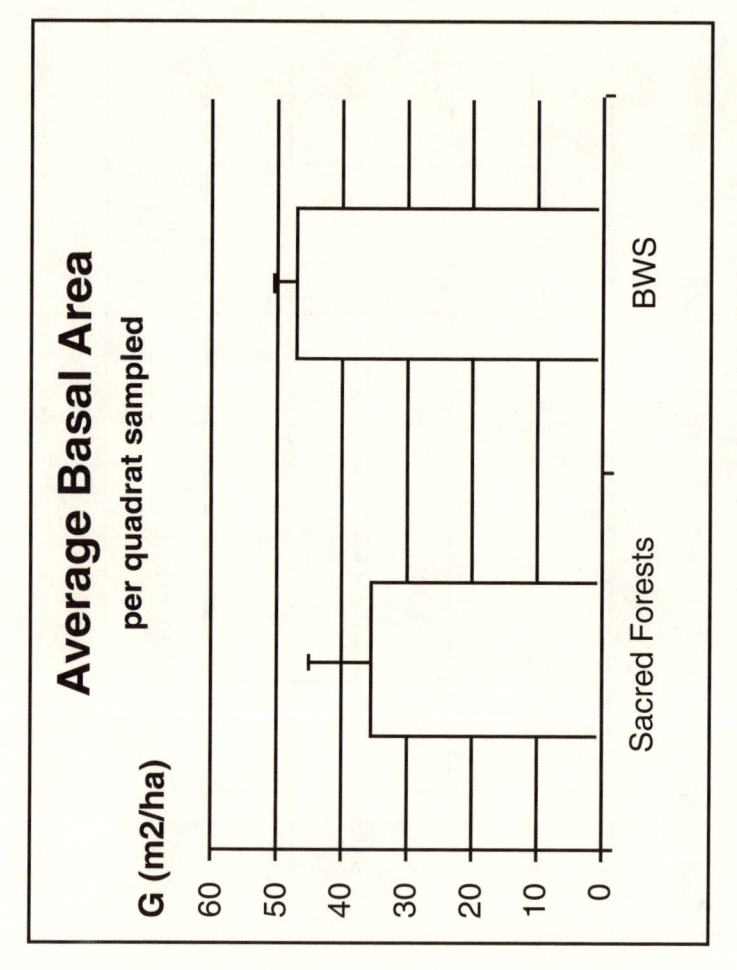

Fig. 5: Average Basal Area per Quadrat. The error bar shows the 95 percent confidence interval

area for the sacred forests (all fragments pooled together) and the BWS (+ 95 percent confidence interval). Differences between sacred forests and BWS are this time less marked. Even so, the basal area is significantly lower in sacred forests (unilateral test, $p = 0.014$—there are 1.4 percent chances of making an error while stating this).

Floristic Composition

The richness of rare and endangered species within sacred forests is one of the main reasons for advocating their conservation. But providing a list of likely-to-be found species is not enough to prove their conservation value. Here we shall analyze three different aspects of the species composition of the canopy in sacred forests: (1) its richness, i.e. the number of species present, (2) the presence of endemics,[3] i.e. the conservation value of the canopy cover and (3) the rank/frequencies, i.e. the relative abundance of the different species, as a measure of diversity.

Species Richness: A complete study of the richness of the forests of the study area is outside the scope of this essay. We consider here the simplest estimator of ecosystem richness: the number of species observed in the sample.

This estimator is very sensitive to the sampling effort: the bigger the sample, the more species observed. In order to compare the richness of both sacred and natural forests, we use species accumulation curves. A species accumulation curve is a plot of the cumulative number of species detected as a measure of the sampling effort (here, the area sampled). But the order in which the samples are added affects the shape of the curve. To get rid of this heterogeneity, we calculate the theoretical value of the expected number of species in any sub-sample that can be extracted from the original data set (Sanders 1968; Hurlbert 1971; Colwell and Coddington, 1994). The freeware EstimateS (Colwell 1997) was used to run the computations.

The curves for the natural forest and the sacred forest are shown in Figure 6. The fact that none of the two curves reaches a plateau shows that the total richness of both forest types is not accounted for. It is nevertheless possible to compare them.

Due to their small area, each individual forest fragment shelters a limited number of species. However, Figure 6 shows that if pooled together, sacred forests harbor 20 percent more species than the BWS for a given area (98 sp. vs. 80 for 1.75 ha sampled). The network of sacred forests shelters more species than an equal area of natural forest.

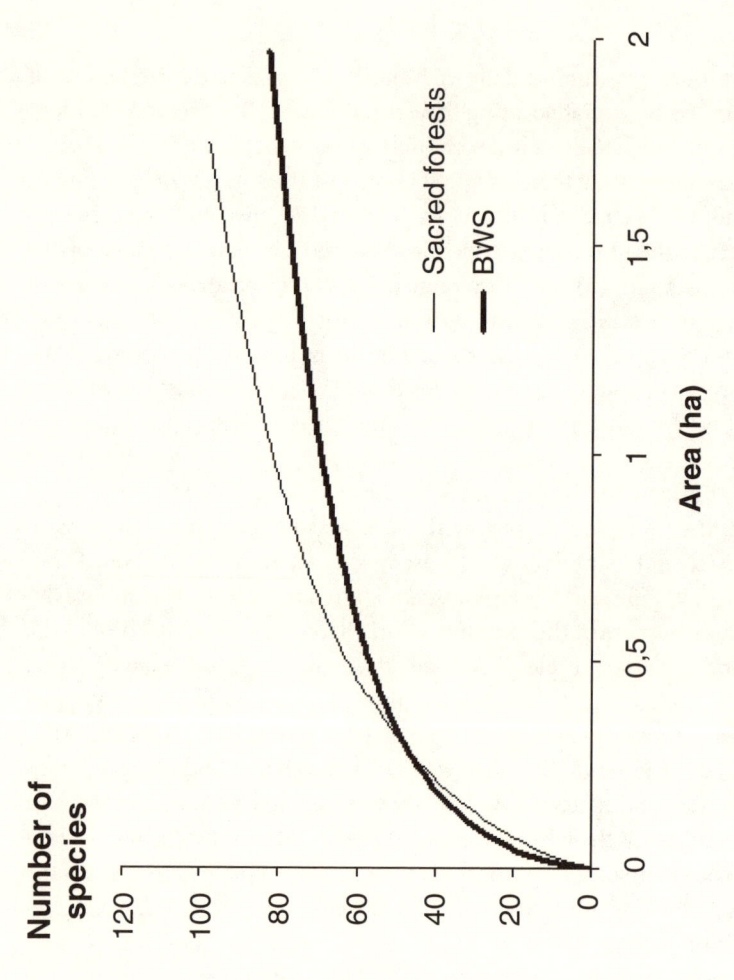

Fig. 6: Species Accumulation Curves Showing the Relationship between Sampled Area and Expected Species Richness in Sacred Forests and the BWS.

Endemics and Richness: Not all the species have the same conservation value. Endemic species, with a narrow distribution area, are more prone to extinction than common, pan-tropical species. The high level of endemism in the Western Ghats is the main reason for their classification as a world's biodiversity hotspot (Myers 1988).

It is possible to build species accumulation curves taking only endemic species in consideration, for both sacred forests and the BWS. The results are shown in Figure 7. This time the sacred forests shelter only 24 endemic species in 1.75 hectares, while the BWS harbors 39. Fragmented forests have lost a third of the endemic tree species. The relative abundance of endemic species in the total population also decreased, as shown in Table II. Both comparisons are highly significant, as shown by the low *p*-values (probability of error).

Table II: Relative Abundance of Endemic Species

Forest	Sacred Forests	BWS	Test
% of individuals	28,6	61,6	$p<0.0001$
% of species	24.5	48.2	$p<0.001$

Species/Rank Curves: In a tropical rainforest, most of the species will be uncommon or rare, whereas a few will be common and constitute the backbone of the plant community. The species/rank diagram lists the species according to their relative abundance (percent of individuals) in the data set.

The species/rank curves of the BWS and sacred forests, and the list of the five dominant species of each forest type are shown in Figure 8. The nature of the floristic composition of both forests is different, as shown by the comparison of the dominant species (pattern coded in Figure 8). The five dominant species of the sacred forests are:

1. *Dimocarpus longan,*
2. *Xanthophyllum flavescens,*
3. *Tabernaemontana heyneana,*
4. *Nothopegia beddomei*
5. *Cinnamomum malabathrum*

In the natural forests, those species behave differently:

§ *Dimocarpus longan,* is no longer dominant , and only occupies the 5th rank

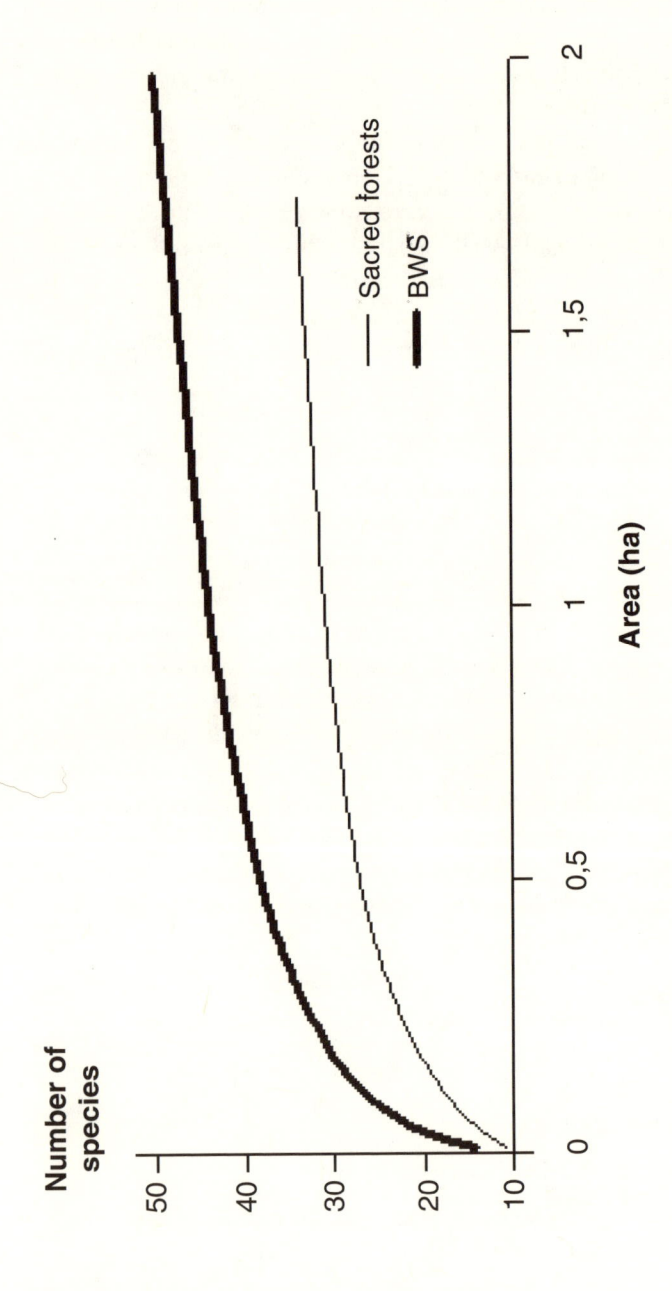

Fig. 7: Endemic Species Accumulation Curves Showing the Relationship between Sampled Area and Expected Endemic Species in the Sacred Forests and the BWS

§ *Xanthophyllum flavescens* becomes rare in the BWS (rank 46)
§ *Tabernaemontana heyneana* is not even present
§ *Nothopegia beddomei* keeps its rank
§ and *Cinnamomum malabathrum* becomes much less frequent (from the 5th rank in sacred forests to the 24th rank in the BWS)

Backbone species of the natural forest suffer a similar fate in sacred forests. The three more abundant species in the BWS, *Palaquium ellipticum* (which gave the forest sub-type its name), *Cryptocarya bourdillonii*, and *Polyalthia coffeoides*, are simply absent from sacred forests.

Ecological Discussion

We could keep on elaborating like this, but the point is already clear. The canopy cover of the BWS is dense and closed. On the other hand, not only are the fragments less dense than the natural forest, they also contain less woody biomass. The canopy of sacred forests is unstructured and has many gaps.

This will have several consequences on the forest dynamics: the gaps and the low density will facilitate the installation of light-demanding species, and the development of grasses, lianas, and climbers. When the old, emergent trees die, lack of recruitment will alter the sealing of the canopy.

The sacred forests in our study area are definitely not undisturbed patches of climax forest, as far as forest structure is concerned. This is coherent with what the scientific literature tells about tropical forest dynamics in small fragments (Laurance and Bierregaard 1997).

Yet the species composition of the canopy may still prove the conservation value of those fragments. *Considered as a network, sacred forests do have a high richness*. This can be explained by a strong heterogeneity of the fragments at all levels: topography, soil, proximity to water, etc. The BWS sample is much more homogeneous. But it must be kept in mind that there is little space outside the sampled area in sacred forests. In many cases, all the richness and diversity was accounted for, sampling errors left aside. That is not the case for natural forests, which form a nearly continuous belt on the ridge of the Western Ghats, thanks to the efforts of the Karnataka forest department.

But the endemic species of the evergreen forest, representing two-thirds of the individuals in the natural forest, are much less abundant in the fragments. *From one-third to one-half of the endemic species have been lost in*

Sacred Forests

% Trees

Dominant species:
1. *Dimocarpus longan*
2. *Xanthophyllum flavescens*
3. *Tabernaemontana heyneana*
4. *Nothopegia beddomei*
5. *Cinnamomum malabathrum*

Species rank

... *figure 8 (contd on p. 215)*

Brahmagiri Wildlife Sanctuary

% Trees

Dominant species:
1. Palaquium ellipticum
2. Cryptocarya bourdillonii
3. Polyalthia coffeoides
4. Nothopegia beddomei
5. Dimocarpus longan

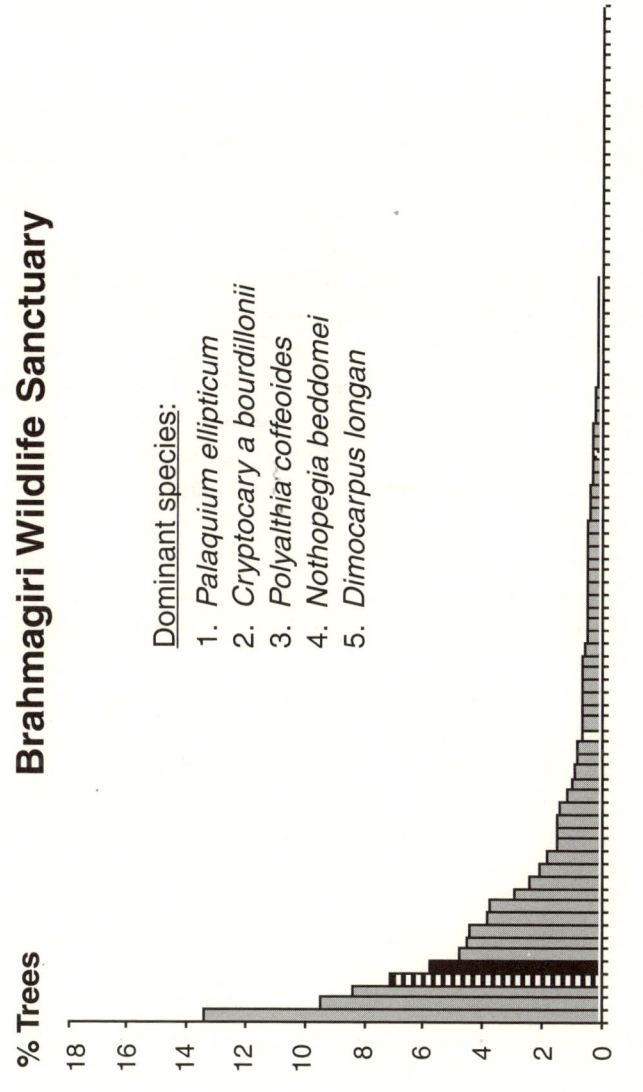

Species rank

Fig. 8: Species/Rank Curves for the Sacred Forests (up) and the BWS (down).

The Five Dominant Species of the Sacred Forest are Colour-coded: *Dimocarpus longan* (■), *Xantho-phyllum flavescens* (▨), *Tabernaemontana heyneana* (■), absent from the BWS, *Nothopegia beddomei* (▥) and *Cinnamomum malabathrum* (□).

sacred forests. This loss is masked by the arrival of new species with wide distribution areas. Most of these will be deciduous and light-demanding species that can establish themselves in the gaps of the canopy, or at the edges of the fragment, and colonize it. Such species have a relatively *low conservation value*, and their overall contribution to the species richness of sacred forests actually tends to diminish their ecological and conservation value.

Finally, the nature of the floristic composition has changed. The backbone species of the natural forest no longer exist in sacred forests. And new species become dominant, sometimes even overdominant (*Dimocarpus longan*). Some species disappear; others have successfully colonized the fragments. The species composition has drifted so far that it can hardly be said that the devarakadus are of the same forest type as the natural forest, far from saying they are remnants of pristine forests, as is routinely said in the literature. Nowhere, in our exhaustive sampling of all sacred forests of the study area, could we find "vegetation in its climax formation [. . .] representation of forest in near virgin condition" (Vartak and Gadgil 1981).

It is worth noting that we discussed the conservation value of a network of sacred forests. Taken individually, each of the fragments has little value. Their individual richness is well beyond that of the natural forest; their diversity is often low, even when considering the total pool of species. In terms of biodiversity conservation and management, it would be almost irrelevant to talk about sacred forests individually. Only when a local population of endemic species is found inside the fragment could this have a meaning.

We draw attention to the fact that a rapid assessment of the biodiversity can lead to misinterpretations. Both richness and diversity are high in sacred forests. Such measures must be balanced by a careful evaluation of conservation value. Several hardy and ubiquitous species do not justify the same conservation effort as one rare or uncommon endemic species.

Ecological significance is only one facet of sacred forests, one that scientists and managers can easily grasp, but quite far from the vision and interests of local inhabitants. Sacred forests are as much ecological objects as social constructions. As Rich Freeman points out: "The modern environmentalist's interest in floristic composition or biodiversity does not inform the institution and maintenance of sacred groves" (Freeman, in Jeffery 1998).

STAKEHOLDERS AND REPRESENTATIONS

Now that we know that sacred forests are not pockets of natural forest, the central question is to determine if the sacredness of the forests provides, per se, a framework of conservation and ecologically sound management practices.

Gadgil and Vartak introduce the notion that the sacred groves are biological hotspots, due to the fact that, out of respect and fear for the deities harbored by them, they are unaffected by human activity: "All the forms of vegetation in such a sacred grove, including shrubs and climbers are supposed to be under the protection of the reigning deity of that grove, and the removal of even a small twig is taboo" (Vartak and Gadgil 1981). We'll see that this representation of sacred forests is not shared by all the actors involved in their management.

Sacred Forests as Resources

Tradition demands that the devarakadus be left untouched, except for "the right to take fire-wood for temple worship, materials for constructing pandals, and ... timber for repairing the temple [that was allowed to] the temple authorities and servants, while the villagers generally have the rights of way and water, of grazing, and of hunting" (Haller 1910).

One part of the ecological survey was to note all traces of human activity in the sacred forests. Paths crossing them were recorded, as well as pits dug up to find edible roots, or cut stems. In sacred forests, 71 ± 9 percent (95 percent confidence interval) quadrats bear evidence of human activity. Sacred forests are not a space left free of the village life. Neighboring villagers do enter these to harvest forest products they cannot find elsewhere, near their homes. The interviews highlighted the different uses of resources in the sacred forests:

Firewood Collection: A family will need two truckloads of firewood per year, mainly for cooking (Interviews 1.5 and 4.1). If this demand cannot be met within the land of the household, other sources need to be found and firewood will be collected from the nearest forest patch. The accessibility and proximity of a sacred forest will determine, then, the amount of biomass collected (Interviews 4.1 and 2.8).

Small Poles and Timber: The harvest of small saplings (often less than 30 cm gbh) is widespread, and accepted by many, since it is not considered as endangering or damaging the forest (Interview 6.2). The felling of large and economically valuable trees, on the other hand, is an outlawed practice. Outsiders from the neighboring state of Kerala are often blamed for this. Both the villagers and the forest department fight against it, but this did not prevent the felling *en masse* of timber from sacred forests (Interviews 1.7, 7.4): "There are no more valuable trees, because the villagers cut them rather than letting them to forest department" (Interview 1.5). Timber extraction with the approval of the forest department and temple committees is possible, though rare. The benefits are then shared between both parties (Interviews 1.1, 7.3). Between the timber smuggling and the legal harvest, "All the valuable trees, rosewood, santal, teak, have already been sold" (Interview 1.3).

Minor Forest Products: A great variety of minor forest products is collected from the sacred forests. Gums, resins (*Canarium strictum*), fruits (*Mangifera indica, Artocarpus heterophyllus, Garcinia gummi-gutta and Sapindus laurifolius*), wild roots, and medicinal plants (*Fabaceae* climbers) are extracted, and sometimes sold in city markets. Such production can supplement household revenue (Interviews 1.6, 1.8, 7.2). The nutrient-rich topsoil of the forests is sometimes removed and used for plant nurseries (Interview 7.2).

Resource Control and Access: As noted by Kalam 2000, accessibility and proximity of a sacred forest is the major factor determining the intensity of different extractions. Most of these uses are opportunistic, and needs are supplemented using the closest forest patch. Since control over access to sacred forests seems less strict than over private forests (Interviews 3.1, 4.1, 7.6) or reserve forests under the rule of the forest department (Interview 7.2), and since sacred forests are at the heart of the village landscape, harvesters often visit them.

Sacred Forests as Space

If the extraction of forest products can lead to conflicts over access to and control of such resources, the land use of sacred forests is not in question. But some actors do have conflicting views challenging this perpective.

Sacred Space: It is not possible to sum up a faith in a few lines. Giving a detailed account of the diversity of cults in sacred forests, and their ritualistic value, is out of the scope of this essay and beyond our abilities. Presented here are only a few elements, extracted from field observations and interviews, which give meaning to the notion of a sacred forest.

This notion is rooted in local history, folklore, and religion: the devarakadus are "God's forests." But two approaches must be distinguished that we would like to label traditional and modern. In the traditional vision, the forest (*kadu*) is essential to faith. Gods are often hunter gods. Aiyappa is the most common (not the Aiyappa of Sabarimala). Temples devoted to him are extremely simple, with no built structure. Most of the time, the *sanctum* is a small clearing in the forest, with some *trishuls* (tridents), and non-iconic representation of the god. Terracotta votive offerings (dogs, sometimes horses) are made. In some cases, blood sacrifices (poultry, goats) can also be offered (Figure 9).

In the modern vision, the temple and the god give all meaning to the devarakadu. The gods (often a form of Shiva, sometimes Bhadrakali) are strictly vegetarian and need a closed and roofed structure. Rituals are very similar to those in the lowlands. The sacred forest is considered the premises of the temple, just as paddy fields are attached to other temples. All the attention, all the resources of the community, will go to "improve" the structures, to establish a permanent *pujari* (Interview 3.2). In some cases, the endowment of land to a priest was mentioned. He could cultivate it, thus clearing the forest (Interviews 2.1, 2.3, 3.2). Only the veto of the forest department can stop this from happening, but, even for the forest department, facing a community united in favor of such endowment may prove difficult.

An informant summed up the differences between these two conceptions:

– What are you looking for when you enter a devarakadu?
– I search peace of mind and comfort. It is the source of my spirituality.
– What difference, then, with a temple?
– It's different. The temple is related to the gods. One goes there to seek their blessings. The devarakadu is associated with nature, and tradition. Temples [in the devarakadus] are a recent addition. (Introduction 7.13)

A good illustration of the arrival of new practices and representations is the appearance of recent structures in the devarakadus. In five of the sacred forests studied, recent structures (erected one to three years back) were present. Constructed using money levied on the community (*terige*), and government grants, such "temple improvements" prove the vitality of devarakadu practices. But, excepting one, such structures were always closed, sometimes even relegating an older shrine with terracotta figures to one

Fig. 9: Traditional Shrine with Terracotta Dogs and
Trishuls (Tridents)—*Kaadu Motte Devarakadu*, Kuttandi Village

side. A closed structure, a vegetarian god, and pujaris, neither of which is present in traditional rituals, are a source of prestige and pride for the community, the village. The center of gravity of the devarakadus is then shifted from forest to temple (see Figure 10 for an example).

Fig. 10: The Temple Expands at the Expense
of the Sacred Forest—*Aiyappa Devarakadu*, Begur Village

To this dichotomy one has to add the social stratification of religious practices, and the visions thus adopted. Different actors pay tribute to different gods, and follow different rituals. The caste system, refuted by the dominant Kodavas,[4] nevertheless dictates who can attend which temple and which devarakadu, and the roles that are to be assumed during rituals. Some sacred forests will thus be traditionally linked to a particular group, caste, or tribe. This adds a further level of complexity to the management regimes of the devarakadus.

Cultivation Space: Forest tends to be considered by the landowners and agriculturists of Kodagu as wasteland that could be turned into a profitable plantation (Interviews 7.6, 1.6). Well-off coffee planters with social weight, whose lands neighbor the devarakadus, may not exclude sacred forests from this representation: "I converted the devarakadu into a coffee estate. Now I have more land, more coffee and my economical situation has improved" (Interview 1.6).

Until recently, forest land had little or no value, the landscape was shaped by paddy fields, where the wealth lay, with adjoining *bane* land on the hilltops.[5] With the advent of large-scale cardamom, pepper and coffee cultivation, this has completely changed. Now the value lies in the coffee estate. Many households do not even bother to work the paddy fields. This new landscape has brought a new representation of what a forest is or should be, and the vision of sacred forests has changed likewise.

Many sacred forests are encroached, appropriated by a neighboring planter for the establishment of a coffee plantation (or by a ginger field when the coffee prices went down recently). The trees are thinned or completely removed, and the land use is then drastically changed (Kalam 2000; personal observation).

Such appropriation is possible because some sacred forests are perceived by the neighboring landowners as open access land. The legal owner is the forest department, hence the government. While few villagers would dare touch temple lands, cheating the government seems, like everywhere, to be a national pastime. Furthermore, there was an ambiguity over who—the revenue department or the forest department—held responsibility over sacred forests (Interview 7.4; Kalam 1996). Hence, the legal owner seemed very far, and unconcerned.

If the sacred forest has no permanent structure (no temple, no festival), if it is associated with a socially low group (Scheduled Caste, Scheduled Tribe), and if the landowner has social weight (being himself from the temple committee of the village for example—Interview 1.6), appropriation will become a distinct possibility (Interviews 1.3, 1.5, 1.6).

This representation of the sacred forest is individual-centered. It views sacred forests as a commodity. The situation is very similar to "the tragedy of the commons" (Hardin 1968), and often leads to conflict, even if it is sometimes suffocated by the social weight of the encroacher.

Other Land Uses within Sacred Forests: There are other uses of the sacred forest that may compete with the two main points of view discussed above.

Sacred Forests as Forests: There is no such thing as one point of view for an administration like the forest department. Management decisions take place according to the perceptions of local foresters within the framework of forest department directives. This leads to different attitudes within the department. In places, the administrator has no interest whatsoever in sacred forests: he sees them as small areas, dispersed, holding the potential of conflict with villagers (Interview 7.3). On occasion, the forest department did take interest in the sacred forests, for extraction and enrichment (plantation) purposes. This did lead to conflict, and the media also played a role here.

Recently, the attitude of the forest department changed, partly due to a genuine interest in conservation, partly due to public pressure (Interview 7.11). Today, sacred forests are considered forests under the control of the forest department, but whose management can be trusted to village communities, via temple committees. The main concern then becomes fighting encroachments and preserving forests (Interviews 7.15, 7.16).

Sacred Forests as Housing Space: This was not present in the study area and could seem anecdotal if it wasn't for the huge impact it had on the discussions with informants and the media. Colonies of laborers from neighboring states (Kerala and Tamil Nadu) were settled by estate owners in a few sacred forests. Buildings, temples, even schools are reported (see Kalam 1996 and 2000 for details). This had a strong symbolic value but, in terms of land use, it happened only in a few places, and was nowhere as widespread as encroachment by local planters (Interview 7.3).

Sacred Forests as Grazing Space: Conversion of bane land into coffee estates, and fencing to prevent crop damage, diminished the amount of available grazing land. For most well-off landowners, this is not a problem, since most of them sold their cattle a few years back and took to mechanization. But for households with cattle and little land, sacred forests provide an alternative to roadsides (Interviews 1.5, 7.2), putting considerable pressure on the forest regeneration.

Sacred Forests as Symbols

The little area the sacred forests represent would let them pass unnoticed were it not for their huge symbolic value. The ecological results raise a series of questions, about what devarakadus represent or are assumed to represent, and why and how they are increasingly used politically.

Sacred Forests as Group Identity Features: Kodagu district has witnessed important changes during the last fifty years. Its population has more than doubled since 1941. This increase is largely due to immigration from neighboring states (Elouard and Guilmoto 2000). Liberalization of the coffee trade and the hike in coffee prices has led to a dramatic increase in the landowner's livelihood and raised labor wages.

These changes have diluted the traditional hierarchical structures (Interviews 1.1, 3.2). Many members of the dominant Kodava community, which emerged as a homogeneous group after colonial rule (Rao and Lokesh 1998), feel that both alien newcomers and an uncaring government, dominated by lowland cities (Mangalore), threaten their position: "The natives of Coorg are in a minority. The migrants have a heavy political weight" (Interview 7.14). This has led many to find in their traditions the source of a renewed identity.[6] "As an answer to the influx of migrants, and their networks of solidarity (specially the Muslims), they [the Kodavas] try to strengthen their local traditions. The devarakadus are a part of this movement" (Interview 7.16). The development of the Kodava Samaj (community gathering halls), the idealization of the *okka*, the joint family system, the writing or reprinting of books dealing with Kodava origins and traditions (Ponnappa 1997; Richter 1870) shape a new nationalism. Faced with rapid changes, some Kodavas find comfort in an idealized vision of the "good old days," while others use it as a ground base to reconstruct a society where they can find their place (Vijaya 2000). This golden tradition, part true part invented, will essentially serve to mark the differences between self and other, between the sons of the soil and the outsiders. It marks a frontier, a boundary that delimits a community of values as well as interests.

The devarakadus are a part of this historiography. The movement for the conservation of the devarakadu gained momentum as it was integrated into mainstream Kodava traditionalism. This explains the importance they have gained in the local media over the last three years: "What we want is to protect the traditional values. This is more important than their [the devarakadus'] ecological value" (Interview 7.13).

Sacred Forests as Political Tools: Devarakadus soon became a political tool, highlighting the lack of concern of the state government and the mismanagement of the forest department (see Anonymous 2000a; Anonymous 2000b; and Anonymous 2001): "Protesting against the large scale encroachment of Sacred Forests . . . to call the attention of the govt. towards the inaction and callousness of the authorities concerned" (*Coffee Land News*, August 21, 2000).

The cause was even embraced by, among others, the CNC (Coorg National Council), the now disgraced separatist party (Interviews 7.1, 7.12, 7.16). Devarakadus were for a moment at the core of Coorgi nationalism.

An organized community with political leverage, such as the Kodavas, could find ways to enforce their vision of sacred forests. They proposed a set of rules to the state government of Karnataka, inspired by the joint forest management plan, to transfer management of sacred forests to village communities. This was done in close association with the forest department, and local NGOs.

The text of these rules would not have been acceptable nor feasible if it benefited only the Kodavas. The notion of group was then expanded to include the other seventeen communities described as native to Kodagu (Interview 7.1). Most of these communities are those that have been dominated by the Kodavas, and few are now as organized or powerful as their former masters.

The study area is located in "Kodagu proper," and in the villages visited, the traditional hierarchy is still very present (Interview 7.6). The temple committees which are to hold responsibility for the management of the sacred forest are comprised almost exclusively of Kodavas or Ammo-Kodavas, a related group. The few non-Kodavas are barely accepted and seldom voice their opinion at meetings (Interviews 1.2, 7.2). Likewise, some of these seventeen communities integrated into the management plan only pay lip service to the project.

The adhesion of the Kodava community to the movement for conservation of sacred forests can then be understood, at least in part, as a way of restating their dominance over the landscape, a dominance that was contested by the arrival of migrants and by the dissolution of old hierarchies. Ecology is far from being the central question.

Sacred Forests as Religious Icons: This point has been addressed partially when considering sacred forests as sacred space. Here we deal with another dimension, less anchored to the landscape and everyday life of the village. This view of sacred forests sees them as temples of the Hindu faith. As such, they deserve the same amount of reverence and protection as any temple. Interestingly, the tenants of this representation are not necessarily concerned with the traditional aspects of sacred forests, since they are not related to mainstream Hinduism.

It is, then, not surprising that groups like the RSS (Rashtriya Swayamsevak Sangh), and other radical Hinduist movements, newcomers to the Kodagu scene, rallied the cause of the conservation of the devarakadus and allied for a while to Kodava traditionalists (Interview 7.16).

Sacred Forests as Sanctuaries of Nature: There is a distinction between natural sanctuaries, which the devarakadus may have been, and sanctuaries of nature, which they have become recently—in the eyes of some. This representation is quite close to the European approach to national parks. It banishes all human activities from the forested area. It fights encroachment, but also extraction and cattle grazing. Biodiversity and strict conservation are its motto.

This has happened recently and is a view which sometimes merges with a religious symbolism. Sacred forests appear then as a proof of ecological wisdom in the old faith and in traditional practices.[6] The differences noted between the idealized representation of sacred forests and their real ecological status is then blamed upon the erosion of values and modern iconoclast consumerism. This representation is more commonly found in the media—in local newspapers as well as scientific papers. It has an ecological back up which makes it politically correct and hence displayable.

CONCLUSION

The positions presented above are archetypal. Most of the actors shape their own representation, taking elements from different visions that suit their beliefs, their knowledge and their desires. But in all situations, sacred forests act as a metaphor.

Arguments about Nature are always arguments about Society. J. Weber, personal communication.

Sacred forests are described as isolated fortresses where the last remnants of tradition and religion stand assaulted by external foes, be they migrants, non-believers, modern values, or for that matter exotic plant species. This is a striking and powerful image that has its roots in concepts and representations that largely overcome the mere problem of the management of some patches of forest. And this is probably the reason for so many heated debates. The representations and the motives in conflict may well be far from the ground-level reality of the sacred forests and from the daily relationship that neighboring habitants establish with them.

Our ecological study shows that there is a great gap between the common image of sacred forests and what is found in the field. Once the old paradigm is shattered, it becomes possible to question the different representations of the stakeholders and their vision of sacred forests.

Does the value of the sacred forest lie, then, in the eyes of the observer? It certainly depends on the geographic scale considered:

§ The resource value of a sacred forest acts at the local level. It takes into account the number of dependent households, the amount of biomass extracted, and the services it provides that cannot be replaced in the immediate neighborhood.

§ The religious and symbolic value also operates at the local level, in the life of the village, its festivals, and its rituals (Figure 11). People will cherish and pay respect to their God, to their temple, and sometimes to their devarakadu. The symbolic representations that have a broader scale do not really focus on the devarakadus, but rather on an idea, a metaphor, and often have very different agendas only marginally concerned with the ground-level reality of sacred forests.

§ The ecological value—if we admit that an ecosystem or a group of ecosystems have an intrinsic value without a human to assess it—lies on a regional scale. A single sacred forest, apart from some exceptional spots, will have little or no conservation value. This is due to the smallness of size that affects forest dynamics, and the strength of the human pressure on it that alters the structure, composition, and dynamics of the canopy. But as a network—provided a minimum number of such forests each with minimal area is conserved—the sacred forests of Kodagu can preserve at least a sizeable portion of the local biodiversity, specially in areas where large tracts of protected forests are unthinkable or unwanted. But

Fig. 11: Gathering at the Annual Festival—the Temple and the Sacred Forest at the Heart of Village Life—*Kundachappa Devarakadu*, Kuttandi Village

it is clear they cannot replace a wider network of large-scale reserves that, luckily, exist at the margins of the district.

The question of the ecological value of sacred forests should not hide the existence of secular forests, government holdings, or private patches of forest not converted into coffee estates—for a variety of reasons. Estimates from satellite imagery tell us that this kind of land use may amount to up to 14 percent of the total forested area of Kodagu, which is eight times more than the area of sacred forests (Elouard and Guilmoto 2000). Work is currently under way to estimate their ecological value, and this will help us determine if the sacredness of the devarakadus provided them with a better framework for conservation or not.

Sacred forests merge environment, history, and religion. As such, they are a keystone in the definition of the relationship between man and nature. Researchers, be they natural or social scientists, and decisionmakers must be aware that the natural sciences can take us only so far in the definition and justification of such an institution. Beyond that, the matter becomes an ideological (religious and/or political) one, and is therefore removed from scientific purview.

NOTES

This work was carried out with a fellowship from the French Institute, Pondicherry (FIP). The Institute and the Ponnampet College of Forestry (University of Agricultural Sciences, Bangalore) provided logistic and administrative support. Mr S. Aravajy, N. Barathan Ravi, and S. Ramalingam from the FIP provided superb fieldwork, as did students of the Ponnampet College of Forestry. Work in the BWS was possible thanks to the collaboration of the Karnataka forest department to whom we express our gratitude.

This work could not have been carried out without the invaluable help of Dr C.G. Kushalappa, who provided not only logistics but also much-needed insights and clear-minded analysis of Kodagu society and ecosystems. We are indebted to him for his friendship, his openmindness, and his ability as an organizer.

1. This sacred forest no longer exists; it was converted some years ago into a coffee estate. It is included in the data set only for reference.

2. This sacred forest was being dismantled when the data was collected. Only a few trees were left.

3. We consider here as endemics those species whose area of distribution is strictly limited to the Western Ghats. They are listed in Ramesh and Pascal 1997.

4. The Kodavas, or Coorgs, are the traditional masters of the land. For literature on them, see Richter 1870 as an introduction.

5. *Bane* is forest land granted for the service of the holding of paddy fields to which it is allotted for grazing purposes, and to provide the leaf manure, firewood, and timber required in the holding.

6. It is interesting to note that the Kodavas refer to European writings for the sources of their traditions. See Rao and Lokesh 1998 for a detailed study.

III
Commodified Nature and National Visions

9

KNOWLEDGE AGAINST THE STATE

Local Perceptions of Government Interventions in Fishery (Kerala, India)[1]

Götz Hoeppe

IF ONE DEFINES "ECOLOGICAL NATIONALISM" AS "WAYS IN WHICH varieties of nationalism are mediated and constructed through reference to the natural," as Sivaramakrishnan and Cederlöf do in their Introduction, then the focus of this essay is on the role of environmental knowledges, both "local" and "global," in this process. In focusing thus, I shall concentrate on what is called "indigenist/regionalist reactions to the expansion of the high-modern nation state." Looking at a community of marine fisherfolk in Kerala, South India, three issues draw attention. First, how did these fishermen perceive state-induced development interventions? Second, do they perceive the post-Independent state government's access to, and use of, environmental knowledge as different from that of the colonial government? Third, has fishermen's "local knowledge" been affected by confrontation with the powerful knowledge of the state? I believe that two examples of state expansion into fisheries may shed some light on this topic, one colonial and the other post-Independent. The first is the ban on the fishery of small oil sardines which was issued over 1943 to 1947 by the government of the (British-ruled) Madras Presidency. The second is a seasonal ban on trawling which has been annually ordered by the state government of Kerala since 1988. My approach is ethnographic, the findings being based on eighteen months of fieldwork in Kerala (in 1999/2000 and 2002), including twelve months of residence in Chamakkala, a fishing village. In addition, I studied published sources from both the colonial and Independent periods.

At first sight, the emerging issue seems to lie in the confrontation of "global" or supposedly "scientific" knowledge with "local" knowledge, the latter being labeled alternatively "indigenous" or "traditional" (for the ups and downs of these terms, cf. Ellen and Harris 2000). Another theme to be explored, in the tradition of Foucault, is the link between these knowledges and discursive power (e.g. Tsing 1993). In any case, one should be wary of a simple dichotomy such as "global" vs. "local." Its apparent straightforwardness and simplicity make one wonder whether we are dealing here with an essentialism which hides more than it reveals (Springer 2000). For example, the global and the local may permeate and modify each other in many ways, eventually becoming indistinguishable: no wonder essentialism has been called the "bad word" of modernity (Daniel 1996: 13). On the other hand, to identify the purposeful, perhaps even strategic, use of essentialization in discourse may be an insightful method of inquiry (Herzfeld 1996). It turns out that the village's fishermen themselves make use of such essentialisms, for example, when contrasting the present "time of progress" (*puroogamicchu kaalam*)—characterized by technological advance and a decline in morality—with "old times" (*paazhaya kaalangal*) of poverty yet moral purity. When considering environmental knowledge within the scope of "power" and "ecological nationalism," the benefits and limitations of essentialization thus become relevant. Knowledge perceived to be scientific might be associated with foreignness and power. Yet by claiming the label scientific for local knowledge, it may gain authority as well. As we shall see, what is considered scientific locally may differ profoundly from that which Western scientists would call scientific.

In line with the forest dwellers discussed in this volume by Morrison, Cederlöf, and Damodaran, Kerala's fishermen have been marginalized by both the colonial and the post-Independent state. They have been fringe dwellers, both geographically as well as with regard to their position in Kerala society. By and large, artisanal fishermen's exclusive right to access marine resources remained unchallenged until Independence in 1947: for them there was no need to articulate this right. However, in recent decades the state has intervened in manifold ways, visible and invisible, within their lifeworld. The changes produced thereby may not be obvious to the outsider (including government representatives), but they are interwoven with local concepts in intricate ways. These may only be properly understood if one considers fishermen's conceptualizations in some detail. These fishermen have understood that their way of relating with the marine environment is increasingly challenged. In such a shifting situation, knowledges themselves are transformed and reiterated, and ambivalences hitherto unknown have emerged.

Let me provide further detail about my fieldwork location. Since 1830, Chamakkala was part of Malabar District, and, thus of Madras Presidency. When Kerala became a state in 1956 through the merger of the kingdoms of Travancore and Cochin with Malabar District, our village came to be located in Trichur District. Most fishermen in the village are Hindus and belong to the Araya caste. Muslims were previously much involved in fish vending and, to a smaller extent, in fishing, but they have largely abandoned these activities in favor of work in countries of the Persian Gulf. Having spent most time with the (male) fishermen of Chamakkala, my findings will be biased toward their views. The language spoken in Kerala is Malayalam; its speakers are called Malayalis. In what follows, transcribed Malayalam words appear in italics.

This essay is arranged as follows. In section II I give an outline of how Chamakkala fishermen conceptualize their environment. In section III I describe their memories and perceptions of the 1943–7 ban on oil sardines, as issued by the Madras department of fisheries. I also consider how the reasoning of this department's scientists led to the ban. In section IV I briefly summarize the changes in the fisheries of Kerala since 1947, and how they led to the installation of an annual ban on the use of trawling boats in 1988. Once more, I am particularly interested in fishermen's perceptions and judgments thereof, and the interactions with putative government knowledge. Some conclusions on the fate of local knowledge in the "time of progress" are made in the final section.

KNOWING THE SEA BY RELATING TO IT

In a most general manner, the ways in which the Chamakkala fishermen conceptualize the sea are characterized by a sense of the interrelatedness of human beings with their marine environment. Their knowledge of this environment is not held to be absolute in any sense, but is continually reconstituted and reiterated by engaging with the sea and working on it.

The sea is commonly referred to as the "west" (*patinjaru*). Fishing is the "[manual] work of the west" (*patinjaththu pani*). In fishermen's speech, the Malayalam word for sea (*katal*) is used less often. Most fishermen agree that the sea is female in character. In their general comments, reflections, and lamentations, older men refer to the sea as "mother" (*amma*) or "sea mother" (*katalamma*). Notably, this is a category of kinship which entails notions of caring and protection. In fishermen's understanding of the sea, these are relevant (see below). Even though there are no temples consecrated to *katalamma*, she is often identified with the goddess (*devi*) of the Hindu pantheon.

Besides this explicit notion of the sea's female nature, fishermen's speech contains many references to its "bodiliness" and "subjectivity." Its "bodiliness" is manifested by what one may call a "physiology of heat." The terms which are used by fishermen to refer to the constitution of the sea are identical to those used when referring to the female human body. A state of heat (*chuutu*), agitation (*kshoobham*), and anger (*koopam*) is opposed to a state of coldness (*thanuppu*) and calmness (*shaantham*). As in the female body, the "heat" of the sea is imagined as varying according to regular patterns.[2] This latter is illustrated by a popular myth in which the seasonal cycle of the "heat" of the sea is considered an expression for the sea's desire for intercourse with (male) river water from the Western Ghats. This desire is cooled by the mountain water (*mala vellam*)—i.e. water which has poured down the Western Ghats during the south-west monsoon (June to August) and which subsequently enters the sea through rivers. When the mountain water enters the sea, the latter is expected to be rough for a few days, but subsequently its heat is supposed to be "cooled." As a consequence fish, thought to prefer cool environments, may now enter the near-coastal inshore waters. Currents in the sea are said to be affected by the mountain water as well. A counter-current from west to east is supposed to carry along small fish.

Another example of the sea's bodiliness is provided by verbs which describe the sea either as (passively) "lying down" (inf. *kitakkuka*) or (actively) "standing up" (inf. *iranguka*). In the case of the latter, the sea in the west is supposed to be situated higher than the beach. Being in contradiction with the commonsensical experience of water flowing down, the notion of a standing sea has been considered an example for the morally constituted power of the sea to protect the people who live in coastal areas. This protective attitude of the sea is commonly ascribed to its innate truthfulness (*sathyam*), a quality composed of notions of benevolence, protectiveness, and provision. It is the *sathyamulla muthal katal*, the "from-the-beginning truthful" one. If defined in this way, truthfulness resembles the nurturance model of motherhood as elaborated by Lakoff (1987: 74f.). And indeed, as we have seen, fishermen do refer to the sea as mother. Yet, unlike in the hunter-gatherer societies considered by Bird-David (1990), where conceptualization of the environment as parents makes their members the mere recipients of a unidirectional "flow" of benevolence (a "giving environment"), Chamakkala fishermen emphasize that the moral, protective behavior of the sea presupposes that fishermen themselves reciprocate, and act in accordance with well-defined rules of morality and purity. As such, one may speak of a morally sanctioned reciprocal relationship between fishermen and the sea. Thus, much emphasis is placed on the sea's "subjectivity" or "agency."

These examples offer some insight into these fishermen's ontology. Rather than being governed by lifeless physical objects and impersonal forces, their world is at least to some extent determined by moral, "personal" interactions. Likewise, their epistemology is in part personalized i.e. their knowledge of the marine world is gained through engaging in social relationships between subjects. This resembles in many ways the concepts of intersubjectivity emphasized in the phenomenology of Heidegger, Merleau-Ponty, and others (cf. Jackson 1998; Ingold 2000).

This perception gains additional significance if we consider the fishermen's self-image as fringe-dwellers in Malayali society. Despite seeing themselves as marginal, for fishermen the sea and the activity of fishing is also a domain of self-representation. When speaking of fishing, they commonly mention its independent character, freeing them from the command of superiors. They are aware that skill is necessary for success in fishing, and they know the uncertainty and danger which it entails, but they are equally aware of the possibility of sudden and immense catches. Courage, "good guts" (*nallu thandeetam*), and bravery (*dhairyam*), which are thought necessary for fishing in the outer sea (*puram katal*), add to a self-image via fishing within which male autonomy, performative skills, and independence are highly valued.[3] These personal traits distinguish fishermen from *kizhakkarans*, the "people of the east," or dwellers inland. Depending on the context, this undifferentiated group may include people from the village, as well as those in nearby or distant towns, and even representatives of the state government. The word denotes people who do not relate to the sea and who cannot therefore know it.

While success or mischance in fishing may be interpreted in the light of these relationships, fishermen know well that neither the sea nor the fish are predictable in any absolute sense. Thus, irregularities of wind, rain, or sea currents are often considered as a "*vikrithi* of nature" (*prakrithi*). *Vikrithi* may be translated as "change, abnormality, vicious attitude or mischief" (Warrier *et al.*, 1999: 972) and is commonly used in contexts of affectionate familiarity between human beings. The behavior of sea and fish cannot be predicted. An old man explains: "If what has to happen does not happen then it is the mischief (*vikrithi*) of nature" (*prakrithi*). The mischievousness of the sea, its irregularities and the impossibility of making predictions about its future behavior, remind fishermen of the limitations of their knowledge. Says Kunhiayyappan, one of the village's oldest fishermen in his mid eighties:

> The *prakrithi* of the sea's fish cannot be explained by us. Sometimes the fish step down [come ashore] and then the heat is not at all a problem for them. The *prakrithi* of the sea, or the *prakrithi* of the fish in the sea: it means how the *prakrithi* of the sky is changing, and in the same manner how the sea and the fish are changing. Our ancestors mention three conditions for this: the rain from the sky, the fish in the sea, and the changes of the *prakrithi* of the sea. These three cannot be predicted by anyone and nobody can do anything against them.

Note that Kunhiayyappan here uses the word prakrithi—often translated into English as "nature,"—in the sense of "character" or "behavior."[4]

Fluctuations in catches and the uncertainties of trying to predict fish behavior are known all too well. Another fisherman, Kunhiraman says: "These are the fish. It is not their habit to build a house and live in it. So they travel from one side to another." Fishermen are familiar with fluctuations in catches of fish particularly in relation to the Malabar oil sardine (Mal. *chaala*; Lat. *Sardinella longiceps* Val.). These are commonly understood as being the fastest fish. When they disappear from the near-coastal inshore sea for weeks, months, or even years, they are said to have migrated to other parts of the Arabian Sea or the Bay of Bengal. Mackerel (Mal. *ayila*; Lat. *Rastrelliger kanagurta*), conceived as slower than the oil sardine, is also known for its migratory habits. Both oil sardines and mackerel are thought to live mostly near the surface of the sea. In contrast, fish perceived as living at the sea's bottom, such as the Malabar sole (Mal. *manthal*; Lat. *Cynoglossus semifasciatus*) and prawn (Mal. *chemmiin*; Lat. *Parapenaeopsis* and *Penaeus* spp.), are understood as too slow to migrate over long distances. They are believed to be more prone to being carried along near-bottom currents. Nevertheless, all fish are thought to prefer a cold and quiet environment. Ideas of the quantity of catches are always linked to thoughts about the location of fish. This conjuncture about the habit of fish migrating over long distances and over long periods makes it impossible to talk of a definite, quantifiable "stock of fish" in the sea.

I should add that the morally constituted reciprocal relationship between these people and the sea is not extended to include fish. Rather, the latter are often called "stuff" (*charakku*) or "matter" (*saadanam*).

Virtually all fishermen in Chamakkala agree that the seasonal regularity of the sea has been profoundly disturbed in recent decades. Since the 1950s, a number of dams have been built in the Western Ghats to store water for irrigation and generate electricity. The construction of these dams in the eastern mountains is widely thought to have disrupted a previously established regularity. The disruption is seen to impede local fisheries in three different ways. First, in the language of their myth mentioned earlier, the near-shore sea remains "hot" instead of being "cooled." The intercourse of waters is needed for the sea to cool; uncooled, the near-shore sea remains unattractive for fish, for, as we saw, fish are believed to prefer cold environments. Second, the hypothetical counter-current which brings small fish is absent. Third, mud brought down by the mountain water may be nutritious and, as such, attractive for fish, but is now lacking.

The view that the sea no longer gets sufficiently rough at the beginning of the south-west monsoon is, to many fishermen, a transformation of their environment, even if this is temporal or seasonal. The change has been enforced from outside, by the construction of the dams. Those who have inflicted this change on the environment are judged suspiciously: it was certainly done by inland people, the *kizhakkarans* ("people of the east"), but it is surmised that the state government was also involved in the construction of the dams and, thus, in the transformation of the sea.

COLONIAL INTERVENTIONS: A BAN ON THE FISHERY OF OIL SARDINES

In the early 1940s an enormous decline in the landings of oil sardines was noticed in Chamakkala and elsewhere along the Malabar coast. Old fishermen remember that for several years no oil sardines were caught at all. This was a serious issue. Locally, oil sardines are (and have been) the most nutritive fish species for the local populace by virtue of its abundance and low price. Occasionally, this fish is called "provider of the family" (*kutumban pularthi*). At the same time, fluctuations in the catches of this fish are well known. Within memory, sudden drops in the catches and, subsequently, years without any catch, have been known.

It came as a surprise to fishermen in Chamakkala when in 1943, the Madras department of fisheries ordered a ban on the capture of small fry and spawners. The prohibitions were threefold and concerned:

(a) the use of the highly destructive boat seine (*mathikolli vala*) during the sardine season from August to April,
(b) the use of the encircling gill net (*mathichaala vala*) during the spawning period in August and September; and
(c) the landing of more than a total weight of 37 kg (one maund) of oil sardines under 15 cms from any single boat during the fishing season (ICAR 1971: 28).

Boat seines and encircling gill nets were the common gear to catch pelagic (i.e. near-surface) fish. The ban was renewed in 1945, when, in addition, the use of boat seines and encircling gill nets was forbidden all year round. Never before had a similar ban been imposed on the marine fisheries of Malabar.

When I learned about the ban during my fieldwork in 1999/2000 I wondered how the older fishermen were judging its usefulness. Did they think the ban benefited anyone? And if so, whom? Kunhiraman, in his mid eighties, remembers:

> In the sea no oil sardine was seen. At that time everybody was saying that the oil sardine was lost, then the police was watching if anybody was fishing oil sardines, and they said that it is forbidden to catch oil sardines. But some [catches of] oil sardine arrived in Kochi and after some time small oil sardines got caught in some people's nets here, and because of this [illegal fishing] some police cases were filed. It is true, the oil sardine was missing for some time, but it came back afterwards. That was when the British were ruling [. . .] Sometimes fish is missing from our sea. Occasionally, fish is not seen for one or two months, and after that it comes here from other regions. The same fish which left may come here again.

Chandran, a man in his late sixties, explains:

> At that time, the oil sardine was missing in the sea for twelve years. [. . .] It may move through the sea, and even to the Eastern sea. That means to Madras. By moving like this, the oil sardine vanished from here. There is only a small possibility that they may turn around and come back here. Thus the

oil sardine became rare. Last year and the year before too [i.e. around 1997/8] the oil sardine was missing a lot. The oil sardine which we got in the market was the oil sardine from Madras. To sell it here, the oil sardine was brought from Madras! Now it has turned to the Northern Sea, that means the Bay of Bengal, and then it reached the Arabian Sea. After breeding and hatching it has multiplied. Now it will be here for some time. It may move to the Southern sea and then we will miss it for three or four years. Less oil sardine was there for five years but this year it came back.

Given the age of this man, he cannot have witnessed the 1943–7 ban; he was relying on hearsay. His reference to the recent decline is correct. Kerala-wide catches of oil sardine plummeted from 190,000 tonnes in 1989 to a mere 1554 tonnes in 1994, a decline of 99.2 percent (Yohannan *et al.* 2000: 6). In Chamakkala, oil sardine catches were thought to have returned to their former level only in 1999.

Ramakrishnan, a man in his mid seventies, recalls:

Oil sardine is the main food of sharks. Previously, catching the oil sardine had been banned by the government. We were not allowed to catch the oil sardine, because the oil sardine was the food of the shark. This was the reason, according to the fisheries department. The order was issued that the oil sardine must not be caught. Those who caught the oil sardine had to be punished. So the oil sardine was caught, but it was secretly transported to faraway places. The sale was done secretly. If we were getting big sharks, then we had to sell them to the fisheries department.

At Independence in 1947, the ban was abolished because of "difficulties encountered in its enforcement, the lack of preventive staff over a long coast line and of similar legislation in adjacent states" (ICAR 1971: 28).

The decline in landings of oil sardines has been memorable. Equally memorable has been the ban and its enforcement, as well as the attempts to bypass controls. According to several men, it was made the duty of the *kadak-kodis*, i.e. local headmen of the Araya caste, to enforce the ban. As such, the colonial government made use of the caste's hierarchical structure. During my fieldwork I realized that most *kadakkodi* families had not had active fishermen for generations. Indeed, many of them had long turned into petty landlords, holders of small government posts and teachers in the state in "fisheries schools." Until today, if one finds English-speaking members of the Araya caste, they are usually members of the families of former *kadakkodis*. As such, the ban of 1943–7 was delegated to members of the same caste which had to control the (low-status) work of their former equals. This situation reminds one of Akhil Gupta's work on the praxis of a North Indian government office of agriculture. Gupta notices that the local population came in touch with the government usually at its lowest levels. These people experience the complex formation of a "state" through their interaction with individuals with whom they may entertain a variety of social relationships. Thus, for them the distinction between "the state" and "the local population" is difficult to identify (Gupta 1995a: 376). The role of the *kadakkodis* during the 1943–7 ban suggests that it was similarly difficult for fishermen to disentangle the colonial state from the local population. At least over the duration of the ban, the boundary of the colonial state, blurred as it may have been, was situated within the fishing community itself (cf. Gupta 1995a: 384).

As the first two men emphasize, fluctuations in the catch have been seen as inevitable, and certainly not a consequence of over-fishing. This seemed in agreement with "local knowledge" about oil sardines and fish more generally. With this understanding in mind, none of the men judged the ban as beneficial for the "recovery" of oil sardine catches observed in 1948 (see below). The ban was, rather, judged as a misconception, as a meaningless endeavour.

Why, then, did the department of fisheries consider the ban necessary? Fishermen were unaware that the ban was the result of the first scientific investigations into the marine fisheries of South India. But how could they know this? After all, during the ban (as well as before), visits of British officials to the seashore were rare and did not involve much interaction with fishermen. None of the old fishermen of Chamakkala can remember that these officials would discuss the reasons for the installation of the ban with them.

In order to shed light on why the fisheries department installed the ban, we must consider in more detail its intentions to develop fisheries. As Sivaramakrishnan and Cederlöf write in their Introduction, the British produced a history of "development interventions where wilderness and wild people have been brought into the fold of progressive possibilities." Fisheries were no exception. From its foundation in 1908, the Madras department of fisheries considered fisheries as needing to be developed in accord with Western technical and scientific knowledge.[5] In that year Frederick Nicholson became the first director of fisheries in Madras. His verdict on the fisheries in Malabar, as in 1916, is worth quoting:

> [The] fishing industry is in the most primitive condition, quite undeveloped in any of the modern methods and allied industries, bound by custom and ignorance, and entirely without initiative in new departures; it is the Government officers only who have a larger knowledge and a certain degree of initiative, and it is, at present, for them to lead the industry and the men, as has been done in the oil and guano development, in canning and other curing and cultural methods, and as will be done shortly in matters of capture; this is the raison d'être, and this only, of the Government Department [of Fisheries]. (Govindan 1916: 2)

Thus, the artisanal fisheries of the Malabar coast were not seen as what they were, but as what they were not—and as what they ought to be. British intervention was based on a paradigm rather different from fishermen's idea of their interrelatedness with their environment. Nicholson believed fishing to be an industry which had to be developed by government. His comparison of fishing with the developments in oil and guano production and the hint at canning technologies suggest that he had in mind the development of Malabar fisheries as export oriented; he did not merely wish to improve the living conditions of fishing folk. Their development was to be based on "fisheries science," then newly emerging in Europe. Of course, "science" was understood as the production of knowledge according to the methodological style inherited within Western modernity, implicitly representing, at any time, the closest possible approximation to "truth" and following a universal (i.e. "global") style of reasoning. If artisanal fishing was indeed regarded as "bound by custom and ignorance" we may safely assume that the British had little interest in consulting fishermen about their ideas on fluctuations in the landings of oil sardines. Indeed, in all the extensive reports published by the British, I found only rare hints of any interest in fishermen's knowledge. It was James Hornell, in 1918 Nicholson's successor as Madras Director of Fisheries, who occasionally seems to have noted fishermen's ideas (Hoeppe, forthcoming). However, it is nowhere visible that this occasional interest has had any influence on the research scheme or on government policies.

Perhaps the administration's interest in local fishing techniques and fishermen's local knowledge would have run counter to the department's intentions. By criticizing the "ignorance" of Malabar fisheries of the day and its "being bounded by old customs," Nicholson delegitimizes its status. In contrast, he notices that only government officers had a "larger knowledge" and a "certain degree of initiative," thus legitimizing the doings of the colonial administration. Such a strategic function of "science" and "scientific knowledge" in the legitimation of British colonial intervention in India has been previously noticed by Kumar (1995: 229).

In 1899, even before Nicholson took up his position, the fish resources of the Madras Presidency had been estimated. A note on the "desirability of developing the agricultural department [of Madras Presidency]" estimated that one million tonnes of fish could be annually caught (Anonymous 1915: 2). This was the first estimate against which future catches came to be measured.[6] Earlier, only exports of fish products (mostly dried fish and fish oil) had been recorded. Now, the aim was to quantify fish landings in a comprehensive way in order to understand the potential of the fishery. Hitherto, catches by the artisanal fishing folk, which were mostly consumed locally, had remained unknown. In 1908 the department of fisheries began to record (or, at least, estimate) the catches of artisanal fishermen and publish them in its annual reports. Quantifying exploitable and exploited resources in this manner is of course a typical activity of the modern state (cf. Scott 1998).

Soon, the numbers in the landings revealed immense fluctuations. Of all varieties of fish caught, fluctuations of oil sardines were the largest. This was particularly unfortunate, for the British had recognized that this fish was the most important nutrient for the local population. In Malabar district, catches of oil sardines were low in 1908–9 to 1911–12, reasonable in 1912–13 to 1913–14, and dropped again from 1914–15 to 1918–19 (Balan 1984: 1). Throughout the 1920s and early 1930s, catches fluctuated widely between 1100 tonnes (in 1931–2) and 41,690 tonnes (in 1933–4: Nair 1952). The fisheries department's Annual Report for 1941 notes somewhat desperately: "So great are the fluctuations [in the catches of oil sardine] that they render the fishery unstable and undependable" (p. 7). Elsewhere, the fluctuations are called "unfortunate and disastrous" (Devanesan 1943: 2). What resounds in these quotes is the colonial state's concern with the food security of its subjects (cf. Vasavi 1999).

When James Hornell was appointed Director of Fisheries in 1918, he initiated scientific research into the nature of these fluctuations. Perhaps the greatest step in this direction was, in 1921, the inauguration of a fisheries research station on West Hill in Calicut: "It is only an institution which gives facilities for laboratory work, study of collections, and for consultation of books, in a word, a Fisheries Research Station that can with a definite plan of work promote, direct and consolidate marine fisheries research" (Devanesan 1943: 1). Studies on the fluctuations of the oil sardine fishery began at the station in 1921 and were directed at learning more about the life cycle of this fish and its spawning grounds. The results were published three years later (Hornell and Nayadu 1924), but were largely inconclusive. Following a decade of immense fluctuations, an improved investigation started in 1930, when D. W. Devanesan was appointed Assistant Director of Fisheries (Biology). Devanesan, a biologist with a doctoral degree from London, was to implement a state-of-the-art program of research at the Calicut station. His specific duty was to address the issue of fluctuations in the fishery of oil sardines. The advance of his research can be traced in the annual reports of the fisheries department until 1942 (apparently, no annual reports were published between 1943 and 1947) as well as in a separate report (Devanesan 1943).

As mentioned, from the viewpoint of local fishermen the border between the colonial state and their caste may have been blurred because of the enforcement of state politics by fellow caste members. One may speculate that, on the other hand, the department of fisheries did not perceive an absolute border between the "colonial government" and the local population. This may be surmised if one notices that Devanesan and other Indian co-workers of the department appear as authors and co-authors of its publications. The title page of Devanesan's 1943 report on his investigations of the oil sardine fishery mentions not only the PhD which he had obtained from the University of London, but calls him "Rao Bahadur," a title given to Indian officers, and addresses him respectfully as "Sahib."

The career of some other of the department's co-workers is equally remarkable. Particularly noteworthy is V.V. Govindan, an Araya man from Kozhikodu, who was hired by Nicholson in 1914 and soon promoted to become the "Assistant Director of Fisheries (West Coast)." By hiring local men the department must have attempted to improve the realization of its development aims. Prior to his promotion as assistant director, Govindan was sent on a journey to Britain and Germany in order to study what Nicholson had called the "modern methods and allied industries" of fishing. As Nayadu and Devanesan did some years later, in 1916 Govindan published a report in the "Madras Fisheries Bulletin" under his own name. Until today, Govindan's career is remembered with much respect in Chamakkala, especially among academically educated Arayas. This was made particularly clear when, in 1978, a "Rao Bahadur V.V. Govindan Memorial Souvenir" was published, this being a 200-page book comprising articles in praise of Govindan's life and work. It was published on the occasion of his birth centenary, in Kaipamangalam, a village south of Chamakkala.

Coming back to the history of oil sardine research in Malabar: while recordings of the annual catches of all fish species continued throughout, Devanesan initiated size measurements of large numbers of oil sardines. In doing this, his aim was to investigate whether or not the fluctuations were due to over-fishing. If years of large catches were indeed followed by years of small sardines, this was a likely conclusion. Devanesan was aware that catches and fish sizes needed to be collected for a number of years before any such relationship could be established. Besides over-fishing, there were two other hypotheses. First, the "migration theory," which assumed that oil sardines migrated temporarily (as the artisanal fishermen surmised); and, second, that shoals of sardines were prevented from entering the coast by specific hydrographical conditions (rainfall, temperature, salinity, etc.). The basic question underlying all these ideas targeted the issue of over-fishing. In 1933/4, according to Devanesan: "unless the Malabar sardine proves to be a distinct local race confined to that coast, the question of depletion by fishing does not arise, though this has often been alleged to be the reason for the scarcity of fish in some years" (cited in the Annual Report for 1941, p. 7). Indeed, if the Malabar oil sardine is a local fish, then its fishery could be influenced by a ban in the fishery. On the other hand, if it is not local, then a regulation, which is only enforced locally, will have limited success. This was the "local race theory." If verified, it implied that one could consider the abundance of oil sardines in terms of a "stock," quantifiable and, thus, in principle, manageable by government regulation. This idea was alien to artisanal fishermen.

Devanesan surmised that the question whether or not the Malabar oil sardine was a local fish could be established in two ways. First, if this was true, its spawning grounds must be located somewhere in the Malabar area.

Second, there ought to be anatomical differences between Kerala oil sardines and those from other parts of the Arabian Sea and the Indian Ocean.

Results of the first investigation were published in the Annual Report for 1935. This reported the discovery of spawning grounds about 15 kms in the sea off Calicut. Resolving the second issue took more time. Oil sardine specimens were collected from Karwar (near Bombay), Karachi, Muscat (Oman), and, later, Aden (Yemen). Some additional specimens were consulted in the collections of the Natural History Museum (London). The differences in anatomy were found to be slight. Hence, an unambiguous conclusion seemed impossible. Nevertheless, Devanesan concluded that the "migration theory" was unlikely and that the "local race theory" may have to be preferred (1943: 36). In other words, he surmised the over-fishing of a local "stock" of oil sardines. This conclusion was drawn not only from the discovery of the spawning grounds, but also from the results of a decade of comparing landings and size measurements. According to the latter, large catches of small, i.e. young, oil sardines (with sizes under 15 cms) in one year resulted in a lack of small oil sardines the next year. Apparently, the fishery of little sardines lowered their contribution to a replenishment of the stock.

It was only at this point that scientists consulted artisanal fishermen. When considering the possible consequences of their insights, researchers at the Calicut station went to local fisherfolk to find out with what sort of net small sardines were caught. This net, it turned out, was the small-meshed boat seine net (mathikollivala). When the scarcity of oil sardines that had been noticed in 1940 and 1941 continued in 1942, the use of this net was banned for nine months per year, starting in 1943. As mentioned above, the ban was renewed and intensified in 1945. Whether or not it was considered a success is not clear from the published sources. However, the ban was removed in 1947. The following year, for whatever reason, the landings of oil sardines had recovered their "normal" levels (cf. Nair 1952; Balan 1984: 1).

The difference between the state's "scientific" knowledge and the fishermen's "local" knowledge may be expressed in different ways. The one presupposes the working of impersonal, "natural" forces, expressed in abstract terms and detached from humans, while the other is based on ideas of the interaction between subjects (including the sea), the morality of causation, and the embeddedness of humans in their environment. The one claims that there is a specific "stock" of fish which can be quantified and regulated by laws, the other that there is no foundation for such a claim.

STATE INTERVENTIONS: TRAWLERS, DAMS, AND MOUNTAIN WATER

In the half century between the end of the ban on the fishery of oil sardines and my fieldwork in Chamakkala, this rift between two schools of knowledge has deepened and given rise to new ambiguities. I shall consider these after a brief survey of the profound changes in Kerala's fisheries. These may be described as follows (for references, cf. Hoeppe, forthcoming). First, the intervention by the "Indo-Norwegian Project" from 1953 into the 1960s. This development project opened the way for the export of local catches, especially prawns, to foreign markets. Previously, prawns had little economic significance. The "pink gold rush" of an export-oriented prawn fishery began, characterized by immense profits for the traders involved. Subsequently, there was a drive toward introducing large numbers of trawling boats. Most of these were owned by financially potent people without a background in fishing.

Second, feeling encroached by this development and noticing an over-fishing of the sea, organizations of South Kerala's Christian fisherfolk responded with violent protest. Hindu and Muslim fisherfolk were much less involved in this agitation. Soon, all artisanal fisherfolk responded with motorizations of their craft and the introduction of more efficient gear.

Third, the state government reacted to fishermen's demands by introducing, in 1980, the Kerala Marine Fisheries Regulation Act (KMFRA), which formally reserved fishing in the near-coastal waters for artisanal fishermen. After examinations of the over-fishing issue by government-appointed committees and a heated public debate, a seasonal ban on trawling has been implemented annually since 1988. Its purpose is to secure the livelihood of artisanal fisherfolk and conserve Kerala's much-exploited prawn resources. Discussions about whether or not the resources are sufficient or exaggerated have been going on ever since.

Fourth, with the liberalization of the Indian economy in 1991, foreign industrial fishing vessels have been permitted to operate in India's EEZ (exclusive economic zone) for joint ventures. The effect of these ships is critically observed and the protests of fisherfolk—aimed at withdrawing licenses for these ships—have been going on since the mid 1990s. Technologically, the adoption of new craft and gear has led to a situation in which the efficiency of "artisanal" fisheries has approached that of trawlers.

All these developments have profoundly affected fishery in Chamakkala. For lack of space, I shall consider only the knowledge involved in the justification of the ban on monsoon trawling, and consider briefly how it was perceived by fishermen in Chamakkala.

The initial debate about the trawling ban resulted from the perception that the immense number of trawling boats was the reason for the artisanal fisherfolk's dwindling catches in the late 1970s. At that time, more than 3000 trawlers were operating in Kerala. While fishermen participated in the protest, the discussion itself ensued mostly between educated Christian activists from South Kerala—who were not engaged in fishing themselves (and who included a prominent Catholic priest)—and the government, i.e. representatives of the fisheries department. The state government (then Congress-led) felt locked between the positions of the fishermen and that of trawler owners, who exerted pressure on the government. Indeed, many artisanal fishermen seemed to perceive the owners of trawlers as their true enemies. The government felt the difficulty of trying to please both sides and decided to rest its decision on the findings of an expert committee which was mostly composed of fisheries scientists (at the same time, it was blamed for procrastination. The first committee, named after its convener Babu Paul, produced its report in 1982. A second one, the Kalawar Commission, presented its results in 1985. In both reports the Central Marine Fisheries Research Institute (CMFRI) in Kochi (Central Kerala), run by the central government, was prominently involved, both through its scientists as well by being a source of data.

To cut a long story short, in this context "science" and "scientific knowledge" assumed a mediating role in a political conflict involving two interest groups as well as the government. Others, however, claimed that " science" was abused as an excuse to delay government decisions or to serve as their apology. Neither the Babu Paul Committee nor the Kalawar Commission arrived at an equivocal recommendation on trawling ban. However, the Kalawar Commission demanded a limitation of the fleet of trawling boats and ring seine units to 1145. This number of units was equal to roughly one-third of the more than 3000 unit fleet. However, this recommendation was ignored by the government, which instigated more protests among the fisherfolk. At the same time, activists supporting the fisherfolk attempted recourse to "science," partly relying on the same institutions as the state government. In the early 1980s they asked a retired deputy director of fisheries from the CMFRI to investigate the issue of over-fishing of prawn resources. He concluded that a three-month ban was necessary to ensure sustainable use of the prawn resources.

A seasonal ban on trawling and purse seining (considered another threat on the resources: the use of a net for encircling large shoals of fish) was installed only after a third committee came to recommend it. This committee was led by Professor N. Balakrishnan Nair, himself a CMFRI fisheries scientist. In order to evaluate the efficiency of a ban on trawling and purse seining, the committee ordered trial bans in the years 1988, 1989, and 1990. In the end, an annual ban of forty-five days has been installed annually since 1991. This is only half the length recommended by the Balakrishnan Nair Committee and is widely judged to be a compromise enforced by the strong political influence of trawler owners. In 1999/2000 and 2002, when I did my fieldwork in Kerala, the annual debate about the ban had turned into an annual political ritual which was performed with much fervor.

While "science," especially "fisheries science," had a prominent role in the public discussion leading to the ban (there never being any doubt that Western, "global" science was implied thereby), local conceptualizations were rarely, if ever, articulated in public. Only in debates about the "common property" nature of the sea, Christian intellectual representatives made an occasional reference to fishermen as the rightful "children of the sea;" an attempt to claim their particular right to its products. This notion reversed the one about katalamma, "sea mother." In fact, from a Chamakkala viewpoint, this was misconceived, since the truthful nature of the sea assured access to its resources for all who behaved truthfully.

For Chamakkala fishermen, this was not the only misconception made in public discourse. While the operation of trawlers has been regarded critically since their first appearance on the sea, perceptions about their effects are remarkably ambivalent. Some men in Chamakkala regard trawlers as almost irrelevant to most local fishing. Knowing that trawling nets scratch the sea bottom, their immediate impact is perceived to be only on bottom-dwelling species. Of course, prawns are known to be bottom dwelling and are financially important. But for many years the dominant fishing technique in Chamakkala has been the ring seine, a technique aimed at catching pelagic (near-surface) fish such as oil sardines and mackerel. Prawns do occasionally come near the surface and may then be caught with a ring seine net. Thus, at first sight, the efficiency of trawlers and ring seines is perceived to be complementary rather than a competition to local fishermen.

Equally profound is that critique of the public debate which brands its focus on the over-fishing issue (and, thus, of the notion of a specific "fish stock") as partial and inadequate. Indeed, from the viewpoint of fishermen's "local knowledge," trawling is only one element in a larger scenario of environmental change inflicted by the government and other agents. A first example is the effect of (motorized) trawling boats to "heat" the sea and thereby chase away fish. If trawlers are operating in the deep sea, fish may be chased toward the shore. This is beneficial for fishermen. On the other hand, trawlers operating near the coast may chase fish into the deep sea. This represents a negative impact on local fishing. Another negative effect is the dispersal of shoals, which is often blamed on the noise or heat of boat engines, mostly trawlers. All species of fish are said to be scared by noise, and thus shoals may dissolve when approached by motor vessels. The influence on fishing is precarious since ring-seine fishing is aiming at (undispersed) shoals of fish.

Altogether, the fishermen of Chamakkala have no doubt that trawling has had a considerable impact on their fishing. However, they consider it in the context of additional interventions which may appear even more profound. The construction of dams in the Western Ghats is a case in point. As mentioned above, these dams are thought to impede the flow of mountain water (*mala vellam*) into the Arabian Sea during the south-west monsoon and, thus, prevent its cooling. Never mentioned in public discourse on the fisheries is the understanding of this process where it is conceived as having an important, even detrimental, impact on fishing. In a sense, the trawling ban may be seen as "completing" the impact on the sea of dams. The lack of mountain water implies an absence of cooling of the near-shore sea, and thus a scarcity of fish. Since fish are considered sensitive to noise, the operation of trawlers and purse seiners in the outer sea after the end of the ban period is supposed to chase the fish to the shore. The duration of the ban is forty-five days for trawlers and about seventy-five days for purse seiners. Both of these ban periods begin in mid June. In early August, and then again in early September, motorized boats re-enter the sea, the effect being to chase fish toward the coast. Thus, a force which drives or attracts fish toward the shore, lacking since the dams were constructed, has been introduced by the government via the trawling ban.

This argument is coherent with "local" knowledge as described above. Moreover, while the public debate about the trawling ban explicitly focused around "scientific" ideas, many fishermen insist that their viewpoint is no less *shaastriyamaayi*, "scientific," than public discourse with its explicit reference to "science." The word shaastriyamaayi is derived from *shaastram*, "science, law." Shared features of "science" and shaastram include the claim to truth, authority, and their association with "power." While "science" is strongly linked to modernity, shaastram may also be understood as classical, scriptural knowledge. The latter is often linked to Brahminical practice. The Vedas, for example, are associated with shaastram, and so is astrology, *jyothishaastram*, which may be translated as "science of light." As such, the semantic fields of "science" (as it is understood in the West and by the Kerala state government) and shaastram are not identical. Unlike "science" and shaastram, fishermen's knowledge is not codified in any written source. However, what they mean by claiming their knowledge as shaastriyamaayi is that it rests on the experience of established regularities no less than that is surmised to be the case for "science." One may wonder whether the acceptability of "science" as a category seems appealing because of its ambivalence. Whatever the case, despite the fishermen's claim to virtually the same essentialized category of knowledge, their views have largely remained unarticulated in public discourse.

CONCLUSIONS

With regard to both interventions by the state in fishery, fishermen's local knowledge was at odds with that on which state interventions were based. In both cases fishermen's knowledge remained unarticulated in local discourse. The difference between the state's "scientific" knowledge and the fishermen's "local" knowledge may be expressed in different ways. The one presupposes the working of impersonal, "natural" forces, expressible in abstract terms and detached from human beings, while the other is based on ideas of the interaction between subjects (including the sea), the morality of causation, and the embeddedness of humans in their environment. The one claims that there is a specific "stock" of fish which can be quantified and regulated by laws, while in the other there is no foundation for such a claim. However, in retrospect the critique of the 1943 oil sardine ban as a misperception of the government is a paradigmatic situation illustrating local skepticism of state interventions. The state and its government are often conflated in fishermen's perception and looked at critically, with considerable skepticism. During my fieldwork, most government policies reached the beach at Chamakkala either through the fisheries department or through the state cooperative society Matsyafed. General comments about the government (and its governance) were rare. More typically, local judgments of government were linked to opinions about specific programs and interventions. Programs to issue loans for the acquisition of boats are one example.

In Chamakkala the first government loans were issued in relation to small cooperative societies and the "society boat program." As mentioned there, the government eventually considered this program as a failure, since the money spent for the program had gone into the pockets of a few. This development did not surprise local fishermen. Indeed, not least because of their previous experience with the system of *kadakoddis*, it is clear to many fishermen that some men are closer to government (and its financial resources) than others, and therefore more likely to benefit from government programs. Yet there does not seem to have been protest against this conduct.

As was the case with "society boats," many loan schedules are introduced along with new technology. Both technology and loans are sometimes associated with government. The *vallams* (large plank-built boats), ring seines, outboard motors and, most recently, the *muduveddis* (small motorized plank-built boats) are examples. Shashi, the middle-aged skipper of a Chamakkala vallam, explains: "At first some people were skeptical. The government had introduced society boats before, but they were not successful, then the *kamba vala* [beach seine] was introduced, but it did not succeed. The government introduces many new things. They go away but the debts stay." This statement reads like advice for a general skepticism toward the government and its involvement in fisheries. The latest example, the muduveddis, were financed through loans in the mid 1990s advanced by Matsyafed.[7] At the same time, muduveddis are often equipped with a mini trawl net (the double net), especially during the monsoon. This means breaking, the Kerala Marine Fisheries Regulation Act, since all trawling, including that done by mini trawl nets, is forbidden during the monsoon season. Fishermen know about this regulation but argue that, due to Matsyafed's tight repayment schedules, they are forced to break the law. No wonder that the fishermen continue to see the government in a rather ambivalent light.

NOTES

1. I thank the fishermen in Chamakkala for their help, cooperation, friendship, and patience during my fieldwork. I am grateful to Mr P.V. Ramamoorthy, former Joint Director of Fisheries, for help with archival work in Madras (Chennai). Comments by Gunnel Cederlöf, K. Sivaramakrishnan, and L.S. Rajagopalan have benefited this text.

2. I shall write "heat" within quotation marks since it is not always understood thermometrically, but may be used figuratively as well.

3. To some extent, this self-image may be regarded as a counter-discourse of the subaltern, a "hidden transcript" in the sense used by Scott 1990.

4. Formally, *prakrithi* is a Malayalam term denoting "nature," at least according to most dictionaries. It stems from the Sanskrit vocabulary. Yet there is no understanding of "nature" as being opposed to "culture" or "society," as a Cartesian dichotomy would suggest. Rather, just as "nature" is perhaps the most complex word in the [English] language—Williams 1985: 219—the usage of *prakrithi* reveals a similar complexity. Even though this word has often been translated as "nature" (e.g. by Shiva 1988: 29ff; Gold 1998: 183; Vasavi 1999: 29), it also refers to "constitution" in a medical sense. Zimmermann 1983: 13f.

5. The impact of the colonial state on fisheries in Chamakkala dates back to the mid nineteenth century. Exports of fish oil from Malabar district to Great Britain (shipped via the harbor in Kochi) began in the 1840s. Day 1865: xxi, xxv. These exports soon became sizeable, amounting to 4140 tonnes over the five-year interval ending in 1863/4. Ibid.: xxi. However, during the entire nineteenth century there were no interventions which could match those initiated by the Madras department of fisheries after 1908.

6. Improved estimations of the exploitable fisheries resources of Madras Presidency were made in the early 1940s. Kurien 1985: A70.

7. The local cooperative has advanced loans to fourteen muduveddi units.

10

SHIFTING CULTIVATION, IMAGES, AND DEVELOPMENT IN THE CHITTAGONG HILL TRACTS OF BANGLADESH

Wolfgang Mey

SHIFTING CULTIVATION EXISTS IN MANY PARTS OF THE WORLD and, though it plays a dominant role in the economy of many societies living in forest areas, it has generally been perceived and discussed most controversially. After decolonialization, this discussion focussed on levels of acquisition of natural resources for state- and nation-building as well as development. This area of the economy has also set the frame for perspectives on peoples of the Chittagong Hill Tracts (CHT) during the time of empire and in the post-colonial states of Pakistan and Bangladesh. The CHT borders Upper Burma to the east and India to the east and north. The area is claimed by twelve different people as their traditional home.[1] Their cultures and languages are rooted in the cultures of their regions of origin, Eastern India and Upper Burma.

Descriptions of this forest land and its inhabitants oscillate between opposite poles. To some it is a lush and luring paradise in the jungle, populated by "innocent" and "happy-go-lucky tribal peoples;" to some it is an underdeveloped area populated by "ignorant tribes" opposed to modern development. At different times, this type of image production has been deployed to legitimize the "legal" acquisition of natural resources in the name of development.

In the academic field, this dichotomized view of "stagnant and backward" tribes people and a dynamic nation-state has been substituted by a more integrated approach (cf. van Schendel 1992a: 95; Baal 2000: 3). This shift has however neither found its way into the development discourse nor into minority policies in Bangladesh. At the base of policies in Bangladesh lie notions of primitiveness and civilization in the cloak of the political language of the nation-state. Such dichotomous views and concepts surface in arguments and views on shifting cultivation and the implementation of development from above and outside, and serve at the same time as a justification for the ruthless exploitation of natural resources in the CHT. An overarching threat to the national unity is taken into account (cf. Baal 2000: 20; Roy 2000, endnote 1: 210).

Development planning and implementation is linked to a particular vision of national history in Bangladesh. Much has been written on this part of Asia in the perspective of mainstream history (van Schendel 1992a; van Schendel, Mey, and Dewan 2000: 297 ff.; van Schendel 2001). However, little is known about subnational, local processes which take place outside the limelight of overarching political processes. Further, little is known about interactions between state administration, agencies, and their representatives on one side, and institutions of local people and their representatives on the other. Development projects in the CHT have been a segment of state- and nation-building in East Pakistan and later Bangladesh. They were based on top-down models, with indigenous knowledge never having been taken into account. Local responses to development from above are a particularly striking example of this one-way communication. All reactions of local people that do not match with expert talk are perceived as "obstruction," "resistance" or "ignorance."

After the peace accord in 1997 between the guerrilla forces of the CHT peoples and the Government of Bangladesh, national and international donor and development agencies have taken up work in the CHT. Reflecting earlier development experiences and their ideological frames, the rethinking of such frames has the potential to help plan development from the perspective of sustainable development, implemented not among "ignorant and backward tribes" but together with, and by, the people of the tracts. These are the "Jummas,"[2] who are defining their needs and identity as "indigenous peoples" (van Schendel 1992b, especially for the conceptual extension which goes along with the term "indigenous;" cf. Roy 2000: 22ff.).[3]

THE CHITTAGONG HILL TRACTS

The hills in the hinterland of Chittagong, bordering Burma and India to the east and north, are the home of twelve different peoples. With the exception of the Tripura, a Bodo-speaking group which came from Hill

Tippera, all had migrated into the CHT from Upper Burma and Eastern India.

The CHT came into the view of the powers in the plains with the extension of Mughal hegemony into the plains of East Bengal, which came to an end in 1664/5. The Mughal political system interfered only marginally with the economic and political structures of the hill peasants. The East India Company extended its hegemony over Chittagong in 1760, but the changes that were implemented in the plains of Bengal during its rule, such as the Permanent Settlement Regulation, did not affect living conditions in the hills. The Company's economic interests centered on the transformation and exploitation of the Bengal peasant economy.

Two different processes characterized population movements in the hilly areas to the east of the plains of Bengal during the late eighteenth and the nineteenth centuries.[4] Bengal's farmers and traders pushed into the hills, while hill peoples living further east and north-east, in what is today Cachar, Mizoram, and Upper Burma, pushed westward, partly in defense of their territories invaded by plains peoples and British tea planters, partly because their territories had been invaded by people living in the CHT (Mey 1980: 93ff.). Raids on Bengal villages and British tea gardens followed in quick succession. Attempts to control the situation by setting up border posts to contain "the wild tribes" beyond a demarcation line, which marked the limit of the British sphere of interest, linked with the aim of creating strong chiefs who could be charged with the defense of the "border" (Ricketts 1853) did not work out. But they succeeded in inducing a structural change in the social system of the hill peoples. A few representatives of kinship groups who were traditionally entitled to receive the "first fruits" of the new harvest from their kinsmen and who enjoyed few privileges (Lewin 1870: 169) succeeded in monopolizing the tax collection in areas under their influence, with the support of the British administration (Ricketts 1853; Hutchinson 1906: 33).[5]

This creation of a stratum of tax collectors from among the hill people, who enforced the payment of a tax (unknown in this shape to hill people) along kinship lines with the support of colonial force marked the beginning of the formation of indigenous political and economic power over kinsmen in formerly egalitarian societies, as also the dismantling of traditional systems of representation and administration (Mey 1980: 72ff.).

The annexation of the hills in 1860 was the result of prolonged disputes over land between forest dwellers, Bengali peasants, and British tea planters. In order to suppress raids by hill people once and forever, the British decided to annex the CHT to British India in 1860 (Lewin 1869: 23; Hunter 1876: 341; Roy 2000: 29). Annexation placed the hill tracts within the realm of pax Britannica and, at the same time, the resources of the area became a target of colonial, e.g. commercial, interests (Lewin 1869: 4 ff., 119 ff.).

Colonial administrators saw themselves confronted with a large number of peoples who were hardly known to them.[6] To colonial officers who conceived the area in terms of "territories," "frontiers," profit and "civilization," life in the CHT was "primitive." The hill peoples were considered "wild races" (Lewin 1870); all these groups were identified as primitive, savage, simple, uncivilized, underdeveloped, and so on (Dewan 1991: 25).

SHIFTING CULTIVATION IN THE CHITTAGONG HILL TRACTS

The hill peoples practiced shifting cultivation (*jhum*) (Lewin 1869: 10ff.), a system of land use which was then widespread in hilly and mountainous areas in South Asia. But shifting cultivation was not just a mode of production to such people, it constituted a way of life which connected various aspects of human existence to a meaningful network of actions and obligations (Life is Not Ours 1991: 88; Roy 2000: 76). The indigenous peasants of the hill tracts considered forest land as common property (Mey 1979: 88, 103; Life is Not Ours 1991: 60), even though the government controlled aspects of its transfer (Roy 2000: 55 ff.).

At the same time, shifting cultivation served as a canvas on which European concepts of civilization and progress were projected. T.H. Lewin, the first deputy commissioner of the CHT and later of the Lushai Hills, painted a thoroughly romantic picture, emphasizing the contrasts with the cultivation made by plains people:

> Although the clearing of a patch of dense jungle is no doubt severe labour, yet the surroundings of the labourer render his work pleasurable in comparison with the toilsome and dirty task of the cultivators of the plains. On the one hand, the hill man works in the shade of the jungle that he is cutting; he is on a lofty eminence, where every breeze reaches and refreshes him; his spirits are enlivened and his labour lightened by the beautiful prospect stretching out before him: while the rich and varied scenery of the forest stirs his mind above a monotone. He is surrounded by his comrades; the scent of the wild thyme and the buzzing of the forest bee are about him; the young men and maidens sing to their work, and the laugh and joke goes round as they

sit down to their mid day meal under the shade of some mossy forest tree. On the other hand, consider the moiling toil of the cultivator of the plains. He maunders along with pokes and anathemas at the tail of a pair of buffaloes, working mid-leg in mud. Around him stretches an uninterrupted vista of muddy rice land; there is not a bough or a leaf to give him shelter from the blazing noon-day sun. His women are shut up in some cabin, jealously surrounded by jungle; and if he is able to afford a meagre meal during the day, he will munch it *solus*, sitting beside his muddy plough; add to this, that by his comparatively pleasurable toil, the hill man can gain two rupees for one which the wretched ryot of the plains can painfully earn, and it is not to be wondered that the hill people have a passion for their mode of life, and regard with absolute contempt any proposal to settle down to the tame and monotonous cultivation of the dwellers of the low-lands. (Lewin 1869: 11)

In spite of this romanticized description of the "hill people," Lewin was the first to equate this method of resource use with waste and the destruction of forest wealth and nomadism (Lewin 1869: 10 ff.), i.e. with aspects that indicated a makeshift, primitive, improvident and unsettled way of life. This projection was part of Lewin's "invention of the primitive" (Kuper 1996: 1ff.) which was in line with aspects of understanding "primitive" society at the time.

The colonial administration realized that this system of land use was incompatible with colonial notions of territories, frontiers, revenue, a market-oriented surplus production, and profits; consequently they recommended its substitution by permanent agriculture "for the purpose of forest conservancy" (Lewin 1887; Mackenzie 1884: 51) but few of them realized the differentiated approach of cultivators to the forest land and the overall (ecological) limitations of the forest land's use (Hutchinson 1906: 51; Hutchinson 1909: 66; Roy 2000: 65).[7]

Especially to the forest department, swidden cultivation was considered a waste of resources and was in contradiction with the notion of a profitable use of the forest. A forest conservator of the 1880s even went as far as demanding that "These people destroy the trees, therefore let them be sent away" (Beames1961: 282). And precisely here, the notions of shifting cultivators and colonial administrators clashed most severely: burning the trees was a *conditio sine qua non* as well as manure for hill peasant agriculture. But the forest department lost no time to establish control over the forest resources. In 1883, one-third of the total forest area had been converted into reserved forests "in which no cultivation is allowed" (Hutchinson 1909: 67).

While the hill people considered the land they cultivated as common property, the colonial administration defined all land as government land (Unclassed State Forest, cf. Roy 2000: 61f.). Its use had to be compensated by rent (plough land) or tax (Life is Not Ours 1991: 59 ff; Roy 2000: 62f.). The colonial economy was after all centrally based on the exploitation of local resources for the system of circulation and profit (teak, tea, rubber, see Hutchinson 1909: 72 ff.; van Schendel, Mey and Dewan 2000: 131 ff.).

Yet, the perception of administrators was far from unilinear. About fifty years after the annexation, the outlook on shifting cultivation was more balanced. The deputy commissioner, S.R.H. Hutchinson, wrote in 1909: "Apart from the fact that a large portion of the population will always Jum, it is doubtful if lands suitable for the cultivation of rice are available on which to settle the population. There is certainly a very great amount of land that can be claimed, but this need not be necessarily suitable for rice cultivation" (Hutchinson 1909: 66). Contradicting the economist's balance sheet, he went on: "The value of forest produce depends entirely on the facilities available for removing the same from its site and placing it on the market" (Hutchinson 1909: 66). The existing infrastructure would not permit a profitable realization of the value of the forest produce.

Also, the alleged nomadism did not stand the test of historical experience: The "great majority of the villages of the district are permanent and have occupied their present site for a great number of years" (Hutchinson 1909: 67; cf. Sopher 1964: 119). F.D. Ascoli spoke in his report on the administration of the CHT a little later, of the necessity to dispel "the fallacy that the cultivation of the hill sides by *juming* must be abolished."[8] J.P. Mills, a government ethnographer in the British civil service, with ample experience as administrator and ethnographer in the Naga Hills and the CHT, put all the prejudiced arguments against shifting cultivation in a nutshell:

> Englishmen do not *jhum*, and in the sixties and seventies of last century English customs were considered model ones, and we were very busy "raising" savages to our own standard by the distribution of flannel waistcoats and chemises, and in trying in general to destroy their culture and substitute for it a caricature of our own.[9]

He concluded that shifting cultivation was "in certain places [...] the only possible method of cultivation." This was a new aspect in the discussion: he perceived the problem from the perspective of arguing a culturally appropriate solution and made a number of proposals aimed at stabilizing and improving this type of economy.[10]

In the twentieth century the ideological basis of the discussion on shifting cultivation in the CHT directed focus on the alleged wastefulness of this mode of production while local measures for forest protection have not been taken into account. Yet the conservation of forest land has always been an aspect of this economy, not as an ecological concept in terms of the preservation of nature, but as a set of necessary actions to prevent substantial damage to forest and swidden lands (Mey 1979: 93 f.; Löffler 1988: 14; Life is Not Ours 1991: 59; Roy 2000: 86 f.).

Village communities and their representatives decided what parts of the jungle were to be cleared, and they set the time-frame for fallow periods—in the "good old days" ten to fifteen years. During this time the soil had sufficient time to recuperate until the next plot was cleared and planted. The recultivation of swidden fields was regulated and offenders fined. Village communities planted their own "reserved forests" to guarantee a continuous supply of raw materials (Pardo and Löffler 1969: 50; Mey 1979: 104 ff.). The indigenous system of land use was, as in many other parts of the mountainous areas of Eastern India and Burma characterized by common access to the land in kinship frames. The economy was mainly based on production for local consumption. Social prestige was acquired by the distribution of agricultural surplus (Stevenson 1943; Leach 1954: 119 ff., 190f.; Parry 1976: 428; Lehmann 1963: 14 ff.; Brauns and Löffler 1986: 225 ff.). The political systems were mostly characterized by flat hierarchies, and segmentation served as an efficient check to the usurpation of power (Lewin 1869: 64 ff.; Mey 1980: 180 f.).

A number of strategies that intended a structural change in the man–land relationship followed the annexation of the hills. Programs were launched to bring the acquisition of forest resources into the mainstream of the colonial economy. This meant, among other things, substituting "wasteful" shifting cultivation by flatland cultivation and, along with it, introducing a new system of land tenure and revenue. Finally, a system of territorial administration and jurisdiction was implemented (Lewin 1887; for a detailed discussion, see Mey 1980: 112 ff.).

This process of structural transformation of political and economic conditions in the hills lasted about forty years and succeeded in substituting the kinship-based self-administration of the CHT peoples with a territorial system of administration under the colonial regime, a change in the hill economy, and an introduction into it of a territorial and hierarchical system of administration.

IMAGE PRODUCTION: CIVILIZING "TRIBALS" AND "NATURE"

Colonial descriptions of the hill peoples' mode of production were linked to descriptions of their "character" or "nature." Correspondingly, divergent and contradicting tendencies echoed overarching views on "wild" people and "wild" nature. Early contact times were marked by military encounters; consequently, hill peoples were seen as wild, nomadic and primitive; but when they were pacified, other qualities surfaced. From the perspective of "progressive" administrator, they were lazy, happy-go-lucky fellows, improvident, but honest and innocent. British post-romanticism had even hoped that the peoples of the CHT, with "education open to them, and yet moving under their own laws and customs [...] will turn out, not debased and miniature epitomes of Englishmen, but a new and noble type of God's creatures" (Lewin 1869: 118). As noted earlier, Lewin was completely taken in by the open, frank and generous way of life of hill people, which compared well with what he described as the conceited arrogance of British colonial society. The reference to the "noble savages" of the hills and the lure of the simple life served as critique of the British lifestyle; Lewin even considered remaining in his beloved hills. During his period in office, in 1860/70, he developed an ever-growing distance from the British way of life and felt more at home with "his" hill people. To him and many others, it seemed they lived a peaceful life in harmony with their neighbors and nature (cf. van Schendel, Mey and Dewan 2000: 88 ff.; for a wider perspective, see Ellingson 2001, especially 342ff.).[11]

Nature charmed the administrators, too.

> The scenery throughout the District is very picturesque, the mixture of hill and valley, densely covered with forest and luxuriant vegetation, yields the most beautiful and varied effects of light and shade. To be viewed at the best it should be seen from the summits of the main ranges, where the apparently boundless sea of forest is grand in extreme. The cultivated areas of the valleys, dotted here and there, appear as islands, carpeted with emerald green, cloth of gold, or sober brown according to the season of the year. The rivers

slowly meandering on their way to the sea, now shimmering like liquid gold, and again reflecting in heavy dark shadows every object within reach, all combine to make a picture not easily forgotten. (Hutchinson 1909: 2)

During the first decades of the twentieth century, the dichotomy between tribal people living close to nature and settled people living a civilized life had receded and given way to a functionalistic view, but it was to surface again after Independence.[12] In the context of state- and nation-building, the national elites of East Bengal/East Pakistan (later Bangladesh) perceived hill peoples' cultures not as a different way of life that existed in its own right and framework, but as customs frozen in time (Sattar 1971: 232; Belal 1989: 52). They were seen as primitive in the sense that they represented a previous stage of development (Sattar 1971: ix, 1, 93, 325; Rajput 1962, 1963, 1965: 8; 1966; Husain 1967: 136, 157, 159). With the exception of the Chakma, the hill peoples were said to be unable to "develop" their own capacities. Their historic fate of standing apart from the development mainstream had to be overcome by development from above. "Tribal culture is now undergoing transitional and qualitative changes. As in other sectors, the Government is making allout efforts to help the tribals to overcome their traditional aboriginality in the field of culture also" (Belal 1989: 53).

Accepting this view, hill societies had no right to their (outdated) cultures. Rather, the "relationship between Bengalis and hill people is seen as one of guardianship, and Bengalis assume the responsibility to 'uplift' their charges, to bring them into contact with the modern world. This 'civilising mission,' akin to the 'white man's burden,' is nowadays translated in terms of development policies carried out or at least nurtured by the state" (van Schendel 1992a: 103). "That the Government is keen to deliver maximum possible good to the tribals is manifest from the fact that a separate Ministry (Division) has been set up for the region" (Belal ed. 1992: 15).

Yet, some doubt existed within this perception of "outdated cultures" which painted hill people into an exotic corner. "Primitive, crude and antiquated customs" (Sattar 1971) had their attractions and it seems as if, behind disapproving descriptions of hill people and their ways of life, there lurks a thrilling temptation of the unknown.

> The major part of our tribal population inhabit the colourful and variegated forests of the district, whose primitive way of life, peculiar tribal organization in society hardened by age-long customs, tradition, ritual and religious

beliefs, separate ethnological identity and comparative impregnability of tractless hills and evergreen forests of the region—all have combined to invest it with an exclusiveness uncommon in other parts of the province. Amid beautiful surroundings of the district about a dozen tribes . . . live in the area on the fringes of civilization—but virtually unaffected by it in comparative isolation . . . The ripples of civilization into these hills have not yet penetrated beyond its surface. (Sattar 1971: ix)

This view is by no means antiquated: "Chittagong Hill Tracts Region is just bewitching because of the picturesque landscape it offers. Its ineffable lush green hills and the valleys are the traditional abode of 13 tribal communities" (Belal 1989: 52).

FORESTS AND THE NATION-STATE

The post-colonial debate on the CHT (Ahmad and Rizvi 1951: 230; Johnson and Ahmad 1957; Ahmad 1964: 67 ff.; Kermani 1953) employs similar oscillating categories. Basic to this perception is again a set of dichotomies: hill peoples lived in an almost empty habitat (Johnson and Ahmad 1957: 160).[13] Their destructive economy (Kermani 1953: 48) was based on a nomadic way of life and they lived close to nature, were innocent, of simple character and helpless, while plains people were crafty and sophisticated. They lived in an overpopulated area, but in the fold of an age-old civilization and were productively engaged in settled agriculture: "in Bangladesh there is a better civilization on the plains, and there is a less developed civilization in the Hills. In the Hills there are some roads, electricity and telecommunications and they are linked to the notion of civilization. The civilizations are the contemporary civilization of Bangladesh versus the tribal culture" (Life is Not Ours 1991: 88 f.).

Discussion of the character of shifting cultivation displays a corresponding time lag. Whatever information on shifting cultivation had been collected over time (cf. Mey 1979; for recent approaches, see Silitoe 1998) virtually nothing was accepted in a substantive discussion on the prospect of swidden cultivation and /or alternative possibilities of land use in the hills (cf. Sopher 1963; 1964; cf. Conklin 1961; Smith 1973; Caesar 1977). In fact, government representatives proved particularly resistant to critique from outside as far as land management policy was concerned (Sopher 1964: 126).

This outlook on the CHT mirrors colonial ambivalence, but the demands of the nation-state demanded top priority. "Wild hills" had to be tamed, subdued and turned into a productive segment of the capitalist market economy. The CHT "may be said to be East Pakistan's land of promise. If the crude, primitive, and shifting cultivation called 'jhum' is replaced by settled cultivation and the problem of soil erosion is met by terracing the hill sides which are extremely fertile, some of the plain's growing population can possibly be absorbed in the thinly populated areas. What we need is a scientific approach and a planned effort firstly, to make the Hill Tracts an agriculturally useful area" (Ahmad and Rizvi 1951: 230). Hill people had to be brought into the national mainstream— defined in terms of economy, religion, and culture: "Tribal culture, as visualized in dances, songs and similar other performances is fascinating . . . But fact remains that things are not always good in their original forms, they need retouching to attain accomplishment" (Belal 1989: 52).

The alleged economic stagnation and unproductiveness of tribal economy surfaced again and legitimated the structural change of hill peoples' economy. In a discussion with members of the CHT Commission in 1991, a military officer emphasized: "Everywhere in the world nomadism is going. We want to give a permanent address and livelihood to the people . . . They are clinging to certain things due to which they remain backward. You cannot preserve them in the stone age, you have to bring them out (Life is not Ours 1991: 80).

It was the "chiefs" or "rajas" who exposed incompetent planning concepts and management,[14] but they, and a few critical voices from outside, were neutralized (Mey 1980: 215). The state was determined to develop the area according to its interests. However, development demanded its tribute: in 1964 a dam and a hydroelectric power plant were completed in the hills. The lake inundated 40 percent of the fertile alluvial lands and displaced 100,000 hill peasants and their families. About 40,000 people were forced to migrate to India (Mey 1980: 214; Dewan 1991: 227 ff.) This population displacement and relocation broke up traditional settlement patterns and led to ever-increasing pressure on scarce and exhausted swidden lands. In 1990 a high military officer admitted that the dam project had been a failure. Logging activities in the hills and the denudation of forest areas had further led to a process of silting and, according to his information, already 25 percent of the catchment area of the lake had filled up with silt (personal communication 1991).

After completion of the dam and the hydroelectric plant, the Pakistan government stepped up its "development activities." It enlisted an eleven-man team of geologists, soil scientists, biologists, foresters, and agricultural engineers to devise a master plan for the integrated development of the area based on what they considered to be optimum land-use possibilities. The team worked for two years with helicopters, aerial photographs, and electronic computers. It concluded that regardless of how well the traditional economic system of shifting cultivation and subsistence production may have been attuned to its environment in the past, today it "can no longer be tolerated" (Webb 1966: 3232). The research team decided that the hill tribes should allow their land to be used primarily for the production of forest produce, for the benefit of the national economy, "because it was not well suited for large-scale cash cropping" (Bodley 1975: 6 f.; for a survey of the development activities of the whole period, see Bertocci 1989: 153 ff.).

The chairman of this planning team was very clear about the future of hill peoples:

> More of the Hill Tribesmen will have to become wage-earners in the forest or other developing industries, and purchase their food from farmers practising permanent agriculture on an intensive basis on the limited better land classes. It is realized that a whole system of culture and age-old way of life cannot be changed overnight, but change it must and quickly. The time is opportune. The maps and the basic data have been collected for an integrated development towards optimum land use. (Webb 1966: 3232)

The schemes proposed in this frame promised to develop and modernize hill peoples' economies. At the basis of such projects was, however, nothing but the aim of bringing hill peoples into the "national mainstream," to "reorganize" the economy of hill people along capitalist lines of production and distribution, e.g. to open up the area to the profit of private and state entrepreneurship (Bertocci 1989: 153 ff.).

Whatever measures were adopted following the Forestal Survey came to an abrupt end in the 1970s when the military forces of Bangladesh began to wage war on the people of the CHT. A large number of massacres forced about 60,000 to 70,000 people to take refuge in neighboring India. Until the end of the 1980s, about 400,000 Bengalis had been illegally settled in the hills with the help of the army on the paddy lands of mostly Chakma and Marma peasants (Mey ed. 1984: 9 ff.; Mey 1991: 24). This large-scale military intervention was answered by the formation of a guerrilla troop recruited from among the tracts people. On the political level, this process was parallel to the creation of "Jumma" identity (van Schendel 1992a). After about twenty years of war, the leadership of the guerrilla forces and the Government of Bangladesh signed a peace accord in 1997.

During these decades, the CHT comprised military areas and it was the army that was—apart from the suppression of the guerrilla activities—charged with the task of carrying out "development." Counterinsurgency policy was defined as "development policy" (Mey 1994: 196). Much that the state and foreign development agencies had been unable to accomplish earlier was then implemented. At this point, the policy of the Bangladesh government was akin to the counterinsurgency strategies which had been implemented in the course of British intervention in Malaysia and the US war in Vietnam (Thompson 1966).

The army began the implementation of this radical change with the structures of proprietorship and targeted the forest lands of the CHT (Life is Not Ours 1991: 77 ff.). Large-scale felling for monoculture plantations led to an overall deforestation of the hills with the aim of monopolizing the natural resources of the hills, the preparation of conditions for a "profitable land use" and the privatization of "developed" areas (Life is Not Ours 1991: 79ff.; Gain 2000: 27ff., 37). Fallow jungle land that from the perspective of the hill people was part of the swidden cycle, and "common land," were all, from the perspective of the government, "unclassed state forest," e.g. land belonging to the state. This land was confiscated and converted into rubber, teak, and softwood plantations financed by international development agencies, owned and run by state agencies, and partly turned into private property. Hill farmers dispossessed in the process took up work in these plantations as day laborers. Whatever was left of the alluvial lands, which had allowed for three harvests a year, was now mostly in the hands of Bengali farmers. Only fruit gardening on deteriorating hill slopes and wage labor is left for hill farmers (Mey 1994: 199ff.; Life is Not Ours 1991: 79 ff.).

However, the army's financial means and capacity to plan and implement development projects were too limited and, moreover, the armed resistance in the hills blocked the overall structural change which was on the army's agenda.

IMAGES, POLICIES AND DEVELOPMENT

So far, I have linked images of CHT people and their roots and histories to a heritage based in colonial and nationalist narratives, the latter being dominated by two major themes in Bangladesh: the "struggle for Bengali nationhood" and "the emancipation of the Muslims" (van Schendel, Mey and Dewan 2000: 297). Apart from the different shadings within the political discourse in Bangladesh, one theme has pervaded the last thirty years of its history: "If there is one thing that has dominated public debates in Bangladesh since 1971, it is the issue of national identity" (van Schendel 2001: 107), and, after 1971, "Bengali nationalism was quickly appropriated by the new Bangladeshi state elite which found nationalist phraseology useful to legitimise its power and policies, discredit its critics as unpatriotic and discipline the 'lower orders' " (van Schendel 2001: 126).[15]

This discourse was by no means uniform over time (cf. van Schendel 1992a and 2001). An important aspect of this debate was the "assumption that Bengali nation and Bangladeshi state are coterminous and that Bangladeshi history can be equated with the history of Bengalis" (van Schendel 2001: 113).

Part and parcel of this debate was the concept of "tribe" which revived dichotomies of "primitive simple and backward tribes" who had no voice of their own; they were not part of (the mainstream) history, they were "frozen in time" (Sattar 1971: 232) and had to be looked after and represented by a benevolent government which acted on behalf of the "tribes people." But what should appear magnanimous at first sight was the paternalistic negation of difference. A.B. Chakma wrote in his memoirs of his youth in the hills:

> In 1975 Sheik Mujibur Rahman the then Prime Minister of Bangladesh paid a visit to Rangamati [then capital of the CHT]. . . . Hundreds of tribal people were brought from distant villages by the local administration to attend a meeting with him. He addressed the tribals as brethren and told them to become Bengalis, to forget the colonial past and join the mainstream of Bengali culture. At this the tribal people left the meeting. (Chakma 1984: 58)

This strategy of inclusion negated difference and on the level of political representation this meant that the "Constitution does not recognise the existence of other national communities in Bangladesh"—this was said in 1972 by Manobendra Narayan Larma, Member of Parliament from the

CHT—"while refusing to endorse the Constitution of Bangladesh" (Jumma Peoples Network 1998: 11 f.; Gain ed. 2000: 100 ff.).

The equation of Bangladeshi history with that of the Bengali population barred hill people from occupying their own position in the national discourse on history and identity, from developing their potential as subjects of their history, and from deploying their point of view and experience and thereby adding a wider approach to historiography in Bangladesh.

The negation of difference had yet another effect. It refused the acceptance of what had been called "indigenous knowledge" into a development discourse.[16] There was a striking difference in the field of economic change. When the hill people found it necessary and compatible with their cultural views, economic change was easily implemented.[17] But when development projects based on concepts of mainstream development discourse were implemented in the hills through government schemes after Independence, they invariably failed (Mey 1980: 210 ff.). As it turned out, the acceptance of indigenous knowledge was barred exactly at a point at which it would have been most needed to reconcile the concepts of shifting cultivators with development discourses.

It is here that the restricted, elitist discourse of the political class in Bangladesh and the discourse on development policy meet and diverge. Development policy for the CHT is conceptualized in two different approaches. The "traditional" approach still holds on to the elitist top-to-bottom ideology, a tool of decision-making of a political class which has regularly displayed its failures. A recent approach understands future development from the perspective of sustainable development. Consent and participation of (indigenous) people are in the center of this new orientation. Two major banks that finance a substantive share of development budget, the World Bank and the Asian Development Bank, are embarking on this road. The World Bank has developed frames to define the outreach of its involvement in projects affecting indigenous peoples:

> The directive provides policy guidance to (a) ensure that indigenous people benefit from development projects, and (b) avoid or mitigate potentially adverse effects on indigenous peoples caused by Bank-assisted activities. Special action is required where bank investment affects indigenous peoples, tribes, ethnic minorities, or other groups whose social and economic status restricts their capacity to assert their interests and rights in land and other productive resources. (Roy 2000: 147)

The Bank's objective toward indigenous peoples is:

> to ensure that the development process fosters full respect for their dignity, human rights and cultural uniqueness. More specifically, the objective at the centre of this directive is to ensure that indigenous peoples do not suffer adverse effects during the development process, particularly from Bank financed projects, and that they receive culturally compatible social and economic benefits. (Roy 2000: 147f.)

Apart from this the Bank has also developed policy guidelines for environmental assessment (EA) which would also be applicable to the CHT: "The purpose of the EA is to improve decision making and to ensure the project options under consideration are environmentally sound and sustainable" (Roy 2000: 148).

The Asian Development Bank, which has in the past financed most of the projects in the CHT, has in recent years been drawing up new guidelines to orient its policy approach. They are in line with the World Bank's Directive 4.20 on Indigenous Peoples; the specific objectives are:

> to ensure that indigenous peoples receive culturally compatible social and economic benefits from development projects, and to avoid or mitigate the adverse effects of such interventions. In the context of development operations where indigenous peoples are affected either beneficially or adversely, Bank policy should ensure, together with the borrowing country government, that proposed activities are (i) commensurate with the needs and demands of affected peoples; (ii) compatible in substance and structure with culture and social and economic organizations; and (iii) conceived, planned and implemented, to the maximum extent possible, with the consent and participation of the affected communities or their genuine representatives. (Roy 2000: 149)

Apart from these global approaches, there are also a number of "civil society initiatives taking place in the CHT" which aim at bringing together people representing different political echelons and to identify the modalities for developmental activities to be undertaken in the CHT (Roy 2000: 183).

Going along with the state monopoly of defining the frames for discourses, development activities that follow a different approach are stalled by the orthodoxy of the center. After the peace accord in 1997,

UNDP has taken the lead in mobilising international support for the CHT, and a need-assessment mission conducted in April 1998 identified components for future activities including agriculture, primary education, technical and vocational education, health, infrastructure and communication. However, a number of donors including the European Commission have indicated their reluctance to commence technical co-operation activities in the CHT before the full and effective implementation of the Peace Accord. The indigenous peoples, including the JSS and other leaders, agree with this position as they believe that any development projects and programmes undertaken under the present circumstances will not be of benefit to the indigenous peoples, or can be formulated, implemented or evaluated with their full and meaningful participation. Their decision is to wait until participatory development processes can be implemented. (Roy 2000: 183)

Yet, one needs to be critical. Such concepts have been discussed for twenty years. In the case of the CHT they were not incorporated into a development discourse. Too many vested interests, and too many powerful interested groups are linked to the "development" of the hills. According to unconfirmed rumors, the Japan Bank for International Cooperation (JBIC) has held dialogs with the Bangladesh government to provide funds for an extension of the hydroelectric power project in the CHT.

Prasanta Tripura confirms a legitimate distrust: "it would be necessary to discern whether those professing allegiance to these notions [of indigenous peoples equal participation] are simply paying lip service, or are genuinely trying to introduce fundamental change in thought and action" (Tripura 2000: 100),[18] and concludes that "as long as 'development' means the uncritical adoption of ideals, models and techniques developed elsewhere, it is very likely that within a few years, the people of the CHT will also have to start thinking not in terms of development alternatives, but in terms of alternatives to development" (Tripura 2000: 100).

NOTES

1. Chakma, Taungchengya, Sak, Marma, Tripura, Khyeng, Bawm, Mru, Khumi, Pangkhua, Uchai, and Lushai (Mizo). With the exception of the Tripura, a Bodo-speaking group which had come from Hill Tippera and the Chakma, and who speak a Bengali dialect, all belong to the Tibeto-Burman language group.

As in other parts of wider India, different terms were used to identify these peoples. The terms varied over time and were so perceived by others in the political discourses of the colony, the empire, the Pakistani and Bangladesh nation-states (cf. van Schendel 1992a, 2001), in all shadings, from "savages" to "indigenous peoples" (Roy 2000; see also Baal 2000: 37).

2. In the course of the migration of Bengali peasants into the hills from the late 1970s and early 1980s, the then underground party which claims to represent all hill peoples of the CHT, namely the PCJSS (Parbotyo Chottogram Jono Shonghoti Shomiti, Chittagong Hill People's Solidarity Association, also Jana Samhati Samiti, in short JSS (van Schendel 1992a: 120) introduced the term "Jumma" (Chittagonian for jhum, shifting cultivation) for the people of the CHT, and "Jumma nation" for all the peoples in the area who are supposed to share common (hill peoples') characteristics and a common identity (cf. van Schendel 1992a: 121 f.; Roy 2000: endnote 14: 210f.).

3. Over the last few years, a new definition of their status has been in use. In post-Independence communications, representatives of the hill people often employed the term "tribe" and "tribal" to point at their ethnic difference. But since they have linked up with human rights discussions, the term indigenous people(s) is preferred as no traces of human settlement, prior to the immigrations of the seventeenth century, have been found (Mey 1980: 38 ff.). The term "indigenous" is preferred by scholars from within the CHT. It gives them rights and standards in line with international conventions that have also been signed by the Government of Bangladesh (Roy 2000: 22 ff. and endnote 18: 211), and, for exactly this reason, this term is carefully avoided by official phrasing in Bangladesh. Government spokesmen maintain that all people in Bangladesh are immigrants and therefore no one can claim the status "indigenous."

4. Phayre 1841: 683 f.; Lewin 1869: 65; Hunter 1876: 51; Hutchinson 1090: 22; Löffler 1964: 556; Bernot 1967: 27, 67, 86; Spielmann 1968: 64 f.

5. Mills 1927: paragraph 12.

6. Cf. also the account of the life and peoples in the CHT written by Francis Buchanan, who undertook a journey "through the Provinces of Chittagong and Tiperah in order to look out for places most proper for the cultivation of Spices in 1798" (van Schendel ed. 1992b: 1). Astonishingly, this account was never used as a major source of information in the early colonial period (van Schendel ed. 1992b: xi).

7. Mills 1927: II, 24.

8. Chakma Raja's Office, Rangamati, Ascoli, F.D., "Report on the Administration of the Chittagong Hill Tracts," Calcutta, 1918, p. 13.

9. Mills 1927: 24.

10. Mills 1927: II, 24 and App. B: 2.

11. Lewin Letters, April 13, 1867, July 10, 1867; April 25, 1869, University of London, Library Collections.

12. Mills 1927: I and II.

13. "As far as its developed resources are concerned, the Chittagong Hill Tracts is as constrained as the most thickly populated district of the plains. The emptiness of the Hill Tracts therefore is a myth." Master Plan 1967, B: 19.

14. Three Chiefs' Report 1963; View of the Three Chiefs 1962.

15. When a delegation of representatives of the peoples of the CHT went to Dhaka to submit their protest against an unbroken series of cruelties perpetrated by paramilitary forces of the Awami Leagie on the hills, President Mujibur Rahman advised the delegation to go home "and do away with ethnic identities." Mey ed. 1984: 127.

16. The issue of indigenous knowledge was formulated in the ethnographic field in a comprehensive approach and vision by Paul Silitoe. Sillitoe 1998. He argued that a "revolution is occurring in the pursuit of ethnography as the development world changes its focus from top-down intervention to a grassroots participatory perspective [. . .] It is increasingly acknowledged beyond anthropology that other people have their own effective 'science' and resource use practices and that to assist them we need to understand something about their knowledge and management systems." Silitoe 1998: 223. He "picks up on the anthropologically self-evident point that effective development assistance benefits from some understanding of local knowledge and practices" and urges "anthropology to become more fully engaged in advancing such understanding." Silitoe 1998: 223. The paper gives a survey of the components of rethinking development from a grassroots participatory perspective and discusses its potential and outreach. Silitoe argues that an "integrated perspective implies a willingness to learn from one another; researchers need to allow all knowledge of a place [. . .] There must be a genuine reciprocal flow of ideas and information among all parties. Motivation will depend in considerable measure on commitment to consensus decision-making and open debate." Silitoe 1998: 230.

17. The British administration had launched a number of schemes to induce hill people to adopt plough cultivation, with very meagre results. But rising population pressure made them soon aware of the necessity of changing their mode of production, and this was done without loans and credits from the administration in the hills. When the Bawm people realized in the 1950s that shifting cultivation would not feed them any more, they took up horticulture and cash crop production in the fashion in which they had seen it in Mizoram with their Lushai (Mizo) "brothers."

18. The new concepts of the World Bank and the Asian Development Bank are by no means new. Participatory research and implementation concepts date back to the 1980s and are linked to the arguments of critical social scientists. They were taken up by a number of NGOs. Cf., for instance, Nebelung 1988; Rahman 1993.

11

FOREST MANAGEMENT IN A PUKHTUN COMMUNITY

The Constructions of Identities

Sarah Southwold-Llewellyn

BOTH COSMOPOLITAN AND NATIVIST VERSIONS OF RIGHTS OVER forests converge in disputes over forest resources in a Pukhtun village in the Hindu Kush of Pakistan. Historically, plural legal frameworks based on both cosmopolitan and nativist concepts have been used to control user rights to the forests. Current international policy discourse on the management of natural resources encourages community-based management through an idealization of community homogeneity, or the assumption that cooperative action can be developed based on common interest.

Concurrently, the Provincial Government of the North West Frontier Province (NWFP) of Pakistan adopted and continues to use the framework of the British colonial administration to claim ownership of all forests. The state's policies have reified the legal rights of local residents through land registration (cf. the essay in this volume by Geiser). This process of reification has been exacerbated by commercial forest harvesting which entitles those with shares in the forests to 60 percent of the revenue. The discourse of the state is used by some royalty shareholders[1] to dis-embed their responsibilities to non-royalty shareholders, making the usufruct rights of non-shareholders less secure.[1] It is also used to articulate conflicts among royalty shareholders. One of the unintended consequences of government policy has been to reinforce patron–client relations and political factions, opening new arenas for disputes and the articulation of identities. Examination of conflicting constructions and practices will illustrate how different elements of the cultural repertoire that is central to Pukhtun identity operate.

A second theme is how both ecology and environmentalism contribute to the historical, changing processes that shape livelihoods and identities.[2] Contrasts between Pukhtun settled in mountainous areas with those settled on the plains call attention to differences in the nature of their political alliances and incorporation with other groups (Vogelsang 2002: 25), and to differences between egalitarian political and economic organization and feudal organization (e.g. A.S. Ahmed 1976, 1980; Barth 1959, 1969b).

Ecology is important in terms of shaping livelihoods. It is also symbolic of the relative weakness of the political position of those living in mountainous regions. Mountains are less desirable and the weakest groups have settled in these areas, resulting in their relative poverty and isolation from cosmopolitan incorporation.[3] Livelihood today is also shaped by environmentalism. The desire of the state to manage their forests has implications for the financial value of forests and access to forests.

Ecology and environmentalism have contributed to the heterogeneity in socio-political organizations, which reflects isolation as well as historical uniqueness. There is heterogeneity among communities throughout the province, as well as in the locality of study, both in the historical distribution of forests and in response to the implementation of government policies. Emergent forms of interactions among users of the forests reflect this diversity.

A third theme is the construction of identities. First, ecology has played a role in how the state construes the Pukhtun. During the colonial period, the Pukhtun were seen as different from the rest of the population in the Raj, being dangerous and warlike (Banerjee 2000: 44–5; 120; cf. Geiser herein). The relative isolation created by the mountainous ecology of the Malakand Division, the most north-west corner of the NWFP, was a major factor that enabled the Pukhtun to withstand colonization by both the Mughals and the British, as well as incorporation into the state of Pakistan for more than twenty years after its creation. Malakand was and is seen as a wild backwater by those from the settled plains of Peshawar and the rest of Pakistan. Their comparative separateness is further demarcated by a plural legal system, which incorporates tribal law and makes exceptions to a unified national code of law. Today, the government remains frightened of the Islamic, Taliban-like political movements in the area, as well as the historic and ethnic identification with a greater Pukhtunistan with the aim of merging the Pukhtun in both Pakistan and Afghanistan into one nation.

A second aspect of identity is the differentiation between shareholder and non-shareholder as a response to the state's policy of land registration and forest management policies. However, this class dichotomy is diluted by other identities, which undermine the foundations of analysis along these lines.[4]

A third aspect of identity is the identity of being a Pukhtun, as manifest in the importance of individual autonomy and hospitality. The ambiguities in these features of their cultural repertoire are articulated in the management of forests and in the creation of factions based on patronage. The second and third aspects of identity intersect, creating new articulations of identities.

The specific focus of this essay is on the access to fuelwood and timber within the Akhund Khel area of Ajmir village. More specifically, I focus on the impact and implementation of state-regulated forest management. The juxtaposition of the constructions and practices of different social actors: government officials (the divisional forest officer, range officer, forest guards); royalty shareholders, and non-royalty shareholders (those from Akhund Khel, those from others *khels*, their tenants, and renters of alpine pastures) will give some insight into the unintended consequences of this intervention with regard to livelihoods and the construction of contested identities.[5]

SWAT DISTRICT AND AJMIR VILLAGE

During the summers of 1993 and 1994,[6] I lived with a family in Ajmir village. There are two nucleated hamlets, each of a single patrilineage (khel), Akhund Khel and Khali Khel. In addition, various other khels are represented by those living outside the nucleated hamlets. This essay concentrates on that part of the village controlled by Akhund Khel who consider themselves to be Miangan (Mias).[7] There are 211 households in the hamlet of Akhund Khel and the surrounding area included in their part of Ajmir. Most of these households are extended households, including adult sons and their families. In addition to a census which included information on *banda* shares and migration, interviews have been conducted with 108 of these households, who represent a cross-section of Akhund Khel, as well as many other khels living in this part of Ajmir. Interviews also have been done with the Khali Khel part of the village and with residents in all the alpine pastures of Ajmir village.

Ajmir lies at the top of the Kana River valley that runs parallel to the Swat River and the Indus. Poor roads and state services are a symptomatic consequence of political disunity, comparative poverty, and the relative isolation of Ajmir. At the time of research, the area was on the north-eastern fringe of Swat District, on the border of Kohistan. It now lies in the recently created Shangla District. (See Map 1 plus those in Geiser's essay.)

The variation in the mountainous Kana Valley questions the facile correlations often made between ecology and socio-political structures. Rather, heterogeneity is suggestive of the importance of historical diversity, as Ajmir illustrates (cf. Sivaramakrishnan and Cederlöf herein). Consequently, I will limit the discussion to the specific situation of my research area and use the concepts used by my informants. The important fact to note with regard to the introduction of new management institutions is the heterogeneity of forms of distribution and management of forest resources.

The founder's only son distributed the land of Ajmir among his sons into eleven shares: each receiving land for cultivation, fodder, and bandas (alpine pastures and forests).[8] The thirty-two bandas in Ajmir were included in this distribution. To give the reader some appreciation of the area, it takes about three hours to walk to the uppermost bandas near to Akhund Khel hamlet and about six hours to walk to the farthest bandas.

The montane production strategy in Ajmir is characterized by transhumance to higher pastures (2500–3000 meters) during the warmer months and the careful balance between crops and fodder production near the permanent settlement (2000 meters).[9] This agro-pastoral system is changing because of population pressure and the natural limits on the possibilities for increasing animal carrying capacity and/or agricultural production. Two common responses are labor migration and decreasing numbers of animals. In Akhund Khel Ajmir, the option of increasing agriculture is pursued by few because of limited labor due to migration as well as limited financial resources. Furthermore, there is not one household that is self-sufficient in grain, or that has more than a few mature buffaloes. Therefore, all households are dependent on supplementary sources of income, almost exclusively based on migration within Pakistan, and on the sale of forest products.

In 1969 Swat was incorporated into the NWFP of Pakistan. The Malakand Division, of which Swat District is part, is a Provincially Administered Tribal Area (PATA).[10] This created a plural legal system in which the state is involved in successively higher levels of jurisdiction: local *jirgas*[11] set up by local disputants, jirgas appointed by the assistant deputy commissioner, the district courts, provincial courts and federal courts.[12] These tiers of judicial

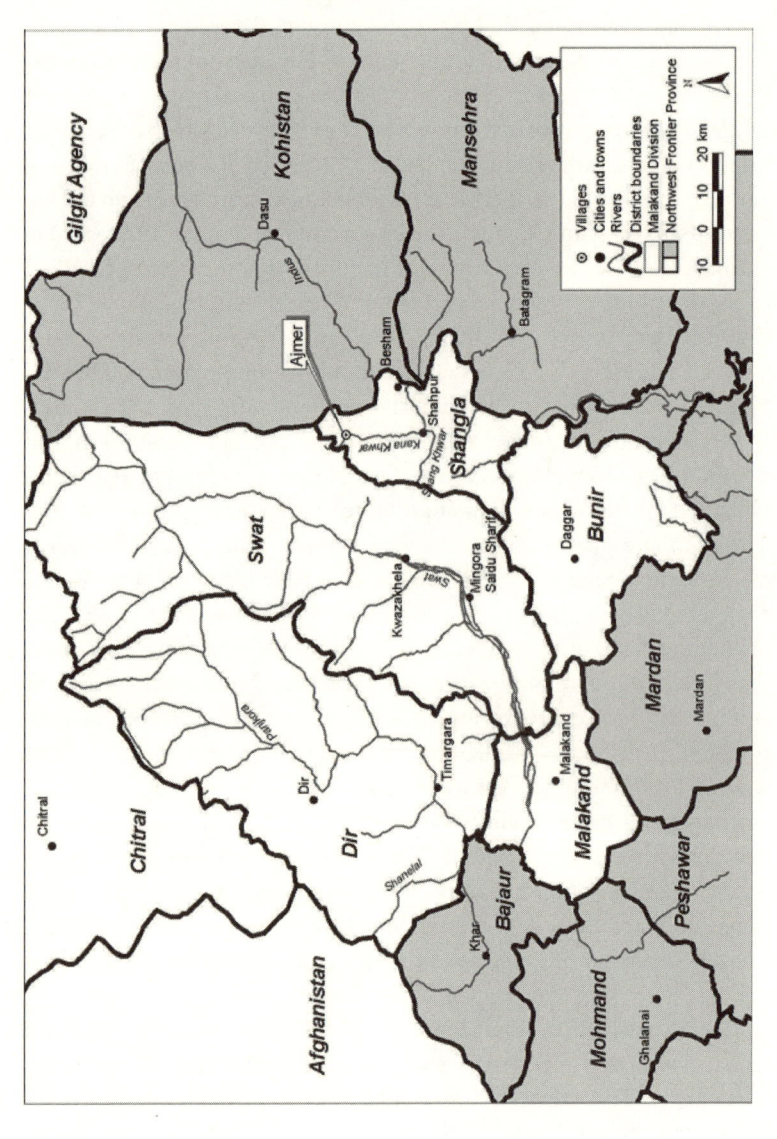

Map 1: Location of Ajmir

power represent tribal law, PATA law administered through civil servants, and the civil and criminal laws of the state at both the provincial and federal levels. Each tier is a potential court of appeal, with the consequence that land disputes often are unresolved after twenty or more years.

A second consequence of incorporation was the state's claim to ownership of the forests and land registration (cf. Geiser herein; and Southwold 2002c). The registration of land entailed registering the forests as separate from other land, including alpine pastures. However, the inherited distribution was based on bandas, which combine forests and alpine pastures as one entity.[13] More fundamentally, the government land records refer to alien concepts of measured areas, not to named, spatial areas.

Land registration symbolizes the convergence of the cosmopolitan (i.e. the state) and the nativist (i.e. local) versions about who has rights to the forests. The utilization of plural legal frameworks to manage the forests represents unresolved conflicts between Pukhtun identity (as perceived by the state) and state administration. It is illustrated further by the lack of correspondence between the state's ideas of land area and those of the nativist (cf. Mey). This divergence is further illustrated in disputes whereby elements of different versions are utilized by shareholders selectively. More fundamentally, land registration has reified land rights. With regard to the forests, it reified the rights of shareholders from non-shareholders (cf. Karlsson).

The Survey of Forests was begun in 1978 and was completed in Ajmir before the late 1980s. The forests are measured and denoted by compartment numbers. A compartment may coincide with the forest in a single banda; but often a single banda forest may include several compartments or one compartment may include several bandas. Although the rightholders are registered as the same as those with a share in the banda, the survey is not always accurate. The survey should stipulate all the individual rightholders to a particular compartment. Sometimes, one of the shareholders is not included. It is up to the shareholders to distribute the royalties, as well as manage the forests. Another problem is that the boundaries of the forest are constantly changing as more forest land is brought into cultivation.

The government Settlement Record (land register), completed in 1985, does not include the forests. The alpine pastures are recorded separately in the land register under the name of an individual owner, in spite of the fact that all bandas have multiple owners. Nor do the bandas correspond with the forest compartments designated by the forest department in the Survey of Forests, partly because they only include the forest portion of the banda. For the local residents, it is their rights to their banda shares (*hissa*) which are the basis of their rights to forest revenues, not their shares in the forest compartment.

FORESTS IN AJMIR

The forests have multifold values. They are the only source of fuel and timber for building, and the major source of supplementary income, after earnings from migration. For all residents of Ajmir, the forests have been commercialized through the sale of timber, fuelwood, roots, bark, and leaves. They are also an important source of wild foods such as green leaves—a major source of vegetables in the diet. There are, however, two factors that have changed the value of forests. The first is the commercialization of the forests controlled by the government (cf. Geiser herein). Ajmir is a comparatively heavily forested area because of poor roads that discourage commercial extraction. The second factor is decreasing forest reserves, partly as a consequence of commercial harvesting as well as population growth. Informal sector extraction is important; but up to the time of research (1994) it was on a comparatively small scale (cf. Geiser for other parts of Malakand).

By law, the state has total control over the management of forests: no one can cut a tree without permission. During 1994, only 360 trees for the entire Kana Valley were allowed for building timber. This is clearly insufficient to meet building needs and stimulates illegal felling. There are no restrictions on plants and leaves. There are only restrictions on roots.

However, the state acknowledges that the same forest land is private property, in several senses of the term.[14] In the Survey of Forests, individuals are cited as owners of specified shares of the forest land. Accordingly, this "owner" (termed a royalty rightholder by the state) is given 60 percent of the revenue from the sale of timber; the state's share is 40 percent.[15] This "ownership" can be inherited and is frequently sold (de facto, not de jure). No one can sell forest land because the state is the sole owner. It is symbolic that the government terms individual owners as royalty rightholders. This royalty distribution can be rescinded at any time.[16] Thus, the position of landowners is tenuous and there is confusion over how these shareholders view their rights.

Rights in the Banda

It is through their rights to the banda that locals claim both usufruct and ownership rights to forests. During the last two to three generations, many Akhund Khel sold their shares in the bandas. Today, only 40 percent of Akhund Khel households "own" a share in a banda. Many of these bandas were bought by the other khels (lineages) in the vicinity where virtually every khel member contributed to buying the banda. They themselves describe their bandas as communal property. The individual's shares are expressed in terms of rupees—i.e. in proportion to the amount paid for the banda. Hence, both inherited shares and the purchased shares in the banda are unequally distributed.

Among Akhund Khel, the area of the banda is subdivided into fractions of a share of the whole banda. One banda is divided into two shares; the others are divided into between five and forty shares. All shareholders have equal use rights to grazing and forests, regardless of their share. For example, someone with one-fifth share of half the banda has as many rights as someone with one-fortieth share to the other half.

There are no instances where the ownership rights of a specific banda are not shared with several others. Any decisions about changes in management must be made—at least in theory—with other shareholders. The profits from logging and rents for grazing are shared. And the risk of over-exploitation of the forest by those needing and selling fuelwood must also be shared. This contrasts with the state's view that shares are individually owned.

In Ajmir, a distinction between fuelwood and timber is made by all actors. However, both are a major source of supplementing subsistence and livelihood. Rights to collect and sell fuelwood and timber characterize the inconsistency in the conceptualizations and the practices of different actors.[17]

ACTORS IN FOREST MANAGEMENT

The Survey of Forests and the Settlement Record reified the legal rights of shareowners, and by implication the management rights of shareholders against non-shareholders. Yet the objectives of the Working Plan for Alpuri, 1984–94 are: "To meet the essential requirements of the local people for timber, firewood and grazing" (p. 63). The Working Plan acknowledges the subsistence rights of local residents. What is not acknowledged or stipulated is the heterogeneity of local rightholders and their practices in forest management with regard to whom they allow access to "their" bandas, and particularly the forests that are part of "their" banda.

This confusion is exemplified by the interpretations of different actors. In this context we can identify different social actors with different sets of interests: the state represented by government officials, shareholders, and non-shareholders. However, analysis based on the conflicting interests, practices and discourses of these different social actors only goes part of the way in understanding why and how these different actors operate in different contexts.

Government Officials

The Divisional Forest Officer (DFO) told me that everyone is allowed to cut fuelwood from the Ajmir area, regardless of whether or not they are shareholders.[18] Fuelwood is defined as dead trees, leftovers from harvesting, and branches. The DFO described his role to protect the forest; but he added that people need fuelwood, timber, grazing, and agricultural land. "We must solve local people's needs before the forest can be preserved." With regard to timber, he told me that if a permit for building timber is granted, a jirga of rightholders must give permission for the tree to be cut.

The implementation of policy is through the local forest guards. The range officer (who holds a position senior to the forest guard) told me that the rules concerning fuelwood are the same throughout Malakand Division. Yet, there is discrepancy about the rights of local residents to collect fuelwood. In many parts of Malakand Division, fuelwood collection is heavily fined. The difference between Bunir District, for example, and Ajmir is due to the discretion of local forest guards. In the Ajmir area, they are tolerant because there is no other source of heating. In Bunir, fuelwood collection is discouraged through fines because of the high consumption and use for seasoning tobacco. However, the implementation of their discretionary powers does not simply reflect different contexts; it also reflects the fact that their individual interpretations of government policy are evident from their different constructions and practices.

One forest guard told me that traditionally there were no restrictions on fuelwood. Today, it is reasonable (*insaaf*) and very just that anyone should cut firewood, but not to sell it because it would deplete the forests. However, this guard said that he will not fine anyone selling firewood and sees about five hundred people per day carrying wood to Ullander (the nearest marketplace) for sale. Furthermore, it is the right of every person to have timber for building. In theory, anyone can get permission to cut trees for building timber; and the royalty shareholder cannot protest. (Note the difference between his interpretation and that of the DFO.) If someone does not have a permit, the forest guard can report him to the forest magistrate who will fine him Rs 500 per tree.

Another guard told me that there were no restrictions at all on collecting fuelwood for domestic use or for sale. The only restrictions are on selling timber, which is mostly done by shareholders at night who are "stealing" their own trees. When he reports them, higher officials receive bribes and do nothing.

A third forest guard told me that there were two forms of fines for cutting down a tree. If you catch someone on the spot, you measure the tree and charge the value of the tree at Rs 50 per foot. The second form involves reporting the person to the forest magistrate. According to him, forest department officers tell them to get the reduced fine on the spot and in this way the forest department gets more money. Forest guards are considered by higher officials to be doing a good job if they receive a lot of fines.

Further inconsistencies in the application of the law were revealed when the third guard told me that forest guards say nothing to those selling fuelwood because of their political alliances with those selling. The same applies to those selling timber. Furthermore, the interpretation of rules for cutting tree branches for fuelwood seems to vary among forest guards. Some told me that a third of the branches must be left on the tree, another that two-thirds must be left.

The view of local residents about forest guards is that they are corrupt and demand bribes reported as Rs 100 to Rs 1000 per tree. Repeatedly, I was told that if they do not pay the bribe, the person caught with timber is sent to court where the fine is Rs 1500–2000, in contrast to the set fine of Rs 500 or Rs 50 per foot reported by government officials.[19]

Although the forest guards are viewed as corrupt and are feared by those collecting and selling wood illegally (mostly non-shareholders), the forest guards themselves are afraid, particularly of the shareholders who are also selling wood illegally. One forest guard told me that there is little he can do to stop timber harvesting because he is one guard against four or five shareholders. There have been incidents elsewhere where forest guards have been killed or beaten up. Guards are afraid to do anything but note the names of offenders and give the information to a higher officer who may fine them. Such fears were supported by a fourth forest guard.

Interpretations of the law vary among different forest guards, as does their implementation of the law. The perceptions of local residents about how forest guards operate, as a social actor, is also different from how the guards see themselves and how higher levels of officials perceive them. "Thus the understandings and motivations of government officials at these local levels crucially mediate how the policies formulated at higher levels are actually presented to their intended beneficiaries" (Springer 2000: 87). In this case, the intermediary role of the forest guards in representing and implementing the policies of the state (i.e. the forest department) is inconsistent and impotent.[20]

In practice, it is up to the shareholder to take fuelwood; it has little to do with the government. Both its local-level forest officers (in this area) and the shareholders give open access to anyone living in the area to cut as much fuelwood as his household requires, without repayment in any form, thus, coincidentally, complying with the objectives of the Working Plan. This, at least, is the stated principle. Shareholders state that it is a moral principle to allow anyone fuelwood; not their right. In practice, this principle is often not applied unless labor and/or political support is given in exchange. The increasing commercial value of timber and government laws against cutting trees are catalysts for reneging on this customary moral principle.

Royalty Shareholders

One of the most difficult aspects of describing resource management is that there is little consistency in management principles. Like the forest guards, there is variation among informants who hold similar positions in the community. Unlike the forest guards, most of whom I interviewed only once, the accounts of individual shareholders varied with each of numerous conversations over a two-year period. Five conflicting constructions about who may collect fuelwood in the bandas, made by one shareholder named Amir, in Ajmir is typical:

(1) Everyone should have access to fuelwood. There are no restrictions. No one needs to ask. How can anyone live here without fuelwood?
(2) Anyone who is a member of the community may collect fuelwood. [Who is a member of the community is a fluid concept.]
(3) Anyone who has paid rent for grazing their animals in the banda can collect fuelwood.

(4) Only those who are given permission by a shareowner can collect fuelwood.
  (a) a shareowner will give permission to anyone who asks
  (b) a shareowner will give permission to anyone who gives him political support
  (c) a shareowner will let anyone collect fuelwood, except his enemies
(5) Only shareholders may collect fuelwood.

To complicate understanding further, the rules of shareholders vary with the shareholder and his level of cooperation with other shareholders. The rules also vary with the relationship between one shareholder and the person asking. It is the fluidity of these "principles" that characterize the management of bandas. On the one hand, they use the discourse of the government of private ownership and forest conservation to extricate themselves from obligations to those who do not have a share. On the other hand, if private shareholders limit access, they will reduce other sources of resources. Allowing others to take fuelwood enhances prestige (symbolic capital), encourages loyal political followers and other forms of patron–client relationships such as those between landlords and tenants. Without clients you cannot develop economic resources such as labor for cultivation or labor for a new enterprise. Therefore, these conflicting constructions are themselves a form of risk management, giving maximum alternative options in the present and for the future.

Anyone with a share in a banda can grant permission to a non-shareholder to cut timber, collect fuelwood, or graze animals. In addition, a shareholder may cut timber for sale or clear the land for cultivation without consulting the other shareholders. The size of the share is important with regard to distributing the rents collected for grazing and most important for distributing the revenues for timber harvested by the state. In recent years, some of the larger shareholders have received sums up to Rs 900,000. Such windfalls have enabled investment in land, housing, and migration to the Middle East. Hence, the larger shareholders want to protect the forests; but given the structure of shareholdership, management practice, and social organization, it is difficult for them, as a group, to cooperate in changing the management of the bandas. That is, they do not act as a social actor with a similar identity related to their social, political and economic interests.

Non-Shareholders

The use by non-shareholders is also recognized: other Akhund Khel, other khels living in this part of Ajmir, tenants, and those who rent grazing rights in the banda. Everyone needs to use the banda for fuelwood. There are, however, differences in the nature of their rights. In practice, those from Akhund Khel and the other khels who have no banda share, or do not have sufficient fuelwood in their own bandas, take fuelwood. Those who are tenants of the cultivated land of banda shareholders usually may take fuelwood from the landlord's banda. Those who stay in the banda with their animals pay a rent (*qalang*) to the shareholders. This entitles them to rights to collect wood. In practice, access is based mostly on relations with a particular shareholder.

On any day, there is a continuous procession of people carrying heavy loads of fuelwood and timber down the mountain from the bandas. Much of it is for sale to supplement subsistence. From the perspective of the shareholders, subsistence needs of non-shareholders are based on household need for fuelwood. From the perspective of the poorest, the sale of forest products is also an important part of their subsistence.

Shareholders have few sanctions. In practice, there are few restrictions on fuelwood, although sometimes a shareholder can tell a relative not to cut firewood because of a dispute with that relative. They also can report to the authorities that a person is cutting a tree for firewood or timber without permission. In spite of these sanctions, limited though they are, it is difficult to stop people from stealing trees at night and selling timber for house construction.

DIFFERENCES IN MANAGEMENT

Nevertheless, there are differences in management among these bandas. This is partly due to the number of shareholders, whether or not the shareholders live in the bandas, and distance from the hamlet. Those closest to the hamlet have fewer trees. The following examples of three bandas will give some insights into the difference and inconsistency in which both shareholders and non-shareholders view their access to particular bandas.

C. Banda

Amir (cited above) is a large shareholder of C. Banda, one hour's walk from the hamlet. He explained that shareowners can restrict cutting green trees, but not collecting dead wood and branches. This complies with government restrictions. The problem is that there is little dead wood.

> If we do not allow our landless relatives to collect wood, there would be a collision between them and us. When it snows, everyone needs a lot of wood. If they have no wood, those without would fight with us. A poor man will be in opposition to me if I do not give him wood. How can we live here if everyone is in opposition?
>
> Those without a share in a banda have no right (*haq*) to fuelwood. Only those with *daufter* [bought or inherited land] have a right, not those who sold their banda share. Rights of shareholders are *kilikana haq* (share honoring right) in which the state gives the shareholder 60 percent of the revenue. The rent paid for each animal to graze in the banda is qalang (rent). If you pay qalang, it is not a right (*haq*), but humanity (*insaniat*) to collect wood.

On another occasion, he told me that they should keep the bandas empty to save the forest. The qalang for one animal (between Rs 10 and Rs 30) is less than the cost of one bundle of wood (Rs 25–40). "We do not need the qalang; but we do need the forest." Furthermore, "Those people who are in opposition (*khalaf*) to me cannot cut trees." There is, however, room for maneuver for non-shareholders to cut wood from C. Banda. One told me that he always asks a shareholder with whom he is on good terms, and not others.

N. Banda

N. Banda is close to the hamlet, is heavily used by all sections of this part of Ajmir, and has the largest numbers of shareholders, most of whom are among the poorer members of Akhund Khel. Mohamad is one of the shareholders and the leader of the political faction of poorer residents. The following is how he described the management of N. Banda:

> If I found a person cutting wood who had not asked, there is no punishment. There is no meeting of the ten shareholders of my ¼ share about those who have given permission to cut wood. There are only the rules and regulations of the forest department, none of our own.[21] Non-shareholders who use my banda for fuelwood have no moral right (*akhlaquie haq*) to fuelwood. I give them fuelwood because they are my neighbors and relatives and cannot go without wood. It is my duty (*faraz*) because they are living here. It is my duty, not their right to fuelwood. Anyone in need can get fuelwood. It is my duty to anyone in need.

Anyone can cut fuelwood, but he must ask first. I expect those who ask to support my political party, otherwise they should ask someone else. The government rules that anyone can cut timber from anyone's banda if they have a permit to do so. Most shareholders will give permission for building timber without a government permit; but if a person is caught by the forest guard, he must pay the fine.

LP Banda

Farman and his brothers are large banda shareholders in LP Banda, one and a half hours' walk away. He told me: "All forests belong to Allah. Everyone has a right. Their own cultivated land, they work for themselves; but the forests are for all. It is a regulation of Islam, and the order of God, that they must be sympathetic to each other."

His tenant told me that he and everyone else is forbidden to cut wood from a part of the banda owned by Farman alone. They only can collect wood in LP Banda in which he has a $1/5$ share with his brothers. Farman and his brothers have made a number of restrictions in their joint banda. In the past, tenants and renters took building wood freely. Now they must ask and pay Rs 500 for one beam. Nor can they sell fuelwood. The landlords have ordered them not to take more than what is needed for their own use; 1994 was the first year in which this restriction was imposed in that particular banda. However, tenants of the different brothers have slightly different terms of tenancy, which is characteristic of the lack of cohesion between the brothers. On the other side, these restrictions are not unreasonable since most of the banda tenants told me that there is not enough grazing in that banda.

Another shareholder, Bashir, brother of Farman, told me: "There are no conflicts between shareholders and users. There are no restrictions over fuelwood. For grazing a rent must be paid." I asked: "People are terrible to each other in many ways, why not over fuelwood?" He said: "Because there is no gas or petrol. And we are all relatives through exchange marriages. Where could they go? Relatives are not restricted. Muslims must help the poor."

In a later interview, Bashir told me that he and his brothers decided that they would allow no more animals and no more fuelwood to be cut in LP Banda; but the brothers would not agree. His brothers said that if they restricted their tenants from collecting wood, their fields would not be cultivated. Further on, he said: "Powerful people do not take from weaker people. Even the powerful want to help the poor, because the poor need help." With prompting he said that it enhances the wealthy's power. But it is also because they fear God who says not to steal from the poor. In contrast, it is interesting to note that Bashir destroyed three houses of tenants living in LP Banda earlier the same year. When asked about it, he said he did not want tenants to stay there because they were selling fuelwood.

ANALYSIS

The lack of consistency in both discourses and actions reflects two issues. The first is how people actually react to specific situations. They draw on a repertoire of constructions to conceptualize their behavior, post facto. For example, why one shareholder allows one person fuelwood, but not another; while, on another occasion, he says that both are entitled to fuelwood. The juxtaposition of these constructions is indicative of changing ideas with regard to management of forest resources. It also illustrates that, in different, specific contexts, individuals conceptualize their actions differently. These different contexts are what Long terms arenas. "*Arenas* are spaces in which contexts over issues, claims, resources, values, meaning and representations take place; that is, they are sites of struggle within and across domains" (Long 2001: 242).

The second issue is the patterns of practices that reflect the history of practice as well as responses to new situations, in this case the changing value of forests. The introduction of state-controlled commercial felling clearly marks the shareholders as a financial interest group. However, their inability to act as a group—as a social actor—is embedded in their history of actions and ideas about the self in relation to others, i.e. their identity.

From the perspective of academic analysis, identity is a descriptive tool for comparison in specific contexts. The notion of identity, especially the notion of ethnic identity, runs the risk of assuming an essentialist homogeneity and uniformity, rather than accounting for the diversity and contradictions of practice. There are, however, several ideas which Pukhtuns label as central to their identity as being Pukhtun. Commonly, they are subsumed under the notion of Pukhtunwali (code of honor or code of behavior). Banerjee argues that

[. . .] We should think of *Pukhtunwali* as providing for the Pathans what Bourdieu has famously called habitus—"a system of lasting, transposable dispositions" that function "as a matrix of perceptions, appreciations and actions" (Bourdieu 1977: 82–3). The practices that it generates vary and are "emergent and unfinished," and the habitus does not determine actions so much as set a basic framework and logic within which actions can be taken in response to the predicaments thrown up by life. (Banerjee 2000: 15)

The cited elements of Pukhtunwali vary (Barth 1969; A.S. Ahmed 1976, 1980; Lindholm 1982; Banerjee 2000). The term is not used in Ajmir; but many of its principles are used to justify behavior. One is hospitality (*melmastia*) or the honorable uses of material goods (Barth 1969: 120). It is often referred to as simply giving hospitality to a guest. However, as Barth points out, "a consistently unilateral host-guest relationship [. . .] entails dependence and political submission by the guest" (1969: 121). When my informants talk about their duty to those who have no shares in the forest, it is partly in reference to the moral rights to subsistence (Scott 1976) or access rights (Peluso 1996: 512), as well as a means to reinforce patron–client relationships. Elsewhere I have explored aspects of this moral economy (Southwold 2002a). Here, I will concentrate on another principle: autonomy. Barth explains that the distinctiveness of Pukhtun culture is based on value orientations which "[. . .] emphasize male autonomy and egality, self-expression and aggressiveness in a syndrome which might be summarized under the concept of honor (*izzat*)" (1969: 120).

In terms of economic self-interest, the shareowners, as a group or coalition of actors, have a common interest in controlling the amount of fuelwood and timber leaving the forests. As a group, most of them acknowledge the needs of everyone to have fuelwood; but it is not in their interest for non-shareholders to sell what is not for their domestic need. Furthermore, many shareholders are selling timber without the agreement of their other shareholders. Yet in practice little can be done to stop the illegal, informal economy because of disunity among shareholders. This lack of cohesion is an integral part of Pukhtun socio-political organization, and identity.

There is a Pukhtun adage which exemplifies segmentary opposition in acephalous patrilineages: I against my brother, my brother and I against our father's brother's sons, my brother and I and our father's brother's sons against our father's father's brothers' sons, etc. One example of self-interest against one's own brothers is that Rashid has sold Rs 200,000 worth of timber from the banda in which he and his brothers are equal shareowners. None of the proceeds have been given to his brothers.

Individual autonomy and self-interest are exemplified by the concepts of *dushmani, badneitei, swazei* and *zud*. A dushman is an enemy or foe, the polar opposite of *dost*, a friend. Badneitei is to have bad thoughts in your heart about other people. Swazei is not wanting someone else to have good things or to be in a good position: it is not wanting something yourself, but preventing someone else from having it. The concept of jealousy in English is defined as: "suspicious or fearful of being displaced by a rival or resentful of or vindictive towards, especially through envy" (*Collins English Dictionary* 1998). The contrast of badneitei and swazei with jealousy is highlighted by the concept of zud: doing what another person does not want you to do and pride in winning, right or wrong.

Amir: "The changing value of bandas is a major source of dushmani in the village. It is only natural because some are getting richer and others getting poorer."[22] Dushmani reinforces patron–client relationships and is a key factor in the inability of shareowners to agree on a common policy in managing their joint bandas. Faheem (a non-shareholder) told me that he can take wood from Amir's banda because he is his friend. Others who are not friends (dushmani) cannot. In answer to questions about special things he would do to represent friendship, he said: "If anybody attacks Amir, then I will support him. I would support him even if I thought he was wrong because he is a friend." What if you are a *dost* of one shareholder and a dushman of another? "If there are five owners, and one is a friend, it is all right because the one shareholder will say that I took his share."

One means of access to fuelwood, as well as a means of sanctions, is linked to patron–client relationships, which by their very nature are divisive. A sanction against stealing can be the threat of violence; yet, the offender will have a protective patron. Likewise, shareowners are only likely to report persons to the forest guards if they are someone else's client. In both cases, there is a risk of conflict between the shareholders, thus having the effect of protecting those involved in the informal economy.

Relations with cultivating tenants are more complex. Akhund Khel landlords need to ask those who are not of their own khel. "No matter how poor, a Mia will not work for others." Since the economy is only partially based on agriculture, tenants, like everyone else, are more dependent on migration, especially since tenants get ¼ share of the crop, plus inputs and fodder.[23] Hence, there is a scarcity of labor, especially since most women of Akhund Khel are excluded from agricultural production activities. One landlord told me that he must give fuelwood and grazing to his tenants, otherwise, "how will my fields be cultivated?" Nevertheless, cultivating tenants are in an insecure position. Few have a tenancy for more than a few years, even though most of them have lived in Ajmir for generations. This general practice reduces the power of tenants, and it is symptomatic of the fluidity of patron–client relations.

As a consequence of badneitei, swazei and zud, cooperation is rare. Mohamad told me that:

> No one in this society will do anything unless they see an advantage for themselves. I will accept the leadership of an outsider, but not an insider. [Amir told me the same.] I am a close relative of Amir, but if Amir asked me to cooperate, I would not, even if it was in my own interest. Whatever Amir says, I will say the opposite. This is zud. It is the custom of us Pukhtun to be jealous. That is why there is no political cooperation and we are changing alliances. There is no development because we do not work together. If one *kada* (family) joins with another—the others will oppose.

Akhund Khel has four, sometimes five, subdivisions based on descent. These sub-khels are mixed in terms of land rights and domicile. Each section has its own leaders and supports different national political parties. Further, there is no consistency in which party subsections of Ajmir support. Whichever political party is in power enables supporters to use force. Several drinking water schemes have been introduced by a succession of political parties through local councils. When the Pakistan People's Party (PPP) was in power, Muslim League supporters in the hamlet were not given pipes. The reverse happened when the Muslim League gained power. This affected the poor as well as the wealthier. Naturally, it led to physical conflict with the use of Kalashnikovs to steal pipes from the opposing faction.

Threat of violence implicitly underlies many relations in Ajmir and affects the management of bandas. As Banerjee notes: "Violence was not some criminal aberration but had a central place in this wider ethnical system" (2000: 154).

The forms of violence, who engages in them, and their dynamics are accordingly expanded and deepened analytically by conceptualizing violence as a sort of habitus.

> As Dumont (1992: 277) puts it: Violence is a habitus . . . at once structured and structuring; structured because the idea of violence results from historical events, stored as the memory of past deeds, of past encounters, of past frustrations; and structuring because the idea of violence informs human actions, determines the acceptability, even the banality of violence, if not the ability to erase the scandal of its occurrence. (Peluso and Watts 2001: 6)

Some of the shareholders are constrained by their fear of what non-shareholders would do if they did not have fuelwood. On the other side, tenants from other khels repeatedly told me that they were afraid of Akhund Khel. The fear and practice of violence works as a counterbalancing force. It may be used to terrorize a weak individual, such as tenants of another khel, or to forge temporary alliances; but it is not used effectively to force one group to comply with another except for brief encounters (e.g. the incidents over water pipes). Hence it has weak potential to protect the self-interest of shareowners, as a coalition of actors.

In this PATA, jirgas are a key institution for resolving disputes. This is the forum in which the different sub-khels come together in an attempt to make joint decisions. In theory, everyone living in Ajmir should be invited; but this is rarely the case. Bashir told me that only Akhund Khel is invited. "There is no need to invite others because others will do what the Mias say." Characteristically, Rashid said that: "Usually the jirgas are not successful because elders are not giving fair decision and do not agree."

It is not surprising that the shareowners of the same banda are unable to act jointly to protect their own financial self-interests. The five brothers who are the joint shareowners of LP Banda are also not united over management of forests. Last year, the son of one (Mia Bacha) cut timber to sell and made a field for his own use. The brother of his father (Farman) asked him not to do this because it belonged to them all. This did not stop his brother's son. When Farman went to talk with him again, he took a Kalashnikov and fired at his uncle. It was then proposed that they divide the forest. After the division, Farman's brother said that he did not get a good piece and demanded to make the banda communal again. Mia Bacha is still cutting the trees as a business. His father's brothers think that this is very bad because it is an area susceptible to landslides and that nothing is being done to stop Mia Bacha. As zud, the other brothers are cutting trees.

CONCLUSIONS

In this essay, I have deliberately submerged the reader into the conversations in which I had to highlight inconsistencies in the way individuals conceptualize access to forest resources as representatives of different social actors. More fundamentally, I have tried to avoid the "[. . .] rigid categories, binary distinctions, and ahistorical truisms" (Scott: 2000: vii), often taken for granted in descriptions of conflicts between indigenous groups and the state.

Although I have adopted an actor-oriented approach, I have been critical of this approach when it has been used to simply map out different actors, as if each actor represented a homogeneous group. Although this is an improvement on looking at local communities and state bureaucracies as if they spoke with one voice, it only partially opens the black box of heterogeneity. This case illustrates how a repertoire of discourses and practices is used in specific arenas, in an attempt to avoid these limitations.

The cosmopolitan and nativist institutional frameworks have been compared in several arenas: land registration, the function of jirgas in implementing dispute settlements, and legislation giving access to forests. The internal inconsistencies in these institutions are made manifest through divergent interpretations of these institutions and the practices of individual social actors: the forest guards who represent the state forest department, shareholders and non-shareholders.

The essay has also dealt with the impact of the state's forest management policies on livelihood and identities. State-controlled felling has dramatically enhanced the livelihoods of shareholders; at the same time making the livelihoods of non-shareholders less secure. The unintended consequences of two interventions—the Survey of Forests and the state-controlled commercial felling—has been to put non-shareholders in a more vulnerable position, even though the explicit aims of the Working Plan should protect them. Further, these two interventions have created new arenas for disputes. Shareholders are unable to unite to protect their rights. Rather, the consequences have been to create new factions, giving non-shareholders continued, if insecure access to forest resources. As Agrawal and Sivaramakrishan note: "[. . .] communities are unavoidably fragmented politically and are located and shaped in wider sociopolitical contexts toward whose construction they contribute" (2000: 10; cf. Karlsson herein). Although regional Pukhtun identity has influenced state policies such as plural legal institutions and granting larger forest royalty shares, this has been due to the influence of powerful Khans in the region and the state's construction of Pukhtun identity. As the case of Ajmir illustrates, alliances are short-lived and are undermined by Pukhtun identity.

NOTES

1. The term shareholder is used because those who "own" shares are not, technically, owners. Royalty rightholders (the government's term) is also confusing because others also have rights, as will be explained in this essay.

2. I am not referring to Dobson's contrast between ecologism and environmentalism. Ecology, like ecologism, changes our relationship with the non-human natural world which influences our social and political life. However, Dobson is referring to political ideology of ecologism, which I am not. Dobson 2000: 2. See also Introduction to this volume.

3. Contrast with Cederlöf and Morrison in this volume, who show how Western trading interests infiltrated the Western Ghats.

4. Cf. Sivaramakrishnan 2001 for a critique of homogeneous class categories in Subaltern Studies.

5. The relations between forest contractors and local royalty owners and the institutional conflicts between the roles of the forest department and the Forest Development Corporation have been excluded from this essay. See Geiser 2001 and 2002.

6. Exploratory research was done throughout Malakand Division for four months during 1991.

7. The Akhund Khel consider themselves to be Miangan, i.e. descendants of a religious Pir. However, unlike many other Miangans, they claim that their land is *mali kahanimat*, i.e. land cleared of non-believers. By their own account, their role was never to mediate disputes, nor do they claim to be Saeeds. Furthermore, their land was inherited and not Tserai. It was not given by a khan, but taken in jihad. Therefore, their position should not be confused with the literature on Swat (e.g. Barth 1959 and A.S. Ahmed 1976). Ajmir Akhund Khel does not claim to be the same patrilineage as other Akhund Khel in Dir and Swat.

8. This division was never changed. In Swat, there was the *wesh*, whereby land was redistributed about every twenty years according to the size of lineage and following. This was never done in Ajmir.

9. For the production strategy see Orlove and Guillet 1985.

10. See Geiser, this volume, for the situation before incorporation.

11. A jirga is often translated as a council of elders. In fact, it can refer to any group brought together to discuss a specific issue or to make decisions.

12. Since the time of research, the PATA has been abolished; and sharia law was introduced and later abolished.

13. Geiser (this volume) discusses that the new Forest Act will give the newly formed Department of Forests, Fisheries, and Wildlife responsibility for management of forests, watershed areas, and rangelands. The claimed interlinkage of these land uses is based on the idea of managing an ecological system.

14. For a discussion of notions of property rights see Gururani 2000 and many others.

15. There are different arrangements in other areas. For example, in bordering Kohistan, local shareholders are given 80 percent of the revenue, while the state receives 20 percent. During the Wali's reign, rightholders were only given 10 percent of the revenue. Several local informants told me that they received Rs 10 per tree. In 1976, the government made the 60 percent concession after fighting in Dir. Manager of Forest Operations, Malakand Circle, Jehangir Khan, August 2, 1994.

16. The Division Forest Officer, Salar Khan, August 2, 1994.

17. There were plans to make Ajmir a model reafforestation area. Free saplings were available; but no one took up the offer in 1993 and 1994. Aside from government officials, only a handful of residents knew about the plan and none had participated. Furthermore, several development projects have been established since my fieldwork. Therefore, I will leave these issues out of my discussion.

18. Interviews on June 28, 1993 and August 2, 1994, with Salar Khan, Divisional Forest Officer for Alpuri, whose area included Ajmir.

19. From observation during the day, I often have seen men dragging logs that are about 3–4 meters long or about 13 feet, which would incur a fine of about Rs 650.

20. See Gururani 2000: 185–8 for a comparative and mostly similar account of the position of forest guards in India.

21. In other areas, e.g. Dir District, there are no individual shares and fines (*nagar*) are levied by a jirga on those found stealing wood.

22. Banerjee 2000: 45 notes that during the colonial period, Pathan violence increased as an egalitarian social order was replaced by feudal hierarchy.

23. A ¼ share is unique to Kana and Alpuri. In the rest of Swat, tenants receive ½ share of the crop.

12

"THERE IS NO LIFE WITHOUT WILDLIFE"

National Parks and National Identity in
Bardia National Park, Western Nepal

Nina Bhatt

INTRODUCTION

THIS ESSAY ANALYZES HOW ONE SEGMENT OF THE NEPALI BUREAUcracy—national park and wildlife officials—construct their identities in the contexts of multiparty democracy and the end of absolutist monarchical rule. Before 1990, allegiance to the king, social mobility through patronage and nepotism, and localized loyalties were the means by which bureaucrats attached themselves to the center. After 1990, Nepali officials' identity is perhaps best understood by the rubrics of development, democracy, and globalization. While these transnational influences are most intelligible in experiences of Western education, professional relations with expatriates, and ubiquitous popular culture forms,[1] here I focus on the ways Nepali national park staff reconstitute their relations, aspirations, and ideologies in the framework of the new democratic polity as compared to the days of monarchical rule. The central question asked is: how does being a conservator of nature inform bureaucratic identity formation? And for Nepal, how do the socio-political realities of monarchy and democratic rule shape this identity formation?

POLITICAL HISTORY

A brief political chronology of Nepal is as follows: the Shah Dynasty (forefathers of the present king) ruled over 1769–1846, at which point a coup by the Rana family diminished the power of the royals.[2] This coup resulted in the Rana family establishing for themselves a hereditary primeministership with control over all powers of state. In 1857, Jang Bahadur Rana formalized this arrangement whereby collateral succession to the primeministership was instituted and remained till the 1950/1 revolution, when the Shah kings regained power. For modern Nepali political history, the period 1962–90 marks the decades when political parties were banned and kings ruled under a partyless "democratic" system. The term "panchayat democracy" used throughout this essay refers to the period prior to 1990, and as we will see it marks a period of meaningful identity formation for the civil servants in question. The role of Nepalese royals from this period on became constitutional. For the purpose of this essay, the period 1951–90 is referred to as the pre-andolan (before democratic revolution).[3]

THE ROYALS AND CONSERVATION

Locating the identity of Nepali wildlife staff has to begin in the context of their historical ties with the monarchy.[4] The pre-revolution (1951–90) accounts show how individual and collective identities were shaped through encounters with royalty, which informed the everyday practices of such staff. For this group, the identification of the king as a Hindu monarch (for many, an avatar of the god Vishnu) also has central importance.[5] But the fact that Nepali kings sanctioned much of Nepal's early conservation efforts is also what resulted in the display of particularly strong regard and allegiance for royals among government officials.[6] The special attention paid to conservation efforts is seen in initiatives taken soon after the overthrow of the Rana regime (Heinen and Kattel 1992a and 1992b). For instance, in 1958 the Wildlife Conservation Act was passed and in 1973 the ruling monarch, King Birendra Bir Bikram Shah Dev, approved the National Parks Act which facilitated the designation and management of four types of protected areas (Heinen and Kattel 1992a and 1992b).[7]

After the 1990 revolution bureaucrats shifted their attention away from monarchy as their object of reform. In the reshuffle for power and in seeking to acquire agency, government servants allied themselves with newly elected politicians and with the bearers of international development aid (expatriate specialists and powerful local NGOs). Because bureaucrats have inherited a legacy of hierarchical rule characterized by networks of royal patronage, political allegiances, and kinship nepotism—engaging with "new" actors (elected politicians, international expatriates, Nepali NGO workers) reveals dilemmas in everyday discourse and practice.

In anthropology, detailing the lives of bureaucrats remains woefully underdone for South Asia. Unlike popular anthropological subject areas, such as caste studies for India,[8] or Sherpa ethnographies for Nepal,[9] the question of how state officials conceptualize social relations as individuals and groups is addressed by relatively few academics (Britan and Cohen 1980; Gupta 1995; Herzfeld 1992; Heyman 1995, 1997, 1999, 2000a). This is despite Nader's call to "study up," as far back as 1972.

Since only a handful of Nepal scholars address processes related to state-making (Goodall 1978; Edwards 1977; Joshi 1983), I extrapolate from Scott's (1985) work among Malaysian peasants; Siu's (1997, with Faure 1995) work in South China, and Tsing's (1993) accounts of state-making at the margins. These observers discuss how individuals and groups appropriate official ideology to their benefit and create complex identities to resist hegemonic powers. By deconstructing categories of power, static identities, and culture, these authors expand, reshape and fragment crucial intellectual concepts for a more multifaceted analysis of social processes across scale, time, and cultures. In his illuminating historical study of the changing culture of forestry and political action in West Bengal, K. Sivaramakrishnan offers a nuanced definition of state-making by referring to the "ideological and organizational power of the central government to penetrate society, exact compliance, and invoke commitment [. . .] which rests on a delicate balance [. . .] in the relationship between state and society" (1999: 5).

BACKGROUND TO NEPALI ADMINISTRATION

In 1951 the Rana administration (founded in 1846 by Jung Bahadur) ended, and with it ended a century of regal isolation and stagnation (Rana 1999; Sever 1993, 1996). Since that time, the Nepali government has projected itself as the purveyor of development, with the consequent result that most Nepalis look upon the state with great expectation—as the source of crucial inputs necessary to enrich their lives (Mishra *et al.* 1983; Mishra 1997; Mishra and Sharma 1983). With the aim of fulfilling these goals, the Government of Nepal Act (1951) provided the constitutional basis for a new political order, which included an increasingly complex bureaucracy modeled after the Indian system (Joshi 1983; Rose and Landau 1977).[10]

The expansion of the Nepalese bureaucracy has been remarkable. In 1849, when the Rana Prime Minister Jung Bahadur was consolidating his rule, the civil service consisted of a mere 2700 officials (Panday 1983, 1989). By 1951, this figure had risen to 7000; by 1989, the expansion reached 90,000 permanent civil service officers and thousands of temporary positions. These numbers do not even include employees serving on development boards and various autonomous and semi-autonomous public agencies, for which data are not available (Panday 1989).[11]

The civil service is divided into the administrative and technical sectors. Within these are gazetted (officer) and non-gazetted (sub-officer) positions.[12] Ethnographic data for this essay is drawn from both groups. For gazetted officials, I concentrate on third, second, and (to a lesser extent) first class officers.[13] Thus I primarily discuss here the category of game scouts, rangers, and game park wardens. Only the latter are of officer rank. Since the national park service is considered a technical component of the civil services (others technical fields include agriculture, engineering, health, and education), most of my data pool consists of technical rather than administrative bureaucrats, although much of these officials' work is arguably more administrative than technical in nature.

JOINING GOVERNMENT SERVICE: DEPARTMENT OF NATIONAL PARKS AND WILDLIFE MANAGEMENT

Game Scouts[14]

Certainly for national parks and wildlife management staff, joining government service was one of the pinnacles in their lives. Bureaucratic life represented prestige, lifelong job security, and power. The glamor of *jagir khanu* (literally, eating a salary) was most often the reason given for wanting to join His Majesty's Government (henceforth HMG) service.[15] For game scouts and rangers, becoming a *karamchari* (government worker) from childhood days had a very strong appeal. This interest in government service was shaped by their fears, combined with respect for HMG officials encountered in youth. A senior game scout from Thumani Post, Bardia National Park, put it this way: "Once one is a government worker, villagers and others—everyone—looks upon you with respectful eyes. As children, when we saw HMG workers, we used to think 'oh if only I were an HMG worker, even I would get the same type of respect,' that was our *rahar* [strong desire] even back then."

Many villagers actively press for an HMG job, applying what is commonly referred to as "source-force." This term (used even by Nepalis who speak no English), refers to pressure applied to achieve one's end, especially in obtaining employment. (The use of cultural techniques of pressure and compliance in the Nepalese context has been documented by scholars such as Brown 1996; Chatterji 1977, 1980; and Panday 1989, 1990.) For most, any government job suffices; the actual position in government is often inconsequential—it is simply getting in that matters. While recruitment for officer rank positions involves a series of exams, non-officers are often recruited through patrons already in government service. Patrons are expected to, and often fulfill, their obligations of helping friends and family with *bharti garne* or getting admitted to government work (Borgström 1980).

To illustrate the degree to which government jobs are highly sought after, a Tharu game scout based in Royal Bardia National Park (Eastern Nepal) discussed the ambivalence with which he was viewed by community members.[16] For fellow Tharus, this game scout represents the state that keeps his fellow villagers from exploiting valuable park resources. Yet, despite regarding him as something akin to a traitor, the men of his village keep soliciting him for jobs: "Depending on how kind or strict I am, fellow villagers say 'he is good' or 'he is bad.' But regardless of our [park's] conflicts with the community, young men keep coming to me for jobs. They keep begging me to get them admitted and so far, I've admitted twenty Tharus into the national park services." While some game scouts recalled exercising personal agency in pursuing a government job, many others felt they just fell into it—at times pushed by family and friends.[17]

Two game scouts with high school degrees, now with the national parks services for over twelve years, said they were very young (below the age of seventeen) when they joined the government. What they recall from their high school days is a lot of pressure to *jagir khanu* [earn government salary]. One of the scouts remembered being yanked out of school without his father's consent by the Bardia game warden and being given a job as a scout. The boy's father (also a game scout) was highly regarded by the warden, thus the warden felt he was doing the family a great favor by taking his son into the services. This game scout, now twenty-nine, agrees: far from regretting the loss of an education, he is grateful for the steady employment.

Game scouts continually recalled their childhood fear of government workers—a fear reinforced by elders of the community. This fear became conflated with respect, a sense of awe. Game scouts today shake their heads in wonderment that they ever felt such fear. With the arrival of bahudal (multiparty democracy), they believe the respect for government service and its officials has greatly declined.[18] As one senior game scout (age forty-two) put it:

> We used to be afraid! At that time, we knew a forest guard. When the forest guard and rhino sepoys came to the jungle, our elders used to say "la, they have come carrying *bandooks* [guns] now if you talk left, right [i.e. nonsense] to us, they'll shoot you bullets." For us, we gave respect to HMG workers. But now, it's not that way. Even in small children, *maryada* [respect] isn't there. They see that the generation elder to them does not respect us, puts government workers down, so they learn the same. Not even a little bit of *maryada* is there anymore.

Rangers

Among game scouts, the deployment of social connections resulted in their being given a government job. For this group, being a government worker meant a great increase in social prestige: alternative options included agricultural labor, factory work, domestic service, or erratic forms of menial employment. But as one moves up the echelons of HMG service (park rangers, clerks, legal aides), one begins to see that individuals in the more elite ranks of service often landed in their positions due to family hardship or personal inability to succeed in other professions. At higher levels of government service, membership is often determined not by free choice but by the lack of other choices.

One middle-aged ranger, for example, said that family poverty had prevented him pursuing higher studies. Once he took a government job and began earning money, he lost his earlier ambitions. Later he became demoralized as he watched successive generations of younger officials surpass him, both academically and professionally.

Another ranger, who had been with the national park service for over fifteen years, had a junior college equivalent degree, but decided not to pursue further education. While traveling to Kathmandu from his village to collect his degree, he already began to feel "left behind" because he realized all his friends were already in government jobs. A chance meeting with a game park warden at a hotel where he was staying led to friendship, and also to valuable career guidance. This student then applied for a ranger position with both the national parks and general forestry services. When accepted at both, he chose wildlife, in part because of his positive impressions of the warden he'd met by accident. Such choice, however, is increasingly a thing of the past: a tighter job market is forcing educated young men to remain in jobs for which they are overqualified.

Park Wardens and Senior Officers

Similar to game scouts and rangers, officer rank staff (i.e. wardens) were drawn to government service for reasons of job security and prestige. But since members of this group could ostensibly have made careers elsewhere (as teachers, professors, engineers, or businessmen), it is the additional perks of government life, especially at the national parks department, that provide key incentives for joining. Such licit perks include foreign travel, the possibility of being sent abroad for an MSc (or possibly a PhD), choice assignments in the field, and finally a plum posting in Kathmandu. The illicit perks of government service, of course, are even more enticing to individuals with a penchant for corruption.

Officers in my data pool enjoyed talking about the power of being an HMG official. When asked about the nature of this power, several pointed to the most basic type of power in the world: the ability to throw someone in jail. A second-class warden from the Solokhumbu district (eastern Nepal) says it was this power which made a profound impression on him while growing up. A former official with the Department of National Parks and Wildlife Conservation (commonly referred to by its abbreviation, DNPWC) said: "I was the third or fourth sherpa ever to join government service. We were always impressed with government officers growing up. It always seemed like they had so much power: whether it was to toss someone in jail or to enable them [illegally] to become citizens." Wardens can at their discretion jail intruders who enter the park for up to fifteen years. This tremendous authority made HMG especially attractive to the warden of Royal Chitwan National Park: "In any work, when force is used, that is power. If a poacher kills a rhino, you punish him [. . .] that is power. We have to use our authority, but use it in the right way. Foresters can't jail people for fifteen years the way we can. Politicians don't have the power of the law but we do—we have HMG's legal power." Others simply enjoy being the *chetra ko boss* (boss of a given locale). Shiv Raj Bhatta, Bardia National Park's warden, said: "I feel this way not because of the authority, the position, but because there is a feeling of leadership. When what I say gets implemented, that is when I feel like a boss. Everyone here has given me the confidence."

In reality, however, it is often the inability to succeed in other fields that forces officers to join the DNWPC. Two wardens (both in their late thirties) said that as high school students they concentrated on the sciences in hope of becoming doctors or engineers. Both were unable to achieve the grades necessary to pursue medical or engineering studies, and were forced to consider other career options. Another warden, a third-class officer in his thirties working for Kanchenjunga National Park, was not embarrassed by his academic failures: "Forestry was my third choice. My marks weren't good enough for either engineering or medicine so I went into forestry. It's O.K. Sometimes when I look at my friends who stuck it out in chemistry or who are in other fields, their lives are so much more luxurious. In such times, I feel I have regrets."

Many officers voiced similar regrets when they compared their lives with those of their friends or, especially in recent years, with those of Nepalis working in similar capacities in the field of international development. These officials often express disbelief at how well their high school friends have done. As one officer put it:

> When I was taking my high school exams, there were four of us buddies. We rented a room and studied together. Do you know "Gurung" [pseudonym] on TV?[19] Well, he was one of the guys. Since I did well on my exams, I thought I should become an MD but it turns out that I didn't do well on the exams. Among the four of us, one buddy failed high school, he was the lazy, stupid buddy. But slowly, he took four years to pass his school, then another four to do his BA and now, he is working on his MA. This friend now drives around in a car. This guy who failed high school now moves around with our minister!

TAKING THE PUBLIC SERVICE EXAMS

By definition, one becomes an HMG officer (as opposed to a scout or ranger) upon successful completion of the public service exams. These national-level exams, which are administered for both gazetted and non-gazetted positions, are the basic requirement for becoming a civil servant. For many, they are also the most difficult hurdle in the process.[20]

For non-officer staff such as *subbas* (office administrators) and park rangers, inability to pass the civil service exams remains a source of preoccupation throughout their careers. It symbolizes their perceived failure as government servants. The importance of passing civil service exams becomes clearer when those who did pass (despite not consequently rising up the ranks) kept recalling this achievement despite the passage of many years. These officers would bring up the names of *saathi/bhai* (friends and relatives) who, unlike them, were unable to pass these exams.

Ironically, many who were unsuccessful in joining government service are now highly successful with international development organizations. They are now far wealthier and enjoy greater professional challenges than their HMG friends. Even more ironic is the fact that those who could not enter HMG are now in charge of disbursing grants, which support park projects as well as the salaries of their government buddies. This places officials in the peculiar position of being both supplicant (because they rely on international aid money for support) and superior (because they have the power to shut aid programs down).

A warden remembers four buddies from college: "They fought for these exams for three or four years [. . .] they could still not pass. They now work in *projects* [referring to international aid work] in the same project office I am working for [on leave], do you understand? They couldn't pass HMG for many years, crossed the age of 35, so joined *projects*."

Despite the disparities *vis-à-vis* NGO workers in pay, perks and even (when it comes to budgetary matters) some degree of power, HMG officials cling to their success in the civil service exams as a key source of pride and comfort. In addition to such intangible factors as respect and local standing, passage carries with it the promise of lifelong security.

"Rajendra," now in his early forties and on leave from the government, works for an international project based in the western plains. Rajendra is in two minds about his experience as a third-class official with the ministry of forests. Despite his ambivalence, however, Rajendra views his entry to government service as one of the greatest achievements of his life. The year he successfully entered competition, about 200 people had applied for fewer than six available slots. "I realize that HMG isn't a well-organized system," he said. "But the truth is, 90 percent of people currently with international *projects* sat for the public service exams. They take three to four days of holiday from work, go to Kathmandu, take the exams, and return to their *projects*."

In another instance, an overqualified candidate repeatedly sat for the civil service exams despite failing them several times over. "Vasant," a ranger assigned to Bardia National Park and on leave because he is pursuing a Master's degree in Europe, could have easily abandoned his quest and found higher paying work in the private sector: he is fluent in English, has extensive field experience, and all the right academic qualifications. Still, he sheepishly admits that he rented a room in Kathmandu to study for and take the *lok sewa* (government exams) so he could become an officer. "There is big difference in becoming an officer you know," he says. "After all, this is Nepal."

Others already within the HMG system (rangers, administrators, clerks) compete hard to become gazetted officers. They express frustration—feel "*dikkha*" (sad), speak of "having big hopes but getting small things"—when they cannot pass the exams. Often this happens when candidates join HMG with expectations or experience at odds with the requirements of the job.

For example, the subba of Bardia National Park is responsible for clerical tasks ranging from keeping track of staff holidays to providing guidelines on government rules and regulations. His educational background, however, is of a more classical bent: he has a degree in Sanskrit Studies from a well-respected college in India, and recites classical *shlokas* at the drop of a hat. His natural aptitude and love is for teaching, but he performs *subba* clerical work as a non-gazetted first-class official because this is where he was able to secure a permanent job.

Bureaucracies can be cumbersome and clumsy beasts. Seldom is there a good match between individual capability and the need of a particular government slot. Because lifelong job security is valued over factors such as effectiveness or efficiency, performance standards can often be low and the work environment can be uninspiring. Park staff often spend much of their time in gossip and tea drinking, while potential change agents (officers with power) are consumed with the ever-present threat of transfers by the political players in Kathmandu. At a more pernicious level, those with power utilize their time and resources to aggressively consolidate their economic and social capital and to entrench their *afno manches* (own people) in strategic positions.

The Sanskritist subba expressed dismay (despite the passage of many years since he had failed his exam) that HMG had asked him questions about geography, and other fields in which he was not terribly informed.[21] Other park staff, alternating between eavesdropping and participating in this interview, wholeheartedly agreed with the subba when he plaintively asserted that it is HMG's *duty* to provide jobs (*rozgari dilaune sarkar ko kam ho*). The assertion was even met with applause: "It's in the constitution," said one administrator. The legal interpretation of the assembled subbas and *khardars* was unanimous. As one put it, "The constitution says HMG will look after the welfare of people and that includes rozgari."

Earning Worth in HMG

Passing the government entry exams (and, to a lesser extent, working in a non-officer capacity) provides park staff with a level of prestige that helps compensate for a relative lack of benefits such as those provided by international NGOs. This prestige is an essential part of what makes HMG work desirable, and is thus a core aspect of officers' personal identity.

For senior government officials in my data pool, being a *hakim* (boss) is a large component of their official persona. It is also something that they feel they would not get from working for *kuires* (slang term for foreigners). Being a *hakim* (boss) can mean having subordinate staff, being based in Kathmandu, enjoying international travel, and often—for many the most important perk—obtaining a foreign degree without the rigors of a genuinely competitive application process. "Ram," a second-class officer, had this to say: "I'm an under secretary with the forest ministry. I'm a section chief of planning. I have karamcharis [staff] who consider me their boss. Any *ban karyalaya* [forest office] I go to, I go as a boss. People respect you, so you get satisfaction. You enjoy this status. Money is one thing, but status is another." For this senior officer, and for junior staff as well, the precise distribution of government perks is of crucial importance—a factor carefully weighed as contributing to or detracting from the attractiveness of their jobs: "I stay in Kathmandu. I have a car that the office gives me to go to the ministry. Petrol is also free. This is also a type of respect. There are a lot of old cars. Some other Class II officers have also gotten it. I can also use it for personal purposes." This is what a senior officer told me.

Pension, job security, food ration, and clothing were especially important to national park staff of all ranks. According to a senior game scout: "After doing service for twenty years, we'll get some help. It's our *adhikar* [right]. Maybe our sons won't look after us. Perhaps our daughters-in-law will beat us. It could be that fellow villagers don't come to our assistance but still—we'll have our pension. That's the guarantee. Other benefits are that we get food ration and clothes. Plus we don't have to pay for rent. All this in the context of Nepal is a big deal."

Knowing your Hakim, Doing *Chakri*: The Politics of Getting Ahead in HMG

The HMG *mahoul* (environment) requires staff at all levels to be attentive of their boss' nature, to engage in chakri (ritualized obsequious behaviors) and to constantly build upon and work connections to ensure that the right transfer, promotion, opportunity for travel, and training occur. The situation is perceived as being so eroded that staff feel compelled to perform chakri merely to ensure the smooth completion of minor transactions (such as obtaining boss' signature for leave). Elsewhere, I detail the negotiation of Nepali government officers within a system tied to politics and nepotism, where connections to the royal house or to INGO expatriates, elected officials, and other politicians determine success.

The daily struggles of government bureaucrats are periodized as falling in pre-democratic Nepal (before 1990) or in post-andolan (after the 1990 revolution). The overall consensus is that getting ahead was a simpler, more straightforward process in the days of the monarchy, if only because politics and political interference had not seeped down to petty levels.

In this section, I discuss how junior government staff understand their relations with their superior officers. I describe how such staff experience their work environment, and the extent to which they find it enabling and empowering—or discouraging and routine.

For junior staff (scouts, clerks, petty administrators), their valuation of a "good" or "bad" boss depends largely on how they feel treated on a personal level. Game scouts say how their superiors address them, provide directives, and encourage them matter a great deal. Being made to perform menial duties, such as laundering clothes, cooking, and running personal errands is demoralizing for staff—an issue that breaks down on lines of class as much as cultural background.[22] Junior park staff I interviewed were extremely preoccupied with *bani/behura* (character, treatment). They were also concerned with whether or not hakims had *sikaune tarika* (instructive styles). People who do *ghamanda* (have inflated egos) or act like they are "*ma thulo chu*" ("I am great") are disliked, regardless of their rank.

Game scouts identify their superiors (particularly park wardens) as either *kada* (strict), or *naram* (kind). The latter is greatly preferred, and far better respected. As one scout explained:

> The former Bardia park warden was very strict, but Bhatta-sir [referring to his current warden] is very kind. Before, scouts did all the work, cooking rice, etc. Now there is some *parivartan* [progress] with him. Bhatta-Sir has hired a cook rather than using game scouts for this purpose. Now everyone has to follow his example. During *panchayat kal ko shasan* [absolute monarchy 1962–90] there was more misuse of scouts. Now people understand. After bahudal [democracy], there is *manav adhikar* [human rights]. Newspapermen go from village to village and ask what is going on.

Other scouts also approved of the example set by warden Shiv Raj Bhatta, whose decision to avoid using subordinates for menial labor forced intermediate-level officers to do likewise. Shiv Raj, who had been the acting warden of Bardia National Park for five years at the time of this research, was seen by many subordinates as a good model of boss behavior:

> *Bardia HQ scout*: What is a good boss? A good boss is someone like Bhatta-sir. *Ramro kam lagaunu huncha* [He makes us do good work]. He gives us no sorrow. Work is our *kartabya* [duty] but the officer has to do good *bolchal* [speak nicely]. *Sabya bhayara bolnu parcha* [they shouldn't scold us]. Bosses shouldn't give us unnecessary *dukkha* [pain]. They shouldn't *pelo* [oppress] us.

Since game scouts are most vulnerable to exploitation by their seniors, they were very sensitive to how they were treated on an everyday basis. Being routinely cursed at (*gaali garnu*), being forced to perform unreasonable chores, and in general being treated in an undignified way resulted in deep resentment. Scouts were especially sensitive to losing public face. In a group interview with game scouts assigned to headquarters in Bardia, this is what they had to say:

> *Boli, bachan* [style of speaking] is the most important thing. It's the same thing said in different ways. To curse someone and to give instruction in a kind manner are two very different things. Because one way saves our *izzat* [honor], then we feel desire for our work. If a boss says "*babu, kam gare ra*

aau, la hera, kati cheetal cha" [son, go and work, go see, how many cheetal—a species of deer—there are] then we like it. The point is, it's all how you make someone do the same work.

Saruwa Garnu—Transfer as Punishment

For many, displeasing bosses can have the dire result of being transferred to a distant or unpleasant area. Because it happens so often, being transferred is a popular topic of discussion among government staff. The dread of being transferred (*saruwa garnu*) or more aptly *faldinu* (to be thrown) to an undesirable place is a fear experienced by government workers in all ministries and among all ranks. I was told that this threat disappears only if one achieves the rank of "secretary," indicating that most government officials operate within the framework of this threat throughout their career. The dread of being sent to a punishment post (often to remote areas), cut off from adequate communications, family, health, and other services, thus results in the perceived need to perform chakri—to please one's boss to earn his favor. Much of the effort of performing chakri is directed with the aim of ensuring a favorable field posting. The geographical area to which an officer is assigned, and the duration of the posting, are often important markers of his social capital.

In fact, in almost all stories of corruption a villain bureaucrat is thrown to dreaded far-flung corners of Nepal (such as Dolpo, Mustang, or Sagarmatha); or, in tales (less common) of bureaucrats taking a principled stance by not caving into chakri, they too are "thrown" into the far corners of the Himalayas. Because officials noteworthy for either virtue or vice risk a bad posting, most officials take the middle path of compliance and inaction. "Bhim," an administrator at Bardia National Park, said that even his well-connected and popular boss Shiv Raj Bhatta was not safe from being "thrown:"

> HMG is all about giving *dhamki* [threats]. For example, if Bhatta-sir gets sent to Rara (a remote area), he'll have difficulty there. And the minister can send him if he gets pissed off. If they like you, they'll keep you in a good place for ten years. Central power is all about giving sorrow to people. For example, the people who are in Kathmandu, they want to keep their power, they want to keep their chair. It is human nature to want that but if someone has spent four years in Jumla, then naturally he should get transferred at the right time. They are not getting transferred. Someone might be staying in

the Maoist district. He should get transferred within a two-year period. Otherwise they will be in trouble. But the department and ministry won't do that. Within the democratic principle, undemocratic practices are being exercised.

Not everyone feels as pessimistic about the irrationality of HMG as Bhim. Most national park officers recognize and are pleased by the advantage of their department compared to most HMG outfits. The department of national parks is small, intimate relationships are forged, and the staff enjoy the patronage of the royal family. Department officials are proud that Nepal has gained international recognition in conservation, through community forestry, buffer zone regulation, and other methods. Royalty has played a key role in highlighting national park and wildlife efforts through relationships with international organizations such as the World Wildlife Fund (WWF).

Compared to other ministries and departments, park officials have a coherent identity whose departmental features include a familial environment, fairness, professional development opportunities, and looking out for one another. Park officials believe these features stand in stark contrast with the attitude of other departments and ministries.

The Performance of Chakri

Regardless of how optimistic national park officials are about their department compared to others, the place of chakri is an entrenched and systemic feature of government interaction which has survived various regimes and political periods (Bista 1991; Fisher *et al.*, 1997; Panday 1999).[23] Park staff acknowledge the central place of chakri and its manifestations. The severity of chakri, its purpose, and features have undergone some transformations but many of its salient features remain.

Senior officers, park wardens, rangers and game scouts describe chakri in the following ways:

- Treat your hakim like a king—no matter how *bekuf* [idiotic] he is.
- Pretend that you don't know anything, and hence are no threat.
- *Namaskar bajai rahanu parcha* [you have to keep banging out salutations].
- Go to your boss's house regularly. [This is a show of deference rather than an annoying invasion of privacy.]
- *Boss ko parivar lai maya dhekaunu parcha* [show affection for your boss' family].

- Give expensive fruits to your boss, but say its from your garden, or your relatives' farm in order to avoid insulting him. If something looks store-bought, it's embarrassing, like you are reducing his izzat [as if he can't afford it].

Game scouts said that chakri for them meant "saying OK to big people all the time, regardless of whether they are right or wrong." For them, it also meant having to do "personal *kam* (work) such as washing their boss' clothes, fetching his rations, going off to such and such a place for errands."

Some time-honored forms of chakri include giving one's boss prized foods, such as clarified butter, smoked fish, bananas, special nuts, and fruit. These small things are intended to yield big returns and must be given in person. All government officials understand chakri etiquette: one must never phone before going to a hakim's house. This will irritate the boss, since phone calls in the local cultural context only happen between *saathi/bhai* (friends/family) or those of equal footing. The appropriate conduct is to wait by the hakim's door until beckoned; depending on rank, the supplicant may be received outdoors rather than permitted to enter the house.

In post-andolan government service, chakri has become worse. Added to behavior aimed at pleasing the boss is the question of hard cash. A twenty-year veteran and second-class officer with the Ministry of Forests and Soil Conservation told me he feels the situation in government is becoming untenable now: "Chakri is the same now, except that people look for cash as well (*paisa pani khoj cha*). For the favor of being sent for an overseas Masters degree, Rs 200 worth of bananas isn't going to cut it. You have to give considerable sums to the minister, secretary, director general or some combination thereof for being sent for an MSc."[24]

But if chakri is as necessary as it appears to be in order to get ahead, there are yet innumerable officials who shy away from it and describe their moral inability to engage in the act. A second-class officer with the ministry of forests told me that he realized it was the "politically strategic thing to do" and that he had the "necessary skills" for it, but that he was incapable of relinquishing his "ego" or "pride."[25] In the words of this particular officer, "Doing chakri is not easy. *Ego lai chodnu parcha* (you have to leave your ego). You have to go and meet [kowtow] with big people."[26]

Such officers who said that they do not do chakri wished most for their careers to work out "normally." In other words, they wanted merit-based promotions and assignments. Surprisingly, these officers expressed a high degree of confidence despite the prevalence of the culture of chakri: "If someone is big, it's because he has power, not because he is superior to me. I feel I am capable in everything. Even if someone throws me (to a remote place), I can do something. I have *bishwas, atman bishwas* [confidence, spiritual confidence]." Officers worry about the implications for their promotions because of chakri. Because promotions are perceived as not being merit based, staff realize that simply having educational qualifications, securing recommendations, and earning points at remote field assignments are not enough. A key factor is being based in Kathmandu in order to grease the wheels. Because being Kathmandu based is considered so crucial to career development, few mid-level or senior officials assigned to the field remain in their stations for very long. During one of my research stints at Bardia (a five-month stay), the senior warden in charge never came to his deputed station once. As a senior official explained to me: "In Nepal, you can't get promoted without source-force. It's worse now, more shrill compared to the panchayat years. To get promoted, you have to stay in Kathmandu. There is no peace, even in the field. But here in Bardia, even mid-ranking officers have not wanted to stay." When promotions do not occur in a timely manner, a deep demoralization sets in. Krishna Man Shrestha, a retired senior warden of Bardia National Park, described the mindset which begins to develop: "When people start to get bypassed for promotion, it becomes embarrassing, especially when those junior to you move ahead. People begin to develop an inferiority complex. An inferiority complex means that you cannot face someone. You won't speak even if you were verbose and confident before. It means you are tongue-tied, you cannot debate someone."

With the diminution of the political role of the palace, park staff feel even less sure that they will be treated fairly. Elsewhere, I detail the experiences of bureaucrats during the pre-andolan period, when bureaucrats (at least in retrospect) feel they exerted greater power. In post-andolan Nepal, many officials feel that chakri has increased, and that politicians formerly unused to power have subjected the promotion process to new levels of abuse.

One ministry of forests official explained that while he never supported the monarchy during the panchayat years, he does feel that the old system at least worked better for the bureaucrats. Now in his mid fifties, he compared his government life in pre- and post-andolan times:

> I have a lot of confidence in myself. I experienced a lot of *bikas* [progress] in my studies, which has given me immense confidence. This makes me not want to do chakri. For instance, I got the Colombo Plan without any source-force.[27] In panchayat times, there was fairness. You have to accept that. Whatever else, there was some fairness. In those days, it was 25 percent *jhelli* [cheating], but 75 percent was fair. Now it's the opposite. Today, I would never be able to go on the Colombo Plan because things work so unfairly. I actually want to thank the panchayat times for that. At least then, people had bishwas [faith or trust] that if they studied, they could do well.

But the transaction of chakri isn't as straightforward as it appears. On one level, the system suggests that the disempowered are forced to make offerings to those who hold real or perceived power over them. In reality, the efficacy of a superior's power is often miscalculated by the supplicant, with the result that the superior feels unfairly obligated and the subordinate feels cruelly betrayed. "Gautam," a second-class officer currently in the monitoring and evaluation wing of the Ministry of Forests, recalls one such incident:

> No one has done chakri to me, I really don't have that much power. It's really people who are at the secretarial level or those who are in administrative positions with the ability to do saruwa [transfers] are the ones with real power. But once a ranger came to me for saruwa, and even that was through my tenant. I didn't accept his ghee and dried fish. They said: "*hoina hazur* [no sir], we didn't even think of such a thing. If you return this, *hamro baijat huncha*" [it will be shameful for us]. They wouldn't take the "gifts" back. There is an element of humiliation involved if they take it back. But it's a total obligation, and becomes a question of your conscience. I always keep my word.

POST-MONARCHY POLITICS AND BUREAUCRATIC IDENTITY CONSTRUCTION

In delineating the difference between pre- and post-andolan Nepal, many staff believe there has been a general undermining of bureaucratic character. When asked to list the features of this loss of character, officials cited increased dishonesty, laxity in job performance, erosion of the code of conduct, and (perhaps most important) the propensity to work for one's personal interest rather than the national good.

Government officials who contend with many levels of managers point to the inability of their superiors to withstand pressures from extra-state agents, including politicians and international donors. Junior officers thus believe that their superiors are now "spineless." Senior officers say they are structurally weaker than in the days of panchayat, when their *aat* (courage) largely stemmed from the fact that they had the backing of the monarchy.

The perception of a weak boss in post-andolan Nepal has serious implications. For instance, when vacancies within the National Park Services need to be filled, the director general of this unit has the legal authority to make assignments (with the approval of his seniors); his judgment is supposed to be the last word, since he would be expected to know the needs of the park better than any outside official. In practice, however, vacancies are seldom filled without external interference. Before 1990, only the highest ranks of the bureaucracy were treated as political plums; in the current era, even low-level jobs are treated as the spoils of politics. This creep downward of patronage appointments has impeded the smooth functioning of the park system.

Since 1990 the phenomenon of external actors interfering in the assignment process has become commonplace. I was able to witness this process in action during the course of my work (1994–6) with the Makalu-Barun National Park in far eastern Nepal. As I watched the maneuvring of various park staff over the course of two years, I saw the combination of chakri and other forms of pressure undermine the morale and efficacy of entire units within the ministries.

Because of the high value placed on HMG jobs, even low-level posts such as driver, clerk, and custodian generate intense lobbying by outside patrons. Director Generals told me they are often threatened with unfair and improper transfers if they fail to allot menial jobs to the applicants selected by powerful Kathmandu agents. The performance and morale of their staff suffer when promotions are seen as overly politicized, but a director general cannot buck the trend lightly. Meanwhile junior staff, not to mention NGO workers and development expatriates, often view Director Generals and their deputies as an unholy alliance, cooking up nefarious deals for their own enrichment while undermining staff morale and harming the national interest. "Ajay," a thirty-eight-year-old officer with the Department of National Parks, saw it this way:

> Once vacancies are announced, the DG (Director General) ought to have the power to appoint people, but it seems that they are unable to withstand any pressure from above—they cave in. Ministers forward petitions of their

favorites who are nine out of ten times unqualified. If positions for the Parks and People Program [a UNDP-sponsored project that was ongoing in Bardia at the time] motivators are vacant, the park warden cannot make assignments even if he has the power. See, the DG had the power, he could have influenced UNDP but then the pressure from above was too much for him. Now the DG feels insulted because UNDP took away this power. It's good that UNDP took away this power but not good for the park system. It means that politicians have no commitment.

The question of how politicians (many recently arrived on the scene) wield such power over bureaucrats is a complex one. Elsewhere, I detail the politician–bureaucrat nexus. Here it is useful to note that no elected politician, from the prime minister down, has the legal authority to remove an HMG official from office. Job security, however, is not the same as life security. HMG staff may be immune from arbitrary firing, but they are still subject to the vagaries of arbitrary transfer, denied promotions, and other potential setbacks. The mere threat of being transferred or undermined in some other manner often propels senior bureaucrats to concede to the demands of political figures. "Pratap" feels frustrated by his own inability to hold the line against political demands: "Why, I don't know. They can't remove me from my job (*hamro jagir khana sakdaina*). So why is it that I cannot stand my ground?"

GOVERNMENTAL IDENTITY

Comparing National Park Staff with Forestry Officials

While staff enter the bureaucracy in different ways, their identify as Nepali bureaucrats is constructed over time and in comparison with specific external groups. The rubrics under which wildlife and national park officials describe, analyze and contest their lives are varied, but are noteworthy for the inherent tension between them: identification of self as steward of Nepali nature and wildlife (in contrast to poachers or others who wish to exploit wildlife resources for their own benefit), and identification of self as defender of national interests in nature management (in contrast to international conservation ideologies often deemed inappropriate to the local context). Park staff contrast themselves with other Nepalis in their identity as defenders of wildlife, but contrast themselves with international wildlife advocates in their identity as Nepalis.

Elsewhere, I analyze how bureaucratic identity is shaped by globalization (including the ways in which national resource management expatriate presence in Nepal, international conservation ideology, and development aid impinge on, interact with, and support a form of Nepali national park identity). In this section, I discuss how and why national park officials (employees of the DNPWC) construct their identities vis-à-vis Nepali foresters (employees of the department of forestry). Foresters and park officials have much in common: they see themselves as stewards of nature, they are government servants in remote field postings, they work for the Ministry of Forests and Soil Conservation; yet, for national park staff, how they differ from foresters is the crux of their personal identity.

Both the Department of National Parks and Wildlife Conservation (DNPWC) and the Department of Forests are subdivisions reporting to the Ministry of Forests and Soil Conservation. DNPWC officials—the group on whom this dissertation is focused, interchangeably referred to throughout as wildlife officials, park officials, *nikunja* (national park) staff—work exclusively in one of the thirteen protected areas of Nepal.[28] The DNPWC is a small department with unusually close ties with the royal house.

In contrast, the Department of General Forests covers all seventy-five districts of Nepal. Besides the obvious difference in scale of operations, there are important differences regarding how members of such similar departments are perceived. Foresters are stereotypically seen as highly corrupt whereas national park staff are not.[29] In my interviews with rangers (non-officers), many had the option of joining either the general forestry sector or the national parks department. Many chose national parks despite knowing they could likely have practiced large-scale corruption with the forestry department. Foresters, on both an individual and institutional basis, are widely seen as engaging in large-scale scams involving timber contracts. The general public often discusses rumors regarding foresters' enormous bungalows and land acquisitions all over the country. Wildlife officials, on the other hand, are seen as *sojho* (straightforward), and *ramro* (good) by the general public—a perception the officials themselves, needless to say, wholeheartedly share.

Many wildlife officials in my data pool noted the difficulties of holding fast against the temptations of corruption in the forestry department. "Suresh," a ranger with Royal Bardia National Park, was formerly assigned to the forest department. He recalled his first assignment with them: "They [foresters] used to drink every night. In the forestry department, if you went to the village, *rakshi* [locally distilled liquor] and chicken used to arrive immediately. It was really bad. To our face, villagers said, '*ranger namaskar*' [ranger salutation] but actually what they were saying was '*ghusiya mora*' [corrupt bastard]."

Officials blame the work culture of the forest services rather than the personal failings of individual foresters. In a thoroughly corrupt environment, the thinking goes, even an honest man would have great difficulty avoiding entanglement in dishonest practices. Suresh spoke of his discomfort with his forestry colleagues:

> It was uncomfortable to me. I had to live with the forest guards because we didn't have any room, no office space. There was a lot of conflict between local people and foresters because of encroachment in the forests. And I thought, if I stay in *ban vibhag* [forest department], even I'll become corrupt. When I saw that the DNPWC advertised for a ranger post, I applied and passed the exam. So I quit forestry. There is a difference between forestry and DNPWC. At that moment, I wanted change. Then I went to Suklaphanta Wildlife Reserve for two years. At least I was far from corruption.

The perception ingrained in both the minds of public as well as government officials is that there is a great moral difference between the two departments. Wildlife officials describe *rastriya nikunja* (national parks) as having honor, and say they don't sell the forests whereas *ban ko manche* (foresters) are reputed as being *izzat bechne manche* (those who sell honor). A senior second-class officer with the soil conservation department (another branch of the Ministry of Forests and Soil Conservation) recalls that at the start of his career he and the rest of his fourteen-student cohort had the option of joining general forestry. Despite the illicit opportunities such a path would have brought, all fourteen of his classmates chose soil conservation because it was reputed to be more intellectually challenging. More importantly, the perception that the soil conservation department was honest compared to general forestry was a major factor in their decision-making process: "Despite the openings in general forestry, we chose soil conservation. Now this is where a person's attitude starts. Even before I started my career, we heard so much about corruption in general forestry. There is much tension there. Soil conservation is dry, there is no corruption."

Officials in general forestry exercise more extensive powers than their wildlife colleagues. Their *pahuch* (reach) is greater because they work in all seventy-five districts. These officials are networked with each other and they are able to exert much greater authority over local people. "Keshab," a ranger with Suklaphanta Wildlife Reserve, remarked that: "Since DFOs [District Forestry Officers] have to interact with *janata* [public], they have more power. The more your job requires you to interact with people, the more power you have. Till the buffer-zone regulations were implemented in 1994,[30] wildlife officials had virtually no contact with local people except in the event that they trespassed as poachers, hunters or for other reasons."

Despite wildlife officials' awareness that they would accrue more money in forestry—sometimes more in a year than they would over the course of their whole lives—park officials felt there was a moral line which they would have trouble crossing. This moral line was often described in physical terms, as an ache, discomfort, or pressure upon the chest, which they would find unbearable. It was a feeling of unease, of feeling uncomfortable:

> Some people just don't like forestry. They consider it to be a *jhamela* [nuisance]. There are *muddas* [court cases] involved, which makes it risky. You can get into trouble. The risk factor especially during the panchayat days was great. There was dacoity with timber. Dacoits had guns. To do *chori* [theft] with timber, it was *dushman ko mole* [one becomes a target of the enemy]. There was a risk of losing your job. Why? Because in stealing timber, you inevitably made enemies in the process.

Tika Ram (real name) is easygoing and hardworking, an upright ranger who has been with the national park services for over fifteen years. He is never tempted by the forest service because of the headaches and games involved:

> There is so much jhamela, mudda, and *mamla* [referring to the headache of court cases]. Some people like being involved in *lafra* [complications] but some people just don't have that nature. Even now, if we [park staff] go to the forest department, it'll be uncomfortable for us to do job. Even now we can go to forest department with the permission of the forest ministry, but it'll be hard for us to eat *jagir* [job] there. Its hard to survive [*tikna garo huncha*]. There is too much headache, isn't that so? People's habits have gone bad in the forest services. "How will money come and go?"—such are the things they are preoccupied with. Your *dimak* [head] becomes like that.[31]

NATIONAL PARKS AND NATIONALISM

Nepali park officials describe their work as dharmic (spiritual), as having to do with maya (love), and as providing the staff with dignity and status as stewards of nature. This loyalty or duty toward nature echoes the sentiments of the Bhutanese and Indian staff, particularly in its conceptualization of government servants dedicating their lives to a cause larger than themselves. In his elegant study of wildlife conservation in India, Rangarajan remarks that "salvaging" the wild was tied to a more "self-confident" notion of Indian nationalism (Rangarajan 2000: 8). The professional irritations of their lives (particularly tensions with local villagers or soldiers,[32] both of which groups they regard as being less than wholly devoted to wildlife conservation) come to be seen as minor hardships. The physical hardships of the forest life are the price park staff pay for the privileges of serving as stewards of a national treasure.

"Kanti," a ranger based in Rambapur Post in Bardia National Park, sees his work as dharmic (spiritual) because he prevents the slaughter of wildlife, helps keep the forests healthy, and helps preserve river systems. Protection of an irreplaceable natural heritage, he argues, is protection of Nepal—his work is different from that of soldiers defending Nepal's borders, but it is no less important. He and his colleagues are defenders of the nation: "Even if poachers might kill some animals, the parks are protected. We feel this is because we are fulfilling our duties—that's what we feel. And we don't feel bad talking forthright, taking credit for this. It's government property."[33]

Yuv Raj Regmi, who has been with the national park services for sixteen years and is currently the warden of Shey Phoksundo National Park, agrees: "Dignity is important for social status. I'm a member of the world's environmental wildlife biology community in the Nepali context and I feel dignity in this. Between the national parks and the forest department, people say that foresters earn money. But people have a better opinion of wildlife officials. I feel I am fulfilling my dignity. In city areas, I feel this way when I talk about my background."[34] The jungle ethos of bravery, hard work, and love of wildlife is what distinguishes national park staff from other government servants: "We are not like the 10am–5pm peons. We are on duty 24 hours a day. We have to be responsible. Rangers, hakims, teach us to be that way. We have love towards this organization. Poachers will finish everything if we're not on duty 24 hours a day. We wouldn't say 'la, bahudal [democracy] is here, we'll only work 10 a.m.–5 p.m.' "

In recalling the sorrow of early years in service, the Bardia ranger Kanti describes his eighteen-day trek to reach Dolpo, a high-altitude park in northern Nepal. Kanti recalls sleeping in buffalo sheds, grinding corn, and being completely cut off. Such experiences are shared by almost everyone in park management, and it is this sort of collective experience which shapes a unique identity.

Esprit de corps is particularly strong in the department of national parks. A small unit which was established at the directive of King Mahendra, the department of national parks is distinguished from most larger government outfits by its collegial atmosphere, supportive familial relationships, and perceived equitable treatment of employees (at least relative to other bureaucracies).[35] Because of the department's size, close relationships develop between senior and junior staff: the director general will often address his juniors as *ba* (a term of affection used by parents with their children).

In these bureaucratic narratives by wildlife officials, the andolan and monarchical rule are clear markers of when a shift in identity takes place. During the monarchy years (at least when viewed from the post-monarchical perspective) bosses were a far sight better than the money-grubbing time-servers who replaced them. In 1991 the entire second tier of the bureaucracy was removed, and people at the bottom jumped to the top; in the minds of many, this resulted in promoting upstarts who indulged in corruption. Stories of vast sums of money changing hands is now a standard narrative. The example set by those at the top is mimicked by those further down. Thus in post-andolan Nepal, as bureaucrats grapple with the immense changes in monarchy, governance, and democracy, ambiguity regarding duties to the park, duties to the nation, and self characterize the experience of bureaucratic subjectivity in the decade of multiparty democracy.

NOTES

1. It can be argued that transnational flows in South Asia were under way starting in the early 1990s. With multiparty democracy in Nepal and the liberalization of governmental restrictions in neighboring India, media (specifically television) changed drastically. Television is one such globalizing medium representing the "space–time compression" (Harvey 1990). With CNN, MTV, and foreign soap operas, large numbers of foreign channels are available in South Asia. The results of this have been a general erosion of the state's stringent control on television, resulting in the loosening of its hold on TV popularity (see Kothari, Suri and Singh 1995).

2. King Gyanendra Bir Bikram Shah Dev (reign 2001–).

3. See Hufton 1993.

4. I would argue that His Majesty's Government (HMG) is synonymous with the royal family especially before multiparty democracy was established in 1991.

5. The problematic nature of Nepal as an explicitly Hindu state and its relationship to the complexities of caste and ethnic tensions are important subjects worthy of a separate monograph. The salience of these issues is seen in that it has been amply debated by Nepal scholars. Noteworthy authors include Caplan 1991; Fisher 1993, 2001; Gaige 1975; Hofer 1978, 1979; Parish 1996; Pfaff-Czarnecka 1997; Quigley 1987 and 1993; Ragsdale 1989; Prakash Raj 1993; Prayag Raj Sharma 1994, 1997; Skar 1995 and von Fürer-Haimendorf 1962.

6. Other legislation relevant to biodiversity conservation include the Forest Act 1993, the Plant Protection Act 1973, the Aquatic Life Protection Act 1961, the Soil and Water Conservation Act 1982.

7. The Wildlife Conservation Act of 1958 provided a legal framework for the protection of the endangered Greater One-horned Rhinoceros and its habitat in Chitwan National Park. See His Majesty's Government, Ministry of Forestry, Department of National Parks and Wildlife Conservation Annual Report of 1999–2000: 2. See also Stracey 1957 and Gee 1959 and 1961. The National Parks Act of 1973 was revised in 1994 to incorporate revenue-sharing provisions generated by parks with local communities.

8. The emphasis on caste is warranted, for it is one of the dominant social and cultural facts of life in India. It seems that today, as in the past, status, rank, hierarchy is understood with reference to caste. The historian Bernard Cohn argues (1987) that caste is ingrained in the social imagination, and this ingrainment is seen through policy such as the affirmative action (the Mandal Commission); or the Dalit movements in western and southern India. See also Cohn 1996. These and other such debates (Pandey 1983, 1990) have great salience for discussions of Hindu backwardness and marginality, and we find that even scholarship of non-Hindu societies, such as the customs of Tibeto-Burman Sherpas (see von Furer-Haimendorf 1964) are often posited *vis-à-vis* the Hindu caste system.

9. von Fürer-Haimendorf 1964; Ortner 1978 and 1989; Fisher 1990; Adams 1996.

10. In fact, King Tribhuvan Bir Bikram Shah requested the technical advice of what is now called the Indian Administrative Service (IAS) to achieve these goals. That Asian bureaucratic systems largely emerged from British imperial traditions and have been discussed by scholars including Braibanti (1966). Richard English (1985) and Asad Husain (1970) elaborate on the relationship of Himalayan state formation with that of British rule in the nineteenth century; most scholars agree that Nepali administration and government practice stem from the influence of monarchy and kingship. Panday 1989; Rose and Fisher 1970; G.R. Sharma 1989; J. Sharma 1997.

11. At present, there are 21 ministries under which at least 48 executive departments carry out the respective functions of government. They run from traditional law and order responsibility, to public works, industry, welfare, and culture (Panday 1989). In social composition, the administration has changed little since the days of Jung Bahadur: the predominance of Brahmins, Chhetris, and Newars continues. In 1854, 98 percent of top civil service posts were held by these groups, and by 1969 the percentage had edged down only to 93 percent. Seddon 1987: 232.

12. This essentially means professional and non-professional staff.

13. Since my research was mainly in the setting of national parks, participant observation occurred mostly with third-class HMG officers (assistant park wardens, assistant ecologists, researchers, among others). Also at the field level, I concentrated on non-gazetted staff including game scouts, rangers, administrators, and clerks. Senior staff (of first- and second-class rank) tended to be Kathmandu-based even if they were posted in the field. Government titles for this rank include senior warden, chief ecologist, and the director general of national park services.

14. The ethnographic materials collected for this chapter derive from research conducted in Royal Bardia National Park (Bardia District, western Nepal) and in the capital city Kathmandu. Bardia National Park was established in 1969 as a hunting reserve. It was designated the Royal Karnali Wildlife Reserve in 1974. In 1982 it became Royal Bardia Wildlife Reserve and finally, in 1989, it was officially declared a national park.

15. I use the abbreviation "HMG" to denote "His Majesty's Government" throughout this essay, in accordance with the customary practice of government officials. The very fact that such usage is far more common than more politically neutral formulations ("the government," "the civil service," etc.) demonstrates the depth of personal identification between park staff and the monarchy.

16. Tharus are the dominant ethnic group living in the buffer zone of Royal Bardia National Park. See Guneratne's (2002) account of Tharu identity. For perspectives of an "outsider" living in these communities, see Guneratne (1999).

17. This holds true for all levels of officials and non-officials that I interviewed. Elsewhere, I shall present narratives by very high-ranking officials who were "pushed" into the services by family and friends.

18. Compare for example with Liechty's (1996) account of urban, middle-class Nepali women's experience of democracy, where they perceive a decline in the respect accorded to them in the public sphere.

19. Pseudonyms are used throughout this chapter (and dissertation) unless full name and rank are given.

20. For discussions on the Nepali government, including its evolution of administration, see Joshi 1983; Edwards 1977; for its failings see Panday 1989 and 1998; for its relationship to monarchy see Rose and Fisher 1970; Shrestha 1975 and 1981.

21. Government officials often anthropomorphize HMG in conversation, referring to the bureaucracy as if it were a personal agent. This is distinct from the identification of the bureaucracy with the person of the king himself.

22. This was a major1 issue when I worked for the Makalu-Barun National Park. There, the misuse of scout labor was a source of conflict among staff as well. The Indian author Khushwant Singh writes poignantly about the public perception of dignity enjoyed by Indian sepoys, in contrast with the private humiliations they undergo at the hands of army officers and their wives at being made to perform undignified chores (such as washing the underclothing of officer's family members).

23. For an excellent discussion which focuses on the body as the primary locus of social power, see Graeber (1997). Graeber's discussion of "joking relations" and "relations of avoidance" (essentially having to do with equality and hierarchy) describes the range of behavior I observed between very junior staff (game scouts and peons) and their bosses.

24. Ministry of Forestry, Kathmandu, Nepal, May 2001.

25. Ministry of Forestry, Interview, April 2000.

26. A former palace secretary gave me his example of waiting outside the gates of a senior Rana official during the Rana regime. He did this everyday for many months so as to show that he was faithful and could be trusted.

27. The Colombo Plan was a regional South Asia cooperation program which facilitated training for South Asian nationals in areas such as medicine, engineering, and forestry services, among others.

28. Protected areas include 9 national parks, 3 wildlife reserves, one hunting reserve. These areas cover about 19 percent of Nepal's lands and are exclusively under the control of the DNPWC.

29. The Ministry of Forestry is divided into five departments. These are 1) department of forestry; 2) department of national parks and wildlife conservation; 3) department of soil conservation; 4) department of research, 5) department of plant resources. Among these, the department of forestry is the most dominant. Their staff comprise 60 percent of all ministry of forestry staff. District forest officers (DFOs) with the department of forests are considered very powerful because they have control over vast areas of forests.

30. Department of National Parks and Wildlife Management Annual Report 1999–2000, His Majesty's Government of Nepal, Kathmandu.

31. Interview at Rambapur Post, Bardia National Park.

32. The Royal Nepalese Army is responsible for park protection in conjunction with the national parks department. Soldiers and game scouts jointly patrol the national parks.

33. Ranger, Rambapur Post, Royal Bardia National Park.

34. Warden Seminar, Bardia National Park, April 2001.

35. The parks department has about 35 officers with 70 rangers, and several hundred game scouts and other staff. In the forestry department, there are about 500 officers, 1000 rangers, and several thousand game scouts. These are approximate numbers (*source*: personal communication with Shiv Raj Bhatta, September 21, 2002).

BIBLIOGRAPHY

Abdul, R., Jan Mohammad, and David Lloyd, eds, 1987, "Introduction Towards a Theory of Minority Discourse," *Cultural Critique*, vol. 6, pp. 11–12.
Adams, Vincanne, 1996, *Tigers of the Snow and Other Virtual Sherpas*. Princeton: Princeton University Press.
Agarwal, Anil, Ravi Chopra, and Kalpana Sharma, eds, 1982, *The State of India's Environment: The First Citizens' Report*. New Delhi: Centre for Science and Environment.
Agarwal, Bina, 1991, *Engendering the Environment Debate: Lessons from the Indian Subcontinent*. East Lansing, Michigan: Center for Advanced Study of International Development.
Agarwal, Bina, 1994, *A Field of One's Own: Gender and Land Rights in South Asia*. Cambridge: Cambridge University Press.
Agarwal, Bina, 1997, "Environmental Action, Gender Equity and Women's Participation." *Development and Change*, vol. 28, pp. 1–44.
Agrawal, Arun, 1999, "Community-in-Conservation: Tracing the Outlines of an Enchanting Concept," in Roger Jeffrey and Nandini Sundar, eds, *A New Moral Economy for India's Forests? Discourses of Community and Participation*. New Delhi and London: Sage, pp. 92–108.
Agrawal, Arun and Clark C. Gibson, eds, 2001, *Communities and the Environment: Ethnicity, Gender, and the State in Community-Based Conservation*. New Brunswick, New Jersey, London: Rutgers University Press.
Agrawal, Arun and K. Sivaramakrishnan, eds, 2000, *Agrarian Environments: Resources, Representations, and Rule in India*. Durham and London: Duke University Press.
Agrawal, Arun and K. Sivaramakrishnan, eds, 2001, *Social Nature: Resources, Representation and Rule in India*. Delhi: Oxford University Press, 2001.
Ahmad, K.S., 1964, *A Geography of Pakistan*. Karachi, Lahore, Dacca: Oxford University Press.

Ahmad, N. and A. Rizvi, 1951, "Need for the Development of Chittagong Hill Tracts." *Pakistan Geographical Review*, Lahore, vol. 6.

Ahmed, A., 2001, *Appeal to Save the Brahmagiris*. http://www.indianjungles.com/210202is.htm.

Ahmed, Akbar S., 1976, *Millennium and Charisma among the Pathans: A Critical Essay in Social Anthropology*. London: Routledge and Kegan Paul.

Ahmed, Akbar S., 1980, *Pukhtun Economy and Society: Traditional Structure and Economic Development in a Tribal Society*. London: Routledge and Kegan Paul.

Ahmed, J. and F. Mahmood, 1998, *Changing Perspectives on Forest Policy. Policy that Works for Forests and People Series No. 1*. IUCN Pakistan and IIED, Islamabad and London.

Aiyer, A.K.Y.N., 1980, *Field Crops of India*. Bangalore: Bappco Publications.

Aloysius, G., 1999, *Nationalism Without a Nation in India*. Delhi: Oxford University Press.

Anderson, Benedict, 1991, *Imagined Communities: Reflections on the Origins and Spread of Nationalism*. London: Verso.

Annual Progress Report of the Forest Administration in Bengal. Calcutta, 1898.

Anonymous, 1915, Papers from 1899 Relating Chiefly to the Development of the Madras Fisheries Bureau, *Madras Fisheries Bulletin*, vol. 1.

Anonymous, 2000a, "Devarakadus: Going Extinct." *Coffee Land News*. Madikeri, no. 1.

Anonymous, 2000b, "Devarakadus: Help Needed." *Coffee Land News*. Madikeri, no. 4.

Anonymous, 2001, "Encroachment of Devarakadus in Chettalli." *Coffee Land News*. Madikeri, no. 4.

Archer, S., 1990, "Development and Stability of Grass/Woody Mosaics in a Subtropical Savanna Parkland, Texas, USA." *Journal of Biogeography*, vol. 17, pp. 453–642.

Areeparampil, Matthew, 1984, "Forest Andolan in Singhbhum," *Jharkhand Movement, Origin and Evolution*. Ranchi.

Arnold, David, 1996, *The Problem of Nature: Environment, Culture, and European Expansion*. Oxford: Blackwell.

Arnold, David and Ramachandra Guha, 1995, "Introduction: Themes and Issues in the Environmental History of South Asia," in David Arnold and Ramachandra Guha, eds, *Nature, Culture, Imperialism: Essays on the Environmental History of South Asia*. Delhi: Oxford University Press, 1995, pp. 1–20.

Baal, Ellen, 2000, *"They Ask Us if We Eat frogs." Social Boundaries, Ethnic Categorisation, and the Garo People of Bangladesh*. Delft: Eburon.

Bahadur, Rai Pati Ram, 1992 (1916), *Garhwal: Ancient and Modern*. Gurgaon: Vintage Books (first published Simla: Army Press).

Bahuguna, Sunderlal, 1987, "The Chipko: A People's Movement," in M.K. Raha, ed., *The Himalayan Heritage*. Delhi: Gian Publishing House, pp. 238–48.

Bahuguna, Sunderlal, 1990, *"Yes" to Life: "No" to Death*. Varanasi: Sarve Seva Sangh Prakashan.

Baker, Christopher John, 1984, *An Indian Rural Economy 1880–1955: The Tamilnad Countryside*. Delhi: Oxford University Press.

Baker, Mark, 2005, *The Kuhls of Kangra: Community-Managed Irrigation in the Western Himalaya*. Seattle and Delhi: University of Washington Press and Permanent Black.

Balan, V., 1984, *The Indian Oil Sardine Fishery: A Review*, Marine Fisheries Extension Series, Technical and Extension Series, no. 60. Kochi: CMFRI, pp. 1–10.

Ball, Valentine, 1985 (1880), *Tribal and Peasant Life in Nineteenth Century India*: First edition London; 1985 edition Delhi: Usha Publications.

Bandyopadhyay, Jayanta and Vandana Shiva, 1987a, "Chipko." *Seminar*, no. 330, pp. 33–9.

Bandyopadhyay, Jayanta and Vandana Shiva, 1987b, "Chipko: Rekindling India's Forest Culture." *The Ecologist*, vol. 17, no. 1, pp. 26–34.

Banerjee, Mukulika, 2000, *The Pathan Unarmed*. Oxford: Oxford University Press.

Barth, Fredrik, 1959, *Political Leadership Among Swat Pathans*. London: University of London Press.

Barth, Fredrik, 1969a, "Introduction," in Fredrik Barth, ed., *Ethnic Groups and Boundaries: The Social Organization of Culture Difference*. Boston: Little, Brown and Co.

Barth, Fredrik, 1969b, "Pathan Identity and its Maintenance," in Fredrik Barth, ed., *Ethnic Groups and Boundaries: The Social Organization of Culture Difference*. Boston: Little, Brown and Co.

Baruah, Sanjib, 1999, *India Against Itself: Assam and the Politics of Nationality*. Delhi: Oxford University Press.

Baruah, Sanjib, 2003, "Citizens and Denizens: Ethnicity, Homelands and the Crisis of Displacement in Northeast India." *Journal of Refugee Studies*, vol. 16, no. 1.

Baviskar, Amita, 1995, *In the Belly of the River: Tribal Conflicts over Development in the Narmada Valley*. Delhi: Oxford University Press.

Bayly, C.A., 1983, *Rulers, Townsmen and Bazaars: North Indian Society in the Age of British Expansion, 1770–1870*. Cambridge: Cambridge University Press.

Bayly, C.A., 1998, *The Origins of Nationality in South Asia: Patriotism and Ethical Government in the Making of Modern India*. Delhi: Oxford University Press.

Bayly, Susan, 1999, *Caste, Society and Politics in India: From the Eighteenth Century to the Modern Age*. Cambridge: Cambridge University Press.

Beames, John, 1961, *Memoirs of a Bengal Civilian: The Lively Narrative of a Victorian District Officer*. London: Chatto & Windus.

Begley, V. and D. dePuma, eds, 1991, *Rome and India: The Ancient Sea Trade*. Delhi: Oxford University Press.

Belal, Khaled, 1989, "The Budding Tribal Culture in CHTs," in Khaled Belal, ed., *The Chittagong Hill Tracts. Falconry in the Hills*. Chittagong: Codec.

Belal, Khaled, ed., 1992, *The Chittagong Hill Tracts. Falconry in the Hills*. Chittagong: Codec.

Bender, Barbara, 1993, *Landscape Perspectives*. Oxford: Berg.

Ben-Habib, Seyla, 2002, *The Claims of Culture: Equality and Diversity in the Global Era*. Princeton: Princeton University Press.

Berndt, Hagen, 1987, *Rettet die Bäume im Himalaya: Die Cipko-Bewegung im Spiegel der indischen Presse*. Berlin: Quorum.

Bernot, Lucien, 1967, *Les Paysans Arakanais du Pakistan Oriental. L'histoire, le monde végétal et l'organisation sociale des réfugiés Marma (Mog)*. Paris, La Haye: Mouton, 2 vols.

Bertocci, Peter J., 1989, "Resource Development and Ethnic Conflicts in Bangladesh: The Case of the Chakmas in the Chittagong Hill Tracts," in Dhirendra Vajpeyi and Yogendra K. Malik, eds, *Religion and Ethnic Minority Politics in South Asia*. London: Jaya Books.

Béteille, A., 1998, "The Idea of Indigenous People." *Current Anthropology*, vol. 39, no. 2, pp. 187–91.

Bhabha, Homi, 1995, *The Location of Culture*. London: Routledge.

Bhatt, Chandi Prasad, 1987, "Green the People: Inaugural Address," in Anil Agarwal, Daryll D'Monte, and Ujwala Samarth, eds, *The Fight for Survival: People's Action for Environment*. New Delhi: Centre for Science and Environment, pp. 1–4.

Bhatt, Nina, 2002, "King of the Jungle: An Ethnographic Study of Identity,

Power, and Politics among Nepali National Park Officials," unpublished PhD thesis, Yale University.

Bhattacharya, Neeladri, 1996, "Remaking Custom: The Discourse and Practice of Colonial Codification," in Romila Thapar, S. Gopal, and R. Champakalakshmi, eds, *Tradition, Dissent and Ideology: Essays in Honour of Romila Thapar*. Delhi: Oxford University Press.

Bird-David, Nurit, 1983, "Wage-gathering: Socio-economic Changes and the Case of the Food-Gatherer Naikens of South India," in P. Robb, ed., *Rural South Asia: Linkages, Change and Development*. Collected Papers on South Asia, no. 5. Centre of South Asian Studies, School of Oriental and African Studies, University of London. London: Curzon Press, pp. 57–89.

Bird-David, Nurit, 1990, "The Giving Environment: Another Perspective on the Economic System of Hunter-Gatherers." *Current Anthropology*, no. 31, pp. 183–96.

Bird-David, Nurit, 1992a, "Beyond the 'Hunting and Gathering Mode of Subsistence': Culture-Sensitive Observations on the Nayaka and other Modern Hunter-Gatherers." *Man* (n.s.), vol. 27, pp. 19–44.

Bird-David, Nurit, 1992b, "Beyond the Original Affluent Society: A Culturalist Reformulation." *Current Anthropology*, vol. 33, no. 1, pp. 25–47.

Bista, Dor Bahadur, 1991, *Fatalism and Development: Nepal's Struggle for Modernisation*. Calcutta: Orient Longman.

Blaikie, Piers and Harold Brookfield, 1987, *Land Degradation and Society*. London and New York: Methuen.

Blank, Jonah, 1994, "Ram and Ram Rajya: The Babri Masjid/Ramjanambhumi Dispute and the Politicisation of a Divinity." *Journal of Vaisnava Studies*, vol. 2, no. 4, pp. 159–74.

Blank, Jonah, 2000 (1992), *Arrow of the Blue-Skinned God: Retracing the Ramayana Through India*. New York: Grove.

Blank, Jonah, 2001, *Mullahs on the Mainframe: Islam and Modernity Among the Daudi Bohras*. Chicago: University of Chicago Press.

Bodley, James, 1997, "Comment," in T.N. Headland, "Revisionism in Ecological Anthropology." *Current Anthropology*, vol. 18, no. 4, August–October.

Bodley, John H., 1975, *Victims of Progress*. London: Cummings Publications Co.

Borgström, Bengt-Erik, 1980, *The Patron and the Panca: Village Values and Panchayat Democracy in Nepal*. New Delhi: Vikas Publishing.
Bouchon, G., 1988, *"Regent of the Sea:" Cannanore's Response to Portuguese Expansion, 1507–1528*. Trans. L. Shackley. Delhi: Oxford University Press.
Bourdieu, Pierre, 1977, *Outline of a Theory of Practice*. Cambridge: Cambridge University Press.
Boxer, C.R., 1969, *The Portuguese Seaborne Empire 1415–1825*. New York: Knopf and Co.
Braudel, F., 1972, *The Mediterranean and the Mediterranean World in the Age of Phillip II*, vol. I. New York: Harper Colophon Books.
Brauns, Claus-Dieter and Lorenz G. Löffler, 1986, *Mru. Bergbewohner im Grenzgebiet von Bangladesh*. Basel, Boston, Stuttgart: Birkhäuser.
Brewer, John and Susan Staves, eds, 1996, *Early Modern Conceptions of Property*. London: Routledge.
Bright, J.S., n.d., *Before and After Independence: A Collection of the Most Important and Soul-Stirring Speeches Delivered by Jawaharlal Nehru During the Most Important and Soul-Stirring Years in Indian History 1922–1957*, vols 1 & 2. New Delhi: The Indian Printing Works.
Britan, Gerald M. and Ronald Cohen, eds, 1980, *Hierarchy and Society: Anthropological Perspectives on Bureaucracy*. Philadelphia: Institute for the Study of Human Issues.
Brosius, J. Peter, 2000, "Endangered Forest, Endangered People: Environmentalist Representations of Indigenous Knowledge," in *Indigenous Environmental Knowledge and its Transformations: Critical Anthropological Perspectives*. Amsterdam: Harwood Academic Publishers.
Brow, J., 1978, *Vedda Villages of Anuradhapura*. Seattle: University of Washington Press.
Brown, T. Louise, 1996, *The Challenge to Democracy in Nepal: A Political History*. London: Routledge.
Bryant, G.J., 1985, "Scots in India in the Eighteenth Century." *The Scottish Historical Review*, vol. 64: 1, no. 177, April, pp. 22–41.
Buchanan, F., 1988, *A Journey from Madras through the Countries of Mysore, Canara, and Malabar*. New Delhi: Asian Educational Services Reprint (originally published 1806).
Burling, Robbins, 1997a, *The Strong Women of Modhupur*. Dhaka: The University Press Limited.

Burling, Robbins, 1997b, *Rengsanggri: Family and Kinship in a Garo Village*. Shillong: Anderson Media and Communications. 2nd edition.

Caesar, Knut, 1977, "Shifting Cultivation an den Feuchtgrenzen des Ackerbaues." *Technische Universität Berlin, Fachbereich Internationale Agrarentwicklung: Agrarentwicklung auf Grenzstandorten der Tropen*. Reihe: Studien, no. iv/17, Berlin.

Calcutta Oriental Christian Spectator, September 29, 1846, "From Our Correspondents, Ootacamund."

Caplan, Lionel, 1991, "From Tribe to Peasant? The Limbus and the Nepalese State." *Journal of Peasant Studies*, vol. 18, no. 2, pp. 305–21.

Caratini, C., J.-P. Pascal, C. Tissot, and G. Rajagopalan, 1990–1, "Palynological Reconstruction of a Wet Evergreen Forest in the Western Ghats (India) from *ca*. 1800 to *ca*. 1400 Years BP." *Current Perspectives in Palynological Research (Silver Jubilee Commemoration Volume of the Journal of Palynology)*, pp. 123–37.

Caroe, Olaf, 1990 (1957), *The Pathans: 550 B.C.–A.D. 1957*. Karachi: Oxford University Press.

Castells, Manuel, 1997, *The Information Age: Economy, Society, and Culture, Volume II: The Power of Identity*. Oxford: Blackwell.

Cederlöf, Gunnel, 1997, *Bonds Lost: Subordination, Conflict and Mobilisation in Rural South India, c. 1900–1970*. New Delhi: Manohar Publishers.

Cederlöf, Gunnel, 2002, "Narratives of Rights: Codifying People and Land in Early Nineteenth-Century Nilgiris." *Environment and History*, vol. 8, no. 3. Isle of Harris: The White Horse Press, pp. 319–62.

Cederlöf, Gunnel, forthcoming 2006, "The Agency of the Colonial Subject: Claims and Rights in Forestlands in Early Nineteenth-Century Nilgiris," in Marine Carrin and Harald Tambs-Lyche, eds, *People of the Jungle: Reformulating Identities and Adaptations in Crisis*. London: NIAS Press.

Chakma, A.B. 1984, "Look Back From Exile. A Chakma Experience," in Wolfgang Mey, ed., 1984, *Genocide in the Chittagong Hill Tracts, Bangladesh*. Copenhagen: IWGIA Document, no. 51.

Chakrabarty, Dipesh, 2000, "Postcoloniality and the Artifice of History: Who Speaks for 'Indian' Pasts?," in Ranajit Guha, ed., *A Subaltern Studies Reader, 1986–1995*. Delhi: Oxford University Press, pp. 263–93.

Chakrabarty, Dipesh, 2001, *Provincializing Europe: Postcolonial Thought and Historical Difference*. Princeton: Princeton University Press.

Champion, H. and F.C. Osmaston, eds, 1962, *E.P. Stebbing's "The Forests of*

India," Vol. IV, Being the History from 1925 to 1947 of the Forests now in Burma, India, and Pakistan. London: Oxford University Press.

Chandran, M.D. Subash, 1998, "Shifting Cultivation, Sacred Groves and Conflicts in Colonial Forest Policy in the Western Ghats," in R. H. Grove, V. Damodaran and S. Sangwan, eds, *Nature and the Orient: The Environmental History of South and Southeast Asia*, Delhi: Oxford University Press.

Chandran, M.D.Subash and J.D. Hughes, 2000, "Sacred Groves and Conservation: The Comparative History of Traditional Reserves in the Mediterranean Area and in South India." *Environment and History*, vol. 6, pp. 169–86.

Chatterjee, Partha, 1993, *The Nation and Its Fragments: Colonial and Postcolonial Histories*. New Delhi: Oxford University Press.

Chatterjee, Partha, ed., 1998, *Wages of Freedom: Fifty Years of the Indian Nation-State*. New Delhi: Oxford University Press.

Chatterjee, Partha, 2001a, "On Civil and Political Society in Post-Colonial Democracies," in Sudipta Kaviraj and Sunil Khilnani, eds, *Civil Society: History and Possibilities*. Cambridge: Cambridge University Press, pp. 165–78.

Chatterjee, Partha, 2001b, "The Nation in Heterogeneous Time." *Indian Economic and Social History Review*, vol. 38, no. 4, pp. 399–418.

Chatterjee, Partha, 2002, *A Princely Impostor? The Kumar of Bhawal and the Secret History of Indian Nationalism*. New Delhi: Permanent Black.

Chaturvedi, Vinayak, ed., 2000, *Mapping Subaltern Studies and the Postcolonial*. London: Verso.

Chaube, Shibanikinkar, 1973, *Hill Politics in North-East India*. Bombay: Orient Longman.

Chaudhuri, K.N., 1985, *Trade and Civilisation in the Indian Ocean: An Economic History from the Rise of Islam to 1750*. Cambridge: Cambridge University Press.

Chotanagpur Unnati Samaj ki Varshik Mahsabha ka Report aur Chotanagpur Adivasi Sabha ka Uthpathi, 1937.

Choudhury, Dhrupad and R.C. Sundriyal, 2002, "Factors Contributing to Marginalization of Shifting Cultivation in North East India. Microscale Issues." *Outlook on Agriculture*, vol. 31, no. 4, pp. 1–15.

Cimino, R.M, ed., 1994, *Ancient Rome and India*. Delhi: Instituto Italiano Medio ed Estreme Oriente.

Clifford, James, 1988, *The Predicament of Culture*. Cambridge MA & London: Harvard University Press.
Clifford, James, 1997, *Routes: Travel and Translation in the Late Twentieth Century*. Cambridge MA and London: Harvard University Press.
Cohn, Bernard, 1987, *An Anthropologist among the Historians and Other Essays*. New Delhi: Oxford University Press.
Cohn, Bernard, 1988, "Beyond the Fringe: The Nation State, Colonialism, and the Technologies of Power." *Journal of Historical Sociology*, vol. 1, no. 2, pp. 224–9.
Colwell, R.K., 1997, *Estimates: Statistical Estimation of Species Richness and Shared Species from Samples*. http://viceroy.eeb.uconn.edu/estimates.
Colwell, R.K. and J.A. Coddington, 1994, *Estimating Terrestrial Biodiversity through Extrapolation*. Phil. Trans. R. Soc. Lond., no. 345, pp. 101–18.
Comaroff, Jean and John Comaroff, 1991, *Of Revelation and Revolution: Christianity, Colonialism and Consciousness in Southern Africa*. Chicago: University of Chicago Press.
Comaroff, Jean and John Comaroff, 2000, "Naturing the Nation: Aliens, Apocalypse, and the Postcolonial State." *HAGAR: International Social Science Review*, vol. 1, no. 1, pp. 7–40.
Condit, R., R.B. Foster, S.P. Hubbell, R. Sukumar, E.G. Leigh, N. Manokaran, S. Loo de Lao, V. LaFrankie, and P.S. Ashton, 1998, "Assessing Forest Biodiversity on Small Plots: Calibration Using Species-Individual Curves from 50ha Plots," in F. Dallmeier and J.A. Comiskey, eds, *Forest Biodiversity Research, Monitoring and Modelling*. Paris: UNESCO, Parthenon, no. 20, pp. 247–68.
Conklin, Harold C., 1961, "The Study of Shifting Cultivation." *Current Anthropology*, vol. 2, no. 1. Chicago.
Conzen, K.N., 1989 "Ethnicity as Festive Culture: The Nineteenth-century German American Parade," in Werner Sollors, ed., *The Invention of Ethnicity*, New York: Oxford University Press.
Coombe, Rosemary, 2005, "Performative Sovereignties: Emergent Properties and Persons under Environmental Neoliberal Governmentalities," in Bill Maurer and Gabrielle Schwab, eds, *Futures of Property and Personhood*. New York: Columbia University Press.
Corbridge, S., 1986, "State, Tribe and Region: Policy and Politics in India's Jharkhand 1900–1980," unpublished PhD thesis, Cambridge University.

Cronon, William, 1991, *Nature's Metropolis: Chicago and the Great West*. New York: W.W. Norton.

Cronon, William, ed., 1995, *Uncommon Ground: Rethinking the Human Place in Nature*. New York & London: W.W. Norton & Company. (Paperback reprint 1996.)

Dale, S.F., 1980, *Islamic Society on the South Asian Frontier: The Mappilas of Malabar 1498–1922*. Oxford: Clarendon Press.

Dalton, E., 1872, *Descriptive Ethnology of Bengal*. Calcutta.

Damodaran, Vinita, 2000, "Review, S. Guha." *Journal of Political Ecology: Case Studies in History and Society*, vol. 7 (http://www.library.arizona.edu/ej/jpe/jpeweb.html).

Damodaran, Vinita, 2002, "Gender, Forests and Famine." *Indian Journal of Gender Studies*, vol. 9, no. 2.

Daniel, E. Valentine, 1996, *Charred Lullabies: Chapters in an Anthropography of Violence*. Princeton: Princeton University Press.

Daniels, Stephen, 1993, *Fields of Vision: Landscape Imagery and National Identity in England and the United States*. Princeton: Princeton University Press.

Danvers, F.C., 1966, *The Portuguese in India: Being a History of the Rise and Decline of their Eastern Empire, Vol. 1*. New York: Octagon Books (originally published 1894).

Das, Jishnu, 2000, "Institutions and Incentives in a Garhwal Village—I: Common Property Regimes in Traditional Societies." *Economic and Political Weekly*, vol. 35, no. 49, pp. 4337–44.

Day, Francis, 1865, *The Fishes of Malabar*. London: Bernard Quaritch.

Demmer, U., 1997, "Voices in the Forest: The Field of Gathering among the Jenu Kurumba," in P. Hockings, ed., *Blue Mountains Revisited: Cultural Studies on the Nilgiri Hills*. Delhi: Oxford University Press, pp. 164–91.

Department of National Parks. 2001. *Annual Report (1999–2000)*. Kathmandu: Department of National Parks and Wildlife Management, Ministry of Forestry.

Desai, P.B., S. Ritti, and B.R. Gopal, 1981, *History of Karnataka*. Dharwad: Kannada Research Institute.

Deshpande, Satish, 2004, *Contemporary India: A Sociological View*. New Delhi: Penguin.

Devanesan, D.W., 1943, "A Brief Investigation into the Causes of the Fluctuation of the Annual Fishery of the Oil-Sardine of Malabar, Sardinella

Longiceps, Cuv. & Val., Determination of its Age and Account of the Discovery of its Eggs and Spawning Ground." *Madras Fisheries Bulletin*, vol. 28, pp. 1–38.

Dewan, Aditya Kumar, 1991, "Class and Ethnicity in the Chittagong Hill Tracts," PhD thesis, McGill University, Montreal.

Diffie, B.W. and G.D. Winius, 1977, *Foundations of the Portuguese Empire, 1415–1580*. Minneapolis: University of Minnesota Press.

Digby, S., 1982, "Maritime Trade of India," in T. Raychaudhuri and I. Habib, eds, *The Cambridge Economic History of India, Vol. I: c. 1200–c. 1750*. Cambridge: Cambridge University Press, pp. 125–59.

Dirks, N., G. Eley, and S. Ortner, eds, 1994, *Culture, Power and History*. Princeton: Princeton University Press.

Dirks, Nicholas, 2001, *Castes of Mind: Colonialism and the Making of Modern India*. Princeton and Delhi: Princeton University Press and Permanent Black.

Dirlik, Arif, 1987, "Culturalism as Hegemonic Ideology and Liberating Practice." *Cultural Critique*, vol. 6.

Dobson, Andrew, 2000 (1997), *Green Political Thought*, third edition. London: Routledge.

Dovers, Stephen R., 2000, "On the Contribution of Environmental History to Current Debate and Policy." *Environment and History*, vol. 6, pp. 131–50.

Dumont, Jean-Paul, 1992, "Ideas on Philippine Violence: Assertions, Negations, and Narrations," in C. Nordstrom and J. Martin, eds, *The Paths to Domination, Resisitance, and Terror*. Berkeley: University of California Press.

Dunn, F.L., 1975, *Rain-forest Collectors and Traders: A Study of Resource Utilization in Modern and Ancient Malaya*. Malaysian Branch of the Royal Asiatic Society, Monograph No. 5. Kuala Lumpur: Royal Asiatic Society.

Echavarnia, F.R., 1998, "Monitoring Forests in the Andes Using Remote Sensing: An Example from Southern Ecuador," in Karl S. Zimmerer and Kenneth R. Young, eds, *Nature's Geography: New Lessons for Conservation in Developing Countries*. Madison: University of Wisconsin Press.

Eck, Diana, 1999, "The Imagined Landscape: Patterns in the Construction of Hindu Sacred Geography," in Veena Das, Dipankar Gupta, and

Patricia Uberoi, eds, *Tradition, Pluralism, and Identity: Essays in Honour of T.N. Madan*. New Delhi: Sage, pp. 23–46.

Edney, Matthew, 1997, *Mapping an Empire: The Geographical Construction of British India*. Chicago: University of Chicago Press.

Edwards, Daniel, 1977, "Patrimonial and Bureaucratic Administration in Nepal: Historical Change and Weberian Theory," PhD dissertation, University of Chicago.

Ellen, Roy, 1986, "What Black Elk Left Unsaid: On the Illusory Images of Green Primitivism." *Anthropology Today*, vol. 2, no. 6, pp. 8–12.

Ellen, Roy, 1993, "Rhetoric, Practice and Incentive in Nuaulu," in Kay Milton, ed., *Environmentalism, the View from Anthropology*. London: Routledge.

Ellen, Roy and Holly Harris, 2000, "Introduction," in Roy Ellen, Peter Parkes and Alan Bicker, eds, *Indigenous Environmental Knowledge and its Transformations: Critical Anthropological Perspectives*. Amsterdam: Harwood Academic Press, pp. 1–33.

Ellingson, Terry Jay, 2001, *The Myth of the Noble Savage*. Berkeley: University of California Press.

Elouard, C. and C. Guilmoto, 2000, "Vegetation Features in Relation to Biogeography," in P.S. Ramakrishnan *et al.*, eds, *Mountain Biodiversity, Land Use Dynamics and Traditional Ecological Knowledge*. New Delhi, Oxford and IBH Publishing, pp. 25–155.

Elwin, Verrier, 1964, *The Tribal World of Verrier Elwin*. Oxford: Oxford University Press.

English, Richard, 1985, "Himalayan State Formation and the Impact of British Rule in the Nineteenth Century." *Mountain Research and Development*, vol. 5, no. 1, pp. 61–78.

Escobar, Arturo, 1997, "Cultural Politics and Biological Diversity: State, Capital and Social Movements in the Pacific Coast of Colombia," in R.G. Fox and Orin Starn, eds, *Between Resistance and Revolution: Cultural Politics and Social Protest Political Ecology*. New Brunswick: Rutgers University Press.

Escobar, Arturo, 1998, "Whose Knowledge, Whose Nature? Biodiversity, Conservation, and the Political Ecology of Social Movements." *Journal of Political Ecology*, no. 5, pp. 53–82.

Escobar, Arturo, 1999, "After Nature: Steps to an Antiessentialist Political Ecology." *Current Anthropology*, vol. 40: 1, pp. 1–30.

Fairhead, James and Melissa Leach, 1998, *Reframing Deforestation. Global*

Analysis and Local Realities: Studies in West Africa. London and New York: Routledge.

Fairhead, James, 2001, "International Dimensions of Conflict over Natural and Environmental Resources," in Nancy Lee Peluso and Michael Watts, eds, *Violent Environments.* Berkeley: University of California Press, pp. 213–36.

Faure, David and Helen Siu, 1995, *Down to Earth: The Territorial Bond in South China.* Stanford: Stanford University Press.

Faure, David and Tao Tao Liu, eds, 1996, *Unity and Diversity: Local Cultures and Identities in China.* Hong Kong: Hong Kong University Press.

Ferry, Luc, 1995, *The New Ecological Order.* Translated by Carol Volk. Chicago: University of Chicago Press.

Final Report on the Survey and Settlement Operations in the District of Hazaribagh, 1917. Patna.

Fisher, James, 1990, *Sherpas: Reflections on Change in Himalayan Nepal.* Berkeley and Los Angeles: University of California Press.

Fisher, James, Tanka Prasad and Rewanta Kumari Acharya, 1997, *Living Martyrs: Individuals and Revolution in Nepal.* Delhi: Oxford University Press.

Fisher, William F., 1993, "Nationalism and the Janajatis." *Himal,* vol. 6, no. 2, pp. 11–14.

Fisher, William F., 1997, "Doing Good? The Politics and Antipolitics of NGO Practices." *Annual Review of Anthropology,* vol. 26, pp. 439–64.

Fisher, William F., 2001, *Fluid Boundaries: Forming and Transforming Identity in Nepal.* New York: Columbia University Press.

Forest Administration Report for Bengal 1882–83. Calcutta, 1897.

Forest Survey of India, 1999, *State of Forest Report.* Dehradun: Government of India.

Foster, W., 1968, *Early Travels in India 1583–1619.* New Delhi: S. Chand and Co. (reprint).

"Forests of Chotanagpur," 1884. *Indian Forester,* no. 10, pp. 590–1.

Fox, R.G., 1969, " 'Professional Primitives': Hunters and Gatherers of Nuclear South Asia." *Man in India,* vol. 49, no. 2, pp. 139–60.

Francis, W., 1908, *Madras District Gazetteers, The Nilgiris.* Madras: Government Press.

Freeman, J.R., 1999, "Gods, Groves, and the Culture of Nature in Kerala." *Modern Asian Studies,* vol. 33, no. 2, pp. 257–302.

Freeman, R., 1994, "Forests and the Folk. Perceptions of Nature in the Swidden Regimes of Highland Malabar." *Pondy Papers in Social Sciences*, no. 15, p. 36.

Frykenberg, R.E., 1979, "Traditional Processes of Power in South India: An Historical Analysis of Local Influence," in R.E. Frykenberg, ed., *Land Control and Social Structure in Indian History*. New Delhi: Manohar, pp. 217–36.

Fuller, C.J. and J. Harriss, 2000, "For an Anthropology of the Modern Indian State," in C.J. Fuller and V. Benei, eds, 2000, *The Everyday State and Society in Modern India*. New Delhi: Social Science Press.

Fürer-Haimendorf, Christoph von, 1962, "Caste in the Multi-Ethnic Society of Nepal." *Contributions to Indian Sociology*, vol. 6, n.s., pp. 12–32.

Fürer-Haimendorf, Christoph von, 1964, *The Sherpas of Nepal: Buddhist Highlanders*. London: John Murray.

Fürer-Haimendorf, Christoph von, 1989, *Tribes of India: Struggle for Survival*. Delhi: Oxford University Press.

Gadgil, M. and V.D. Vartak, 1975, "Sacred Groves of India: A Plea for Continued Conservation." *Bombay Natural History Society Journal*, vol. 72, pp. 312–20.

Gadgil, M. and R. Guha, 1992, *This Fissured Land: An Ecological History of India*. Delhi: Oxford University Press.

Gadgil, Madhav, 2001, *Ecological Journeys: The Science and Politics of Conservation in India*. New Delhi: Permanent Black.

Gaige, Frederick H., 1975, *Regionalism and National Unity in Nepal*. Berkeley: University of California Press.

Gain, Philip, 2000, "Life and Nature at Risk," in Philip Gain, ed., *The Chittagong Hill Tracts. Life and Nature at Risk*. Dhaka: Society for Environment and Human Development.

Galey, Jean-Claude, 1990, "Reconsidering Kingship in India: An Ethnological Perspective," in J.-C. Galey, ed., *Kingship and the Kings*. Chur: Harwood Academic Publishers, pp. 123–87.

Garcia, Claude, 2003, "Sacred Forests of Kodagu: Ecological Value, Social Role and Implications for Biodiversity Conservation." PhD thesis, University Claude Bernard Lyon 1.

Gardner, P.M., 1985, "Bicultural Oscillation as a Long-Term Adaptation to Cultural Frontiers: Cases and Questions." *Human Ecology*, vol. 13, no. 4, pp. 411–32.

Gardner, P.M., 1991, "Foragers' Pursuit of Individual Autonomy." *Current Anthropology*, vol. 32, no. 5, pp. 543–72.

Gardner, P.M., 1993, "Dimensions of Subsistence Foraging in South India." *Ethnology*, vol. 32, pp. 109–44.

Gassah, D. S., 1998, *Traditional Institutions of Meghalaya: A Study of Doloi and His Administration*. New Delhi: Regency Publications.

Gee, E.P., 1959, "The Great Indian Rhinoceros in Nepal: Report of a Fact Finding Survey, April–May." *Journal of the Bombay Natural History Society*, vol. 56, no. 3, pp. 484–510.

Gee, E.P., 1961, "History of the Rhinoceros Area in Nepal." *Cheetal*, vol. 4, no. 1, pp. 16–29.

Geiser, Urs, 2000, "Working on Power: Actors' Practices of Improving Control over Forest Resources in North-West Pakistan," paper presented at the 16th European Conference on Modern South Asian Studies, Edinburgh, September 6–9, 2000.

Geiser, Urs, 2001, "Reading Participation in Forest Management through 'Modern' and 'Post-modern' Concepts; Or Where to Start Normative Debates?," in Hilary Povey and Michel Blanc, eds, *Food, Nature and Society: Rural Life in Late Modernity*. Aldershot: Ashgate.

Geiser, Urs, 2002, "Contested Forests in North-West Pakistan: Present-day Struggles and the Role of the 'Colonial,' " paper presented at the 17th European Conference on Modern South Asian Studies, Heidelberg, 9–14 September.

Ghosh, S., 2001, "Sacred Groves and their Role in Plant Conservation." *Science and Culture*, vol. 67, nos. 11–12, pp. 347–9.

Ghurye, G.S., 1943, *The Aborigines So-called and their Future*, Delhi.

Gibson, Clark C., Margaret A. McKean and Elinor Ostrom, eds, 2000, *People and Forests: Communities, Institutions, and Governance*. Cambridge MA and London: The MIT Press.

Giddens, Anthony, 1979, *Central Problems in Social Theory: Action, Structure and Contradiction in Social Analysis*. London and Basingstoke: Macmillan Press.

Giddens, Anthony, 1991, *Modernity and Self-Identity: Self and Society in the Late Modern Age*. Cambridge: Polity Press.

Gilroy, Paul, 1987, *There Ain't No Black in the Union Jack: The Cultural Politics of Race and Nation*. London: Hutchinson.

Gimaret-Carpentier, C., R. Pélissier, J.P. Pascal and F. Houiller, 1998, "Sampling Strategies for the Assessment of Tree Species Diversity." *Journal of Vegetation Science*, no. 9, pp. 161–72.

Giri, Helen, 1998, *The Khasis under the British Rule (1824–1947)*. New Delhi: Regency Publications.

Gleig, George Robert, 1830, *Life of Major General Sir Thomas Munro*. London, 3 vols.

GoNWFP, 1999, NWFP Forest Policy 1999, NEDA, ITC, SDC, Government of NWFP Forestry, Fisheries and Wildlife Department, Peshawar, Pakistan.

GoNWFP, 2002, *Forest Vision—2025*, by Naseem Javed, Ayaz Khattak, Alamgir Gandapur, Abdullah Khattak, Iqbal Syal, Ghazi Marjan; guided by Khalid Sultan, Secretary Environment, NWFP, and Muhammad Abbas Khan, Minister Environment NWFP. Government of NWFP, Peshawar, Pakistan.

Gold, Ann Grodzins, 1998, "Sin and Rain: Moral Ecology in Rural North India," in Lance Nelson, ed., *Purifying the Earthly Body of God: Religion and Ecology in Hindu India*. Albany: SUNY Press, pp. 165–95.

Gold, Ann G. and Bhojuram Gujar, 2001, *In the Time of Trees and Sorrows: Nature, Power and Memory in Rajasthan*. Durham: Duke University Press.

Goodall, Merrill R., 1978, "Bureaucracy and Bureaucrats: A Few Themes Drawn from the Nepal Experience," in James Fisher, ed., *Himalayan Anthropology: The Indo-Tibetan Interface*. Paris: Mouton.

Gordon, Robert W., 1996, "Paradoxical Property," in John Brewer and Susan Staves, eds, *Early Modern Conceptions of Property*. London: Routledge.

Goswami, M.C. and D.N. Majumdar, 1972, *Social Institutions of the Garo of Meghalaya: An Analytical Study*. Calcutta: Nababharat Publishers.

Goswami, Manu, 2002, "Rethinking the Modular Nation Form: Toward a Sociohistorical Conception of Nationalism." *Comparative Studies in Society and History*, vol. 44, no. 4, pp. 770–99.

Government of Nepal, 2000, *National Planning Commission Secretariat: Statistical Pocket Book*. Kathmandu: Central Bureau of Statistics.

Govindan, V., 1916, "Fishery Statistics and Information, West and East Coasts, Madras Presidency." *Madras Fisheries Bulletin*, vol. 9.

Gow, Peter, 1995, "Land People, Paper," in E. Hirsch, ed., *The Anthropology of the Landscape, Perspectives on Place and Space.* Oxford: Oxford University Press.

Graeber, David, 1997, "Manners, Deference, and Private Property." *Comparative Studies in History and Society*, vol. 39, no. 4, pp. 694–728.

Grove, Richard, 1995, *Green Imperialism: Colonial Expansion, Tropical Island Edens and the Origins of Environmentalism, 1600–1860.* Cambridge: Cambridge University Press.

Grove, Richard, 1997, *Ecology, Climate and Empire: Colonialism and Global Environmental History, 1400–1940.* Cambridge: White Horse Press.

Grove, Richard, 1998, "Indigenous Knowledge and the Significance of Southwest India for Portuguese and Dutch Constructions of Tropical Nature," in R. Grove, V. Damodaran, and S. Sangwan, eds, *Nature and the Orient: The Environmental History of South and South East Asia.* Delhi: Oxford University Press.

Guha, Amalendu, 1991, *Medieval and Early Colonial Assam.* Calcutta: K.P. Bagchi and Co.

Guha, Ramachandra, 1983a+b, "Forestry in British and Post-British India: A Historical Analysis." *Economic and Political Weekly*, vol. 18, no. 44, pp. 1882–96 and nos. 45–6, pp. 1940–7.

Guha, Ramachandra, 1989, *The Unquiet Woods: Ecological Change and Peasant Resistance in the Himalaya.* Delhi: Oxford University Press.

Guha, Ramachandra, 2000, *Environmentalism: A Global History.* New Delhi: Oxford University Press.

Guha, Ramachandra and Juan Martinez-Alier, 1998, *Varieties of Environmentalism: Essays North and South.* New Delhi: Oxford University Press.

Guha, Sumit, 1999, *Environment and Ethnicity in India, 1200–1991.* Cambridge: Cambridge University Press.

Guha, Sumit, 2003, "The Politics of Identity and Enumeration in India, c. 1600–1990." *Comparative Studies in Society and History*, vol. 45, no. 1, pp. 148–67.

Guneratne, Arjun Upali, 2002, *Many Tongues, One People: The Making of Tharu Identity in Nepal.* Ithaca: Cornell University Press.

Guneratne, Katherine Bjork, 1999, *In the Circle of the Dance: Notes of an Outsider in Nepal.* Ithaca: Cornell University Press.

Gupta, Akhil, 1995a, "Blurred Boundaries: The Discourse of Corruption, the Culture of Politics and the Imagined State." *American Anthropologist*, vol. 22, pp. 375–402.

Gupta, Akhil, 1995b, "The Song of the Nonaligned World: Transnational

Identities and the Reinscription of Space in Late Capitalism," in Akhil Gupta and James Ferguson, eds, *Culture, Power, Place: Explorations in Critical Anthropology*. Durham: Duke University Press.

Gupta, Akhil, 2004, "Imagining Nations," in David Nugent and Joan Vincent, eds, *A Companion to the Anthropology of Politics*. Oxford: Blackwell, pp. 267–81.

Gurdon, P.R., 1906, *The Khasis*. London: Macmillan.

Gururani, Shubhra, 2000, "Regimes of Control, Strategies of Access: Politics of Forest Use in the Uttarakhand Himalaya, India," in Arun Agrawal, and K. Sivaramakrishnan, eds, *Agrarian Environments: Resources, Representations, and Rule in India*. Durham and London: Duke University Press.

Habermas, Jürgen, 1989, *The Structural Transformation of the Public Sphere: An Inquiry into a Category of Bourgeois Society*. Cambridge: Polity Press.

Haines, H.H., 1910, *The Forest Flora of Chotanagpur*. Calcutta.

Haller, G., 1910, *Land Re-Settlement Report*. Mercara.

Hamilton, Paul, 2002, "The Greening of Nationalism: Nationalising Nature in Europe." *Environmental Politics*, vol. 11, no. 2, pp. 27–48.

Hardiman, David, 1987a, "The Bhils and Shahukars of Eastern Gujarat," in *Subaltern Studies V: Writings on South Asian History and Society*, ed. R. Guha. Delhi: Oxford University Press, pp. 1–54.

Hardiman, David, 1987b, *The Coming of the Devi: Adivasi Assertion in Western India*. Delhi: Oxford University Press.

Hardiman, David, 1994, "Power in the Forest: The Dangs, 1820–1940," in David Arnold and David Hardiman, eds, *Subaltern Studies VIII: Essays in Honour of Ranajit Guha*. Delhi: Oxford University Press.

Hardin, G., 1968, "The Tragedy of the Commons." *Science*, no. 162, pp. 1243–8.

Hardt, Michael and Antonio Negri, 2000, *Empire*. Cambridge: Harvard University Press.

Harkness, Henry, 1832, *A Description of a Singular Aboriginal Race Inhabiting the Summit of the Neilgherry Hills or the Blue Mountains of Coimbatoor, in the Southern Peninsula of India*. London: Smith, Elder, and Co.

Harvey, David, 1990, *The Condition of Postmodernity*. Cambridge: Blackwell Press.

Headland, T.N., 1997, "Revisionism in Ecological Anthropology." *Current Anthropology*, vol. 18, no. 4, August–October.

Heinen, Joel T. and Bijaya Kattel, 1992a, "Parks, People, and Conservation:

A Review of Management Issues in Nepal's Protected Areas." *Population and Environment: A Journal of Interdisciplinary Studies*, vol. 14, no. 1.

Heinen, Joel T. and Bijaya Kattel, 1992b, "A Review of Conservation Legislation in Nepal: Past Progress and Future Needs." *Environmental Management*, vol. 16, no. 6, pp. 723–33.

Heitzman, J., 1997, *Gifts of Power: Lordship in an Early Indian State*. Delhi: Oxford University Press.

Hembram, P.C., 1983, "Return to the Sacred Grove," in K.S. Singh, ed., *Tribal Movements in India*. Delhi: South Asia Books.

Herzfeld, Michael, 1992, *The Social Production of Indifference: Exploring the Symbolic Roots of Western Bureaucracy*. Chicago: University of Chicago Press.

Herzfeld, Michael, 1996, *Cultural Intimacy: Social Poetics in the Nation-State*. London: Routledge.

Heske, Franz, 1931, "Probleme der Walderhaltung im Himalaya." *Tharandter Forstliches Jahrbuch*, vol. 82, pp. 545–94.

Heyman, Josiah, 1995, "Putting Power in the Anthropology of Bureaucracy: The Immigration and Naturalisation Service at the Mexican-United States Border," *Current Anthropology*, vol. 36, no. 2, pp. 261–87.

Hill, R.D., 1969, "Pepper-Growing in Johore." *The Journal of Tropical Geography*, vol. 28, pp. 32–9.

Hirch, Erich, 1995, *The Anthropology of the Landscape*. Oxford: Oxford University Press.

Hirschman, Albert O., 1970, *Exit, Voice, and Loyalty: Responses to Decline in Firms, Organizations, and States*. Cambridge, Mass.: Harvard University Press.

Hobsbawm, E.J. and T. Ranger, 1992, *The Invention of Tradition*. Cambridge: Cambridge University Press.

Hockings, P., 1980, *Ancient Hindu Refugees*. New Delhi: Vikas.

Hockings, P., 1985, "Advances in the Social History of Peninsular Tribes," in R.E. Frykenberg and P. Kolenda, eds, *Studies of South India*. Madras: New Era Publications, pp. 217–38.

Hockings, P., ed., 1989, *Blue Mountains: The Ethnography and Biogeography of a South Indian Region*. Delhi: Oxford University Press.

Hockings, P., ed., 1997, *Blue Mountains Revisited: Cultural Studies on the Nilgiri Hills*. Delhi: Oxford University Press.

Hoeppe, Götz, forthcoming, *Conversations on the Beach: Debating Local Knowledge and Environmental Change in South India*. Oxford/NewYork: Berghahn Books.

Hofer, Andras, 1978, "A New Rural Elite in Central Nepal," in James Fisher, ed., *Himalayan Anthropology: The Indo-Tibetan Interface*. Paris: Mouton.

Hofer, Andras, 1979, *The Caste Hierarchy and the State in Nepal: A Study of the Muluki Ain of 1854*. Innsbruck: Universitatsverlag Wagner/ Ergenbnisse Des Forschungsunternehmens Nepal Himalaya, vol. 13, no. 2.

Hoffmann, J., 1906, *Encyclopaedia Mundarica*. Calcutta.

Hooker, Joseph Dalton, 1854, *Himalayan Journals; or Notes of a Naturalist*, vol. II. London: John Murray.

Hoftun, Martin, 1993, "The Dynamics and Chronology of the 1990 Revolution," in Michael Hutt, ed., *Nepal in the Nineties*. Delhi: Oxford University Press.

Hornell, James and M. Ramaswami Nayadu, 1924, "A Contribution to the Life-History of the Indian Sardine, with Notes on the Plankton of the Malabar Coast." *Madras Fisheries Bulletin*, vol. 17, pp. 129–97.

Hough, James, 1829, *Letters on the Climate, Inhabitants, Productions, &c. &c. of the Neilgherries or Blue Mountains of Coimbatoor, South India*. London: John Hatchard & Son.

Hunter, W.W., 1876, *A Statistical Account of Bengal. Volume VI. Chittagong Hill Tracts, Chittagong, Noákhálí, Tipperah, Hill Tipperah*. London: Trübner & Co.

Hurlbert, S.H., 1971, "The Non-Concept of Species Diversity: A Critique and Alternative Parameters." *Ecology*, vol. 52, pp. 577–86.

Husain, Asad, 1970, *British India's Relations with the Kingdom of Nepal*. London: Allen & Unwin.

Husain, Kazi Zaker 1967, "Expedition to Chittagong Hill Tracts." *Journal of the Asiatic Society of Pakistan*, vol. 12, no. 1, Dacca.

Hutchinson, R.H. Sneyd, 1906, *An Account of the Chittagong Hill Tracts*. Calcutta: Bengal Secretariat Book Depot.

Hutchinson, R.H., Sneyd, 1909, *Eastern Bengal and Assam District Gazetteer. Chittagong Hill Tracts*. Allahabad: Pioneer Press.

ICAR, 1971, *Report on Sardine and Mackerel Resources*. Delhi: Indian Council for Agricultural Research.

Ingold, Tim, 2000, *The Perception of the Environment: Essays in Livelihood, Dwelling and Skill*. London and New York: Routledge.
Ives, Jack D. and Bruno Messerli, 1989, *The Himalayan Dilemma: Reconciling Development and Conservation*. New York: Routledge.
Jackson, Michael, 1998, *Minima Ethnographica: Intersubjectivity and the Anthropological Project*. Chicago: University of Chicago Press.
Jacoby, Karl, 2001, *Crimes against Nature: Squatters, Poachers, Thieves, and the Hidden History of American Conservation*. Berkeley: University of California Press.
Jain, Shobita, 1984, "Women and People's Ecological Movement: A Case Study of Women's Role in the Chipko Movement in Uttar Pradesh." *Economic and Political Weekly*, vol. 19, no. 41, pp. 1788–94.
Jeffrey, Roger, ed., 1998, *The Social Construction of Indian Forests*. Edinburgh: Centre for South Asian Studies, and Delhi: Manohar Publishers.
Jeffrey, Roger and Nandini Sundar, eds, 1999, *A New Moral Economy for India's Forests? Discourses of Community and Participation*. New Delhi/Thousand Oaks/London: Sage Publications.
Jewitt, Sarah, 2002, *Environment, Knowledge and Gender: Local Development in India's Jharkhand*. Hampshire: Ashgate Publishing Ltd.
Johnson, B.L.C., and N. Ahmad, 1957, "Geographical Record. The Karnafuli Project." *Oriental Geographer*, July. Dacca.
Joshi, Nanda Lal, 1983, *Evolution of Public Administration in Nepal: Lessons and Experiences*. Kathmandu: Ratna Pustak Bhandar.
Juhé-Beaulaton, D. and B. Roussel, 1992, "Les forêts sacrées de l'Afrique de l'Ouest," in A. Lorgnier, ed., *Forêts*. AGEP Publishers, pp. 250–3.
Jumma Peoples Network, 1998, *Population Transfer and Implantation of Bengali Settlers. The Threat to the Survival of the Jummas*. New Delhi: Asok Buddha Vihar.
Kalam, M.A., 1996, *Sacred Groves in Kodagu District of Karnataka (South India): A Socio-Historical Study*. Pondicherry: French Institute of Pondicherry.
Kalam, M.A., 2000, "Devarakadus and Encroachments," in P.S. Ramakrishnan, U.M. Chandashekara *et al.*, *Mountain Biodiversity, Land Use Dynamics and Traditional Ecological Knowledge*. New Delhi, Oxford and IBH Publishing Co. Pvt. Ltd, pp. 44–53.
Kar, P.C., 1982, *The Garos in Transition*. Delhi: Cosmo Publications.

Karlsson, Bengt G., 2000, *Contested Belonging. An Indigenous People's Struggle for Forest and Identity in Sub-Himalayan Bengal*. Richmond: Curzon Press.

Karlsson, Bengt G., 2001, "Indigenous Politics: Community Formation and Indigenous Peoples' Struggle for Self-Determination in Northeast India." *Identities*, vol. 8, no. 1, pp. 7–45.

Karlsson, Bengt G., 2003, "Anthropology and the 'Indigenous Slot': Claims to and Debates about Indigenous Peoples' Status in India." *Critique of Anthropology*, vol. 23, no. 4, pp. 403–23.

Kaviraj, Sudipta, 1984, "On the Crisis of Political Institutions in India." *Contributions to Indian Sociology*, vol. 18, pp. 223–43.

Kaviraj, Sudipta, 1992, "The Imaginary Institution of India," in Partha Chatterjee and Gyanendra Pandey, eds, *Subaltern Studies VII: Writings on South Asian History and Society*. Delhi: Oxford University Press, pp. 1–39.

Kermani, W.A., 1953, "Chittagong Hill Tracts." *Pakistan Review*, vol. 2, no. 1.

Keys, William, 1812, "Topographical Description of the Neelaghery Mountains," in H. B. Grigg, *The Manual of Nilagiri District*, 1880, pp. xlviii–li.

Khasi National Celebration Committee, 1994, *Lest We Forget: Indigenous Peoples' Year 1993*. Shillong: Sevenhuts Enterprise.

Khattak, G.M., 1987, *Issues in Forestry*, Report to the Kalam Integrated Development Project. Peshawar.

Klingensmith, Daniel, 2003, "Building India's Modern 'Temples': Indians and Americans in the Damodar Valley Corporation, 1945–60," in K. Sivaramakrishnan and Arun Agrawal, eds, *Regional Modernities: The Cultural Politics of Development in India*. Stanford: Stanford University Press, pp. 122–42.

Kothari, A., Saloni Suri, and Neena Singh, 1995, "People and Protected Areas: Rethinking Conservation in India." *The Ecologist*, vol. 25, no. 5, pp. 188–94.

Krengel, Monika, 1989, *Sozialstrukturen in Kumaon: Bergbauern im Himalaya*. Stuttgart: Steiner Verlag Wiesbaden.

Kumar, Dharma 1982, *The Cambridge Economic History of India, Vol. 2: c. 1757–c. 1970*. Delhi: Orient Longman.

Kumar, Pradeep, 2000, *The Uttarakhand Movement: Construction of a Regional Identity*. New Delhi: Kanishka Publishers.

Kumar, Purushottam, 1991, *Mutinies and Rebellions in Chotanagpur*. Patna.

Kuper, Adam, 1996 (1988), *The Invention of Primitive Society: Transformations of an Illusion*. London and New York: Routledge.

Kurien, John, 1985, "Technical Assistance Projects and Socio-Economic Change: Norwegian Intervention in Kerala's Fisheries Development." *Economic and Political Weekly*, vol. 20, pp. A70–A88.

Kushalappa, C.G. and S. Bhagwat, 2001, "Sacred Groves: Biodiversity, Threats and Conservation," in R.U. Shanker, K.N. Ganeshaiah, and K.S. Bawa, eds, *Forest Genetic Resources. Status, Threats and Conservation Strategies*. New Delhi: Oxford and IBH Publishing, pp. 21–9.

Lakoff, George, 1987, *Women, Fire and Dangerous Beasts: What Categories Reveal about the Mind*. Chicago: University of Chicago Press.

Laungaramsri, Pinkaew, 2001, *Redefining Nature: Karen Ecological Knowledge and the Challenge to the Modern Conservation Paradigm*. Chennai: Earthworm Books.

Laurance, W.F. and R.O. Bierregaard, eds, 1997, *Tropical Forest Remnants. Ecology, Management and Conservation of Fragmented Communities*. Chicago: University of Chicago Press.

Leach, E.R., 1954, *Political Systems of Highland Burma. A Study of Kachin Social Structure*, London School of Economics. Monographs on Social Anthropology. London: University of London.

Leach, M., 1992, "Women's Crops in Women's Spaces," in E. Croll and D. Parkin, eds, *Bush Base: Forest Farm, Culture, Development and the Environment*. London: Routledge.

Leach, Melissa and James Fairhead, 1996, *Misreading the African Landscape*. Cambridge: Cambridge University Press.

Lee, R.B. and R. Daly, eds, 1999, *The Cambridge Encyclopedia of Hunter-Gatherers*. Cambridge: Cambridge University Press.

Lehmann, F.K., 1963, *The Structure of Chin Society*. Urbana: University of Illinois Press.

Leshnik, L.S., 1974, *South Indian "Megalithic" Burials, the Pandukal Complex*. Wiesbaden: Franz Steiner Verlag.

Lewin, Thomas Herbert, 1869, *The Hill Tracts of Chittagong and the Dwellers Therein; with Comparative Vocabularies of Hill Dialects*. Calcutta: Bengal Printing Company.

Lewin, Thomas Herbert, 1870, *Wild Races of Southeastern India*. London: Gilbert and Rivington.

Lewin, Thomas Herbert, 1887 (No 533, dated Rangamattie, the 1st July 1872), "From Captain T.H. Lewin, D.C., To: The Commissioner of Chittagong," in *Selections from the Correspondence of the Revenue Administration of the Chittagong Hill Tracts*. Calcutta: Bengal Secretariat Press.

Lewis, Martin W., 1992, *Green Delusions: An Environmentalist Critique of Radical Environmentalism*. Durham and London: Duke University Press.

Lieberman, David, 1996, "Property, Commerce, and the Common Law: Attitudes to Legal Change in the Eighteenth Century," in John Brewer and Susan Staves, eds, *Early Modern Conceptions of Property*. London: Routledge.

Liechty, Mark, 1996, "Paying for Modernity: Women and the Discourse of Freedom in Kathmandu." *Studies in Nepali History and Society*, vol. 1, no. 1, pp. 201–30.

Life is Not Ours, 1991, *Land and Human Rights in the Chittagong Hill Tracts, Bangladesh. The Report of the Chittagong Hill Tracts Commission.* Distributed by IWGIA/Copenhagen and Organizing Committee Chittagong Hill Tracts Campaign, Amsterdam.

Lindholm, Charles, 1982, *Generosity and Jealousy: The Swat Pukhtun of Northern Pakistan*. New York: Columbia University Press.

Lindholm, Charles, 1996, *Frontier Perspectives: Essays in Comparative Anthropology*. Karachi: Oxford University Press.

Linkenbach, Antje, 1998, "Forests in Garhwal and the Construction of Space," in Roger Jeffery, ed., *The Social Construction of Indian Forests*. New Delhi: Manohar, and Edinburgh: Centre for South Asian Studies, pp. 79–105.

Linkenbach, Antje, 2000, "Anthropology of Modernity: Projects and Contexts." *Thesis Eleven*, 41–63.

Linkenbach, Antje, 2002a, "Shaking the State by Making a (New) State: Social Movements and the Quest for Autonomy." *Sociologus*, vol. 1, pp. 77–106.

Linkenbach, Antje, 2002b, "A Consecrated Land: Local Constructions of History in the Garhwal and Kumaon Himalayas, North India," in Axel Harneit-Sievers, ed., *A Place in the World: New Local Historiographies from Africa and South Asia*. Leiden: Brill.

Linkenbach, Antje, forthcoming, *Forest Futures: Global Representations and Ground Realities in the Himalayas*. New Delhi: Permanent Black.

Löffler, Lorenz G., ed., 1988, *Bedrohte Zukunft. Bergvölker in Bangladesh*. Zürich: IWGIA Lokalgruppe.

Löffler, Lorenz G., 1964, "Chakma und Sak. Ethnolinguistische Beiträge zur Geschichte eines Kulturvolkes," *Internationales Archiv für Ethnographie*. Leiden.

Long, N. and J.D. van der Ploeg, 1989, "Demythologizing Planned Intervention: An Actor Perspective." *Sociologica Ruralis*, vol. 29, nos. 3/4.

Long, N., 2001, *Development Sociology: Actor Perspectives*. London: Routledge.

Long, N. and A. Long, eds, 1992, *Battlefields of Knowledge: The Interlocking of Theory and Practice in Social Research and Development*. London: Routledge.

Louis, Roger William, 1999, "Introduction," in Robin W. Winks, ed., *The Oxford History of the British Empire. Historiography*. Oxford: Oxford University Press.

Lowenthal, D., 1991, "British National Identity and the English Landscape." *Rural History*, vol. 2.

Ludden, David, 1985, *Peasant History in South India*. Princeton; Princeton University Press.

Ludden, David, 1993, "Orientalist Empiricism: Transformations of Colonial Knowledge," in Carol A. Breckenridge and Peter van der Veer, eds, *Orientalism and the Postcolonial Predicament*, Pennsylvania: University of Pennsylvania Press.

Ludden, David, 2000, "Agrarian Histories and Grassroots Development in South Asia," in Arun Agrawal and K. Sivaramakrishnan, eds, *Agrarian Environments; Resources, Representations and Rule in India*. Durham: Duke University Press, pp. 251–64.

Ludden, David, ed., 2001, *Reading Subaltern Studies: Critical History, Contested Meaning, and the Globalisation of South Asia*. New Delhi: Permanent Black.

Mackenzie, Alexander, 1884, *History of the Relations of the Government with the Hill Tribes of the North East Frontier of Bengal*. Calcutta: Home Department Press.

Mackenzie, John M., 1988, *The Empire of Nature: Hunting, Conservation and British Imperialism*. Manchester: Manchester University Press.

MacKenzie, John M., 1993, "Essay and Reflection: On Scotland and the Empire." *The International History Review*, vol. 15: 4, November, pp. 714–39.

MacKenzie, John, 1997, *The Empire of Nature: Hunting, Conservation and British Imperialism (Studies in Imperialism)*. Manchester: Manchester University Press. Reprint.

Macpherson, Evans, 1820, "Report Submitted to John Sullivan, Collector of Coimbatore," in H.B. Grigg, 1880, *The Manual of Nilagiri District*, pp. lv–lx.

Majumdar, D.N., 1982, "The Garo National Council," in K.S. Singh, ed., *Tribal Movements in India*. New Delhi: Manohar.

Malhotra, K.C., S. Chatterjee, S. Srivastava, and Y. Gokhale, 2001, *Cultural and Ecological Dimensions of Sacred Groves in India*. New Delhi: Indian National Science Academy.

Malhotra, K.C., Y. Gokhale, and K. Das, 2001, *Sacred Groves of India: An Annotated Bibliography*. Delhi: Indian National Science Academy.

Malik, Bela, 2003, "The 'Problem' of Shifting Cultivation in the Garo Hills of North-East India, 1860–1970." *Conservation and Society*, vol. 1, no. 2, pp. 287–315.

Man, E.G., 1983, *Sonthalia and the Santhals*. Delhi: Mittal Publications.

Marak, Julius L.R., 2000, *Garo Customary Laws and Practices*, 2nd edition. New Delhi: Akansha Publishing House.

Mariotti, A. and E. Peterschmitt, 1994, "Forest Savanna Ecotone Dynamics in India as Revealed by Carbon Isotope Ratios of Soil Organic Matter." *Oecologia*, no. 97, pp. 475–80.

Master Plan for the Chittagong Hill Tracts Development Project. Plan B, 1967, "Chittagong Hill Tracts Project, Phase 1, 1966–67 to 1974–75." Dacca: East Pakistan Agricultural Development Corporation.

Mathew, K.S., 1983, *Portuguese Trade with India in the Sixteenth Century*. Delhi: Manohar.

Mawdsley, Emma, 1996, "Uttarakhand Agitation and Other Backward Classes." *Economic and Political Weekly*, vol. 31, no. 4, pp. 205–10.

Mawdsley, Emma, 1997, "Nonsecessionist Regionalism in India: The Uttarakhand Separate State Movement." *Environment and Planning*, vol. 29, pp. 2217–35.

Mawrie, Barnes L., 2001, *The Khasis and their Natural Environment: A Study of the Eco-Consciousness and Eco-Spirituality of the Khasis*. Shillong: Vendrame Institute Publications.

McLaren, Martha, 1993, "From Analysis to Prescription: Scottish Concepts of Asian Despotism in Early Nineteenth-Century British India." *The International History Review*, vol. 15, no. 3, August, pp. 469–501.

McLaren, Martha, 2001, *British India and British Scotland, 1780–1830*. Ohio: The University of Akron Press.
Merchant, Carolyn, 1992, *Radical Ecology: The Search for a Liveable World*. London: Routledge.
Mey, Almut, 1979, "Untersuchungen zur Wirtschaft in den Chittagong Hill Tracts (Bangladesh)," dissertation, Veröffentlichungen aus dem Übersee-Museum Bremen, Reihe D, Völkerkundliche Monographien, vol. 6, Bremen.
Mey, Wolfgang, 1980, "Politische Systeme in den Chittagong Hill Tracts, Bangladesh," dissertation, Veröffentlichungen aus dem Übersee-Museum Bremen, Reihe D, Völkerkundliche Monographien, vol. 9, Bremen.
Mey, Wolfgang, ed., 1984, *Genocide in the Chittagong Hill Tracts, Bangladesh*. Copenhagen: IWGIA Document, no. 51.
Mey, Wolfgang, 1991, *Vielleicht sind diese Dinge die einzigen Spuren, die wir hinterlassen. Die bedrohte Zukunft der Bergvölker in Bangladesh*. Reihe: Hintergründe und Materalien 13, museumspädagogischer dienst Hamburg, Verlag Galgenberg.
Mey, Wolfgang, 1994, Entwicklungshilfe als Mittel zur Bekämpfung von Autonomiebestrebungen," in Dieter Conrad and Wolfgang-Peter Zingel, *Bangladesh. Dritte Heidelberger Südasiengespräche*. Stuttgart: Franz Steiner Verlag.
Mies, Maria and Vandana Shiva, 1993, *Ecofeminism*. New Delhi: Kali for Women.
Mills, A.J.M., 1985 (1853), *Report on the Khasi and Jaintia Hills*. Shillong: North-Eastern Hill University Publications.
Mills, J.P., 1927, "Report on the Chiefs of the Chittagong Hill Tracts; Proposals Regarding the Chiefs, with Appendix," unpublished manuscript, University of London, School of Oriental and African Studies.
Mishra, Chaitanya and Pitambar Sharma, 1983, "Foreign Aid and Social Structure: Notes on Intra-State Relationships," in *Foreign Aid and Development in Nepal, Proceedings of a Seminar October 4–5, 1983*. Kathmandu: Integrated Development Systems.
Mishra, Chaitanya, 1997, "Development Practices in Nepal: An Overview," in Krishna B. Bhattachan and Chaitanya Mishra, eds, *Development Practices in Nepal*. Kathmandu: Tribhuvan University.
Mitra, Amit, 1993, "Chipko, an Unfinished Mission." *Down to Earth*, April 30, pp. 25–36.

Mohapatra, Prabhu, 1991, "Class Conflict and Agrarian Regimes in Chota Nagpur, 1860–1950." *Indian Economic and Social History Review*, vol. 28, no. 1, pp. 1–42.

Morris, Brian, 1982a, "The Family, Group Structuring, and Trade among South Indian Hunter-Gatherers," in *Politics and History in Band Societies*, ed. E. Leacock and R. Lee. Cambridge: Cambridge University Press, pp. 171–87.

Morris, Brian, 1982b, *Hill Traders: A Socioeconomic Study of the Hill Pandaram*. New Jersey: Athlone Press.

Morrison, K.D., 1994a, "Reconstructing Fire History through Size-Specific Analysis of Microscopic Charcoal: The Last 600 Years in South India." *Journal of Archaeological Science*, vol. 21, pp. 675–85.

Morrison, K.D., 1994b, "Intensification of Production: Archaeological Approaches." *Journal of Archaeological Method and Theory*," vol. 1, no. 2, pp. 111–59.

Morrison, K.D., 1995, *Fields of Victory: Vijayanagara and the Course of Intensification*. Berkeley: Contributions of the University of California Archaeological Research Facility, no. 52.

Morrison, K.D., 1996, "Typological Schemes and Agricultural Change: Beyond Boserup in Precolonial South India." *Current Anthropology*, vol. 37, pp. 583–608.

Morrison, K.D., 1997, "Commerce and Culture in South Asia: Perspectives from Archaeology and History." *Annual Review of Anthropology*, vol. 26, pp. 87–108.

Morrison, K.D., 2002a, "Historicizing Adaptation, Adapting to History: Forager-Traders in South and Southeast Asia," in K.D. Morrison and L.L. Junker, eds, *Forager-Traders in South and Southeast Asia: Long-Term Histories*. Cambridge: Cambridge University Press.

Morrison, K.D., 2002b, "Introduction: South Asia," in K.D. Morrison and L.L. Junker, eds, *Forager-Traders in South and Southeast Asia: Long-Term Histories*. Cambridge: Cambridge University Press.

Morrison, K.D. and L.L. Junker, eds, 2002, *Forager-Traders in South and Southeast Asia: Long-Term Histories*. Cambridge: Cambridge University Press.

Mosse, David, 2003, *The Rule of Water: Statecraft, Ecology, and Collective Action in South India*. Delhi: Oxford University Press.

Munasinghe, Viranjini, 2002, "Nationalism in Hybrid Spaces." *American Ethnologist*, vol. 29, no. 3, pp. 663–92.

Munda, R. and B. Prasad Kesari, 2003, "Recent Developments in the Jharkhand Movement," in R.D. Munda and S. Mullick, eds, *Jharkhand Movement, Indigenous Peoples' Struggle for Autonomy in India*. Copenhagen: Transaction Publishers.

Murthy, M.L.K., 1994, "Forest Peoples and Historical Traditions in the Eastern Ghats, South India," in B. Allchin, ed., *Living Traditions: Studies in the Ethnoarchaeology of South Asia*. New Delhi: Oxford and IBH, pp. 205–18.

Myers, N., 1988, "Threatened Biotas: 'Hot Spots' in Tropical Forests." *The Environmentalist*, vol. 8, no. 3, pp. 187–208.

Nader, Laura, 1972, "Up the Anthropologist: Perspectives Gained from Studying Up," in Dell Hymes, ed., *Reinventing Anthropology*. New York: Random House, pp. 284–311.

Nag, Sajal, 2002, *Contesting Marginality: Ethnicity, Insurgency and Subnationalism in North-East India*. New Delhi: Manohar.

Nair, R.V., 1952, "Studies on the Revival of the Indian Oil Sardine Fishery," in *Proceedings of the Indo-Pacific Fisheries Council*, 4th Meeting (Quezon City, Philippines), Section II. Bangkok: IPFC Secretariat, pp. 115–29.

Nandy, Ashis, 1990, *The Intimate Enemy: Loss and Recovery of Self Under Colonialism*. Delhi: Oxford University Press.

Nandy, Ashis, 2001, "Contending Stories in the Culture of Indian Politics: Traditions and the Future of Democracy," in Ashis Nandy, *Time Warps: The Insistent Politics of Silent and Evasive Pasts*. New Delhi: Permanent Black, pp. 13–35.

Nash, June C., 2001, *Mayan Visions: The Quest for Autonomy in an Age of Globalization*. New York: Routledge.

Nash, Manning, 1989, *The Cauldron of Ethnicity in the Modern World*. Chicago: University of Chicago Press.

Nathan, Dev, 2000, "Timber in Meghalaya." *Economic and Political Weekly*, January 22, pp. 182–6.

Nebelung, Michael, 1988, *Mobilisierung und Organisation von Kleinbauern und Landarbeitern im ländlichen Bangladesh*. Berlin: Verlag für Wissenschaft und Bildung.

Neeson, Jeanette M., 1993, *Commoners: Common Right, Enclosure and Social Change in England, 1700–1820*. Cambridge: Cambridge University Press.

Nehru, Jawaharlal, 1999, *The Discovery of India*. Centenary Edition. Delhi: Oxford University Press.

Nichols, R., 2001, *Settling the Frontier. Land, Law, and Society in the Peshawar Valley, 1500–1900*. Oxford: Oxford University Press.

Nilakanta Sastri, K.A., 1975, *A History of South India*, 4th edition. Madras: Oxford University Press.

Noble, W.A., 1989, "Nilgiri Prehistoric Remains," in P. Hockings, ed., *Blue Mountains: The Ethnography and Biogeography of a South Indian Region*. New Delhi: Oxford University Press, pp. 102–32.

Nongbri, Tiplut, 2001, "Timber Ban in North-East India: Effects on Livelihood and Gender." *Economic and Political Weekly*, May 26, pp. 1893–1900.

Nongbri, Tiplut, 2003, *Development, Ethnicity and Gender: Select Essays on Tribes in India*. Jaipur and New Delhi: Rawat Publications.

Nongkynrih, A. Kyrham, 2002a, *Human Development in Khatar Shnong*. Shillong: Don Bosco Press.

Nongkynrih, A. Kyrham, 2002b, *Khasi Society of Meghalaya: A Sociological Understanding*. New Delhi: Indus Publishing Company.

Nora, Pierre, 1996, *Realms of Memory: The Construction of the French Past*, English language edition edited and with a foreword by Lawrence D. Kritzman. Translated by Arthur Goldhammer. New York: Columbia University Press.

North, D. C., 1990, *Institutions, Institutional Change and Economic Performance*. Cambridge, New York, Melbourne: Cambridge University Press.

NRB, 1999, National Reconstruction Bureau, Introduction, http://www.nrb.gov.pk/info/chairmans-message.htm; accessed December 2000.

NWFP Forest Department. *Working Plan for Alpuri: 1984–94*.

O'Brien, Karen L., 1998, *Sacrificing the Forest: Environmental and Social Struggles in Chiapas*. Boulder and Oxford: Westview Press.

Ong, Aihwa, 2000, *Flexible Citizenship*. Berkeley: University of California Press.

Orlove, Benjamin S. and David W. Guillet, 1985, "Theoretical and Methodological Considerations on the Study of Mountain Peoples: Reflections on the Idea of Subsistence Type and the Role of History in Human Ecology." *Mountain Research and Development*, vol. 5, no. 1, pp. 3–18.

Ortner, Sherry, 1978, *Sherpas through their Rituals*. Cambridge: Cambridge University Press.

Ortner, Sherry, 1989, *High Religion: A Cultural and Political History of Sherpa Buddhism*. Princeton: Princeton University Press.

Panday, Devendra Raj, 1983, "Foreign Aid and Nepal's Development: An Overview," in *Foreign Aid and Development in Nepal*. Kathmandu: Integrated Development Systems.
Panday, Devendra Raj, 1989, "Administrative Development in a Semi-Dependency: The Experience in Nepal." *Public Administration and Development*, no. 9, pp. 315–29.
Panday, Devendra Raj, 1998, *Transparency in the Context of Good Governance*. Lalitpur: Administrative Staff College.
Panday, Devendra Raj, 1999, *Nepal's Failed Development: Reflections on the Missions and the Maladies*. Kathmandu: Nepal South Asia Center.
Pandey, Gyanendra, 1983, "Rallying Round the Cow: Sectarian Strife in the Bhojpuri Region, c. 1888–1917," in Ranjit Guha, ed., *Subaltern Studies II: Writings on South Asian History and Society*. Delhi: Oxford University Press, pp. 60–129.
Pandey, Gyanendra, 2001, *Remembering Partition: Violence, Nationalism, and History in India*. Cambridge: Cambridge University Press.
Parajuli, P., 1998, "Beyond Capitalised Nature: Ecological Ethnicity as an Area of Conflict in the Regime of Globalisation." *Ecumene*, vol. 15, no. 2, pp. 186–217.
Pant, Govind Ballabh, 1922, *The Forest Problem in Kumaon: Forest Problems and National Uprisings in the Himalayan Region*, with a Commentary by Ajay S. Rawat. Nainital, U.P.: Gyanodaya Prakashan.
Pardo, S.L. and L.G. Löffler, 1969, "Shifting Cultivation in the Chittagong Hill Tracts, East Pakistan." *Jahrbuch des Südasieninstituts der Universität Heidelberg*, Wiesbaden.
Parish, Steven, 1996, *Hierarchy and Its Discontents: Culture and the Politics of Consciousness in Caste Society*. Philadelphia: University of Pennsylvania Press.
Parry, J.H., 1963, *The Age of Reconnaissance*. New York: Signet.
Parry, J.W., 1962, *Spices: Their Morphology, Histology, and Chemistry*. New York: Chemical Publications.
Parry, N.E., 1976 (1932), *The Lakhers*. Aizawl: Tribal Research Institute (reprint).
Pascal, J.-P., 1982, *Forest Map of South India—Mercara Mysore*. Karnataka and Kerala Forest Department and French Institute of Pondicherry.
Pascal, J.-P., 1986, *Explanatory Booklet on the Forest Map of South India*. Pondicherry: French Institute of Pondicherry.

Pascal, J.-P., 1988, *Wet Evergreen Forests of the Western Ghats in India: Ecology, Structure, Floristic Composition and Succession.* Travaux de la Section Technologique et Technique, Institut Français de Pondichéry, XX: 365.

Pascal, J.-P. and B.R. Ramesh, 1987, *A Field Key to the Trees and Lianas of the Evergreen Forests of the Western Ghats (India).* Pondicherry: French Institute of Pondicherry.

Pathak, Akhileshwara, 1994, *Contested Domains: The State, Peasants and Forests in Contemporary India.* New Delhi: Sage (in association with The Book Review Literary Trust).

Pathak, Shekhar, 1991, "Society, System and Environment in the Himalaya," in Ajay S. Rawat, ed., *History of Forestry in India.* New Delhi: Indus Publishing, pp. 326–36.

Pathak, Shekhar, 1998, "State, Society and Natural Resources in the Himalaya: Dynamics of Change in Colonial and Post-Colonial Uttarakhand," in Irmtraud Stellrecht, ed., *Karakorum—Hindukush—Himalaya: Dynamics of Change*, Part II. Köln: Rüdiger Köppe Verlag, pp. 167–86.

Pearson, M.N., 1981, *Coastal Western India: Studies From the Portuguese Records.* XCHR Studies Series No. 2. New Delhi: Concept Publishing.

Peers, Douglas M., 1995, *Between Mars and Mammon: Colonial Armies and the Garrison State in India 1819–1835.* London, New York: I.B. Tauris Publishers.

Pels, Peter, 1999, "The Rise and Fall of the Indian Aborigines: Orientalism, Anglicism, and the Emergence of an Ethnology of India, 1833–1869," in Peter Pels and Oscar Salemink, eds, *Colonial Subjects: Essays on the Practical History of Anthropology.* Ann Arbor: Michigan University Press.

Peluso, Nancy Lee, 1996, "Fruit Trees and Family Trees in an Anthropogenic Forest: Ethics of Access, Property Zones, and Environmental Change in Indonesia." *Comparative Studies in Society and History*, vol. 38, pp. 510–48.

Peluso, Nancy Lee and Michael Watts, 2001, "Violent Environments," in Nancy Lee Peluso and Michael Watts, eds, *Violent Environments.* Ithaca and London: Cornell University Press, pp. 3–38.

Peluso, Nancy Lee and Peter Vandergeest, 2001, "Genealogies of the Political Forest and Customary Rights in Indonesia, Malaysia, and Thailand." *The Journal of Asian Studies*, vol. 60, no. 3, August 2001, pp. 761–812.

Pemberton, John, 1994, *On the Subject of "Java."* Ithaca: Cornell University Press.
Perrett, Roy W., 1998, "Indigenous Rights and Environmental Justice," *Environmental Ethics*, vol. 20, no. 4, January.
Pfaff-Czarnecka, J., 1997, "Vestiges and Visions: Cultural Change in the Process of Nation-Building in Nepal," in David N. Gellner, J. Pfaff-Czarnecka, and John Whelpton, eds, *Nationalism and Ethnicity in a Hindu Kingdom: The Politics of Culture in Contemporary Nepal*. London: Harwood Academic Publishers, pp. 419–70.
PFRI, 2000, *Provincial Forest Resource Inventory, North-West Frontier Province. Draft Final Report*. KFW Kreditanstalt für Wiederaufbau.
Phayre, A.P., 1841, "Account of Arakan." *Journal of the Asiatic Society of Bengal*, vol. 13, no. 1, Calcutta.
Poffenberger, M., 1985, "The Resurgence of Community Forest Management in the Jungle Mahals of West Bengal," in D. Arnold and R. Guha, eds, *Nature, Culture and Imperialism*. Delhi: Oxford University Press.
Ponnappa, K.C., ed., 1997, *A Study of the Origins of Coorgs*. Bangalore.
Porath, Nathan, 2000, "The Re-appropriation of Sakai Land: The Case of Shrine in Riau (Indonesia)," in A. Abramson and D. Theodossopoulos, eds, *Land, Law and Environment: Mythical Land, Legal Boundaries*. London: Pluto Press.
Povinelli, Elizabeth, 2002, *The Cunning of Recognition: Indigenous Alterities and the Making of Australian Multiculturalism*. Durham, N.C.: Duke University Press.
Prasad, Archana, 2003, *Against Ecological Romanticism: Verrier Elwin and the Making of an Anti-Modern Tribal Identity*. New Delhi: Three Essays Collective.
Pratap, Ajay, 2000, *The Hoe and the Ax: An Ethnohistory of Shifting Cultivation in Eastern India*. Delhi: Oxford University Press.
Quigley, D., 1987, "Ethnicity Without Nationalism: The Newars of Nepal." *European Journal of Sociology*, vol. 28, pp. 152–70.
Quigley, D., 1993, *The Interpretation of Caste*. Oxford: Clarendon Press.
Rackham, Oliver, 2001, *Trees, Wood and Timber in Greek History*. Oxford: Leopard's Press.
Ragsdale, Todd, 1989, *Once a Hermit Kingdom: Ethnicity, Education and National Integration in Nepal*. Kathmandu: Ratna Pustak Bhandar.
Rahman, M. Anisur, 1993, *People's Self-Development. Perspectives on Participatory Action Research*. Dhaka, London, New Jersey: Zed-Books.

Rai, Savitha, 2003, "Hazardous Waste is Shipped from India to US Recycling Plant." *New York Times*, International/Asia Pacific Section, May 7.
Raj, Prakash, 1993, "National Integration or Destabilisation in Nepal?" *Economic and Political Monthly*, vol. 11, no. 5, pp. 30–3.
Rajan, Ravi, 1998, "Imperial Environmentalism or Environmental Imperialism? European Forestry, Colonial Foresters and the Agendas of Forest Management in British India 1800–1900," in Richard Grove, Vinita Damodaran and Satpal Sangwan, eds, *Nature and the Orient*. Delhi: Oxford University Press, pp. 324–71.
Rajput, A.B., 1962, "A Trek in the Hills of Chittagong." *Pakistan Quarterly*, vol. 10, no. 4.
Rajput, A.B., 1963, "Among the Murungs in Bandarban Forest." *Pakistan Quarterly*, vol. 11, no. 3.
Rajput, A.B., 1965, *The Tribes of Chittagong Hill Tracts*. Karachi, Dacca: Pakistan Publications.
Rajput, A.B., 1966, "The Primitive Arts of Pakistan." *Pakistan Quarterly*, vol. 14, no. 1.
Ramakrishnan, P.S., 1992, *Shifting Agriculture and SustainableDevelopment: An Interdisciplinary Study from North-Eastern India*. Man and the Biosphere Series, vol. 10, Paris: UNESCO/The Parthenon Publishing Group.
Ramakrishnan, P. S., U. M. Chandrashekara, C. Elouard, C.Z. Guilmoto, R.K. Maikhuri, K.S. Rao, S. Sankar and K.G. Saxena, 2000, *Mountain Biodiversity, Land Use Dynamics, and Traditional Ecological Knowledge*. New Delhi, Calcutta: Oxford and IBH Publishing.
Ramakrishnan, P.S., K.G. Saxena, and U.M. Chandrashekara, eds, 1998, *Conserving the Sacred for Biodiversity Management*. New Delhi: Oxford and IBH Publishing.
Ramaswamy, V., 1985, *Textiles and Weavers in Medieval South India*. New Delhi: Oxford University Press.
Ramesh, B.R., and J.P. Pascal, 1997, *Atlas of Endemics of the Western Ghats (India)*. Pondicherry: French Institute of Pondicherry.
Rana, Pramode Shamshere, 1999, *A Chronicle of Rana Rule*. Kathmandu: Nepal Lithographing Company.
Ranchi District Gazetteer, Calcutta, 1917.
Rangarajan, Mahesh, 1996, *Fencing the Forest: Conservation and Ecological Change in India's Central Provinces 1860–1914*. Delhi: Oxford University Press (hardback).
Rangarajan, Mahesh, 1999, "Troubled Legacy: A Brief History of Wildlife

Preservation in India." *Occasional Paper No. 44*. Delhi: Nehru Memorial Museum and Library.

Rangarajan, Mahesh, 1999, *Fencing the Forest: Conservation and Ecological Change in India's Central Provinces 1860–1914*. Delhi: Oxford University Press (paperback).

Rangarajan, Mahesh, ed., 1999, *The Oxford Anthology of Indian Wildlife: Hunting and Shooting (Volume I); Watching and Conserving (Volume II)*. Delhi: Oxford University Press.

Rangarajan, Mahesh, 2000, "Battles for Nature: Contesting Wildlife Conservation in 20th Century India," paper presented at Tallahassee Florida State University. German-American Historical Institute Seminar, December 1–2.

Rangarajan, Mahesh, 2001, *India's Wildlife History: An Introduction*. New Delhi: Permanent Black.

Rao, B.S. and K.M. Lokesh, 1998, *Coorg Invented*. Madikeri, Forum for Kodagu Studies.

Rawat, Ajay Singh, 1989, *History of Garhwal 1358–1947: An Erstwhile Kingdom in the Himalayas*. New Delhi: Indus Publishing Company.

Rawat, Ajay Singh, ed., 1991, *History of Forestry in India*. New Delhi: Indus Publishing.

Rawat, Ajay Singh, 1992a, *History and Growth of Panchayati Forests in the Kumaon Himalaya*. New Delhi: Centre for Contemporary Studies. Nehru Memorial Museum and Library, Occasional Papers on Perspectives in Indian Development: 31.

Rawat, Ajay Singh, 1992b, *History of Forest Management in Tehri Garhwal State*. New Delhi: Nehru Memorial Museum and Library, Occasional Papers on Perspectives in Indian Development: 32.

Ray, H., 1986, *Monastery and Guild: Commerce under the Satavahanas*. New Delhi: Oxford University Press.

Reid, A., 1993a, *Southeast Asia in the Age of Commerce: 1450–1680, Volume Two, Expansion and Crisis*. New Haven: Yale University Press.

Reid, J.A., 1912, *Final Report on the Survey and Settlement Operations in Ranchi 1902–1910*. Calcutta.

Ribbentrop, B., 1899, *Forestry in British India*, Calcutta.

Richards, J.F., James Hagen, and Ed Haynes, 1985, "Changing Land Use in Bihar, Punjab and Haryana, 1850–1970." *Modern Asian Studies*, vol. 19, no. 3, pp. 699–732.

Richter, G., 1870, *Gazetteer of Coorg*. Delhi: Low Price Publications.

Ricketts, H., 1853, "Report on the Forays of the Wild Tribes of the Chittagong Frontier, 1847," two reports, in *Selections from the Records of the Bengal Government*. Calcutta: Bengal Secretariat Press.

Ricketts, Henry, 1855, "Report on the Agency Administration," in *Bengal Selections*, vol. XX. Calcutta.

Rose, Leo and M. Fisher, 1970, *The Politics of Nepal: Persistence and Change in an Asian Monarchy*. Ithaca: Cornell University Press.

Rose, Leo, 1971, *Nepal: Strategy for Survival*. Berkeley: University of California Press.

Rose, Leo and M. Landau, 1977, "Bureaucratic Politics and Development in Nepal," in B.N. Panday, ed., *Leadership in South Asia*. Delhi: Vikas Publishing House.

Roy, A.K., 1979, "Sal Means Jharkhand, Sagwan Means Bihar." *Sunday* (weekly) Calcutta, April 8.

Roy, A.K., 1980, "Gua Massacre of Tribals." *Economic and Political Weekly*, vol. 15, no. 38, p. 1123.

Roy, Arundhati, 2004, *An Ordinary Person's Guide to Empire*. Cambridge: Southend Press.

Roy, Rajkumari Chandra Kalindi, 2000, "Land Rights of the Indigenous Peoples of the Chittagong Hill Tracts, Bangadesh." Copenhagen: IWGIA Document, no. 99.

Roy, S.C., 1925, *The Birhors*. Ranchi.

Roy, S.C., 1928, *Oraons Religion and Customs*. Calcutta.

Saberwal, Vasant K., 2000, "Environmental Alarm and Institutionalized Conservation in Himachal Pradesh, 1865–1994," in A. Agrawal and K. Sivaramakrishnan, eds, *Agrarian Environments*. Durham and London: Duke University Press.

SAFI, 2000, *Charter of Demands. Sarhad Awami Forestry Ittehad*. Islamabad: Sungi Development Foundation.

Sahadevan, P.C., 1965, *Cardamom*. Kerala: Agricultural Information Service, Department of Agriculture.

Sahlins, Marshall, 1992, *Anahulu: The Anthropology of History in the Kingdom of Hawaii*. Chicago: University of Chicago Press.

Sainath, P. 1996, *Everybody Loves a Good Drought: Stories from India's Poorest Districts*. Delhi: Penguin.

Sahlins, Marshall, 1995, *How "Natives" Think about Captain Cook, For Example*. Chicago: University of Chicago Press.

Saklani, Atul, 1987, *The History of a Himalayan Princely State: Change, Conflicts and Awakening. An Interpretative History of Princely State of Tehri Garhwal, U.P.; A.D. 1815 to 1949 A.D.* Delhi: Durga Publications.

Sanders, H.L., 1968, "Marine Benthic Diversity: A Comparative Study." *American Naturalist*, vol. 102, pp. 243–82.

Sangma, Milton S., 1981, *History and Culture of the Garos*. New Delhi: Books Today.

Saraswati, A.R., 1926, "Political Maxims of the Emperor Poet, Krishnadeva Raya." *Journal of Indian History*, vol. 4, no. 3, pp. 61–88.

Sarin, Madhu, 1996, *Joint Forest Management: The Haryana Experience*. Environment and Development Series. Ahmedabad: Centre for Environment Education.

Sarkar, Sumit, 2000, "Orientalism Revisited: Saidian Frameworks in the Writing of Modern Indian History," in Vinayak Chaturvedi, ed., *Mapping Subaltern Studies and the Postcolonial*. London: Verso, pp. 239–55.

Sattar, Abdus, 1971, *In the Sylvan Shadows*. Dacca: Saqib Brothers.

Sax, William S., 2002, *Dancing the Self: Personhood and Performance in the Pandava lila of Garhwal*. New York: Oxford University Press.

Schama, Simon, 1995, *Landscape and Memory*. New York: A.A. Knopf.

Schendel, Willem van, 1992a, "The Invention of the 'Jummas': State Formation and Ethnicity in Southeastern Bangladesh." *Modern Asian Studies*, vol. 26, no. 1, pp. 95–128.

Schendel, Willem van, ed., 1992b, *Francis Buchanan in Southeast Bengal (1798)*. International Specialized Book Services.

Schendel, Willem van, 2001, "Who Speaks for the Nation? Nationalist Rhetoric and the Challenge of Cultural Pluralism in Bangladesh," in Willem van Schendel and Erik J. Zürcher, eds, *Identity Politics in Central Asia and the Muslim World: Nationalism, Ethnicity and Labour in the Twentieth Century*. London, New York: I.B. Tauris Publishers.

Schendel, Willem van, Wolfgang Mey, and Aditya K. Dewan, 2000, *The Chittagong Hill Tracts: Living in a Borderland*. Bangkok: White Lotus Press.

Scott, James C., 1976, *The Moral Economy of the Peasant: Subsistence and Rebellion in South East Asia*. New Haven: Yale University Press.

Scott, James C., 1985, *Weapons of the Weak: Everyday Forms of Peasant Resistance*. New Haven: Yale University Press.

Scott, James C., 1990, *Domination and the Arts of Resistance: Hidden Transcripts*. New Haven: Yale University Press.

Scott, James C., 1998, *Seeing Like a State: How Certain Schemes to Improve the Human Condition Have Failed*. New Haven: Yale University Press.

Scott, James C., 2000, "Foreword," in Arun Agrawal and K. Sivaramakrishnan, eds, *Agrarian Environments: Resources, Representations, and Rule in India*. Durham and London: Duke University Press.

Seddon, David, 1987, *Nepal: A State of Poverty*. New Delhi: Vikas Publishing House.

Seligman, C.G. and B.Z. Seligman, 1911, *The Veddas*. Cambridge: The University Press.

Sengupta, Nirmal, ed., 1982, *Fourth World Dynamics, Jharkhand*. Delhi.

Sever, Adrian, 1993, *Nepal Under the Ranas*. Delhi: Oxford University Press.

Sever, Adrian, 1996, *Aspects of Modern Nepalese History*. New Delhi: Vikas Publishing House.

Sewell, R., 1982 [1900], *A Forgotten Empire (Vijayanagar): A Contribution to the History of India*. Delhi: Asian Educational Services, reprint.

Shanin, Teodor, 1997, "The Idea of Progress," in Majid Rahnema and Victoria Bawtree, eds, *The Postdevelopment Reader*. London: Zed, pp. 65–72.

Sharma, Anju, Richard Mahapatra, and Clifford Polycarp, 2002, "Dialogue of the Deaf," *Down to Earth*, vol. 11, no. 9, pp. 25–33.

Sharma, Ganesh Raj, 1989, "Monarchy and the Democratic Development in Contemporary Nepal," in Kamal P. Malla, ed., *Nepal: Perspectives on Continuity and Change*. Kirtipur: Tribhuvan University.

Sharma, Jan, 1997, *Democracy Without Roots*. Delhi: Book Faith India.

Sharma, Kumud, n.d., "Role and Participation of Women in the 'Chipko' Movement in the Uttarakhand Region in Uttar Pradesh," in Kumud Sharma and Meera Velayudhan, *Women in Struggle: Two Case Studies of Peasants and Workers*. New Delhi: Centre for Women's Development Studies.

Sharma, Mukul, 2001, "Nature and Nationalism." *Frontline*, February 16, pp. 94–6.

Sharma, Mukul, 2002, "Saffronizing Green." *Seminar* 516 August, pp. 26–30.

Sharma, Prayag Raj, 1994, "Bahuns in the Nepali State." *Himal*, vol. 7, no. 2, pp. 41–5.

Sharma, Prayag Raj, 1997, "Nation-Building, Multi-Ethnicity, and the Hindu State," in David N. Gellner, J. Pfaff-Czarnecka, and John Whelpton, eds, *Nationalism and Ethnicity in a Hindu Kingdom: The Politics of Culture in Contemporary Nepal.* London: Harwood Academic Publishers, pp. 471–9.

Shiva, Vandana, 1988, *Staying Alive: Women, Ecology and Survival in India.* New Delhi: Kali for Women.

Shrestha, M.K., 1975, "Administrative Innovations under King Birendra." *Prashasan: The Nepalese Journal of Public Administration,* February.

Shrestha, M.K., 1981, "Policy Reforms in Nepalese Civil Services." *Prashasan: The Nepalese Journal of Public Administration,* November.

Silitoe, Paul, 1998, "The Development of Indigenous Knowledge. A New Applied Anthropology." *Current Anthropology,* vol. 39, no. 2.

Simpson, E.H., 1949, "Measurement of Diversity." *Nature,* vol. 163, p. 688.

Singh, K.S., ed., 1983, *Tribal Movements in India,* vol. 2. Delhi: South Asia Books.

Sinha, A. C., 1993, *Beyond the Trees, Tigers and Tribes: Historical Sociology of the Eastern Himalayan Forests.* New Delhi: Har-Anand Publications.

Sinopoli, C.M. and K.D. Morrison, 1996, "Dimensions of Imperial Control: The Vijayanagara Capital." *American Anthropologist,* vol. 97, no. 1, pp. 83–96.

Siu, Helen F., 1996, "Remade in Hong Kong: Weaving Into the Chinese Cultural Tapestry," in David Faure and Tao Tao Liu, eds, *Unity and Diversity: Local Cultures and Identities in China.* Hong Kong: Hong Kong University Press, pp. 177–97.

Siu, Helen F., 1997, "Recycling Tradition: Culture, History and Political Economy in the Chrysanthemum Festivals of South China," in Sally Humphreys, ed., *Cultures of Scholarship.* Ann Arbor: University of Michigan Press, pp. 139–85.

Sivaramakrishnan, K., 1995, "Colonialism and Forestry in India: Imagining the Past in Present Politics." *Comparative Studies in Society and History,* vol. 37, no. 1, pp. 3–40.

Sivaramakrishnan, K., 1997, "A Limited Forest Conservancy in Southwest Bengal, 1864–1912." *The Journal of Asian Studies,* vol. 56, no. 1, pp. 75–113.

Sivaramakrishnan, K., 1998, *Regional Development Regimes and Local Knowledge: The Production of Scientific Forestry in Bengal, 1893–1939.* Yale Working Paper series.

Sivaramakrishnan, K., 1999, *Modern Forests: State-Making and Environmental Change in Colonial Eastern India.* Delhi: Oxford University Press.

Sivaramakrishnan, K., 2000, "Crafting the Public Sphere in the Forests of

West Bengal: Democracy, Development, and Political Action." *American Ethnologist*, vol. 27, no. 2, pp. 431–62.
Sivaramakrishnan, K., 2001, "Situating the Subaltern: History and Anthropology in the *Subaltern Studies Project*," in David Ludden, ed., *Reading Subaltern Studies: Critical History, Contested Meaning, and the Globalisation of South Asia*. Delhi: Permanent Black.
Sivaramakrishnan, K., 2002, "Conservation Crossroads: Indian Wildlife at the Intersection of Global Imperatives, Nationalist Anxieties, and Local Assertion," in Mahesh Rangarajan and Vasant Saberwal, eds, *Battles over Nature: Science and the Politics of Wildlife Conservation*. New Delhi: Permanent Black, pp. 388–417.
Sivaramakrishnan, K., 2003, "Nationalism and the Writing of Environmental Histories." *Seminar*, vol. 522, February, pp. 25–30.
Sivaramakrishnan, K., 2004, "Postcolonialism: Nature, and the Politics of Difference in India," in David Nugent and Joan Vincent, eds, *A Companian to the Anthropology of Politics*. Oxford: Blackwell, pp. 367–82.
Sivaramakrishnan, K. and Arun Agrawal, eds, 2003, *Regional Modernities: The Cultural Politics of Development in India*. Stanford: Stanford University Press.
Skar, Harold O., 1995, "Myths of Origin: The Janajati Movement, Local Traditions, Nationalism and Identities in Nepal." *Contribution to Nepalese Studies*, vol. 22, no. 1, pp. 31–42.
Skaria, Ajay, 1999, *Hybrid Histories: Forests, Frontiers and Wildness in Western India*. Delhi: Oxford University Press.
Smith, Christiaan, 1973, "Planned Shifting Cultivation. A Case Study of Shifting Cultivation and Regional Development in Northern Tanzania." *Zeitschrift für ausländische Landwirtschaft*, vol. 12, no. 1, Berlin.
Smith, Mark, 1999, *Ecologism*. Minneapolis: University of Minnesota Press.
Sökefeld, Martin, 1999, "Debating Self, Identity, and Culture in Anthropology." *Current Anthropology*, vol. 40, no. 4, pp. 417–47.
Sollors, W., 1989, *The Invention of Ethnicity*. New York: Oxford University Press.
Sopher, D.E., 1963, "Population Dislocation in the Chittagong Hills." *Oriental Geographer*, vol. 53.
Sopher, D.E., 1964, "The Swidden/Wet Rice Transition Zone in the Chittagong Hills." *Annals of the Association of American Geographers*, vol. 54, no. 1.

Southwold-Llewellyn, S., 2002a, "The Changing Value of Forests: Conflicts within the Moral Economy of a Pukhtun Community in NWFP, Pakistan," paper presented for the Panel: Social Change and the Moral Economy. European Association of Social Anthropologists, Copenhagen, August 14–17.

Southwold-Llewellyn, S., 2002b, "The Unintended Consequences of Government Controlled Forest Harvesting on Rural Livelihoods and Sociopolitical Relations: A Case of an Agro-pastoralist Community in NWFP, Pakistan," paper presented at the 17th European Conference on Modern South Asian Studies, Heidelberg, September 9–14.

Southwold-Llewellyn, S., 2002c, "Rights to Forests and Alpine Pastures: The Consequences of Land Registration in Shangla District, NWFP, Pakistan," Conference on Land Registration and Spatial Planning in Transition Countries, Wageningen, October 31–November 1.

Spencer, Metta, 1998, "When States Divide," in Metta Spencer, ed., *Separatism, Democracy and Disintegration.* Lanham, Md: Rowman and Littlefield, pp. 43–68.

Spielmann, Hans-Jürgen, 1968, "Die Bawm-Zo. Eine Chin-Gruppe in den Chittagong Hill Tracts (Ostpakistan)," dissertation, Ruprecht-Karl-Univiersity, Heidelberg.

Springer, Jenny, 2000, "State Power and Agricultural Transformation in Tamil Nadu," in A. Agrawal and K. Sivaramakrishnan, eds, *Agrarian Environments: Resources, Representations, and Rule in India.* Durham: Duke University Press, pp. 86–106.

Srinivas, M.N., ed., 1951, *Religion and Society among the Coorgs of South India.* Oxford: Oxford University Press.

Stebbing, E.P., 1926, *The Forests of India, Volumes I–III.* New Delhi: A.J. Reprints Agency, reprint 1982.

Stein, Burton, 1982, "South India: Some General Considerations of the Region and its Early History, in T. Raychaudhuri and I. Habib, eds, *The Cambridge Economic History of India, Vol. 1: c. 1200–c. 1750.* New Delhi: Orient Longman, pp. 14–42.

Stein, Burton, 1989, *Thomas Munro: The Origins of the Colonial State and His Vision of Empire.* Delhi: Oxford University Press.

Stevenson, H.N.C., 1943, *The Economics of the Central Chin Tribes.* Bombay: The Times of India Press.

Stewart, M.A., 1991, "Rice, Water and Power: Landscapes of Domination

and Resistance in the Low Country, 1790–1880," *Environmental History Review*, vol. 15, no 3, Fall, pp. 46–64.
Stiles, D., 1993, "Hunter-Gatherer Trade in Wild Forest Products in the early Centuries AD with the Port of Broach, India." *Asian Perspectives*, vol. 32, no. 2, pp. 153–67.
Stokes, Eric, 1959, *The English Utilitarians and India*. Cambridge: Cambridge University Press.
Stokes, Eric, 1974, *The Peasant and the Raj: Studies in Agrarian Society and Peasant Rebellion in Colonial India*. Oxford: Oxford University Press.
Stracey, P.D., 1957, "On the Status of the Great Indian Rhinoceros in Nepal." *Journal of the Bombay Natural History Society*, vol. 54, no. 3, pp. 763–6.
Subrahmanyam, Sanjay, 1984, "The Portuguese, the Port of Basrur, and the Rice Trade, 1600–50." *Indian Economic and Social History Review*, vol. 21, pp. 433–62.
Subrahmanyam, Sanjay, 1990, *The Political Economy of Commerce: Southern India, 1500–1650*. Cambridge: Cambridge University Press.
Subrahmanyam, Sanjay, 1993, *The Portuguese Empire in Asia, 1500–1700: A Political and Economic History*. London: Longmans.
Subrahmanyam, Sanjay, 2001, "Statemaking and History-making in Early Modern South India," in Sanjay Subrahmanyam, *Penumbral Visions: Making Politics in Early Modern South India*. Ann Arbor: University of Michigan Press, pp. 186–219.
Subrahmanyam, Sanjay, 2002, "Profiles in Transition: Of Adventurers and Administrators in South India, 1750–1810." *Indian Economic and Social History Review*, vol. 39, nos. 2 and 3, pp. 197–231.
Subramanian, Ajantha, 2003, "Mukkuvar Modernity: Development as a Cultural Identity," in K. Sivaramakrishnan and Arun Agrawal, eds, *Regional Modernities: The Cultural Politics of Development in India*. Stanford: Stanford University Press, pp. 262–85.
Suleri, Q. A., 2001, *Regional Study on Forest Policy and Institutional Reforms; Final Report of the Pakistan Case Study*. Manila, The Philippines: Asian Development Bank.
Sultan-I-Rome, 1999, "Merger of Swat State with Pakistan: Causes and Effects." MARC Occasional Papers No. 14. Modern Asia Research Centre. Geneva: IUED.
Sundar, Nandini, 1997, *Subalterns and Sovereigns: An Anthropological History of Bastar, 1854-1996*. New Delhi: Oxford University Press.

Sundar, Nandini, 2000, "Unpacking the Joint in Joint-Forestry Management." *Development and Change*, vol. 31, no. 1, pp. 255–79.

Sundar, Nandini and Roger Jeffrey, 1999, "Introduction," in Roger Jeffrey and Nandini Sundar, eds, *A New Moral Economy for India's Forests? Discourses of Community and Participation*. New Delhi and London: Sage, pp. 15–54.

Sutton, Deborah, 2002, "Horrid Sights and Customary Rights: The Toda Funeral on the Colonial Nilgiris." *Indian Economic and Social History Review*, vol. 39, no. 1, pp. 45–70.

Thapar, Romila and Majid Hayat Siddiqui, 1991, "Tribals in History: The Case of Chota Nagpur," in Dipankar Gupta, ed., *Social Stratification*. Delhi: Oxford University Press, pp. 419–28.

Thomas, T., Peter Sheppard, and Richard Walter, 2001, "Landscape Violence and Social Bodies: Ritualised Architecture in a Solomon Islands Society." *Journal of the Royal Anthropological Institute*, vol. 7, no. 3.

Thompson, E.P., 1991 [1963], *The Making of the English Working Class*. London: Penguin Books.

Thompson, E.P., 1993, *Customs in Common: Studies in Traditional Popular Culture*. New York: The New Press.

Thompson, Sir Robert, 1966, *Defeating Communist Insurgency. The Lessons of Malaya and Vietnam*. New York, Washington: Frederick A. Praeger.

Three Chiefs' Report, 1963, "Three Chiefs Report on Rehabilitation and Development of Chittagong Hill Tracts." Chakma Raja's Archive, Rangamati.

Tiwari, B.K., S.K. Barik, and R.S. Tripathi, 1999, *Sacred Forests of Meghalaya: Biological and Cultural Diversity*. Shillong: Regional Centre, National Afforestation and Eco-Development Board, North-Eastern Hill University.

Tripura, Prashanta, 2000, "Culture, Identity and Development," in Philip Gain, ed., *The Chittagong Hill Tracts. Life and Nature at Risk*. Dhaka: Society for Environment and Human Development.

Tsing, Anna Lowenhaupt, 1993, *In the Realm of the Diamond Queen: Marginality in an Out-of-the-way Place*. Princeton: Princeton University Press.

Tucker, Richard P., 1982, "The Forest of the Western Himalayas: The Legacy of British Colonial Administration." *Journal of Forest History*, July, pp. 112–23.

Vail, Leroy, 1989, *The Creation of Tribalism in Southern Africa*. Berkeley: University of California Press.

Vartak, V.D. and M. Gadgil, 1981, "Studies on Sacred Groves along the Western Ghats from Maharashtra and Goa: Role of Beliefs and Folklore," in S.K. Jain, ed., *Glimpses of Indian Ethnobotany*. New Delhi: Oxford and IBH, pp. 272–94.

Vasan, Sudha, 2002, "Ethnography of the Forest Guard: Contrasting Discourses, Conflicting Roles and Policy Implementation," *Economic and Political Weekly*, vol. 37, no. 40, October 5, pp. 4125–33.

Vasavi, A.R., 1999, *Harbingers of Rain: Land and Life in South India*. New Delhi: Oxford University Press.

View of the Three Chiefs' Report, 1963, "View of the Three Chiefs on Post-War Reconstruction." Chakma Raja's Archive, Rangamati.

Vijaya, T.P., 2000, "Contemporary Society and Land Tenure: The Social Structure of Kodagu," in P.S. Ramakrishnan, U.M. Chandrashekara *et al.*, *Mountain Biodiversity, Land Use Dynamics and Traditional Ecological Knowledge*. New Delhi, Oxford and IBH Publishing Co. Pvt. Ltd., pp. 44–53.

Vogelsang, W., 2002, *The Afghans*. Oxford: Blackwell.

von Lengerke, H. and F. Blasco, 1989, "The Nilgiri Environment," in P. Hockings, ed., *Blue Mountains: TheEthnography and Biogeography of a South Indian Region*. Delhi: Oxford University Press, pp. 20–78.

Wallerstein, I., 1974, *The Modern World System, Vol. 1*. New York: Academic Press.

Ward, B.S., 1821, "Geographical and Statistical Memoir of a Survey of the Neelgherry Mountains in the Province of Coimbatore," in H.B. Grigg, 1880, *The Manual of Nilagiri District*, pp. lx–lxxix.

Warner, Katherine, 1991, *Shifting Cultivators: Local Technical Knowledge and Natural Resource Management in the Humid Tropics*. Rome: FAO/ Forest, Trees and People, Community Forest Note 8.

Warren, Louis, 1997, *The Hunter's Game: Poachers and Conservationists in Twentieth-century America*. New Haven: Yale University Press.

Washbrook, David, 1999, "India, 1818–1860: The Two Faces of Colonialism," in Andrew Porter, ed., *The Oxford History of the British Empire: The Nineteenth Century*. Oxford: Oxford University Press.

Webb, W.E., 1966, "Land Capacity Classification and Land Use Planning in the Chittagong Hill Tracts of East Pakistan." *Proceedings of the Sixth World Forestry Congress*, vol. 3, Madrid.

Weber, Thomas, 1988, *Hugging the Trees: The Story of the Chipko Movement*. Delhi: Viking.

Weiner, Myron, 1978, *Sons of the Soil: Migration and Ethnic Conflict in India*. Princeton: Princeton University Press.

Whitcombe, Elizabeth, 1972, *Agrarian Conditions in Northern India, I*. Berkeley: University of California Press.

Whitehead, J., 2002, "Mapping History onto Landscape: Space against Place in the Narmada Valley." *Economic and Political Weekly*, vol. 37, April 4.

Williams, Raymond, 1985, *Keywords: A Vocabulary of Culture and Society*, revised edition. New York: Oxford University Press.

Wilson, Jon, 2000, "Governing Property, Making Law: Land, Local Society and Colonial Rule in Bengal, c. 1785–1830," unpublished PhD thesis, Faculty of Modern History, University of Oxford.

Woodburn, J., 1980, "Hunters and Gatherers Today and Reconstructions of the Past," in E. Gellner, ed., *Soviet and Western Anthropology*. New York: Columbia University Press, pp. 95–117.

Wootton, David, ed., 1996, *Modern Political Thought: Readings from Machiavelli to Nietzsche*. Indianapolis/Cambridge: Hackett Publishing Company.

Xaxa, Virginius, 1999, "Tribes as Indigenous Peoples of India." *Economic and Political Weekly*, December 18, pp. 3589–95.

Yohannan, T.M., P.N. Radhakrishnan Nair, N.G.K. Pillai, and P.L. Ammini, 2000, *Marine Fisheries in Kerala*, mimeo draft as appendix for Balakrishnan II Report.

Yorke, M.P., 1976, "Decisions and Analysis: Political Structure and Discourse among Ho Tribals of India," PhD thesis, School of Oriental and African Studies, London.

Zagarell, A., 1994, "State and Community in the Nilgiri Mountains," *Michigan Academician*, vol. 26, no. 1, pp. 183–204.

Zagarell, A., 1997, "Megalithic Graves of the Nilgiri Hills and the Moyar Ditch," in P. Hockings, ed., *Blue Mountains Revisited: Cultural Studies on the Nilgiri Hills*. Delhi: Oxford University Press, pp. 23–73.

Zagarell, A., 2002, "Gender and Social Organization in the Reliefs of the Nilgiri Hills," in K.D. Morrison and L.L. Junker, eds, *Forager-Traders in South and Southeast Asia: Long-Term Histories*. Cambridge: Cambridge University Press, pp. 77–104.

Zimmermann, Francis, 1983, *Remarks on the Conception of the Body in Ayurvedic Medicine, South Asian Digest of Regional Writing*, vol. 8, pp. 10–25.

Zoller, Claus Peter, 1994, "Saying Good-bye the Himalayan Way," in Dilip Chitre *et al.*, eds, *Tender Ironies: A Tribute to Lothar Lutze*. New Delhi: Manohar Publishers.

Zoller, Claus Peter, 1996, "Die Panduan. Ein mündliches Mahabharata-Epos aus dem Garhwal-Himalaya," Habilitation thesis, University of Heidelberg.

INDEX

Page numbers in italics indicate figures

A'chik National Volunteers Council
   (ANVC) 174, 176
Abbott. Col J. 96
Aboriginal rights. *See* indigenous rights
Absolutism 74
Act(s)
   Draft Forest (1999), NWFP 90, 91,
      111n.9
   Forest (1878), NWFP 101, 106
   Forest (1927), NWFP 106, 107
   Government of Nepal (1951) 299
   Indian Forest (1865) 100, 101
   Kerala Marine Fisheries Regulation
      253
   Land Transfer (1971), Meghalaya 178
   National Parks, Nepal 298
   Private 72
Adivasi(s) 24, 30, 43
   assertion of indigeneity 8, 25
   concept of 127
   identity. *See* Adivasi identity
   political significance of the term 142,
      143
   protest movements 33. *See also* protest
      movements
Adivasi identity 21, 116
   emergence of 142
   political orientation under JMM 132
   politicization of 140
   role of Christian missionaries 128
   regional 129–30, 132, 134
   See also Tribe(s)/tribal(s)
Adivasi Mahasabha 128–9, 130

Afghanistan 275
Agrawal, Arun 116, 171
Agriculturalists 48
   foragers and, interdependence
      between 13, 47, 50, 63
Agriculture
   expansion in Western Ghats 48,
      53–5
   expansion of, effect on forests in
      Nilgiris 55
   settled *vs.* shifting agriculture 173,
      258–9, 261
   swidden. *See* Shifting cultivation
   wet rice 47, 49, 54
Aiyappa, Lord 219
Ajmir (NWFP) 276, 277, *278*
   agro-pastoral system, change in 277
   forest survey 279–80
   individual ownership of forests 280
   state control over forests 279, 280
   state controlled commercial felling
      in 280
   value of forests 280
   rights to fuelwood. *See* fuelwood
   See also Bandas
Akhund Khel, NWFP 276, 277
   sub-khels of 292
   rights in banda 281, 286. *See also*
      Bandas
All Bodo Students Union 5
Allen, W.J. 125
Aloysius, G. 24
Alpine pastures, of NWFP. *See* Bandas

American Indians
  subsistence conservation practices of 139
  relationship with Amazonian landscape 127
Amuktamalyada 55
Anderson, Benedict 6, 23
Aralam Wildlife Sanctuary 204
Araya caste 241
Archer, William 126
Areeparampil, Father Mathew 135, 138
Arnold, David 30
Artisanal fisherfolk. *See* Kerala fisherfolk
Ascoli, F.D. 260
Asian Development Bank, policy regarding indigenous people of CHT 270–1
Autonomous district councils in Meghalaya 27, 171, 175, 176
  creation of 175
  forest management by 173, 182, 195n.51
  jurisdiction over land and forest 171, 175
  opposition to 177
  timber trade under 191
Autonomy
  movements. *See* movements
  tribal, under Sixth Schedule of Indian Constitution 27, 175, 176, 180
Ayan (grass allowance) 81

Babri Mosque 24
Babu Paul Committee, on fisheries in Kerala 249
Badaga shifting cultivators 55, 67, 82, 83
  and Toda, social relations between 82–3
  land rights of 67
Badneitei, concept of 291
Bahadur Jung 299, 300
Bahuguna, Sunderlal 25, 159, 160
  views on development 160
Balakrishnan Nair Committee, on trawling 250

Ball, Valentine 117, 121
Bandas (alpine forests and pastures), NWFP 276, 277, 279, 295n.1
  as communal property 281
  effect of violence on management of 292–3
  impact of state-controlled commercial felling on shareholders of 289, 294
  management of, differences between shareholders 282, 285–91, 292, 293–4
  non-shareholders access to 274, 281, 283, 285, 286, 294
  ownership of 279–80
  reification of rights in 281
  relationship between shareholders and tenants 291–2
  right to shares in 280, 281
  royalty shareholders. *See* royalty shareholders
Bangladesh 1, 4, 256
  and Bengali nationalism 268
  nation-building and development planning in 256
  negation of tribal identity in 268–9
  population movements in hills of 257
  state developmental intervention in the hills 26, 27
  state perception of tribal culture 263, 265, 266, 268
  tribals *vs.* plains people 264
  World Bank policy regarding indigenous people of 270–1
  See also Chittagong Hill Tracts
Bannerjee, Mukulika 289
Bant tribe 57
Barbhum 120
Bardia National Park 34–5
Barth, Fredrik 290
Baruah, Sanjib 175
Bauris 131
Bayo Urubanka River 122
Ben-Habib, Seyla 9
Bengali nationalism, in Bangladesh 268
Bhabha, Homi 140
Bharatiya Janata Party 9, 141

INDEX

Bhatt, Chandi Prasad, views on human–forest relationship 159
Bhatt, Nina 34
Bhattacharya, Neeladri 75
Bhils 58, 73
Bhurty system of revenue assessment 81
Birendra, Bir Bikram Shah Dev, King 298
Birhors 123
Birsa Munda uprising in Chotanagpur 125, 126
Birsa Seva Dal 132, 137
Boat seines, ban in Kerala 240, 247, 250
Bodley, James 116
Bodoland 6
Bongas 123
Brahmagiri Wildlife Sanctuary 200, 204
  canopy cover of 213
  dominant species in 211, 213, *215*
  endemic species in 211, *212*
  species richness of 209, *210*
  structural analysis of 206, *207*, *208*
Brahmins as landowners 57
Brandis, D. 98, 100
Brewer, John 72
British
  annexation of Chittagong Hill Tracts 257–8
  aspirations over Malakand Division in NWFP 97–8
  control over Nilgiris 67
  demand for Malabar teak 72–3
  East India Company. *See* East India Company
  property rights in Nilgiris 20. *See also* Nilgiri Hills
  relations with tribals of Malakand Division in NWFP 101
  settlement in Nilgiris 66, 67, 68
  territory, in pre-Partition Pakistan 93, *94*, 96
  timber requirements, debates over 98–9
  See also Colonial
Buchanan, Francis 56

Bureaucracy
  Nepalese. *See* Nepalese bureaucracy
  forest, in NWFP. *See* Forest bureaucracy

Calicut 51
Cannanore 51
Caratini, C. 49
Cardamom
  cultivation 57, 59–60
  Roman market for 47
  trade in 51, 53
Cartaz, system of 52
Castelle, Manuel 21
Cederlöf, Gunnel 14, 17, 20, 43, 233, 242
Central Marine Fisheries Research Institute 249
Chakmas 116, 263, 267
  identity of 116
Chakma, A.B. 268
Chakrabarty, Dipesh 23
Chakri, in Nepal 308, 310, 315
  cash as form of 312
  culture of 311–14
  features of 311–12
  promotions and 313
Chamakkala fisherfolk. *See* Kerala, fisherfolk of
Chamakkala fishing village 233, 235
Chamier, H.J. 78, 79
  notion of the Toda 80
Chatterjee, Partha 5, 23
Chaukidari tax 126
Chenchus 58
Cherrapunji 171, 186
Chin people 26
Chipko movement 152, 153, 157, 158–62
  debates on importance of forests and 160
  emergence of public sphere 161
  evolution of political awareness and 160–1
  nature as a dimension in 160
Chitral, NWFP 92
Chittagong Hill Tracts (CHT) 116, 255, 256, 264

Asian Development Bank policy
    in 270–1
British annexation of 257–8
colonial intervention in 25–6
colonial migration strategies 26
colonial perception of people of 258,
    262
dam project in 265–6
dismantling of communities in 26, 27,
    257, 269
ecological warfare in 26
effect of development intervention
    on 26
Forestal Survey of 266
forest conservation, role of village
    communities in 261
forests of 25
indigenous knowledge, negation in
    development activities 256, 269
indigenous land use system 261. See
    also shifting cultivation
Jumma identity 256, 267, 272n.2
kinship-based administration in 257,
    261–2
landscape, colonial description
    of 262–3
military intervention in 266–7
monoculture plantations in 267
natural resources, colonial exploitation
    of 260
natural resources, state exploitation for
    nation building 255, 256
peace accord between guerrillas and
    Bangladesh government 256, 267
political and economic transformation,
    post annexation 261–2
reserved forests of 26, 259–60
shifting cultivation in 26, 255, 256,
    258, 259, 261
state development policies in 263,
    265–6
state development policy, traditional
    vs. recent approach 269–71
state development projects in 256, 270
tribal culture, state perception of 263,
    265, 266, 268

tribal economy, state intervention
    in 266
tribal economy, structural changes
    in 261, 265, 266
tribals of 255, 256–7, 263–4, 272n.3
tribals vs. plains people in 264
Chittagong Hill Tracts Commission
    265
Chola empire 57
Chotanagpur 20, 115
    adivasis of. *See* Adivasi
    changes in land-use patterns 119,
        144n.21
    conservation programme in 119–20,
        138–9, 140, 144n.22
    deforestation during colonial rule 118,
        119, 121
    forest communities of 123–4
    forest reservation in, effect on
        indigenous people 121
    forests of 116, 122–3
    forests of, importance in local
        economy 123, 117
    growth of landlordism in 120
    indigenous land rights in 121
    Jesuit missions, role in 115
    landscape 115, 116, 122
    landscape and Chotanagpuri
        identity 122, 133
    landscape and people, symbiotic
        relationship 124, 125
    landscape, memories of and cultural
        resistance 125, 126. *See also* Protest
        movements
    migration into 120
    military reasons for preservation of
        forests 122
    protest movements in 125–6, 133. *See
        also* Protest movements
    sacred groves of 123–4
    village and rural hierarchies in 17
    See also Jharkhand; Jharkhand Mukti
        Morcha; Jharkhand Party
Chotanagpur Unnati Samaj 128
Chotanagpuri identity 122, 133
Citizenship 17

and nation state 9, 14
cultural-ethnic identity and 25
Civic nationalism 6, 9–10
and ecologism 10
Clan land, conversion into private land in Khasi Hills 173
Cleghorn, Hugh 144n.22
report on trans-Indus timber trade in Malakand 96–7
Clifford, James 133
Coastal entrepôt cities in south-west India, importance of 51–2
Cochin 51
Coffee 202
appropriation of Kodagu sacred forests for cultivation of 221–2
Colonial
attitude towards shifting cultivation 24, 66
control of forests in NWFP, justification for 99–100
description of CHT landscape 262–3
development interventions 242
development interventions, in Kerala fisheries. *See* Fisheries in Kerala
empire(s) 18, 20
encounter with NWFP 95–6
expansion in Western Ghats 44
expansion, impact on environment 11
forest policy 119
intervention in Nilgiris. *See* Nilgiri Hills
interventions in Chittagong Hill Tracts 25–6, 260
knowledge, identity formation, and 11
law 75
perception of Pukhtun 275
redefinition of forest rules in Hazara 96
rule. *See* Colonial rule
schematization of landscapes 94
Colonial rule 17
deforestation in Chotanagpur during 118–19, 121
ethnographic codification under 79–80

identity formation in South Asian forests and 21
law and 20
Commercial foraging 62
Common land, enclosure in Britain 72, 77
Common law, and custom 75
Common rights 121, 145n.26
Communities. *See* Indigenous communities
Community forest management 171–2
criticism of 27, 171
in Garo hills 170–2
in Meghalaya 170–2, 173, 182, 195n.51
in Nepal 34
of sacred forests 33, 225
in NWFP 91
Community, notion of 27, 171–2
Congress Party
Adivasi Mahasabha and, relationship between 129, 130
Jharkhand Party and, relationship between 129, 130–1, 147n.70
Tana Bhagat movement and 126–7
tribal opposition to 128–9
tribal policy in post-Independent India 131
Conservation
in Chotanagpur 119–20, 138–9, 140, 144n.22
need for 66
in Nepal, role of monarchy and 34, 298, 311
role of indigenous communities in 28, 261, 137, 139, 140
shifting cultivation and 261
Coorg National Council 224
Coorg. *See* Kodagu 33
Cosgrove, W. 122
Cronon, William 188
Cultural
ethnic identity, and citizenship 25
identity and territorial affinity 9
resistance, remembered landscape and 125, 126

Culture
  indigenous people's perception of 125
  landscape and 146n.41
  nation-building and, disagreements regarding 24
  nation state and 9
  power and 141
Custom
  common law and 75
  user rights and 77
Customary rights *vs.* public good 78, 79, 80

Dalits 24
Damodar Valley Corporation 2, 4
Damodaran, Vinita 16, 17, 21, 189
Dam(s)
  in Chittagong Hill, effects of 265–6
  impact on local fisheries in Kerala 239, 251–2
  Keol Karo, resistance to 137, 142, 149n.90
  Narmada, effect on indigenous rights 142
  Tehri 25
Debbarma, P.K. 176
Decline and Fall of the Roman Empire, The 18
Deep ecology, concept of 160
Deforestation
  effect on wildlife 118–19
  in Chotanagpur during colonial rule 118–19, 121
  in Meghalaya 170–1, 173
  in Santhal Parganas 119
Department of Forests, Fisheries and Wildlife (DFFW), NWFP 90, 91, 92
  contemporary forest reforms and 110
  See also Forest bureaucracy, in NWFP
Department of National Parks and Wildlife Conservation, Nepal (DNPWC) 303, 304
  See also National Park and wildlife staff
Deshpande, Satish 6
Devanesan, D.W. 245, 246, 247

Devarakadus. See Kodagu sacred forests
Dhandak of Rawain 157
Dhebar Report 131
Diku 126
  JMM attitude towards 134
  migration into Bihar 131
  notion of 134
  status in Jharkhand 135
Dir, NWFP 92
Displacement, effect of 29
Donor-supported development projects in NWFP 90, 109
Dovers, Stephen 12
Draft Forest Act (1999), NWFP 90, 91, 111n.9
Drury, George 83

East India Company (EIC) 66, 67, 68, 70, 78
  claim to land and resources 15
  contradictions within, regarding land conflicts in Nilgiris 70, 78–9, 82–3
  control over Chittagong Hills 257
  land conflicts and 3
  monopoly over forests of Malabar 73, 75
  sovereign rights over Toda land 84, 85
  See also British colonial
Ecological
  awareness, among indigenous people. *See* Indigenous communities
  imperialism 19
  mobilization, and nationalist sentiment 9
  nationalism. *See* Ecological nationalism
  networks, nation and 2
  vandalism, in Singhbhum 138, 139
  warfare in Chittagong Hills 26
Ecological nationalism 4, 6, 7–8, 9, 10, 25, 28, 35, 36
  creation of quasi states and 22
  definition 6, 43–4, 233
  indigenist. *See* Indigenist ecological nationalism
  nature and 44

new spheres of 36
nature devotion and 6
Ecologism 7
  civic nationalism and 10
  ecology and 7
  environmentalism and, contrast between 7
  ethnic nationalism and 10
Ecology 7
  ecologism and 7
  impact on livelihoods 275
  nationalism and 7
  political 11, 14, 38n.29
  role in construction of Pukhtun identity 275
  socio-political structures and 275, 277
  as symbol of political weakness 275
Ellen, Roy 187
Elliott, Daniel 83
Elphinstone, Mountstuart, influence of Scottish Enlightenment on 73, 74
Empire(s) 18, 19, 20
  colonial 18, 20
  globalization and 19
  imperialism and 19
  liberalism and racism as basis of 20
  redefinition of 19–20
  strategy of pacification 26
Encyclopaedia Mundarica 128
English Common law 15
  absolute rights to land under 77
Environment
  conservation of, role of indigenous people 28, 261, 137, 139, 140
  cultural identity and, affinity between 7
  degradation, role of indigenous people in 3, 187
  impact of colonial expansion on 11
  Indian scholarship on 23
  national security and 25
  policies regarding, role of historical enquiry 12
  transformation in India 1–2

Environmental
  history. *See* Environmental history
  knowledge 233. *See also* indigenous knowledge
  NGOs 33
  research, role of history in 11, 12
Environmental history 11–12, 13, 21–2, 23, 35, 110n.1
  of NWFP forest bureaucracy 92, 110. *See also* Forest bureaucracy
  political ecology and 44
  of Uttarakhand 152. *See also* Uttarakhand
  of Western Ghats 44. *See also* Western Ghats
Environmentalism
  ecologism and, contrast between 7
  global, and ethnic movements 137
  impact on livelihood 275
  religious chauvinism and 24–5
  socio-political structures of NWFP and 275, 277
Essentialism 23, 234
Ethnicity and ethnic politics 135, 140, 148n.80, 148n.81
Ethnic identity, notion of 289
Ethnic movements
  and global environmentalism 137
  See also Movements; protest movements
Ethnic nationalism 6, 9, 10, 20, 125
  and ecologism 10
Ethnicity 148n.80, 148n.81
  and ethnic ideologies 115
  as a political platform 135
Ethnological science 75
Ethnonationalism 14, 33, 55
  and metropolitan-secular nationalism 33, 34
European knowledge, debates regarding 18–19
Exotic
  plants, and secular nationalism 4
  tree species in Kodagu 202

Federation of Khasi States 177
Fisherfolk. *See* Kerala, fisherfolk of
Fisheries Research Station, Calicut,
    establishment of 245
Fisheries science, development of 243
Fisheries, in Kerala
    Babu Paul Committee on 249
    colonial intervention in 242–3, 244
        See also Malabar oil sardines
    government loans for motorized
        boats 253
    Indo-Norwegian Project on 248
    Kalwar Commission on 249
    state intervention in 253–4. *See also*
        Fishing trawlers, seasonal ban on
Fishing trawlers
    ambivalence regarding effects of 250–2
    Balakrishnan Nair Committee on 250
    industrial protest against 248–9
    over-fishing by, protest against 248,
        249
    seasonal ban on 233, 248, 249, 250
Flatland/permanent agriculture. *See*
    Agriculture
Forager(s) 13, 47, 50
    intermediate brokers and 56, 57
    long distance trade and 13, 14. *See also*
        Forager-traders
    lowland agriculturists and, interde-
        pendence between 13, 45, 50, 63
Forager-traders 14, 45, 61
    identity of 63
    lifestyle of 62
    specialized 47, 48, 50, 61
Foraging, commercial 62
Foraging foods 117
Forest Act (1878), NWFP 101, 106
Forest Act (1927), NWFP 106, 107
Forest(s)
    of Ajmir (NWFP), value of 280
    alpine, in NWFP. *See* Bandas
    andolan, in Singhbhum 135–7, 138,
        139
    bureaucracy in NWFP. *See* Forest
        bureaucracy
    of Chotanagpur. *See* Chotanagpur

clearance for agriculture 55
community management of. *See*
    Community forest management
conflicts over 44, 121. *See also* Protest
    movements; Chipko movement
conservation. *See* Conservation
contractual system of trade in products
    of 56–7
deforestation of. *See* Deforestation
degradation, role of indigenous
    communities in 3. *See also*
    Deforestation
deities, in Uttarakhand 154–5
department, of Pakistan 34
economic value of 117, 123, 153–4
effect of expanding agriculture on
    55
EIC monopoly over, Munro's criticism
    73, 75
exploitation for timber 119. *See also*
    Timber
exploitation of 119, 120, 121, 152
Garo Hills and 183
guards, local residents view of 283, 284
indigenous knowledge of. *See* Indi-
    genous knowledge
indigenous rights to and environmen-
    tal interests, conflict between
    139–40
of Kodagu 200, 228. *See also* Kodagu
    sacred forests
landscape, colonial construction
    of 116–17
local perception in Uttarakhand
    153
management 27, 31
management, by autonomous district
    councils in Meghalaya 173, 182,
    195n.51
management, under scientific
    forestry 120
of Meghalaya. *See* Meghalaya
military reasons for preservation
    of 122
of NWFP. *See* North West Frontier
    Province. *See also* Malakand; Swat

people and, relationship between 153–6
personal *vs.* public interest 99
policies, and national integration 31
policy, colonial 119
political ecology of 27
products, as tribute 57, 58
products, trade in. *See* Trade
protected, in Singhbhum 138–9
recreational value of 53, 156–7
religious and symbolic significance 124, 125, 154, 155
reservation, effect on indigenous people 121. *See also* Reserved forests
reserved. *See* Reserved forests
rights to, and environmental interests, conflict between 139–40
rules, colonial redefinition in Hazara 96
sacred. *See* Sacred forests
as shared space 167n.4
of South Asia 3
of South India, decline in area 55
Survey in Chittagong Hills 266
of Swat 97, 102–3, 106–7
symbolic significance of 154, 155
temples, in sacred forests 219, *220, 221, 227*
temples, in Uttarakhand 154, 155
of Trans-Indus region 102, 104. *See also* Malakand; Swat
of Western Ghats 63
women and, relationship between 155–6
Forest bureaucracy, in NWFP 90, 91, 93–4, 107, 110
challenge to authority of 92
justification for 100, 107–8, 109
nationalism and 109
power of 94–5
resistance to 95
Freeman, Rich 32, 216
Fuel wood 281, 282, 290
access to, and patron–client relationship 285, 290, 291
collection, inconsistency in policy implementation in NWFP 282–4
conflicting views regarding access to 284–5
moral principle behind access to 284
See also Bandas

Gadgil, Madhav 32, 217
Game Scouts, National Parks Service of Nepal 300
chakri and 312
and government service 301–2
relationship with senior officials 308–9
See also National Park and Wildlife staff
Gandhi, Mahatma 127
Ganga river 151, 164
Garcia, Claude 32, 33
Garo Hills 70
ban on felling. *See* Supreme Court ban on felling in Meghalaya
causes of militancy in 173–4
demand for Garoland in 174, 175, 176
ecological crisis in 173–4
economic underdevelopment of 174–5
forest cover of 183
illegal felling in reserved forests of 182
private ownership of land in 173
shifting cultivation in 190
Garo National Council (GNC) 174
Garo Nationalism 174
Garoland, demand for 174, 175, 176
Garos 170, 178
Geiser, Urs 14, 15, 31
Ghatwals 120
Ghurye, G.S. 131
Gibbon, Edward 18
Gibson, Alexander 144n.22, 172
Gilroy, Paul 133
Globalization 7
appropriation of natural resources and 8
and empire 19

Goa 51
  effect of Portuguese involvement in rice trade on 53
Gordon, Robert 71
Government service, in Nepal 302–3, 307
  desire for 300, 301
  Game Scouts and 301–2
  illicit perks of 303
  lobbying by outside patrons 315–16
  National Park wardens and 303–4
  non-gazetted officers in 300, 301
  perks of 307–8
  politicization of promotions 315
  power and prestige of 302, 303, 307
  rangers and 302–3
  recruitment of gazetted officers 301
  recruitment of non-officers 301
  'source force' and 301, 313
  staff evaluation by senior officials 308–9
  transfers as punishment 310, 316
  See also Nepalese bureaucracy
Government of Nepal Act (1951) 299
Govindan, V.V. 245–6
Gow, Peter 122, 127
Green primitivism, concept of 187, 188
Grove, Richard 19, 66
Gudu, right of 83–4, 85
Guha, Sumit 14, 17, 58, 142
  views on tribal communities 188–9
Guinea, reforestation of Kissidougou landscape 117
Gupta, Akhil 5, 242
Gurdon, P.R. 186
Gurkhas 26

Habermas, Jürgen 161
Hardiman, David 116
Hardt, Michael 19
Harkness, Henry 80
  description of the Toda 81
Harriss, J. 108
Hazara, colonial redefinition of forest rules in 96

Hazaribagh 120, 122
Hereditary bondage, in Santhal Parganas 120
Heritage, conservation of 33
Hill Pandaram 46
Hill people. *See* Tribes; Upland people
Historical enquiry, and environment policies 12
History
  critique of 23
  environmental research and 11, 12
  environmental. *See* Environmental history
  occupational, of Western Ghats 49–50
  identity formation and 28–9
Ho tribals 115
Hobsbawn, E.J. 134
Hockings, Paul 47, 55, 69
Hoeppe, Götz 16, 17
Hoffmann, J. 128
Hooker, Joseph Dalton 186
Hornell, James 243, 245
Hos tribals 16, 117, 123, 124, 136
Hough, Reverend James 66, 80
Hume, David 74
Hunter gatherers. *See* Foragers
Hutchinson, S.R.H. 260
Hynniewtrep National Liberation Council 176

Identity/identities 145n.30
  adivasi 21, 116, 128
  Chakma 116
  Chotanagpuri 122, 133
  contested, and landscape 36
  cultural, and environment, affinity between 7
  cultural, and territorial affinity 9
  ethnic, notion of 289
  formation in Jharkhand 29
  formation, dispossession of nature and 29
  Jumma, in Chittagong Hills 256, 267, 272n.2
  Khasi 33

landscape and 9, 10
lost, notion of 11
Munda 21
nation and 2, 5, 21, 22
national, and autochthony 22
national, and nation-state 5
nationality and 21
of forager-traders, in Western Ghats 61, 63
of National Park and wildlife staff in Nepal 298, 311, 316, 317, 320, 321
of Nepalese bureaucrats 297, 298
Pahari 162, 163, 164, 166
place-based, and indigeneity 29
political processes and 10–11
politics of 6–7
politics of, and nationalism 24
Pukhtun 27–8, 274, 275–6, 289
regional. *See* Regional identity
role of memory and history in formation of 28–9
sacred forests, role in formation of 200, 224. *See also* Sacred forests
South Asian 11, 21
struggle in North-East India over 5
Uttarkhandi 168n.17
Imperialism 18, 19
India 4
  absence of nation in 24
  effect of federalism on mega projects 4
  environmental transformation and mega projects 1–2
  forest management in 31
  forest policy and national integration 31
  manifestations of metropolitan-secular nationalism in 31
  Nehru's vision of 30–1
  participatory development programmes in 34
  pluralism in 6
  south-west coastal areas of 46. *See also* Malabar; Western Ghats
  as a state system 24
Indian Constitution, Sixth Schedule of 27, 175, 176, 180

Indian Forest Report (1999) 183, 184
Indian Forest Act (1865) 100, 101
Indigeneity 25, 36
  and place-based identity 29
  adivasi 8, 25. *See also* adivasi
  notion of 17, 116
Indigenist
  view of nature 7–8
  reaction to state appropriation of natural resources 35, 36
Indigenist ecological nationalism 8, 25
  vs. metropolitan-secular nationalism 30
  commodification of environment and 33
Indigenous communities/peoples 189–90
  alignment with development projects 9
  attachment to land 28
  autonomy movements and 115. *See also* Movements
  in Bangladesh, World Bank, policy regarding 270–1
  in Chittagong Hills, Asian Development Bank policy regarding 270–1
  claim to natural resources 27, 188, 191
  dismantling of, in Chittagong Hills 26, 27. *See also* Tribals, state perception of
  ecological awareness among 28
  effect of forest reservation on 121
  effect of integrationist policies on 26
  environmental conservation and 28, 137, 139, 140, 261. *See also* Community forest management
  environmental degradation by 3, 187–8
  environmental knowledge. *See* Indigenous knowledge
  environmental management and 87. *See also* Community forest management
  importance of forest economy for 117, 123, 153–4
  knowledge of landscape 189, 190, 191

knowledge of forest environment 123
land rights of. *See* Land rights
nature and, relationship between 125, 187
perception of culture 125
place attachments of 28
resource management skills of 28
rights of. *See* Indigenous rights
See also Tribes/tribals
Indigenous conservation movements. *See* Conservation
Indigenous identity. *See* Identity
Indigenous knowledge 116, 256, 269
of fisheries *vs.* scientific knowledge 234. *See also* Kerala fisherfolk
of forests 123
of landscape 189, 190, 191
and management of natural resources 16
of sea. *See* Kerala fisherfolk
Indigenous nations, notion of 17
Indigenous Peoples, United Nation's Declaration on Rights of 177
Indigenous rights
cultural struggle for 140
effect of Narmada dam on 142
to forests, and environmental concerns, conflict between 139–40
to land. *See* Land rights
to nature, and political autonomy, link between 27
political struggle for 143. *See also* Protest movements
vs. public good 20, 67, 68, 72, 78, 79, 80
to self determination in north-east India 175, 176–7
See also Rights; Land rights
Indigenous tribes *See* Tribes/tribals; Indigenous communities
Indigenousness, politics of 21
Indo-Roman trade 47, 48
Indus river, NWFP 276
timber trade along 96, 97
Ingold, Tim 28
views on indigenous people 189–90

Ingoldian dwelling perspective 189–90
Intermediaries, role in spice trade 56, 57
Izzat (honour), concept of, among Pukhtuns 290

Jageshwar temple 164
Jaintia hills 170, 183
Jaintia tribe 170, 177, 194n.27
James Hough, Reverend 66
Jamshedpur 131
Jenmi rights in land 73
Jesuit missions in Chotanagpur 115
Jewitt, Sarah 13
Jharkhand 21
environmental vandalism in 138–9
identity formation in 29
movement 141, 142
problems in governance 141, 150n.101
state, demand for 128, 130, 132, 137, 147n.61
status of *diku* in 135
Jharkhand Mukti Morcha (JMM) 132, 135, 137
attitude towards *diku* 134
forest *andolan* and 137
revival of sacred grove festival by 133
Jharkhand Party 129, 130, 132, 135
alignment with non-Adivasi groups 129–30, 132
demand for Jharkhand state 130, 147n.61
relationship with Congress 129, 130–1, 147n.70
Jhum cultivation. *See* Shifting cultivation
Jirgas 277, 282, 293, 296n.11
Joint forest management 31, 140
Jumma identity, in CHT 267, 272n.2
Jungle Katao andolan. *See* Forest, andolan in Singhbhum

Kabul river, timber trade along 96, 97
Kadakkodi, role in enforcing oil sardine ban in Kerala 241–2, 253
Kadar/Cadar tribe 46, 56–7, 58
Kaghan 96, 97

INDEX

Kalam Tribal Agency 92
Kalam (Swat Kohistan) 106
Kalam, M.A. 218
Kalwar Commission, on fisheries in Kerala 249
Kana river valley, NWFP 276, 277
Kanara 46
  kingdoms of 52
  Portuguese demand for rice of 52
  rice production in 51
Kannikar tribe 47
Karlsson, Bengt G. 27, 28, 29
Karumba tribe 46
Kashmir 30
Katalamma (sea mother) 236, 250
Kaviraj, Sudipta 23
Keol Karo Dam, resistance to 137, 142, 149n.90
Kerala, backwater transport system 46
Kerala, fisherfolk of 16, 233, 234, 235, 250, 251
  conceptualization of sea 235–7
  effect of development projects on 16, 26
  female conceptualization of sea 235–6
  knowledge of marine world 237, 238–9, 240–1
  rights to marine resources 233, 250
  self image 237
  society boat programme and 253
  state intervention in lifestyle of 234–5
  See also Fisheries, in Kerala
Kerala fisheries, and Indo-Norwegian Project 248
Kerala Marine Fisheries Regulation Act 248, 253
Keriahs 123
Khali Khel, NWFP 276
Khan, Malik Allah Yar 103
Khasi(s) 170, 177, 173, 194n.27
  conversion to Christianity 187
  demand for self-determination 177
  identity 33
  native states 177
  opposition to amendment of Land Transfer Act (1971) 178
  See also Khasi Hills
Khasi Hills 170
  clan land, conversion into private land 173
  desertification of 185
  forest cover in 183
  iron-smelting industry in 186, 197n.73
  land ownership and management system in 181
  private ownership of land in 173
  sacred forests of 33, 186–7, 191
  uranium mining in, debate regarding 178, 179
Khasi Students Union (KSU) 177, 181
Khasis, The 186
Khel (patrilineage) 276
Khuntkhatti tenure 120
Kissidougou landscape, reforestation of 117
Klingensmith, D. 4
Knowledge
  colonial, and identity formation 11
  European, debates regarding 18–19
  indigenous. *See* Indigenous knowledge
  scientific 243
Kodagu district 200, *201*, 226, 228
  average annual rainfall 200, *202*
  change in tree cover 202
  coffee estates/plantations in 202, 221–2
  dry season, length of *203*
  forest cover 200, 228
  growth of exotic tree species 202
  influx of migrants into 224
  landscape transformation 202
  reserved forests of 200
  sacred forests of. *See* Kodagu sacred forests
Kodagu sacred forests 203, 204, 226, 228
  appropriation for coffee cultivation in 221–2
  canopy cover of 213
  caste system and 221

change in species composition, effect of 216
conservation value of 213, 216, 228
as cultivation space 221
dominant species of 211, *214*
ecological significance of 216, 227
endemic species of 211, *212, 213, 216*
forest department attitude towards 222–3
as grazing space 223
as housing space 223
human activity in 217–18
Kodava traditionalism and 224, 225
management by village communities 33, 225
new species in 216
as open access land 222
politicization of 224–5
as religious icons 225
resource use in 217–18, 227
sacralization of 33
as sacred space 218–21
as sanctuaries of nature 225–6
species richness of 209, *210*
structural analysis of 206, *207, 208*
symbolic value of 223
temples of 219, *220, 221, 227*
traditional notion of 219, *220*
Kodava community 33
Kodava Samaj 224
Kols 126
Kolis 58
Konkan coast 46
Kosi river fair 25
Krishna Janambhumi 25
Krishna, Lord 24
Kumaon 163, 164

Lakoff, George 236
Land
attachment to, and political mobilization 28
classification of 4
colonial claim to 15
common rights to 77
common, enclosure of 72, 77
community management *vs.* private ownership 191
conflict over, in Nilgiris 72, 78–9, 82–3
degradation of, role of forest communities in 3. *See also* Shifting cultivation
humans and, relationship between 45
indigenous system of use in Chittagong Hills 261. *See also* shifting cultivation
indigenous people and, relationship between 187, 189
indigenous peoples claim to 176, 177
ownership in Meghalaya 171, 172–3
private *vs.* communal property 71–2
registration policy in NWFP 274, 275, 279
rights to. *See* Land rights
settlement programme in NWFP 107
struggle over, in North-East India 5
tribal rebellions over 128. *See also* protest movements
See also Landscape
Land rights
absolute 72
of Badaga 67
in Chotanagpur 121
and English Common law 77
jenmi 73
in Nilgiris 15, 20. *See also* Nilgiri Hills; Toda
in north-east India 176–7
in NWFP 15, 27, 274, 279
tribal, and indigeneity 17
of women in Meghalaya 170
Land Transfer Act (1971), in Meghalaya 178
Landlordism, in Chotanagpur 120
Landscape
of CHT, colonial description of 262–3
colonial schematization of 4
concept of 122
contested identities and 36
culture and 146n.41
identity formation and 9, 10
imagined *vs.* managed 30, 31

indigenous communities' knowledge
  of 189, 190
  as lived experience 118, 122, 125,
    127
  nation and 2
  of Nilgiris 65–6
  and people, symbiotic relationship in
    Chotanagpur 124, 125
  racialization of, in Nilgiris 80
  regional identity and 17
  remembered, and cultural resistance 125, 126
  romantic visions of, and anti colonial
    nationalism 30–1
  See also Land
Larma, Manobendra Narayan 268
Law
  colonial rule and 20
  custom and 71
  English Common 77
Leach-Fairhead thesis 117
Lewin, T.H. 258, 259
  view of hill people of Chittagong
    Hills 262
Liberty, and authority, balance between
  74
Liberalism *vs.* racism, in Nilgiris 20. *See
  also* Nilgiri Hills
Linkenbach, Antje 16, 24, 29
Local knowledge. *See* Indigenous
  knowledge
Long, N. 289
Lost places, memories of 29–30
Lowland agriculture. *See* Agriculture
Ludden, David 3
Lushai
  tribe 26
  hills 258
Lushington, Stephen, R. 76, 78
Luxury goods, trade in 54
Lyngdoh, Paul 177

Macaulay, Thomas Babington 18
Mackerel 238
Madras Government 73, 78
  absolute control over land in

Nilgiris 15, 68, 69, 86. *See also*
  Nilgiri Hills
department of fisheries. *See* Madras
  fisheries department below
differences with district administration
  in Nilgiri 15, 20, 66, 67, 68, 70
interest in Malabar teak 72–3
Madras fisheries department
  ban on Malabar oil sardine fishery. *See*
    Malabar oil sardines
  fishery development in Kerala 242–4
Mahabharata, enactment in Uttarakhand
  164, 167n.8
Mahajans, exploitation of jungles by 120,
  121
Mahendra, King 321
Mahua tree 122
Malabar 46
  loss of *jenmi* rights in 73
  oil sardines. *See* Malabar oil sardines
  pepper production in. *See* Pepper
  sole 238
  spice trade in. *See* Spice trade
  teak, British demand for 72–3
  trade in forest products. *See* Trade
Malabar oil sardines 238, 241
  ban on fishery of 233, 239, 240–8, 253
  decline in landings 239, 241
  fluctuations in catch 238, 242, 244–5,
    246–7
  local knowledge of 240–2
  local knowledge *vs.* scientific
    knowledge of 247
  local perception of ban on fishery
    242
  overfishing as cause of fluctuations in
    catch 246–7
  research on 245, 246–7
  role of *Kadakkodis* in enforcing ban on
    fishery of 241–2
Malakand Division, NWFP 31, 92, *93*, 96,
  97, 102, 277
  British aspirations over 97–8
  Cleghorn's report on 96–7
  difficulty in implementing forest policy
    in 105

forests, exploitation by natives 102, 104
forests, NWFP Forest Department report on 102
inconsistencies in implementation of forest policy in 282–4
isolation of 275
plural legal system in 274, 275, 277, 279
protected forests of 106–7
relations between British and tribals in 101
timber supply from 100–1
See also Swat; NWFP
Malcolm, John, influence of Scottish Enlightenment and 73, 74
Man, E.G. 119
Manas Tiger sanctuary 5
Maoists 34
Maoris 125
Marak, Julius L.R. 172
Marma 267
Marwaris 126
Matsyafed cooperative society 253
Mawphlang sacred forest 186
McLaren, Martha 74, 75
Megahalya 28, 170
  Autonomous district councils in. *See* Autonomous district councils
  community forest management in 170–2. *See also* autonomous district councils
  deforestation in 170–1, 173
  forest cover in 183–4
  forest department 182, 183
  forest reserves in, opposition to 174
  forests of 170, 171
  Garo Hills of. *See* Garo Hills
  indigenous movements for political autonomy 27, 174, 175, 176, 177
  indigenous tribes, debates regarding 178
  jhum cultivation in 172, 185
  Khasi hills of. *See* Khasi Hills
  land ownership in 172–3
  land rights of women in 170
  private control of forests 27, 171, 173
  reserved forests in 171
  sacred forests of 33, 186–7
  statehood for 176
  timber ban in. *See* Supreme Court ban, on felling in Meghalaya
  timber extraction in, effects of 185
Megahalya Land Transfer Act (1971) 178
Metropolitan-secular ecological nationalism 7–8, 25, 33, 35, 36
  ethnonationalism and 33, 34
  ethno-regional ecological nationalism and, relationship 33, 34
  vs. Indigenist nationalism 30
  modern nation state and 8, 31, 35, 36
Mey, Wolfgang 25
Mia 291
Miangan 276, 295n.7
Mills, A.J.M. 186
Missionaries, role in indigenous identity formation 128, 146n.53
Mizo 26
Morrison, Kathleen 13, 17
Movement(s) 27
  Adivasi 33
  autonomy, in Uttarakhand 152, 153
  autonomy, in Meghalaya 27, 175, 176
  forest, in South Asia 3
  Jharkhand. *See* Jharkhand
  resistance, among Mundas 125, 126
  sub-national 5
  subaltern 23
  See also Protest movements
Muivah, Apam 176
Mukkuvar fisherfolk 9
Multiculturalism 22
Mundas 16, 21, 120, 123, 128
  resistance movements by 125, 126
Munro, Thomas 71, 73, 74, 78
  criticism of EIC monopoly over forests 73, 75
  defence of indigenous law and administration 74–5, 78
  influence of Scottish Enlightenment on 73–4, 75
  support of *jenmi* rights 73

INDEX

views on EIC monopoly over timber trade 75
views on free market 75
Murree 96, 97
Murthy, M.L.K. 58
Musharraf, General 92
Muslim League, Adivasi Mahasabha and 129
Muthuvan 47

Naga 175, 193n.18
Nair, N. Balakrishnan 250
Nanda Devi Biosphere Reserve 161
Nandy, Ashis 23
Narmada Bachao Andolan 142
Narmada dam, effect on indigenous rights 142
Nash, Manning 134
Nation(s) /nationhood/nationality 2, 3, 21, 30
   absence of, in India 24
   ancient past and 2
   and citizenship 14
   and ecological networks 2
   identity and 2, 5, 21, 22
   imagination of 2, 3, 5
   indigenous, notion of 17
   landscape and 2
   nature and 2, 22, 28, 35, 191
   notion of 2
   political mobilization and 23
   postcolonial notion of 5
   utopian 2
   See also Nation state
Nation state
   appropriation of nature by 7–8. *See also* State appropriation of nature
   citizenship and 9
   culture and 9
   development interventions by 3. *See also* State development policies
   metropolitan-secular ecological nationalism and 8, 31, 35, 36
   modern, Nehru and 30–1
   national identity and 5
   nationalist resurgence and 21
   regional assertions and 17, 18
   strategy of integration and 26
   See also State
National integration, and nature 2, 7–8, 17
National Park and Wildlife staff, in Nepal 300, 320
   forestry staff and, contrast between 317, 318–19, 320
   government service and. *See* Government service, in Nepal
   identity of 298, 311, 316, 317, 320, 321
   nationalism of 34–5, 320–1
   ties with monarchy 298
National Park Service, Nepal. *See* Nepal, Department of National Parks and Wild Life Conservation
National Parks Act, Nepal 298
Nationalism 3, 5, 21, 34, 109, 174
   Bengali 268
   civic 6, 9–10
   competing, in Western Ghats 44, 63
   conflicting 5
   contemporary 22
   ecological. *See* Ecological nationalism
   ecology and 7
   elite, absence of cultural sensitivity in 24
   ethnic 6, 9, 10, 20, 125
   identity politics and 24
   ideology of 7
   indigenist ecological. *See* Indigenist ecological nationalism
   Metropolitan-secular. *See* Metropolitan-secular nationalism
   of National Park staff in Nepal 34–5, 320–1
   nature and 3, 35–6
   Nepali 34–5, 320–1
   new perspectives regarding 22
   political 24
   secular 4
   study of, in South Asia 23
   vernacular 44

Nature/natural resources
  colonial appropriation in the
    Nilgiris 15. *See also* Nilgiri Hills
  colonial exploitation in Chittagong
    Hills 260
  colonial perception of 86
  commodification of 33, 34
  community management of 274. *See
    also* Community forest manage-
    ment
  contest over 3, 29, 36
  control over, role of power in 11
  devotion to 3, 6, 25, 44
  devotion, and nationalist aspirations
    2, 3
  as dimension in Chipko movement
    160
  dispossession of, and identity forma-
    tion 29. *See also* Identity formation
  ecological nationalism and 44
  as economic resource 5, 159
  effect of development projects on 29
    See also State development projects
  gendered characteristics of 16, 235–7
  as heritage 5
  humanity and 3, 159
  hybrid 188
  iconographies of and claims to place
    36
  identity formation and. *See* Identity
  indiginistic view of 7–8
  indigenous people and, relationship
    between 117, 125
  indigenous people's claim to 27, 188,
    191
  as lived relationship 118
  management of, role of local know-
    ledge 16. *See also* Indigenous
    knowledge
  memories of 2
  Metropolitan-secular view of. *See*
    Metropolitan-secular ecological
    nationalism
  nation and 2, 22, 28, 35, 191
  national integration and 2, 7–8, 17
  nationalism and 3, 34, 35–6
  objectification of 154
  politics and 2–3
  politics of, and ethnic mobilization
    172
  rights of pastoralists over 20. *See also*
    Toda, land rights
  rights to, *vs.* public good 20, 67, 68, 78,
    79, 80
  rights to, and movements for
    autonomy. *See* Movements
  role of women in management of
    13
  significance for *paharis* of Uttarakhand
    165–6
  state appropriation of. *See* State
    appropriation of nature
  struggle over 5, 28
  See also Forests; Land; Landscape
Natural boundaries and territorial
  allegiances 4
Nayadi 47
Nayakas 124
Neelgherry Exhibition, Poona 70
Neeson, Jeanette 72, 77
Negri, Antonio 19
Nehru, Jawaharlal 30–1, 151
Nepal 1, 4
  bureaucracy in. *See* Nepalese bureau-
    cracy
  chakri, culture of. *See chakri*
  civil service 300, 305. *See also* Nepalese
    bureaucracy
  community forestry programmes
    in 34
  conservation efforts of monarchy 298,
    311
  conservation programmes in 4
  Department of Forests 317, 318–19,
    320, 324n.29
  Department of National Parks and
    Wild Life Conservation 297, 300,
    303, 304, 311, 315, 317, 321. *See
    also* National Park and wildlife
    staff
  government service in. *See* Govern-
    ment service

His Majesty's Government (HMG) 323n.15. *See also* Government service
Ministry of Forests and Soil Conservation 317
National Park Service 300, 315, 321
National Parks Act 298
nationalism in 34–5, 320–1
NGO workers in 305
panchayat democracy in 298
political history of 297–8
politicians of, power over bureaucrats 316
post-*andolan* social conflicts in 34
public service examination in 304–6
Rana administration, end of 299
Rana family of 298
Shah dynasty of 297
Wildlife Conservation Act (1958) 298
Nepalese bureaucracy/bureaucrats 297, 300
  expansion of 300
  formation of 299
  identity of 297, 298, 316, 317
    politicians and 298, 316
  post-*andolan* 314–15, 321
  ties with monarchy 298, 321
  See also Government service
Nepalese monarchy, conservation efforts of 34, 298, 311
Nicholson, Frederick 243, 244
Nilgiri Hills 15, 46, 55, 72
  bhurty system of revenue assessment in 81
  colonial administration, contradictions in 15, 66, 67, 68, 70
  colonial appropriation of nature 15
  conflicts over European migration into 73
  conflicts over land in 72, 78–9, 82–3
  contractual system of trade in 56
  early British settlers in 76
  effect of agricultural expansion on forests of 55
  European settlement in 66, 67, 68
  land rights in. *See* Toda, land rights

  land settlement by Sullivan. *See* Sullivan
  landscape of 65–6
  megaliths of 49
  property rights of British settlers 20
  property rights in, and sovereignty, debates over 69, 77–9
  proprietary rights in land 15
  racialization of landscape 80
  sovereign rights of Madras Govt in 69
  subject's rights *vs.* public good 20, 67, 68, 72, 79
  Toda pastoralists of. *See* Toda
  See also Ootacamund
Noble, W.A. 49
Nomadism 259, 265
Nongbri, Tilput 179, 180
Non-shareholders of banda, in NWFP. *See* Bandas
Nora, Pierre 28
North-east India
  autonomy movements in 27, 175, 176
  forest management in 27
  insurgency groups in 176
  land rights in 176–7
  right to self determination 176–7
  state exploitation of natural resources in 176–7
  struggle over identity 5
  See also Meghalaya
North West Frontier Province of Pakistan (NWFP)
  Ajmir village 276, 277, *278*
  Akhund Khel. *See* Akhund Khel
  Alpine forests of. *See* Bandas
  Bandas. *See* Bandas
  colonial encounter with 95–6
  colonial justification for control over forests in 99–100
  commercial forest harvesting in 274
  community participation in forest management 91
  conflict over forest management procedures in 92
  contemporary forest reforms and DFFW 110

creation of 101
Department of Forests, fisheries and Wildlife (DFFW) 90, 91
donor-supplemented development projects in 90, 109
Draft Forest Act (1999) 91
forest administration in 15
forest and revenue legislation under British rule 31
forest bureaucracy in. *See* forest bureaucracy, in NWFP
Forest Department 101, 105. *See also* Forest bureaucracy, in NWFP
forest reforms in 90–2, 95
forest management, heterogeneity in 277, 282
forest management rules 106–7
forest rights in 274. *See also* Bandas
forests of 90, 91, 95
forests of, Parnell's report 102–3
Indus river 276
Kana river valley 276, 277, 280
Khali Khel 276
land registration policy in 274, 275, 279
land rights in 15, 27, 274, 279
land settlement programme 107
Malakand Division of. *See* Malakand Division
nationalization of forests 31
Parnell's report on forests of 102–3
patron–client relationship in. *See* Patron–client relationship in NWFP
plural legal system in 274, 275, 277, 279
proprietary rights in 15
reification of legal rights over land and forests 274, 279
rules for forest management 106–7
Shangla district 277, *278*
state controlled commercial felling in 274, 289, 294
state ownership of forests 274, 279
Survey of Forests 279–80, 281
Swat district. *See* Swat district

Swat river 96, 97, 276
timber trade in 96, 97. *See also* Malakand; Swat
Trans-Indus region of. *See* Malakand
tribal law in 275, 279
working plans in NWFP, non-implementation of 105–6, 107, 109

Ootacamund 66, 67, 68
conflict over cantonment land 83, 84
purchase by John Sullivan 69
Oraons 16, 128
resistance movements in Chotanagpur 126
Tana Bhagat Movement and 126–7
Oraon, Sibu 126
Oriental Christian Spectator 85
Orientalists 74
vs. Utilitarians 75

Pahari identity 162, 163, 164
role of nature in construction of 166
vs. Uttarakhandi identity 168n.17
Paharis 16, 24
identity of. *See* Pahari identity
patriotic dimension of 164–5
vs. plains people 152, 163–4
political awareness among 161
regional identity of 162, 163, 164
struggle for a separate state 165
Pakistan 4, 14, 26, 274, 275
abolition of princely states 106
British territory in 93, *94*, 96
forest department 34
forest policy and national integration 31
forest management in 31
North West Frontier Province of. *See* NWFP
participatory development programmes in 34
post-independence forest reports 108
Palamau 120, 122
Paliyan 46
Panchayat democracy in Nepal 298
Parnell, report on forests of Swat 102–3

Pascal, J.P. 32, 33
Pastoralists 3
  rights over nature 20
  See also Toda pastoralists
Patron-client relationship in NWFP 27, 276
  access to fuel wood and 285, 290, 291
  divisive nature of 291
  fluidity of 292
  politicization of 274
Pemberton, John 23
Pepper 59
  cultivation of 58–9, 61, 64n.7
  demand for 52
  effect of Portuguese rice trade on extraction of 52
  increase in production of 53–4
  Roman market for 47
  trade 46, 48, 51, 52
  wild 57, 59, 61
Permanent Settlement of land and revenue 71
Perrett, Roy 139–40
Peshawar 96
  Forest Division, creation of 103
Plantations, raising of 99
Plural legal system, in NWFP 274, 275, 277, 279
Political
  activism, and identity politics 6–7. *See also* Movements
  autonomy. *See* movements
  ecology 11, 14, 27, 35, 38n.29, 44
  nationalism 24
  society, concept of 161–2, 166
Politics, nature and 2
Portuguese 14, 15, 51
  demand for forest products 52
  involvement in rice trade 52, 53
  spice trade and 54
  use of intermediaries in spice trade 57
Povinelli, Elizabeth 28
Power, and resource control 11
Prawns 238, 248, 250–1
Private Acts 72

Private property and economic growth, connection between 74, 78
Property rights 72
  of British settlers in Nilgiris 21
  debates regarding 70–1
  individual *vs.* public good 20, 67, 68, 72, 79, 80
  in Nilgiris, debates over 77–9
  of Toda. *See* Toda land rights
Protest movements 33
  Birsa Munda uprising 126
  Chipko. *See* Chipko Movement
  in Chotanagpur 115, 125–6, 133
  Dhandak of Rawain 1929/30 157
  forest andolan in Singhbhum 135–7, 138, 139
  Munda rebellion 125
  Narmada Bachao Andolan 142
  in Santhal Parganas 132
  Tamar rebellion 125
  Tana Bhagat Movement 126–7
  See also Movements
Provincially Administered Tribal Area (PATA) 277, 293
Public sphere, notion of 161
Pukhtuns
  colonial perception of 275
  concept of honor among 290
  identity. *See* Pukhtun identity
Pukhtun identity 27–8, 274, 289
  formation of 275–6
  influence on state policy 295
Pukhtunistan, Greater 275
Pukhtunwali, notion of 28, 289–90
Purse seining, ban on use of 250
Purulia–Ranchi railway 121

Quasi-states 22

Rahman, Sheikh Mujibur 268
Rajan, Ravi 120
Ramayana, enactment in Uttarakhand 164
Ramjanambhumi 24
Rana family of Nepal 298
Rana, Jung Bahadur 298

Ranchi 131
Ranger, T. 134
Rangers, National Park Service, Nepal 300, 302–3
Rashtriya Swayamsevak Sangh (RSS) 25
Rawain village in Uttarakhand, protest movement in 157
Raya, Krishna Deva 55
Regional identity 21
 of Adivasis 129–30, 132, 134
 landscape and 17
 of Paharis 162, 163, 164
 rights and 6
 shaping of 17
Regionalism 24, 25
Reserved forests 119, 121
 in CHT 26, 259–60
 in Meghalaya 171
 of Kodagu 200
Reverty, Captain 97
Rice 51, 52, 54
 cultivation, in Chittagong Hills 260
 trade, in south-west coastal India 53, 54
Ricketts, H. 119
Rights
 aboriginal. *See* Indigenous rights
 to banda shares in NWFP. *See* Bandas
 common 121, 145n.26
 customary. *See* Indigenous rights
 indigenous. *See* Indigenous rights
 jenmi 73
 land. *See* Land rights
 legal, and regional specificity 15
 to marine resources. *See* Kerala fisherfolk
 to nature, and movements for autonomy 27. *See also* Movements
 to nature, and rights of livelihood 10
 private *vs.* public good 20, 67, 68, 72, 79
 property. *See* Property rights
 proprietary, over land. *See* land rights. *See also* Property rights
 regional identity and 6

of Toda pastoralists over nature 20. *See also* Toda
 tradition and 9
 user, and custom 77
Ring seines 250–1
River linking project 1, 2
Roy, Arundhati 1
Royal Bardia National Park 301, 317, 320
Royal Chitwan National Park 303
Royalty shareholders 280, 283, 295n.1
 conflicting views regarding access to fuel wood 284–5
 conflicts among 274
Rumbold, William 81
Ryotwari system of settlement 71, 80–1

Sacred forests 31–2, 33, 122, 133, 199, 225
 of Chotanagpur 123–4
 cultural value of 199
 ecological value of 199
 effect of human pressures on 32
 female spirits of 123
 festivals of 124, 125
 festivals, politicization of 133
 floristic composition of 32
 identity formation and 200, 224
 of Khasi hills 33, 186–7, 191
 of Kodagu. *See* Kodagu sacred forests
 local history and 32
 as managed forests 32
 management by village communities 33
 of Meghalaya 33, 186–7
 preservation of 137
Sacred groves. *See* Sacred forests
Sahlins, Marshall 122, 125
Sahrul puja 133
Sal tree 122, 135
Sangma, Sonaram R. 174
Santhal Parganas
 debt bondage in 120
 effects of deforestation in 119
 resistance movement in 126, 132
Santhals 26, 126
Sarhad Awami Forestry Ittehad (SAFI) 91–2

Sarna. See Sacred forests
Schendel, William van 25
Scientific forestry 118
   forest management under 120
   impact on tribal economies 118
   impact on women's subsistence 118
Scientific knowledge 243
   vs. indigenous knowledge 234, 252–3
Scott, James C. 299
Scottish Enlightenment 20, 73–4
Sea
   as common property 250
   effect of dams on seasonal regularity of 239
   female conceptualization of 235–6
   fishermen's local knowledge vs. scientific knowledge 252–3
   moral and protective nature of 236–7
   as mother 16, 236, 250
   unpredictability of 237–8
Secondary traders, role of 56, 57
Secular nationalism 4
Seeley, J.R. 18
Sen, Amartya, capability approach 140, 149n.96
Seng Khasi 177
Settlement Record 279, 281
Shah dynasty of Nepal 297
Shah, Abdul Jabbar 102
Shanin, Teodor 29
Sharma, Mukul 25
Shifting cultivation/cultivators 3, 27, 47, 61, 180, 181, 190, 260, 264
   Badaga 67
   in CHT 26, 255, 256, 258, 259, 261
   conservation of forests and 261
   contradictions in colonial attitude towards 24
   effect of colonial policies on 66
   effect on forest ecosystem 185
   forest department's view of 259
   in Meghalaya 172, 174
   vs. permanent cultivation 173, 261
   vs. settled cultivation, Lewin's view 258–9
   support for 260–1
   unsustainability of 190–1
   in Western Ghats 27, 50
Singh, Jaipal 130, 131, 147n.60
Singhbhum
   felling for railway sleepers 119
   forest andolan in 135–7, 138, 139
   forests of 122
   indigenous conservation movements in 139, 140
Sinha, A.C. 170, 171, 185, 186
Siu, Helen 299
Sivaramakrishnan, K. 18, 31, 43, 79, 80, 116, 233, 242
Skaria, Ajay 142
South Asia
   conflicting nationalisms in 5
   forest movements in 3
   forests of 3
   formation of nation states in 21
   identity formation in 11
   identity formation under colonial rule 21
   nationalisms in 23
   postcolonial, effect of development in 29
   regional environment of 4
   seasons 3–4
   study of nationalisms in 23
South India
   coastal areas of. See Malabar; Western Ghats
   decline in forest area 55
   forager-traders of. See Forager-trader
   local self-governance in 51
Southwold-Llewellyn, Sarah 27, 34
Spice trade 45, 46, 54
   effect on tribals 58
   expansion of 48, 53
   expansion, effect on upland economies of Ghats 61
   role of intermediaries in 56, 57
   See also Cardamom; Pepper
Sri Lanka 47

State-making 299
State
  appropriation of natural resources. *See* State appropriation of nature
  development policies. *See* State development policies
  intervention in regional polities 25
  ownership of forests in NWFP 274, 279
  perception of tribal culture of Chittagong Hills 265, 266, 268
  system, *vs.* state idea 108
  See also Nation state
State appropriation of nature/natural resources 7–8, 30
  globalization and 8
  indigenist reaction to 35, 36
  nation-building and 255, 256
  national integration and 7–8
  in North-East India 176–7
  for political and economic control 9
  in Uttarakhand 16
State development policies/projects 3
  alignment of communities with 9
  in Chittagong Hills 26, 27, 263, 265–6, 269
  donor-supported 90, 109
  effect on postcolonial South Asia 29
  effect on nature 29
  effect on Kerala fisherfolk 16, 26, 234–5
  intervention in Kerala 234–5, 253–4. *See also* Fishing trawlers
Staves, Susan 72
Stebbing, E.P. 96, 98, 99
Stewart, Dr J.L. 100
Sthala Purana 14, 32
Subaltern social movements 23
Subaltern Studies 23
Sub-khels 291
Sub-national movements 5
Subrahmanyam, Sanjay 14
Subramanian, Ajantha 9
Sullivan, John 68, 71, 72, 77, 81
  defence of Toda land rights 69, 70, 76, 79, 80, 82–3

  H.J. Chamier's criticism of 78, 79
  land settlement in Nilgiris by 76
  purchase of Ootacamund 69
Supreme Court ban, on felling in Meghalaya 174, 191
  consequences 179–80, 181
  criticism of 180–1
  debates regarding 179–83, 184, 186
  support for 181, 182
Survey of Forests, in NWFP 279, 280, 281
Swat district 92, 101–2, 277, *278*
  felling in, arrangement between Wali and British 104
  forests of 97, 102–3
  government control over forests of 106–7
  incorporation into NWFP 277, 279
  land registration policy in 279
  Wali of 102, 104, 105
  See also Malakand
Swat Kohistan 106
  working plan 103–5
Swat river, timber trade along 96, 97, 276
Swazei, concept of 291
Swell, G.G. 176
Swidden agriculture. *See* Shifting agriculture

Tagore, Rabindranath 30
Tamar rebellion 125
Tana Bhagat movement 127–7
Tax farmers as revenue collectors 56
Teak plantations, protest against 135–7
Tehri Dam 25
Territorial allegiances and natural boundaries 4
Thompson, E.P. 77
Timber 290
  ban, in Meghalaya. *See* Supreme Court ban
  British requirement, debates over 98–9
  demand for railway sleepers 119
  in NWFP 96

INDEX

right to, in NWFP 281, 282, 283, 285, 286
as source of revenue in Meghalaya 173
trade. *See* timber trade
Timber trade
along Kabul river, NWFP 96, 97
along Swat river, NWFP 96, 97, 276
in Meghalaya 191
Munro's views on EIC monopoly over 75
Trans-Indus, Cleghorn's report on 97
Toda 15, 65, 66, 67, 70, 72, 85, 86
and Badaga, social relations between 82–3
authority, dismantling of 86
Chamier's notion of 80
conflict with colonial government over land 82–3
Henry Harkness' description of 81
of Kashmund 81
of Khodanaud 82, 83
land rights of. *See* Toda, land rights
loss of land 67, 82
of Malnaud 82
perception of early European presence in Nilgiri Hills 76
rights of pasturage 84, 85
See also Nilgiris
Toda, land rights 67, 68, 69, 71
codification of 85
disqualification of 80
government regulation on 84
individual *vs.* common 83
Lushington's views 76
Sullivan's defence of 69, 70, 76, 79, 80, 82–3
See also Nilgiri Hills
Trade 51, 52
cardamom. *See* Cardamom
contractual system of 56–7
expansion in early colonial period 53–4
Indo-Roman 47, 48
long distant 14, 44, 48, 50. *See also* Forager-traders

pepper. *See* Pepper
rice. *See* Rice
role of intermediaries in 56, 57
south-west coastal 51–2
spice. *See* Spice trade
timber. *See* Timber trade
utilitarian *vs.* luxury goods 54
Tradition, and rights 9
Trans-Indus region. *See* Malakand Division
Trawlers. *See* Fishing trawlers
Tree(s)
exotic species in Kodagu 202
farming, concept of 160
fruit bearing 122–3
plantations 173
Tribal(s)/tribe(s) 43, 44, 45, 47, 48–9, 115, 116
autonomy for, under Sixth Schedule of Indian Constitution 27, 175, 176, 180
of Bihar, decline in population 132
of Chittagong Hills 26, 255, 256–7, 263–4, 272n.3
of Chittagong Hills, state perception of 263, 265, 266, 268–9
culture 128
economies, effect of scientific forestry on 118
economy, state intervention in Chittagong Hill Tracts 261–2, 265–6
economy, structural changes in Chittagong Hill Tracts 261, 265, 266
of Ghats, integration with lowland politics 57, 58
hinduization of 141
importance of *sal* for 135
integration with lowland politics 14
integration with regional political economies 188–9
kingdoms 58
land rights of, and indigeneity 17
law, in NWFP 275, 279

loss of land in post-independent India 131
lowland agriculturalists and, interdependence between 13, 47, 50, 63
of Malakand Division, relations with British 101
of Meghalaya, debate regarding indigenousness 178
opposition to Congress Party in Chotanagpur 128–9
policy in post-independent India 131
politics 14
rebellions over land 128. *See also* Protest movements
reservation for 43
resistance movements under JMM 132
of South India 44, 45
traditions, reinvention of 133–4
vs. plains people in Chittagong hills 264
of Western Ghats 46, 47, 50
See also Indigenous communities
Tribute, of forest products 57, 58
Tripura, Prasanta 271
Tsing, Anna Lowenhaupt 299

United Nation's Declaration on Rights of Indigenous Peoples 177
Upland people, of Western Ghats
economy of, effect of long distant trade on 14. *See also* Trade
and lowland agriculturists, relationship between 52, 53–5, 63
ethnic identities of 61, 63
Urali Ulladan 47
Utilitarian goods, trade in 54
Utilitarians 74
vs. Orientalists 75
Uttarakhand 29, 141, 151
cash crop cultivation in 154
economic significance of forests of 153–4
environmental history of 152
forest exploitation in 152
forest rituals and politics, relationship between 155
forest temples in 154, 155
forests and people, relationship between 153–6
forests, connection with Pandavas 155
forests, local perception of 153
forests, recreational value of 153, 156–7
forests, symbolic significance of 154, 155
forests, women and 155–6
hill people of. *See* Paharis
identity formation in. *See* Pahari identity
local forest deities in 154–5
movement for political autonomy 152, 153
natural wealth of 151
protest movements in 152–3. *See also* Chipko movement
religious significance of 151, 154, 164
state appropriation of natural resources in 16
state of, demand for 162
Uttaranchal 24, 25

Vartak, V.D. 217
Veddas 47
Vernacular nationalisms 44
Vijayanagra empire 51, 55
Village communities. *See* Indigenous communities
Vrindavan 24
Vrindavan Forest Revival Project 24

Wadud, Miangul Abdul (Wali of Swat) 102, 105
Washbrook, David 74
Western Ghats 13, 14, 20, 44, 46
agriculture expansion in 48, 53–5
cardamom cultivation in. *See* Cardamom
competing nationalisms in 44, 63
foragers of. *See* Foragers; Forager-traders

forests of 63
imperial expansion in 44
long distant trade in forest products of 44, 50. *See* Trade; Forager traders
occupational history of 49–50
paleoenvironmental analysis of 49–50
pepper cultivation in. *See* Pepper
spice trade in. *See* Spice trade
swidden agriculture in 50
tribes of 46, 47
upland people of. *See* Upland people
Wet rice agriculture 47, 49, 54
Wild food *vs.* cultivated food 117
Wilderness and state development interventions 3
Wildlife Conservation Act (1958), Nepal 298
Wilson, Jon 75

Women
 effect of forest reservation in Chotanagpur on 121
 importance of forests for 155–6
 knowledge of jungles 123
 management of nature and 13
Working Plan for Alpuri, objectives 281–2
Working plans in NWFP, non-implementation of 105–6, 107, 109
World Bank, policy regarding indigenous people in Bangladesh 270–1
World Wildlife Fund 311

Xaxa, Virginius 175, 178

Yamuna river 151, 164
Yorke, Michael 117, 124
Youzufzai Pathans 101

Zud, concept of 291, 292, 294